www.wadsworth.com

www.wadsworth.com is the World Wide Web site for
Thomson Wadsworth and is your direct source to dozens
of online resources.

At *www.wadsworth.com* you can find out about supplements, demonstration software, and student resources.
You can also send e-mail to many of our authors and
preview new publications and exciting new technologies.

www.wadsworth.com
Changing the way the world learns®

FROM THE WADSWORTH SERIES IN SPEECH COMMUNICATION

third edition

Essentials of Public Speaking

Cheryl Hamilton

THOMSON
★
WADSWORTH

Australia • Canada • Mexico
Singapore • Spain • United Kingdom
United States

THOMSON

™

WADSWORTH

Communication Editor: Annie Mitchell
Publisher: Holly J. Allen
Senior Development Editor: Greer Lleuad
Assistant Editor: Aarti Jayaraman
Editorial Assistant: Trina Enriquez
Senior Technology Project Manager: Jeanette Wiseman
Senior Marketing Manager: Kimberly Russell
Marketing Assistant: Andrew Keay
Marketing Communications Manager: Shemika Britt
Project Manager, Editorial Production: Jennifer Klos
Executive Art Director: Maria Epes
Print Buyer: Doreen Suruki

Permissions Editor: Kiely Sisk
Production: Mary Douglas, Rogue Valley Publications
Text Designers: Patricia McDermond and Delgado Design, Inc.
Photo Researcher: Roberta Broyer
Copy Editor: Susan Defosset
Cover Designer: Denise Davidson
Cover Image: Images top to bottom: ©Photodisc Red; ©Comstock
    Images; ©Stone/Mike Powell; ©DigitalVision
Cover Printer: Phoenix Color Corp.
Compositor: Stratford Publishing Services
Printer: Courier Corporation/Kendallville

Printed in the United States of America
2 3 4 5 6 7 09 08 07 06

For more information about our products, contact us at:
Thomson Learning Academic Resource Center
1-800-423-0563
For permission to use material from this text or product,
submit a request online at
http://www.thomsonrights.com
Any additional questions about permissions can be submitted
by e-mail to thomsonrights@thomson.com.

Library of Congress Control Number: 2004118284

Student Edition: ISBN 0-534-64780-4
Instructor's Edition: ISBN 0-495-00467-7

Thomson Higher Education
10 Davis Drive
Belmont, CA 94002-3098
USA

Asia (including India)
Thomson Learning
5 Shenton Way
#01-01 UIC Building
Singapore 068808

Australia/New Zealand
Thomson Learning Australia
102 Dodds Street
Southbank, Victoria 3006
Australia

Canada
Thomson Nelson
1120 Birchmount Road
Toronto, Ontario M1K 5G4
Canada

UK/Europe/Middle East/Africa
Thomson Learning
High Holborn House
50–51 Bedford Row
London WC1R 4LR
United Kingdom

Latin America
Thomson Learning
Seneca, 53
Colonia Polanco
11560 Mexico
D.F. Mexico

Spain (including Portugal)
Thomson Paraninfo
Calle Magallanes, 25
28015 Madrid, Spain

Essentials of Public Speaking, Third Edition,
is dedicated to Dr. Charles J. Deur, M.D., F.A.C.P.
(practice limited to oncology and hematology).

b r i e f
c o n t e n t s

unit one

Foundations

Can you identify the myths about public speaking?

Some of the following statements are sound public-speaking principles based on research discussed throughout this book; other statements are misconceptions often thought to be true by beginning speakers.

Directions: If you think the statement is generally accurate, mark it T; if you think the statement is a myth, mark it F. Then compare your answers with the explanations at the end of Chapter 1. You can also take this quiz online at the Essentials of Public Speaking website and, if requested, e-mail your responses to your instructor.

_____ 1. In persuasive speeches, your most important tools are logic and evidence.

_____ 2. Good speakers rarely get nervous.

_____ 3. Visual aids are nice but are not essential to a good speech.

_____ 4. Speakers should be experts in the field on which they are speaking.

_____ 5. Red is an excellent color for highlighting graphs and for emphasizing key data.

_____ 6. Audiences consider male speakers to be more credible than female speakers.

_____ 7. Passing around handouts during the speech helps to keep the audience's attention.

_____ 8. In a small conference room when the audience is seated around a table, the speaker should stand.

_____ 9. Wearing bright, colorful clothing and accessories adds to your power and credibility as a speaker.

_____10. Only accomplished public speakers can deliver effective presentations.

Public Speaking, Ethics, and You

F l a s h b a c k

From the beginning of recorded time, educated people have been skilled public speakers. For example, educated Greeks and Romans studied **rhetoric**—the art of persuasive public speaking. The first known handbook of speaking was Aristotle's *Rhetoric*. In it he divided speaking into the following three categories: **forensic** (speaking in court), **deliberative** (political or legislative speaking), and **epideictic** (ceremonial speaking). Your taking this course shows that speech training is equally important today.

D O YOU ENJOY MAKING SPEECHES? IF YOUR ANSWER IS NO, YOU ARE NOT ALONE. Not only do many people not enjoy speaking in public, they dislike and even fear it. You may be thinking, "It doesn't matter that I don't know how to give a speech; my job and personal life won't require it." Are you sure? In this chapter, we'll look at the potential roles of public speaking in your life, as well as the elements and ethics of the communication process.

> Before reading this chapter, complete McCroskey's Personal Report of Communication Apprehension (PRCA) questionnaire under Student Resources for Chapter 1 at the Essentials of Public Speaking website. Turn in your scores to your instructor. All scores will be kept completely confidential.

Public Speaking: What Roles Can It Play in Your Life?

As you become successful in your career, get involved in your community, and pursue various activities or causes, you will be surprised at how many opportunities you will have to give speeches. These opportunities can enhance your personal development, influence society, and advance your career.

Enhancing Your Personal Development

One of the greatest benefits of learning to give a good speech is the personal satisfaction it brings. It's a wonderful feeling to be able to stand in front of a group of people and present a well-organized, dynamic speech that your listeners obviously appreciate. Also, once you learn to give effective speeches, you can stop dreading the possibility that someone will ask you to speak. For example, on the first day of class, a student told me that she had dropped the course five times before and would probably drop it again because she simply couldn't give a speech. But when she looked at the confidence-building techniques covered in the course, she was intrigued enough to give it a try—with great success. ➤ *See Chapter 2 for more on confidence building.*

Being able to speak in public will also give you more control over your life. That is, knowing how to research, conceptualize, organize, and present your own arguments helps you get your ideas across to others. In addition, learning to analyze audiences and to adapt your ideas and arguments to them makes you a more flexible communicator and a better critical thinker (Allen, Berkowitz, Hunt, & Louden, 1999). Moreover, knowing how to evaluate the persuasive arguments of others keeps you from feeling manipulated. In short, although you may find it difficult to believe right now, learning to speak in public can be beneficial to you personally.

Influencing Your World

Learning to give speeches can also be beneficial to society. Because our form of government depends on citizen participation, opportunities to speak are almost limitless. Start with your own neighborhood. Many neighborhoods hold regular meetings to discuss and solve community problems, such as setting up a crime watch program. Similarly, citizens can address key issues at city council and school board meetings. The same goes for campus issues, such as the student council's stance on a faculty member's dismissal, the English club's position on political correctness, or the campaign to keep the library open for longer hours—all are situations requiring public speaking. Even college courses often require you to share information with the class or make an oral presentation. It's hard to find a situation that wouldn't benefit from public speaking.

Some examples of people who are influencing their world through public speaking are:

- Jody Williams, founder of the International Campaign to Ban Landmines and winner of 1997 Nobel Peace Prize.

- Sally Ride and Mae Jemison, NASA astronauts who have both set up science programs for kids.

- Lisa Beamer, whose husband Todd died during the September 11 terrorist attacks on the United States and author of *Let's Roll! Ordinary People, Extraordinary Courage.*

- Bob Love, top scorer for the Chicago Bulls in the 1970s, whose debilitating stutter prevented him from speaking to the media and receiving speaking endorsements. When an injury ended his basketball career, the only job he could get with his stutter was washing dishes and bussing tables at a restaurant. At the age of 45, under the direction of a speech therapist, Bob learned to manage his stutter and is now the Director of Community Affairs for the Bulls and gives over 300 presentations per year (Moore, 2004).

Bob Love, Director of Community Affairs for the Chicago Bulls, uses his public-speaking skills to have a positive impact on the world.

© AP/Wide World Photos

Advancing Your Career

Not only is learning to speak in public personally satisfying and beneficial to society, but it can also advance your career. In 1987, AT&T and Stanford University set out to identify the one question that best predicted a person's earning power (Sandholtz, 1987). To the surprise of the researchers, it was "Do you enjoy giving speeches?" Those who enjoyed speaking in public were earning the highest salaries; those who said, "You've got to be kidding!" were making much less. The National Association of Colleges and Employers (2004) conducts a survey of employers each year about the qualities/skills employers look for in new hires. As they have every year, the results of the latest NACE survey support the AT&T/Stanford survey results: **communication skills** (speaking and writing) are ranked by employers as the most important skills.

Although most of us expect that executives in large corporations such as Microsoft and General Motors would have to give speeches, smaller businesses also need employees who are skilled in public speaking. For example, salespeople must present their products to customers. Even some assembly-line workers participate in decision making and formally present group ideas to management. The fact is, no matter what job you choose, you will need the speaking skills discussed throughout this book (Richmond & Roach, 1992; Russell, 1992).

Speakers' Bureaus Many organizations have their own speakers' bureau, which they use as a public relations tool. A **speakers' bureau** is made up of employees who have expertise in some aspect of the company and are willing to share it with interested groups. Lockheed Martin, Dow Chemical, Xerox, the United States Army and Navy, and most colleges and universities are a few of the organizations that communicate with the public through speakers' bureaus.

Oral Communication Skills If you still aren't convinced that public speaking will be important in your particular career, consult one of the periodical guides or databases in your college library and look for articles written by people in your profession about oral communication skills. For example, a brief search for engineering articles found the following information:

- A survey of engineers concluded that engineers spend more than half of each day communicating (Vest, Long, & Anderson, 1996).

- An engineering task force study ranked oral communication skills second in importance after problem recognition/solution skills and more important than technical skills (Evans, Beakley, Crouch, & Yamaguchi, 1993).

- In a recent survey of engineers, over 50 percent of them listed public speaking as the most important oral communication skill for success—more important than meetings, interpersonal communication, training, or selling (Darling & Dannels, 2003).

- The Accreditation Board for Engineering and Technology (ABET) now includes communication skills (including speaking) as a standard for evaluating college engineering programs in the United States (Koehn, 2001; Williams, 2001, 2002).

- The director of the Stevens Institute of Technology (Farr, 2000) made this observation: "In this age of planning boards, public hearings, and marketing presentations, an engineer will never assume a leadership role within his or her organization without the ability to communicate clearly and confidently" (p. 6).

Learning to speak was certainly a benefit for one engineer who enrolled in a 6-week public-speaking seminar I taught through the training department at Bell Helicopter Textron. Although reluctant at first, less than 2 months later she was promoted to senior engineer because, as her boss stated, her presentations were "so professional." (See also Allen, 2000.)

Although you may not yet feel comfortable giving formal speeches, you most likely already give informal talks fairly often. Common examples include giving information about an assignment to classmates who missed the previous class or suggesting an idea to your boss. Therefore, even though you may not have realized it, you already have many of the skills necessary for successful public speaking.

The Right Speech for the Occasion

The types of speeches you may be asked to give—whether in class, at work, or in your community—fall into three basic categories: informative, persuasive, and special occasion speeches.

Informative Versus Persuasive Speeches

If your intent is simply to make listeners aware of a subject or to present some new ideas or information, your presentation is an informative one. In other words, **informative** speeches promote understanding of an idea or convey a body of related facts. They can also demonstrate how to do or make something. Examples of topics for informative speeches include the following:

- Performing the Heimlich maneuver
- The effects of stress on your body
- Using the Internet for profit
- Sexual harassment in college classrooms

By contrast, **persuasive speeches** seek to influence beliefs, choices, or opinions. Examples of topics for persuasive speeches include these:

- Everyone should make out a will.
- Norton is the most effective virus protector.
- On-campus parking lots should be expanded.
- Daily exercise is necessary for health.

You need to determine whether your speech is informative or persuasive before you begin preparing it because the two types require different approaches. Nevertheless, only a thin line separates informative and persuasive presentations. Persuasive presentations must inform as well as persuade. How can speakers persuade listeners unless they are informed of the facts? In the same way, many informative presentations indirectly persuade listeners to take action. For example, an informative speech may be so interesting or enlightening that listeners decide to follow up on the information or make some change in their lives. → *See Chapters 12 and 13 for more on informative and persuasive speaking.*

Special Occasion Speeches

Special occasion speeches give a sense of distinction to important events in our lives. These speeches are given at such events as weddings, company award ceremonies, and funerals. Halle Berry's 2004 Academy Award acceptance speech, President Reagan's eulogy for the victims of the Challenger explosion, and Mayor Giuliani's speech to New Yorkers after the September 11 terrorist attacks are all examples of special occasion speeches. You might be called on to introduce a new student to the class, accept an award, or pay tribute to a retiring professor—these are also special occasion speeches. To learn more about the special occasion speeches you are most likely to give, read Special Occasion Speaking under the Book Resources at the Essentials of Public Speaking website.

The Communication Process and the Public Speaker

As noted earlier, you may have studied communication in another course—English, perhaps. But you probably have not viewed communication from a public-speaking perspective. By understanding the communication process, you will be able to anticipate and minimize possible misunderstandings.

The *Oxford English Dictionary* lists the Latin root of *communicate* as *communicare,* which means "to make common to many, share." According to this definition, when people communicate, they express their ideas and feelings in a way that is understandable (common) to other people. Therefore, **communication** is a process in which people share thoughts, ideas, and feelings in understandable ways. The model in Figure 1.1 shows the basic elements of the communication process: speaker/listeners, stimulus and motivation, message encoding and decoding, codes, feedback, environment, and noise. Let's look at each of these elements to see how they relate to your speaking success.

Speakers/Listeners

Although the speaker is generally considered to be the sender of the message and the listeners to be the receivers, both are simultaneously sending and receiving throughout the speech. As audience members listen, they are sending messages through laughter, frowns, bored looks, or sometimes questions. Similarly, while you are speaking, you also are receiving audience responses and adjusting your speech to them. Adjustments might include speaking louder, giving a more detailed explanation, showing a visual aid you had originally planned to omit, or adding another example.
→ *Being able to interpret your audience's nonverbal cues is so important to speaking success that additional discussions are included in Chapters 3 and 10.*

Stimulus and Motivation

Before people make an effort to communicate, they must be sufficiently stimulated and motivated. A stimulus triggers a thought, which triggers the desire to communicate. However, a stimulus alone is not enough to prompt communication; sufficient motivation (or desire) is also necessary. To illustrate, think about how many times an instructor has asked a question in class, and even though you thought you knew the answer—that is, you were stimulated—you did not respond. Perhaps you were not sufficiently motivated—that is, you saw no personal benefit in answering. Or perhaps you saw a greater benefit in not answering—you were afraid of being criticized by the professor or looking foolish by risking a wrong answer. Of course, if you knew that the professor graded on class participation, your motivation to answer would probably be greater.

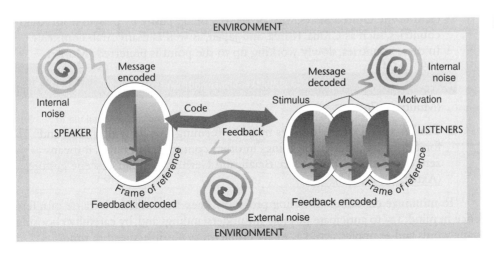

Figure 1.1

Basic Model of Communication

The difference among the verbal, visual, and vocal codes can be illustrated in the following example. Suppose you have purchased a new outfit for a special occasion. As the occasion draws nearer, however, you begin to wonder if the outfit is appropriate and you ask a friend for advice. When the friend responds, "It looks great on you!" do you breathe a sigh of relief at the words? Or do you look closely at your friend's facial expression and listen carefully to the tone of voice for any indication that your friend may not mean what he or she is saying? For example, a slight raise of the eyebrows and a brief pause after the word *great* could reverse the meaning of the comment. Studies have found that when adults attempt to determine the meaning of a statement, they rely more on vocal and visual cues than they do on the words that are actually spoken (Archer & Akert, 1977; Burgoon & Hoobler, 2002; Thompson, Driscoll, & Markson, 1998). Unfortunately, too many speakers think that the only important code is the verbal one and tend to overlook the other two. Effective speakers make sure they send the same powerful message by all three codes. ➔ *See Chapter 3, page 50, for more specific information about codes.*

Feedback

When you evaluate your own speaking behavior, when you ask a friend to give an opinion about a practice speech, or when audience members respond to your presentation, you are experiencing feedback. **Feedback** is verbal, visual, and vocal re-

What does the feedback from this audience tell you about the speaker?

© Sepp Seitz/Woodfin Camp & Associates, Inc.

teachers, police officers, [...]
that senators, congressp[...]
scored fairly low; their e[...]
those rated as the bott[...]
salespeople, HMO mana[...]
little faith in the honesty[...]

Examples of Uneth[...]

Unfortunately, we don't [...]
loss of public confiden[...]
Contra affair, and the i[...]
scandals including Enr[...]
Com, Arthur Anderson, [...]
Stephen Glass (*New Re[...]
York Times); and the que[...]
Martha Stewart, to nam[...]

Let's look at a few [...]

Case 1: In December[...]
of the U. S. Olympic C[...]
In May 2002, Baldwin [...]
in her official biograph[...]
an alumni magazine (*N[...]
bachelor's from the Un[...]
sity. Actually, she had a[...]
torate and no degree f[...]
enough for the positio[...]

Case 2: In 2001, onl[...]
O'Leary resigned as th[...]
his resume: (1) that he [...]
versity, and (2) that he [...]
shire. Both claims (whi[...]
inaccurate—he took o[...]
for New Hampshire ([...]

sponses to messages. Not only is feedback helpful for *self-monitoring* (evaluating and modifying your behavior until it meets your expectations), but it is the only way you can know whether listeners have interpreted your message the way you intended it to be interpreted. Usually feedback from an audience is visual (such as facial expressions or posture) or vocal (such as a collective sigh, laughter, or groans). Occasionally a listener will make a verbal comment or ask a question. Without feedback, you don't know whether your message has been interpreted correctly. Therefore, as a speaker, you want to pay close attention to the feedback from your audience.

Environment

The **environment** includes the time, place, and physical and social surroundings in which the speech occurs (Holm, 1981). A speech during dinner time (when people wish they were eating) or right after lunch (when they might be feeling groggy) will probably be less successful than one given in the morning or later in the evening. The size of the room, the brightness of the lights, the room temperature, and the comfort and arrangement of chairs can also affect the success of a speech. For example, 40 people crowded into a small conference room gives the impression that the speaker must be really good to attract such a crowd; but the same 40 people scattered in an auditorium gives the impression that the speaker must not be very compelling. An effective speaker plans and controls the environment as much as possible. → *Adapting visual aids to various speaking environments is discussed in Chapter 10.*

Noise

Anything that interferes with communication by distorting or blocking the message is called noise. **External noise** includes distractions in the environment, such as people talking, lighting that is too bright or too dim, and even poor grammar. **Internal noise** refers to distractions within the listener, such as headaches, preoccupation with problems, or lack of knowledge about the topic. Internal noise can also affect you as a speaker. If you are tired from studying too late the night before or if you are worried about your speech, you are experiencing internal noise. When possible, select speaking environments that are relatively free of external noises, and provide stimulus and motivation to divert your audience's attention from their internal noise.

As you can see, successful communication involves more than just talking and listening—it's hard work and requires careful preparation. However, the reward of all the work and preparation is an enthusiastic, powerful speech. Successful speakers

- Stimulate and motivate their listeners.

- Encode their presentations for each different audience.

- Try to make their visual and vocal codes reinforce their verbal message.

- Pay careful attention to audience feedback.

- Control the speaking environment and possible noise factors as much as possible.

In addition to preparing a speech that communicates with your audience, you also have the obligation of being an ethical speaker.

Case 3: In 1987, Senator Joseph Biden of Delaware had a good chance of winning the Democratic presidential nomination. In a debate before a crowd at the Iowa State Fair, he delivered an especially powerful closing statement that was almost word for word from a political ad by Neil Kinnock, a British Labour party leader (Cramer, 1992). When the press compared tapes of Biden's rousing conclusion and Kinnock's ad, they found that even the gestures and pauses were the same. When the press discovered a few other inconsistencies in his past, Biden's presidential bid was over (Jaksa & Pritchard, 1994).

Case 4: In their book *Communication Ethics: Methods of Analysis,* Jaksa and Pritchard (1994) report the following media incident:

> On November 17, 1992, NBC's "Dateline" featured a controversy over General Motors' 1973–1987 pickup trucks. The models during those years were designed with fuel tanks mounted on the sides of the vehicle. "Dateline" set out to show that this location renders the tanks highly vulnerable to leaks and fiery explosions on side impact. Seen by an estimated 17 million viewers, a short segment of the feature showed a side collision with one of the pickups resulting in just such an explosion.
>
> Unfortunately, "Dateline" failed to make clear to its viewers that its consultants had installed remote-control, electrical "igniters" under the two pickups it tested. Initially denying that it had improperly "rigged" the explosion, NBC eventually extended an elaborate apology to General Motors and viewers for its misleading footage. (p. 61)

The Costs of Unethical Behavior

Not only has each of these cases further eroded public confidence in politicians, professionals, and the media and deprived the country of possible role models, but the people involved have seen an end to their dreams.

Sandra Baldwin lost the chance to influence the direction of Olympic sports (Marshall, 2002) and saw an end to her dream to "have a lasting effect on the emergence of women in leadership roles, not just in my country, but around the world" (Baldwin, 2000). Although he was immediately hired as the defensive coordinator for the Minnesota Vikings by his good friend, head coach Mike Tice, George O'Leary "forfeited the chance to be part of a grand football tradition" ("Great Exaggerations," 2001, p. 32)—one that very few coaches will ever have—and lost the trust and respect of many people. Senator Biden lost his chance to be president of the United States. Although he is still a senator, the respect and trust needed to become president have been lost and may never return. As for NBC and "Dateline," their reputation for fair and accurate reporting was seriously damaged, and only an elaborate on-air apology kept them from being sued (Jaksa & Pritchard, 1994, p. 62). In addition, the president of NBC, Michael Gartner, as well as the show's executive producer, senior producer, and story producer, were pressured into resigning (*Facts on File,* 1993, p. 250).

Exaggeration, Distortion, and Plagiarism

As these examples illustrate, to be an ethical speaker, you must be careful to tell only the truth, without exaggeration or distortion. Listeners expect the truth from public speakers. Unfortunately, when speakers feel pressured or insecure, they may abandon ethical standards and exaggerate or distort the facts. **Exaggeration** is overstating or

Use InfoTrac College Edition to further investigate the costs of unethical acts. Do a keyword search on *cheating, lies,* or *plagiarism* and look for at least three relevant articles. Prepare a brief review of each to share with your class. You can access InfoTrac College Edition through the Essentials of Public Speaking website by using the passcode on the card included in your copy of this book.

Technology Tip for Speakers

Set Your PowerPoint Presentation to Open Automatically in PowerPoint Show

Whether you have experience or are completely new to public speaking, begin now to learn a presentations tool—I recommend Microsoft PowerPoint. PowerPoint is great for designing visual aids especially when you plan to use photos or transparencies. Even when you don't plan to use visuals, PowerPoint is still a great speaker tool because it helps you organize your ideas and can even serve as speaking notes. → *See the Technology Tip in Chapter 9 for more on using PowerPoint.*

Most speakers save their PowerPoint slides as a PowerPoint Presentation (.ppt), which is the program default. The drawback is that when you double-click on your presentation icon, PowerPoint first opens its software; then it opens your presentation, leaving it in edit mode; then you must click the Slide Show button to launch your presentation into full-screen mode. Your audience is watching all this and may not be overly impressed.

If, however, you save your presentation as a PowerPoint Show (.pps—go to File, Save As, choose PowerPoint Show, and click Save), a double-click on your presentation icon will immediately show a full-screen view of your opening slide. Another way to accomplish the same thing is to change the file extension from .ppt to .pps. To test this tip, prepare one or two slides, save them as both PowerPoint Presentation (.ppt) and PowerPoint Show (.pps) on a floppy disk, and then double-click on each icon to open it. To exit from full-screen mode, press the Escape key. (If you prefer, select the Speech Template available on the Essentials of Public Speaking website and follow the instructions above.)

---

presenting facts as more important than they are; **distortion** is misrepresenting or twisting facts, or stating that they are true when they are only partially true. Both exaggeration and distortion are forms of lying and, as such, are unethical. For example, can Ken Lay, creator and chief of Enron for 15 years and the 31st Enron executive to be indicted for fraud (Schnurman, 2004), be believed when he says that he didn't know that his company had a "massive scam" going on? Or what about Martha Stewart, who was convicted of "trying to thwart a government investigation" into illegal stock sales (Beltran, 2004)? As a public speaker, you must keep in mind that exaggeration and distortion are only half a step away from overt lying.

In addition to doing careful research and reporting only the truth, you must be careful not to plagiarize. **Plagiarism** is using the ideas of others (whether paraphrased or word for word) without giving them credit. If you read an article or see a TV program and then use the information from it in your speech without citing the source, you are plagiarizing—even if you paraphrase the content. Using materials obtained from the Internet without giving credit is also plagiarism. *A senior pastor of a church in Keene, New Hampshire,* took parts of sermons and some entire sermons from the Internet without giving credit ("Pastor Resigns," 2004). As a result, his congregation lost trust in him and he resigned. *A North Carolina school board chairman* used a large part of a speech he found on the Internet in his commencement address, thinking that since the speech was not attributed to anyone, it was all right to use it.

However, the speech was given by Donna Shalala in 1998 when she was U.S. Secretary of Health and Human Services (Manzo, 2004). The board chair resigned his position. Plagiarism is serious for students as well. *A student journalist* for the *Iowa State Daily* was fired after it was found that he plagiarized parts of at least eight articles—most of his information was taken from the *Minneapolis Star-Tribune* ("Students Caught," 2004). A college student who plagiarizes any part of a speech will receive a failing grade for the speech and maybe for the course, and may even be expelled. → *Chapter 6 discusses how to conduct your research to avoid accidental plagiarism.*

Classroom Ethics

In one of my public-speaking classes, I asked students to come up with a code of ethics acceptable to everyone in the class. One student didn't see why everyone was so hung up on ethics when using facts and statistics. After all, he said, speaking is entertainment. Why shouldn't he make up information if it made the speech more entertaining? Another student said that in a previous speech class, she had fabricated a detailed account of her grandmother dying from cancer as an attention-getter. The illustration had touched her audience; several people even had tears in their eyes. The student felt that if she had used a hypothetical example, the speech would not have been as moving or effective. She admitted, however, that her audience was upset and felt manipulated when they realized she had lied about her grandmother. As you can imagine, a lively discussion followed. The discussion ended with the class agreeing that although there is an entertaining element to speaking and that the desire to touch an audience is strong, the end does not justify the means. Several of them also said that they would have trouble trusting or respecting a classmate who fabricated or plagiarized information in a speech. Therefore, the class decided to create their own code of ethics. See Table 1.3 for a partial Code of Ethics list the class approved. What would you add to the list?

Keep in mind that ethical behavior in the classroom is no different than ethical behavior in the office. What you practice now is what you will feel comfortable

Table 1.3

Code of Ethics for Public-Speaking Class (Partial List)	
Speaker	**Audience**
1. Always show up when scheduled to speak.	1. Support speaker—no homework or daydreaming.
2. Show respect by being prepared.	2. Be on time; take job as audience evaluator seriously.
3. Respect audience opinions.	3. Respect speaker's opinions
4. Be honest—no plagiarism, exaggeration, or distortion of facts or visuals. Cite sources.	4. Be open-minded; don't take offense during speeches or class discussions.
5. Limit use of Internet sources.	5. Don't distract speaker in any way.
6. Carefully research all sides of topic.	6. Give honest, tactful critiques (strengths/weaknesses).

doing in the real world. I urge you to think seriously about developing your own personal code of ethics during this course. Don't wait until an ethical problem arises—you may not be prepared to handle the situation. The following advice is offered by Dennis A. Gioia (1992), a bureaucrat involved in Ford's decision not to recall the Pinto even though they knew its gas tank could burst into flames in rear-end collisions at speeds as low as 25 miles per hour:

> . . . develop your ethical base now! Too many people do not give serious attention to assessing and articulating their own values. People simply do not know what they stand for because they haven't thought about it seriously . . . be prepared to face critical responsibility at a relatively young age, as I did. You need to know what your values are . . . so that you can know how to make a good decision. Before you do that, you need to articulate and affirm your values now, before you enter the fray. I wasn't really ready. Are you? (Trevino & Nelson, 2004, pp. 131–132)

Sample Student Speech: "Closet Artifacts" by Monica E. Wolfe

In the following sample speech, student Monica Wolfe discusses how her collection of T-shirts reflects important events in her life. Her assignment specified a 2- to 3-minute speech on one or more artifacts that, if found by an archaeologist in the future, would reveal the most about her. This speech, which was the first speech Monica gave to her public-speaking class, was transcribed from the videotape filmed in class. To read a second artifact speech, "The Ishii Stick" by Eddie Osburn, look under Additional Speeches for Analysis on the Essentials of Public Speaking website. Chapters 4, 8, 11, 12, 13, and 14 of this text also feature sample student speeches. ➔ *See the Quick Start Guide for a discussion of the artifact speech and other types of introductory speeches.*

SAMPLE SPEECH

CLOSET ARTIFACTS

by Monica E. Wolfe

IN THIS BOX ARE the archaeological ruins of my closet. As my very southern mother says, "You can tell a lot about a lady by her closet." Although I don't think this is what she had in mind, I'm going to let the T-shirts in my closet tell you about me. My T-shirts will show how my life has changed from my first try at college to world travel as a flight attendant to settled married life and another go at college.

continued

SAMPLE SPEECH (continued)

I was born and raised in Austin, Texas. I had never been anywhere but Austin so, of course, I went to the University of Texas. I joined a sorority [T-shirt] and went for two years until they hounded me to say what my major was going to be but I had no idea.

So I left and became a flight attendant for Continental Airlines [T-shirt]. While I was a flight attendant, I had a lot of great experiences. I went to Australia [T-shirt] which I loved—got to hug a koala bear. I went to Mexico [T-shirt] and all around the United States.

One of the best things about being a flight attendant is on a trip I met this T-shirt [T-shirt]. His name is John and he is from Newport Beach, California. This is a pretty ragged [T-shirt] because it's his favorite T-shirt. John is a pilot—at the time for Continental Airlines as well, so we had the chance to work together and travel together.

On one of our trips we went to Hawaii [T-shirt] and while we were in Hawaii, we decided to combine our closet space and got married.

A few months after we got married, he decided to get a new job with American Airlines [T-shirt] and this is how we ended up in the Fort Worth/Dallas area [Cowboy T-shirt].

After we were here for about one year, we took another vacation to Ruidoso, New Mexico [T-shirt], and I taught him to ski, which was very interesting. We had a really good time.

When we got back from Ruidoso, I had to wear this shirt [maternity T-shirt]. I know it looks plain but after 9 months, I had this shirt [T-shirt turned around to show baby T-shirt pinned on it]. She is now 2 years old and the joy of our lives.

As you can see, the T-shirts found in the archaeological ruins of my closet tell a lot about my life. But this last shirt is the shirt that we all wear [imaginary T-shirt held up] because we are unsure of what it says or where we are going but we hope that it will be as well worn as all of these [imaginary T-shirt added to stack of other shirts].

Summary

Throughout life, you will have many opportunities to give speeches that can benefit your career, your self-esteem, and even society. There are three basic types of speeches:

- Informative speeches, which promote understanding of an idea, convey a body of related facts, or demonstrate how to do or make something

- Persuasive speeches, which influence opinions or choices

- Special occasion speeches, which are given at such events as weddings and award presentations

To minimize misunderstandings between you and your audience, you need to pay particular attention to your and their frames of reference (background and experiences). Different frames of reference increase the probability that speakers and audience members will have difficulty interpreting one another's messages.

Consider the three types of communication codes—verbal, visual, vocal—as inseparable. Communication is greatly improved when speakers use all three codes effectively. Studies have found that when people attempt to determine the meaning of a statement, they rely more heavily on vocal and visual cues than on verbal cues. Be especially careful to avoid exaggeration, distortion, and plagiarism; all are unethical and may cause others to consider you untrustworthy.

Essentials of Public Speaking Online

Use the Essentials of Public Speaking website at **http://communication. wadsworth.com/hamiltoneps3** for quick access to the electronic study resources that accompany this chapter. When you get to the Essentials home page, click on "Student Book Companion Site" in the Resource box. The Essentials website features the Test Your Knowledge Quiz on page 1, the PRCA (Personal Report of Communication Apprehension) questionnaire described on page 21, the unit on Special Occasion Speaking discussed on page 6, InfoTrac College Edition, the Suggestions for Practice and Critical Thinking activities and the InfoTrac College Edition activities that follow, a digital glossary, and review quizzes.

Key Terms

communication 7
communication skills 4
decoding 8
deliberative speaking 2
distortion 16
emoticon 9
encoding 8
environment 11
epideictic speaking 2

ethical 12
ethical speaker 12
exaggeration 14
external noise 11
feedback 10
forensic speaking 2
frame of reference 8
informative speech 6
internal noise 11

persuasive speech 6
plagiarism 16
rhetoric 2
speakers' bureau 6
special occasion speeches 6
verbal code 9
visual code 9
vocal code 9

Suggestions for Practice and Critical Thinking

1. If you haven't completed the PRCA (Personal Report of Communication Apprehension) questionnaire at the Essentials of Public Speaking website, do so now and turn in your scores to your instructor. You will retake the questionnaire during the last week of class, compare your "before" and "after" scores, and analyze your progress. Scores will be kept confidential.

2. Make a list of the opportunities to give speeches that came your way in the past year (whether or not you accepted) in your community, your campus, your classes, your job, clubs or organizations (including religious ones), and volunteer work. If you spoke in any of these settings, what was the outcome?

If you didn't give any speeches last year, what benefits could have resulted if you had agreed to speak? Share your list with a classmate.

3. Select one of the types of beginning speeches described in the Quick Start Guide and prepare a 2- to 3-minute speech. Also prepare a brief outline to hand in to your instructor. Practice giving your talk several times.

4. Begin a list of speech topics to use during the course. Carry a notepad or a few notecards in your purse or wallet. When you think of, read, or hear about a topic that interests you, write it down along with the source when relevant. With this habit, you will be ready when topics are needed.

5. In groups of four or five, decide on a code of ethics for your class (See Table 1.3 for examples). If you are using InfoTrac College Edition, use it prior to the class discussion to locate at least two articles that focus on codes of ethics in current use. If a keyword search using *code of ethics* doesn't locate what you need, check for additional keywords by entering *ethics* as a subject guide search.

6. Select someone in your class whom you don't know personally. For 15 minutes or less, interview each other to find out all the normal information people usually share (for example, major and minor field of study, home state, marital status, and hobbies). In addition, find out something unusual or unique about each other. This could be something that is true today or something that happened years ago (for example, one of you is from a family of 10, fought in Iraq, or reads five books each week). When your interview time is up, use the information you have gathered to introduce one another to the class.

7. Check out the following websites. You can access these sites under Student Resources for Chapter 1 at the Essentials of Public Speaking website.

   • Go to the SpeakersQuest site. Scroll down and click on "Speaker's Bureau," then click on "VideoZine" and listen to one or more speeches available on streaming video. A different speaker is highlighted each week. If you don't have streaming video, download a free player at RealPlayer.

   • For the complete text of Reagan's *Challenger* eulogy, check out ReaganLibrary.com's speech page under "Ronald Reagan" tab.

   • For more on nonverbal communication, see the page Exploring Nonverbal Communication at the University of California, Santa Cruz website. Also check out The Nonverbal Dictionary by David B. Givens. Click on "Entries" to access articles about various topics in nonverbal communication.

   • Without vocal and nonverbal cues to aid meaning, e-mail messages can be difficult to understand. At the Beginner's Guide to Effective Email website, Kaitlin Duck Sherwood suggests adding smileys, pause equivalents, and creative punctuation to e-mail in place of gestures. For recommended emoticons for e-mail communication, see Windweaver.com/emoticons.

   • The ethics in various professions found in Table 1.2 is updated every year or two around December and February by the Gallup Organization at Princeton. To check for new ethics polls, as well as many other interesting polls, visit the Gallup Organization's home page. Type in "nurses remain at top" in the site search box.

   • Look at the "Code of Professional Ethics" produced by the National Speakers Association, whose members include hundreds of professionals who give 20 or more paid speeches a year.

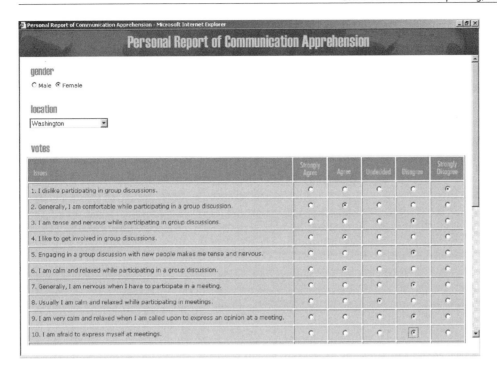

Quiz Answers

Answers to Unit I Quiz on page 1: Test Your Knowledge About Public Speaking.

1. *False.* Although logic and supporting evidence are important in persuading others, research has indicated that these alone are not enough to sway most listeners. In fact, one study found that most audience members couldn't distinguish the logical arguments in a presentation from the illogical ones (Bettinghouse & Cody, 1997). For example, if the speaker used words and phrases that implied a logical progression of thought (such as "It is obvious that," "Therefore," and "As a result"), people judged the speech to be logical even if it was not. Moreover, when listeners favored the speaker's proposal and/or considered the speaker to be credible, they were likely to judge the speech as convincing. No matter how strong your logic and evidence may be, your most persuasive tool is to relate your arguments to the personal and organizational needs of your listeners. ➡ *Chapter 15 has more on methods of persuasion.*

2. *False.* Although good speakers may feel more positive about speaking than inexperienced ones, every new situation causes a certain amount of "butterflies" for all speakers. Good speakers view this feeling as a sign that their body is gathering the additional energy needed for a dynamic speech; poor speakers see it as a sign that they are falling apart and are going to do a lousy job. Good speakers also know they will feel more confident if they are well prepared. Success is more likely when you have researched your audience, have carefully supported your main ideas for this particular audience, have prepared professional-looking visual aids, and have anticipated possible questions and objections. In general, the more you prepare and practice, the more confident you will be. ➡ *Chapter 3 offers more information on coping with speech anxiety.*

3. *False.* The role of visual aids may be one of the biggest misconceptions of all. Although you can give a speech without visual aids, research has indicated that we learn and remember more when we can "see" the speaker's ideas at the same time we "hear" them. This is especially true for speeches that are technical or cover complicated information, such as "How a 747 Gets Off the Ground" or "Three Football Plays Everyone Should Know." Visuals are so powerful that audience members are more likely to remember what they saw than what they heard. Make sure your visual aids are accurate and directly related to what you want the audience to remember. Use of visual aids is the rule, not the exception. ➔ *Chapter 10 focuses on how to develop and use visual aids.*

4. *False.* You don't have to be an expert to give an excellent talk on a subject. In fact, sometimes experts are so immersed in the subject matter that they have difficulty communicating to a general audience. In some cases, you might arrange to have an expert available to answer technical questions, or you could refer technical questions to the appropriate person for a later response.

5. *False.* Although red is an attention-getting color, using it on visual aids has one big problem—some members of your audience may be color-blind to reds and greens. Most people with red-green color blindness are men, but some are women. Blue is a safer color for emphasizing points.

6. *True.* Although gender stereotypes are definitely waning, audiences unfortunately still generally consider male speakers more knowledgeable and credible than female speakers. One source points out that "on professional newscasts, males are viewed as more credible anchors than females [and that] 92 percent of commercial voice-overs employ male voices" (Rozema & Gray, 1988).

7. *False.* Giving out handouts during a speech almost always ensures audience inattention. The distractions that are created as papers are passed around make it almost impossible to pay attention to the speaker, and audience members may begin reading and tune out the speaker. Unless listeners need the handout while you are talking, pass it out at the end of the speech.

8. *True.* Normally, the only time the speaker should sit down is if he or she is blocking the audience's view of visual aids. Standing gives speakers a better view of audience reactions and adds to their authority. If a speaker is seated, everyone appears to have equal status, and listeners may interact with one another rather than to listen to the speaker. If they are argumentative, they are also more likely to argue with one another, as well as with the speaker.

9. *False.* Colorful clothing and accessories are appropriate in some situations (for example, the fashion industry), but many businesses prefer conservative colors and minimal accessories. Dress consultants advise: (1) jackets and suits broadcast professionalism, and (2) darker jackets or suits convey more authority (Egodigwe, 2003; Greenleaf, 1998; Maysonave, 1999; Molloy, 1996). If your organization is more casual or you wish to downplay your authority, choose a lighter color or remove your jacket before or during the presentation.
➔ *Chapter 11 contains more information on delivery and appearance.*

10. *False.* Accomplished public speakers have learned the do's and don'ts of effective speaking through trial and error. There is nothing mysterious about this knowledge. Even someone who has never made a speech before, can give an effective presentation simply by following the guidelines presented in this book.

2

Building Speaker Confidence

*Flash*back Isocrates, a Greek contemporary of Plato and Aristotle, is one of the prestigious Ten Attic Orators. However, he suffered from speaker anxiety and had a voice that wouldn't project. Even so, he founded the first permanent and financially successful school of rhetoric. For over 50 years his graduates became prominent citizens. Most scholars agree that his program of study and his philosophy of educating "the good man skilled in speaking" have greatly influenced education even to the present time (Conley, 1990, p. 20).

I F THE THOUGHT OF GIVING A SPEECH MAKES YOU ANXIOUS, YOU AREN'T ALONE! A 2001 Gallup poll found that fear of public speaking is the number two fear of Americans—only the fear of snakes is greater (Brewer, 2001). A national study of students in public-speaking classes found that 20 percent have severe public speaking anxiety, or PSA (Robinson, 1997). Their anxiety may even begin the minute the professor makes an assignment (Behnke & Sawyer, 1999). Unfortunately, people who experience a high level of anxiety in communication situations are at a great disadvantage compared to more talkative, confident people. People who feel comfortable expressing themselves are perceived as more competent, make a better impression during job interviews, and are more likely to be promoted to supervisory positions than anxious people are (Richmond & McCroskey, 1998).

The reason that speaker confidence creates a positive impression (whereas high anxiety causes a negative one) is that when we speak, we are communicating in three ways—verbally, visually, and vocally. Our verbal message may be clear and well organized, but when we are nervous, listeners are more likely to focus on negative vocal and visual cues (such as lack of eye contact, poor posture, hesitant delivery, and strained vocal quality). But when we are confident and our verbal, visual, and vocal signals are in harmony, we are more likely to be believed. According to Bert Decker, author of *You've Got to Be Believed to Be Heard:*

> Believability is an emotional quality. . . . If you don't believe in someone on an emotional level, little if any of what they have to say will get through. It will be screened out by your distrust, your anxiety, your irritation, or your indifference. Even if the facts and content are great by themselves, they are forever locked out because the person delivering them lacks believability. (Decker & Denney, 1993, pp. 35–36)

Therefore, if we want people to believe us when we speak, if we want to enhance the positive impressions we make, we need to build up our confidence. Fortunately, studying public speaking can help build speaking confidence (Robinson, 1997; Rubin, Rubin, & Jordan, 1997). This chapter will give you some suggestions on how to manage communication anxiety—and more specifically, speaker anxiety—in order to develop a more confident, professional delivery.

Understanding Anxiety

Before you can manage your anxiety, you need to know what kind of anxiety you have—situational or trait. **Situational anxiety**—often referred to as *state anxiety* (Booth-Butterfield & Booth-Butterfield, 1992; Motley, 1995)—is anxiety caused by factors in a specific situation (for example, speaking before a new audience or in front of the boss or being graded while speaking). **Trait anxiety** (Beatty, Balfantz, & Kuwabara, 1989; Daly & Friedrich, 1981) refers to the internal anxieties an individual brings to the speaking situation (for example, feelings of inadequacy in a group or fear of looking like a fool in front of others). In other words, situational anxiety is caused by a new or different situation, whereas trait anxiety is caused by feelings inside the speaker that exist regardless of the situation. Your own anxiety may be situational, trait, or a combination of the two.

Situational Anxiety

Feeling nervous in a new communication situation is perfectly normal. Telling a troublesome employee that he is fired, interviewing for a position, and presenting a controversial idea to your classmates are all situations that can trigger butterflies in the stomach. Any time we become anxious, afraid, or excited, our body gets ready for action:

> First, the heart begins pumping more blood to the brain, the muscles, and skin. Blood is also diverted away from the stomach and intestines in order to supply those same organs. As a result, the digestive system slows to a crawl, and the central nervous system, heart, and muscles receive extra oxygen and energy necessary for clear thinking, quick reaction, and intense physical exertion. At the same time, the pupils of the eyes dilate to produce sharper vision, the level of blood sugar rises to provide added energy, and the skin perspires in order to flush out excess wastes and to cool the body. (Bostrom, 1988, p. 55)

As alarming as all that may sound, we should be glad for this extra boost. Can you imagine an athlete with absolutely no anxiety before a big game? His or her performance no doubt would fall far short of winning the "big prize."

Neither age nor experience seems to cure situational anxiety. Well-known people who have acknowledged feeling nervous before new speaking situations include journalist Mike Wallace, former CEO Lee Iacocca, evangelist Billy Graham, and talk show host Katie Couric. Yet all these people achieved speaking success. One key to their success may be that they learned to view the symptoms of situational anxiety as normal excitement necessary for dynamic communication. With this positive attitude, anxiety not only becomes manageable but often disappears completely. Poor communicators, who tend to view the symptoms of situational anxiety with

fear and as further proof that they are poor speakers, often find that their anxiety becomes worse as the speech proceeds.

Trait Anxiety

Whereas practically everyone experiences situational anxiety, fewer people experience trait anxiety. Trait anxiety, often referred to as *communication anxiety* or *apprehension,* is a more personal, internal feeling about communication. You can determine your level of trait anxiety from your Communication Apprehension (CA) score on James McCroskey's PRCA, the Personal Report of Communication Apprehension (McCroskey, 1982). ➤ *Recall that in Chapter 1 you took the PRCA, located under Student Resources for Chapter 1 at the Essentials of Public Speaking website.*

People with high trait anxiety often (1) feel that they are different from other speakers ("I'm more nervous than anyone else in my class"), (2) have a history of negative speaking experiences (whether real or perceived), and (3) consider themselves to have subordinate status to others (Beatty, 1988; Beatty et al., 1989). Let's look at each of these characteristics and see how they can be overcome.

Dissimilarity As you look at classmates in your speech class, you may say to yourself, "Everyone else looks confident. I must be the only one who is really nervous about speaking." One researcher took an informal survey of students enrolled in public-speaking classes and found that one-third of them felt that "they experienced the highest anxiety levels of all those enrolled in the course" (Beatty, 1988).

The belief in dissimilarity obviously is false. We wrongly assume that we are different from everyone else because no one else seems to be nervous. Although some people do show outward signs of nervousness, most nervousness is internal and is barely obvious to an audience (Carrell & Willmington, 1998). The best way to prove this to yourself is to see yourself on videotape. Most people are amazed that their inner turmoil is only slightly visible or not visible at all.

Speaking History If your prior speaking experiences have been mostly positive, you are less likely to have high trait anxiety. However, if you have had a negative speaking experience in the past, you may feel that there is a good chance that it could happen again. Feeling that you are going to do poorly as a speaker because you have always been a poor speaker is a vicious cycle. Researchers have found the public-speaking section of the PRCA to be a good reflection of a person's speaking history (Beatty, 1984). If you have a high PRCA score, especially a high public-speaking score, I urge you to pay particular attention to the section on managing trait anxiety later in the chapter.

Subordinate Status Not only do highly anxious speakers consider themselves to be subordinate to the person in charge, but they also, because they generally have low self-esteem, feel subordinate to their audience. For example, people who worry that their audience will know more about their topic than they do will feel subordinate. To overcome this feeling, first find two or more expert sources that agree with your viewpoint and cite them during your speech. Second, personalize your speech with at least one personal story or experience to show your own unique slant on the topic.

Once you have identified which type of anxiety is causing your lack of confidence, you can do something to correct or manage it. Although situational anxiety is easier to manage than trait anxiety, both can be controlled.

Managing Situational Anxiety

Accept the fact that every speaking situation will cause butterflies. According to the legendary journalist Edward R. Murrow, "The only difference between the pros and the novices is that the pros have trained their butterflies to fly in formation" (Bostrom, 1988, p. 57). The following suggestions will help you control your butterflies (Hamilton, 2005, pp. 129–130).

Prepare and Practice

Nothing will make you more nervous than knowing you are not adequately prepared. After all, isn't your nervousness really fear that you will look foolish in the eyes of your coworkers, classmates, or friends (Bippus & Daly, 1999)? Preparation makes such a possibility less likely. Lilly Walters (1993), speech consultant and author of *Secrets of Successful Speakers,* estimates that careful preparation can reduce anxiety by as much as 75 percent! Unfortunately, perhaps because they feel overwhelmed, anxious people prepare less rather than more thoroughly (Daly, Vangelisti, & Weber, 1995).

To prepare properly, first analyze your audience and plan your presentation and visual aids for this particular group. Next, prepare easy-to-follow notes. Using these notes, rehearse your presentation three or more times from beginning to end—*always speaking out loud.* Mentally thinking through your speech is not the same as practicing aloud. Your practice environment should be as close as possible to the actual speaking environment. For example, if you will be standing during your presentation, stand while practicing; if you will be using visual aids, practice using them. As you rehearse, time yourself to see if you need to shorten or lengthen the presentation. Practice allows you to eliminate the unexpected from the speaking situation (Buss, 1980). Finally, anticipate possible questions and prepare answers for them. Knowing that you are well prepared will help ease much of your anxiety (Behnke & Sawyer, 1999; Daly, Vangelisti, Neel, & Cavanaugh, 1989; Daly et al., 1995). ➡ *See the Quick Start Guide at the beginning of the text for a brief overview of how to prepare a speech. Chapters 12 and 13 discuss in detail how to prepare for informative and persuasive speeches.*

Warm Up First

Just as singers warm up their voices and athletes warm up their muscles before a performance, you'll want to warm up your voice and loosen your muscles before giving your presentation. A variety of techniques can help you do this. For example, sing up and down the scale the way singers do before a concert. Read aloud a page from a book, varying your volume, pitch, emphasis, and rate. Do stretching exercises such as touching your toes and rolling your head from side to side. Practice various gestures such as pointing, pounding your fist, and shrugging your shoulders. These warm-up exercises will help you relax and ensure that you are ready to perform at your best (Richmond & McCroskey, 1998).

Use Deep Breathing

One quick way to calm your nervousness is deep breathing. Take a deep breath through your nose, hold it while you count to five, and then slowly exhale through your mouth. As you exhale, imagine that the stress and tension are slowly draining down your arms and out your fingertips, down your body and legs and out your toes. Repeat the process a second or third time if needed. Deep breathing slows the

Putting your audience at ease right from the start will help you to relax and set the tone for the rest of the speech.

© Bob Dammrich/The Image Works

heartbeat and lowers tension, making us feel more in control (Pletcher, 2000). A good time to use deep breathing is right before you go to the front of the audience to begin your presentation. ➔ *A more detailed explanation of deep breathing is given in the section Exercises in Positive Imagery, Exercise 1, later in the chapter.*

Plan an Introduction to Relax You and Your Listeners

Most speakers find that once they get a favorable audience reaction, they relax. This is one reason that many speakers start with humor—it relaxes them as well as their listeners (Detz, 2000). If a humorous introduction is inappropriate or you are not comfortable with humor, relate a personal experience. One engineering speaker advises that since "stories travel further and faster than facts," a story makes a great introduction (Anderson, 1999, p. 88). Whatever your preference, make your introduction work to put you and your audience at ease. ➔ *See Chapter 7 for a detailed discussion of attention-getting introductions.*

Concentrate on Meaning

Instead of worrying about how you look or sound and whether you are impressing your audience, center your energy on getting your meaning across. Make sure your listeners are following the organization of your speech and understanding your points. Pay close attention to their nonverbal reactions. If they look confused, explain the idea in different words or add another example. A speaker who is concentrating on the listeners soon forgets about being nervous. ➔ *Chapter 3 contains a detailed discussion of listeners and how to "read" their nonverbal reactions.*

Technology Tip for Speakers

**Boost Your Confidence—
Use Electronic Visual Aids**

Although any type of visual aid can help an anxious speaker feel more confident—by keeping your hands busy, shifting audience attention from yourself, and assisting your memory—electronic visuals are the best. If you have state-of-the-art visual aids, how can you not feel more confident? Although electronic visuals may at first seem complicated, you will soon find that they are easy to prepare, easy to revise (even at the last minute), easy to use, and they help with organization. And they're fun!

For electronic presentations the easy way (using Microsoft PowerPoint):

- *Open your speech template* (adapted from PowerPoint's AutoContent Wizard for speech preparation). Get your speech template from the Student Resources for Chapter 2 at the Essentials of Public Speaking website. Download or copy/paste it into your PowerPoint data file. Each time you open PowerPoint and click on "Open an existing presentation," the template will appear.

- *Type in your outline* (a rough idea is all you need to begin—polish it later). The speech template will open to Outline view (see Figure 2.1). As you type the outline, basic slides are prepared ready for you to customize them. (For basic and advanced customizing suggestions, use the PowerPoint Speaker's Guide in the Student

Figure 2.1
**Speech Template
in Outline View**

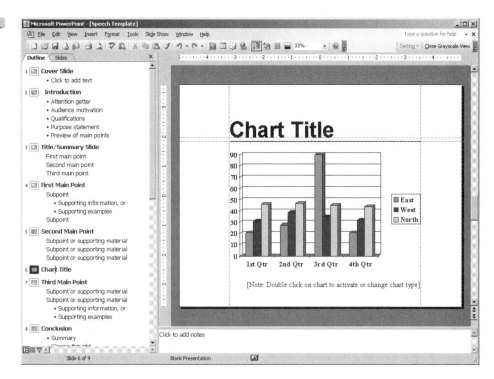

Resources for Chapter 2 at the Essentials of Public Speaking website.) ➜ *Also see the Technology Tip for Speakers in Chapter 9 for more information about customizing PowerPoint slides.*

■ *View your outline in slide form* by clicking on the Slide Sorter View button (bottom left of screen; see Figure 2.2). Double-click on any slide to return it to Slide view for changes. Any changes you make to individual slides will update the outline; also, any changes to the outline will update your slides. Note: This outline on PowerPoint is a rough draft only. You will want to give your instructor a more polished outline with transi-

tions, references, introduction, and conclusion. ➜ *See Chapter 8 for suggestions for a more polished preparation outline.*

■ *View the presentation in full-screen form* by clicking the Slide Show button (to exit, press the Escape key). Move through the slides in your presentation by clicking the mouse or pressing the space bar. Practice moving back and forth between slides simply by pressing the number of the desired slide plus the Enter key.

With just a little practice, you will be able to offer professional-looking presentations with a confidence you didn't think was possible.

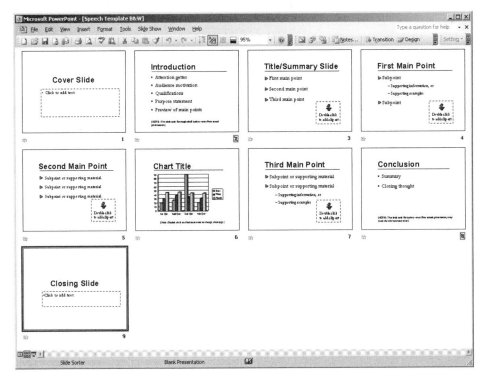

Figure 2.2

Speech Template in Slide Sorter View

Use Visual Aids

Researchers have found that anxious speakers feel more confident when they use visual aids (Ayres, 1991). For one thing, *visual aids give you something to do with your hands* such as changing transparencies, holding an object, or pointing to information on a screen or chart. Of course, to appear really confident, you will need to practice smoothly shifting from one visual to the next while talking and maintaining eye contact with your audience.

Visual aids also shift audience attention away from you—at least for a few seconds. To illustrate this point, have a classmate or your instructor put up an interesting transparency or computer visual while continuing to talk about something unrelated to the visual. Try to look only at the speaker, not at the visual. The urge to look at the visual is overwhelming, isn't it? Although the shift in audience attention to the visual is brief, it gives you time to relax and regroup.

Finally, *visual aids make it almost impossible to forget what you want to say.* If you suddenly forget your next point, all you have to do is put up the next visual and you will instantly remember what you want to say. Also, you don't need to worry about remembering specific facts or statistics if that information is included on a text or graphic visual. In addition, speakers using flipcharts can write notes lightly in pencil on the chart, and speakers using transparencies can write notes on the transparency frames. Be sure to keep your notes brief—key words or phrases are usually enough.

Use Positive Imagery

Researchers have found that positive imagery (discussed in the next section) is not only beneficial for managing trait anxiety, but also helps control situational anxiety as well (Ayres, Heuett, & Sonandre, 1998).

Managing Trait Anxiety: Positive Imagery

Although there are several techniques for managing trait anxiety, most of them require the help of trained professionals. Positive imagery (also called visualization or mental imagery) simply requires the use of your imagination and is a successful technique that you can do on your own. Researchers have found positive imagery to be easy to use and to have a long-term effect (Ayres, 1988; Ayres & Ayres, 2003; Ayres & Hopf, 1989, 1990; Ayres, Hopf, & Ayres, 1997; Bourhis & Allen, 1992). With **positive imagery**, you create a positive, vivid, and detailed mental image of yourself giving a successful and confident speech. When you imagine yourself speaking confidently, you become more confident just as you would if you had actually given a successful speech.

When I ask students and seminar participants to say out loud together, "I am an excellent speaker," most of them say they feel like phonies, and some of them can't even say the words. How about you? Try saying, "I am an excellent speaker," and make it sound as though you mean it. If we can't even say it, how can we expect to do it? Once you begin to see yourself as a good speaker, you will find that it is easier to be a good speaker.

Although positive imagery has only recently been applied to speaker confidence (Beatty, 1984), it has been used successfully in sports for years. One of the first studies of positive imagery investigated its effects on basketball players. Students were di-

Use InfoTrac College Edition to learn more about managing anxiety. Locate several articles on communication anxiety by using the keywords *positive imagery, visualization, visualizing,* or *mental imaging.* Which keyword gave you the most articles?

vided into three groups. Group 1 was told to practice shooting baskets 20 minutes a day. Group 2 was told not to touch a basketball but to spend 20 minutes a day imagining themselves shooting baskets; if they imagined a "miss," they were to correct it and continue practicing. Group 3 had no physical or mental practice of any kind. After 3 weeks, the students in the three groups were tested. The students who had practiced neither physically nor mentally had not improved at all. But the students who had practiced mentally had improved by the same amount as those who had practiced physically—about 24 percent (Richardson, 1952, p. 56).

In 1989, sports psychologist Jim Loehr reported that 80 to 85 percent of top athletes used positive imagery as part of their training. That percentage appears to have increased over the years. For example, basketball great Michael Jordan, golfers David Duval and Tiger Woods, figure skaters Sarah Hughes and Kristi Yamaguchi, and gymnast Mary Lou Retton are just a few of the athletes who make regular use of positive imagery.

Mary Lou Retton, winner of several individual gold medals in the 1984 Olympics, is a good example of an athlete successfully using positive imagery. Retton needed a perfect 10 on her last vault in order for Team USA to win gold in gymnastics:

> She had to get a perfect score, a 10, or lose it all—lose the dream, the gold, the team pride, everything. She closed her eyes for a few seconds, then got into position, ran like a demon on fire, and nailed a perfect 10 off the pommel horse to clinch the gold medal for herself and Team USA. When asked by reporters afterward what she was thinking when she closed her eyes before her run to victory, she told them she saw herself doing every motion precisely, flawlessly, and achieving a perfect score. (Hansen & Allen, 2002, p. 52)

One of my students from several years ago is a good example of a speaker with high trait anxiety successfully using positive imagery. Monica (not her real name) told me at the end of the first day of class that she would probably drop the class when we got to the first individual speech—she had already dropped the class five times previously—because there was just no way she could ever give a speech. I encouraged her to read the chapter on building speaker confidence and to begin using positive imagery. With great hesitation, she agreed. Monica gave the first speech (a great accomplishment), although she was obviously nervous. With each speech she improved and by the final persuasive speech was a different person. Not only was she selected by the class as the *most improved* speaker, she was also voted as the *best* persuasive speaker. As Monica accepted the award, she proudly told the class that she had given a report in her psychology class as well. The applause was thunderous.

Why Positive Imagery Works

According to Gail Dusa, president of the National Council for Self-Esteem, "Visualization, in many ways, is nothing more complicated than involving your imagination in goal-setting. It's not hocus-pocus or magic. When you use your imagination to enhance goal-setting you get fired up, excited. This enthusiasm equips you with more mental energy to put into the task" (McGarvey, 1990, p. 35).

This mental energy has many of the same effects as physical action. Researchers have known for some time that "vividly experienced imagery, imagery that is both seen and felt, can substantially affect brain waves, blood flow, heart rate, skin temperature, gastric secretions, and immune response" (Houston, 1997, p. 11). Using brain-imaging technology, neuroscientists demonstrated why visualization works for athletes. In this study, athletes who imagined a movement activated the same areas in

Athletes such as golfer Tiger Woods commonly use positive imagery to enhance performance. Here, Tiger is checking the lay of the green for his putt and visualizing the path he wants the ball to take.

© AP Wide World Photos

the brain as athletes who performed the actual movement (Kosslyn et al., 1999; Stephan et al., 1995). Another recent study found similar results in the language sphere—both imagined and spoken words activated the same prefrontal and premotor areas of the brain (Wise et al., 1991). Of course, visualization alone doesn't turn athletes into winners. They practice long and hard as well. In the same way, using positive imagery is unlikely to turn you into a confident, polished speaker unless you also prepare and practice your speech carefully.

Another way that positive imagery works is more difficult to explain. Psychologists tell us that the role of our subconscious mind is to keep us true to our "picture" of ourselves (Maltz, 1960). Every time we react to something we have done or respond to a compliment or criticism, we are sending messages to our subconscious about how we see ourselves. Our present thoughts and words determine our picture of ourselves, which in turn shapes our future reactions. In other words, we act as the person we "see" ourselves to be. If you say to yourself, "I don't see myself as a confident speaker," then you won't be one.

According to the authors of *The Mental Athlete,* "If you 'visualize' yourself as a mediocre athlete, if you go into a workout or competition 'seeing' yourself performing on an average level or slower or less perfectly than those around you, this is the way you will perform in reality" (Porter & Foster, 1986, p. 71). They asked runner Mary Decker Slaney, who fell during the 3,000-meter race in the 1984 Olympics, if she had visualized the race. They report, "She said she had dreamed about it and visualized it for weeks, even months. She paused, and then said, 'But I never saw myself finishing the race'" (Porter & Foster, pp. 22, 24).

On the other hand, Alpine skier Jean Claude Killy (winner of gold medals in three Olympic events) reports that one of his best performances occurred after an accident prevented him from practicing on the snow and his only practice was to ski the course mentally (Sheikh, 1983).

Mastering Positive Imagery

So far we have defined *positive imagery* and discussed why it works. This section will show you how to use positive imagery to manage your own trait anxiety and begin to see yourself as a confident speaker. The method discussed here is used across the nation in many athletic programs, business seminars, and coaching sessions (Porter, 2003; Porter & Foster, 1986; Tice, 1980; Tice & Quick, 1997; Tice & Steinberg, 1989).

Step 1: Develop the Habit of Positive Self-Talk Is your self-talk negative? When you make a mistake, what do you say to yourself? "There I go again. It's just like me to mess up like this!" When someone compliments you on a speech, do you reject it by saying, "Oh, it was just dumb luck," or "Well, I did mess up on my visual aids"? Dr. Kay Porter (Porter & Foster, 1986; see also Porter, 2003), who teaches mental training techniques to athletes, says that an athlete's self-talk between points and between games can make the difference between winning and losing. She uses herself as an example of what not to do:

> In the years between age 10 and 22, I played tennis. While I never quite mastered my tennis game, I mastered the negative game totally, doing everything that I have spent the last few years teaching people not to do. I choked, blew my concentration, cursed myself, mentally abused myself, and considered myself a total loser when it came to tennis. I was a master of self-defeat. (Porter & Foster, p. 225)

Instead, use only positive self-talk. If you are in the middle of a speech and suddenly realize that you have forgotten to use your visual aid for the first main point, use positive self-talk: "That's not like me. The next time I'll practice using my visuals." And when you are complimented for your speech, accept the compliment without dwelling on whatever faults you think it had. Say, "Thank you, I worked hard on that speech" even if you feel it was not perfect.

With positive self-talk, you also avoid saying, "I have to/ought to/need to . . ." Such thinking only makes you feel obligated to do certain things, and your subconscious tries hard to get you out of it. Think about what happens when you say to yourself, "I have to get up early to prepare tomorrow's report." How many times have you been so sleepy that you couldn't drag yourself out of bed? The trick is to substitute positive trigger words for negatives ones: "I want to/like to/enjoy/choose to . . ." For example, instead of saying, "I've got to work on my speech," say, "I want to prepare my speech" or "I'm looking forward to finishing my speech" or simply "I've decided to finish my speech." It's amazing how using positive words instead of negative ones can change your attitude. Instead of spending your time resisting the task, you can now complete it and go on to enjoy something else without feeling guilty.

Step 2: Refocus Negative Mental Pictures Into Positive Ones To begin the refocusing process, look two or three months into the future (perhaps to the end of the semester) and picture yourself as the speaker you would like to be. What specific speaking characteristics would you like to possess? To help you see the "ideal you," imagine that you are giving a speech to a class or club 3 months from now. How do you look, sound, and feel? How is the audience responding? Are you confident, organized, and dynamic?

Get a complete picture of the "ideal you" in your mind. As a guide, here are just a few speaking characteristics you might want to achieve:

- Look audience members in the eye
- Feel relaxed and confident
- Sound dynamic
- Keep a loud volume and my voice from shaking
- Use visual aids without dropping one or misusing the remote
- Not worry so much about what my audience thinks of me

- Give speeches that are organized and easy to follow

- Remain confident during Q & A (question and answers)

When you have completed your list of desired characteristics, use them as the basis for writing 5 to 10 positive statements that describe you as though the future has arrived and the changes you want have already occurred. Avoid "I want/I will/I hope . . ." Instead, use present tense, action verbs, and words that will trigger positive feelings. See how the desired speaking characteristics from the above list were turned into sample positive statements:

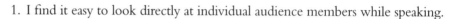

> **Stop reading at this point and make a list of the speaking characteristics you wish to develop.**

1. I find it easy to look directly at individual audience members while speaking.

2. I feel as relaxed and confident giving a formal speech as I do entertaining good friends in my own living room.

3. My delivery is as dynamic and enthusiastic as it is when I talk about an exciting football game.

4. When presenting speeches, my voice is strong and steady and loud enough to be easily heard.

5. I handle visual aids confidently and smoothly.

6. While speaking, I do not worry about pleasing everyone; rather, I please myself with what I have to say.

7. I give speeches that are clear, understandable, and well organized.

8. I find question-and-answer sessions stimulating and enjoyable.

As you write your positive statements, be sure to get rid of negative wording. For example, instead of "I will try to make eye contact with audience members when I speak," say, "I make direct eye contact with audience members when I speak." Instead of "I won't let large audiences scare me," use a positive image and say, "I enjoy giving speeches regardless of the size of the audience."

Once you have completed your positive statements, begin visualizing them. Every morning and evening for about a month, *read* the statements out loud. After reading each one, take a few seconds to close your eyes and mentally *picture* yourself being the person the statement describes. Make this mental picture as detailed and vivid as possible (Ayres, Hopf, & Ayres, 1994; Marks, 1999). At the same time, *feel* relaxed, confident, and competent. For example, for the statement "I find it easy to look directly at individual audience members while speaking," see yourself standing confidently in front of the room looking directly at various audience members as you give a clear, well-organized, and entertaining talk. For the statement "I handle visual aids confidently and smoothly," see yourself standing confidently beside the overhead projector or computer, calmly placing and removing transparencies or using the computer remote or space bar. Feel a sense of satisfaction in your performance.

For positive imagery to work—to refocus the negative pictures you have of yourself into positive ones—you must do more than merely read your statements. For change to occur, you need to *say them* (concrete words), *see them* (vivid mental

To increase speaker confidence, mentally picture yourself on the day of your presentation, looking good, feeling confident, and giving a great presentation.

© Anne Dowie

pictures), and *feel them* (Zagacki, Edwards, & Honeycutt, 1992). To put it another way, words + vivid mental pictures + feelings = confidence. If you have trouble with the "feeling" part of some of your positive statements, build feeling cues into them. For example, if you can't "feel" confident while looking listeners in the eye, think of a situation in which you do feel confident making eye contact and add it to your statement: "It's as easy for me to make direct eye contact with my audience as it is when I _____."

One student commented that she viewed her past speaking history like a videotape. Although she couldn't erase any of her past failures, she could tape over them with both real and imagined speaking experiences. Once she had taped over all the negative experiences, she started to see herself as a good speaker and actually began to enjoy speaking.

Step 3: Don't Compare Yourself to Others   No matter who you are or how long you have been speaking, there will always be people who are better speakers than you are. At the same time, you will always be better than some people. It's not a contest between you and the other students in your class. If someone gives a really outstanding speech right before yours is scheduled, resist the temptation to say, "There's no way I can follow such a good speech. I can never be that good." Your goal isn't to be better than other speakers. Your goal is to be the best speaker you can be—you are competing only with yourself.

On the other hand, it's perfectly all right to borrow techniques from other speakers (students as well as professionals). For example, if the colors Jack used on his visuals made them come alive, you might try using the same colors. Or if Alounsa's gestures seemed especially sincere and expressive, you might try using similar ges-

> ## *Remember*
>
> ## To create positive mental images . . .
>
> - Look two or three months into the future.
> - Picture yourself as the "ideal" speaker you would like to be.
> - Write five to ten positive statements that describe this "ideal" you.
> - Twice a day for four weeks, read, visualize, and feel yourself successfully performing each statement.

tures. You may even wish to ask Alounsa if she uses any special techniques or has any pointers for you. Borrowing public-speaking ideas and practices from a person is not the same as wanting to be that person. It is simply another tool for becoming the best speaker you can be.

If you use positive imagery as outlined here, in about 4 weeks you will begin to feel comfortable with the "new" you (Tice & Quick, 1997). By taping over your past negative experiences and fears, you will begin to think of yourself as a "good" speaker who actually "enjoys" giving speeches.

Exercises in Positive Imagery

In addition to visualizing your positive statements, tape yourself reading the following positive imagery exercises. For the best results, play this tape at least once a week and the night before each scheduled speech. As you listen, see and feel yourself giving a successful speech. Two recent studies found that speakers who used similar visualization exercises even once had less communication anxiety than did speakers who did not use them or who used some other anxiety-reduction method (Ayres & Hopf, 1985, 1989; see also Bourhis & Allen, 1992). Exercise 1 is based on Ayres & Hopf (1989).

Exercise 1

It's important to get in the mood to visualize. Close your eyes and get as comfortable as you can in your chair. For the next 10 minutes or so, try to keep an open body posture with your feet flat on the floor and your arms resting comfortably but not touching. Now, take in a deep breath . . . hold it as you count slowly to three . . . and exhale slowly. As you exhale, feel the tension in your neck and shoulders draining down your arms and out your fingers; feel the tension in your back and hips draining down your legs and out your toes. Take another deep breath . . . hold it . . . and slowly release it through your mouth (if possible). Feel the tension leaving your body. Now one more time, breathe deeply . . . hold it . . . slowly exhale and begin normal breathing.

Imagine yourself at the sink in your bathroom. You lean toward the mirror to get a better look at your face. Do you see your face? The mirror suddenly clouds over. When it clears again, you are looking through the mirror into the future. You can see yourself getting up on a day when you are going to give a particularly important speech. You jump out of bed full of energy, full of confidence, and looking forward to the day. You are putting on one of your favorite outfits, which makes you feel professional and confident. See how good you

look and feel? Imagine yourself arriving relaxed at the speaking site. When you arrive, people comment on your appearance and how relaxed you appear. You feel thoroughly prepared for this presentation. You have researched carefully, have professional visual aids, and have practiced several times. Now see yourself standing or sitting in the room where you will make your speech, talking very comfortably and confidently with others in the room. Everyone seems friendly and supportive. You feel absolutely sure of your material and of your ability to present the information in a forceful, convincing, positive manner. It's time for the speech. See yourself walk confidently to the front and smile at the audience. They smile back. You set up your visual aids and begin your presentation.

Now see yourself speaking. Your introduction goes the way you had planned. You are dynamic, forceful, and interesting. Your speaking rate is just right; your pauses and emphasis couldn't be better; your gestures and body movements are powerful. As you flow from one main point to the next, the audience smiles and nods. They are really paying attention and seem impressed by your visual and verbal supporting material. As you wrap up your main points, you have the feeling that it could not have gone better. The audience applauds with enthusiasm. Do you hear the applause? Now see yourself answering questions with the same confidence and energy you displayed in the actual speech. The speech is over. People come up and shake your hand and congratulate you. You accept their thanks in a relaxed and pleased manner. You are filled with energy, purpose, and a sense of well-being. Congratulate yourself on a job well done!

The future fades, and the mirror again shows your reflection—but the confident smile remains on your face. Now take a deep breath . . . hold it . . . and slowly let it out. Do this several more times and slowly return to the room.

If you can't "see" yourself while doing this exercise, don't be concerned. Positive imagery is easier for some people than for others (Isaac & Marks, 1994). If you have difficulty seeing any images at all, "think of what it might be like if you could see the pictures you're thinking about" (Carr-Ruffino, 1985) and concentrate on the "feeling" part of the exercise.

The next exercise was adapted from a seminar participant who highlighted specific speaking qualities that she wanted to develop (Hamilton, 2005, p. 133). You may want to write your own positive imagery exercise and tailor it to your specific goals. Begin with the relaxation and deep breathing described in Exercise 1. When you feel relaxed, play your taped version of this next exercise and imagine yourself as the person being described.

Exercise 2

I am looking at myself sitting in my usual seat in speech class on the day of my first speech. It is my turn to speak. As I rise from my seat, I direct the butterflies of excitement in my stomach into positive energy. I can do this because I have practiced carefully and know I am well prepared. As I turn to face my fellow classmates, I draw in a deep breath, stand up straight, and begin to speak. An aura of confidence radiates from within as I speak. My body is relaxed. My breathing is paced. My motions are fluid, and my gestures are graceful. My shoulders stay relaxed and down. My voice is steady and strong. It is pitched low and is well modulated and easy for everyone to hear. My eyes scan from student to student, drawing their complete attention. My mind is rested and calm, allowing my words to flow evenly and to be clear and concise.

As I speak, I easily remember each point of my speech. I can see the outline of my speech clearly in my mind and refer to my notes only briefly. I make use

of dramatic pauses to stress important points within the speech. It is obvious that the class understands what I am saying and that they are enjoying my speech. My words continue to flow smoothly, and my transitions are especially good. Each idea is spoken clearly and confidently. There are no mistakes.

As the speech winds down, my words are chosen carefully and powerfully. The audience is paying complete attention. I end with a bang! I know from the enthusiastic applause and positive comments that my speech has been a total success! I pause, and then ask if there are any questions. As I rephrase each question, I continue to feel relaxed and confident. My answers are brief and to the point. I can tell the audience is impressed with the visual aid I use to answer a question. When the Q & A is over, I pause for effect, and then present my final wrap-up. Again the audience applauds with enthusiasm. I feel proud and confident as I walk back to my seat.

Other Methods for Managing Trait Anxiety

Positive imagery isn't the only method for reducing trait anxiety, although it is one of the few methods that you can use on your own. Other confidence-building methods, which are usually offered as a repeated seminar or 1-hour semester course, include systematic desensitization, cognitive restructuring, and rhetoritherapy—a form of skills training (Richmond & McCroskey, 1998). All these methods require some help from trained professionals. Your college may offer seminars or workshops in one or a combination of these methods. If your anxiety level is especially high, you may find that one or more of these methods combined with positive imagery may work better for you (Allen, Hunter, & Donohue, 1989, p. 63; Dwyer, 2000; Kelly & Keaten, 2000). Let's take a brief look at each of these methods.

Systematic Desensitization

According to its originator (Wolpe, 1958), **systematic desensitization** simply means learning to feel relaxed instead of anxious. It has two basic steps: (1) learning to relax, using deep muscle relaxation and breathing (McCroskey, 1972; Richmond & McCroskey, 1998), and (2) learning to remain relaxed while visualizing a series of communication situations that progress from low anxiety to high anxiety (Friedrich, Goss, Cunconan, & Lane, 1997). Deep muscle relaxation involves tensing and then relaxing various muscle groups. Richmond and McCroskey (p. 101) suggest that the following muscle groups each be tensed for approximately 5 to 10 seconds, followed by 10 to 15 seconds of relaxation.

1. *Hands:* clench and unclench right hand, then left hand.

2. *Biceps and triceps:* bend right hand upward at wrist, pointing fingers toward ceiling, relax, then left hand; bring both hands up toward shoulders, flex biceps, then relax.

3. *Shoulders:* shrug shoulders, hold, relax.

4. *Neck:* push head against chair, relax; lean forward, relax.

5. *Mouth:* press lips tightly together, then relax.

6. *Tongue:* extend, hold, retract.

7. *Tongue:* press roof of mouth, relax; press floor of mouth, relax.

8. *Eyes and forehead:* close eyes tightly, relax; wrinkle forehead, relax.

9. *Breathing:* inhale, hold, exhale.

10. *Back:* arch back, hold, relax.

11. *Midsection:* clench muscles, hold, relax.

12. *Thighs:* clench muscles, hold, relax.

13. *Stomach:* suck in stomach, hold, relax.

14. *Calves and feet:* stretch out both legs, hold, relax.

15. *Toes:* point toes toward ceiling, hold, relax; point toes downward, hold, relax.

Once you are relaxed, you begin visualizing various communication situations that your instructor or trainer has helped you develop, moving from the least threatening to the more threatening ones. Low-anxiety situations might include hearing that you will be giving a speech later in the semester, being assigned a speech that is due in two weeks, or researching speech sources in the library. Higher-anxiety situations might include rehearsing your speech, arriving at the classroom on the day of your speech, and walking to the front of the classroom to give your speech (Koester & Pucel, 1993).

If at any time during the process you begin to feel tense and anxious, you stop visualizing and reestablish a relaxed state. When you can maintain this relaxed state without effort, try visualizing the situation again. You continue this process (which will take many sessions) until you can visualize all problem situations without anxiety.

Cognitive Restructuring

Cognitive restructuring is based on the assumption that speaking anxiety is a result of irrational thoughts that produce negative images and unrealistic expectations about speech making (Ellis, 1962; Meichenbaum, 1977, 1985). According to Joe Ayres and Tim Hopf, irrational thoughts that contribute to speaker anxiety include "believing that everyone must like your speech, that everyone should be persuaded by your speech, and that, if you mispronounce one word, everyone will think you are uneducated" (1993, p. 31). Cognitive restructuring has three parts: (1) identifying irrational self-talk that produces speaker anxiety, (2) developing alternative coping statements to replace these irrational thoughts, and (3) practicing using the coping statements in stressful situations, such as group discussions or speaking situations (Fremouw & Scott, 1979; Meichenbaum, 1985).

Rhetoritherapy

Rhetoritherapy focuses on speaking skills more than feelings. As developed by G. M. Phillips (1977, 1991) and refined by Keaten and Kelly (2000), it covers communication skills in interpersonal, small-group, and public-speaking situations (Kelly, 1989; Kelly, Phillips, & Finch, 1995). The skills needed for public speaking include many of the same skills needed in interpersonal and group settings. The less threatening one-on-one interpersonal situations are covered first, then group situations, and finally the more threatening public-speaking situations. Ideally, as your skills increase, your anxiety decreases.

In focusing on skills, rhetoritherapy deals with goal analysis. You are asked to (1) identify reasonable speaking goals, (2) determine specific behaviors or practices needed to complete each goal, and (3) develop procedures for judging the success of each goal (Kelly, 1989; Kelly, et al., 1995). For example, one goal might be to improve your delivery skills. Specific behaviors for this goal might be to speak loud enough to be heard, to use gestures while speaking, and to make direct eye contact with as many audience members as possible (Ayres & Hopf, 1993, pp. 72–73). The goal might be judged to have been achieved when audience evaluations of your speech indicate that your volume was good, your gestures were effective, and at least half the listeners found your eye contact to be direct and sincere.

Summary

"I am relaxed and in control while giving speeches" is a good positive statement to sum up this chapter. There is no reason to let nervousness and anxiety consume us when we speak. Taking control of nervousness and anxiety is much easier once we can identify it.

Situational anxiety is something almost everyone experiences in new situations. We can manage this type of anxiety by preparing and practicing, warming up, concentrating on our message, planning introductions that relax us as well as our audience, using visual aids effectively, and using positive imagery.

Trait anxiety is the personal fears that we bring to a speaking situation. Although it is more difficult to control than situational anxiety, trait anxiety can be effectively managed through positive imagery. Positive imagery, which requires the use of your imagination to create a positive, vivid, and detailed image of yourself giving a successful speech, can be used without professional help and is long lasting. Successful use of positive imagery includes three basic steps: (1) concentrate on positive self-talk, (2) refocus negative mental pictures into positive ones, and (3) don't compare yourself with others—just be the best speaker you can be.

Trait anxiety can also be reduced through systematic desensitization, cognitive restructuring, and rhetoritherapy. Each of these methods requires some help from trained professionals. If positive imagery doesn't seem to work for you, ask your professor if instruction in one of these other methods is available. With a little time and effort, your situational or trait anxiety can be managed so that you can give confident, successful speeches.

Essentials of Public Speaking  *Online*

Use the Essentials of Public Speaking website at **http://communication. wadsworth.com/hamiltoneps3** for quick access to the electronic study resources that accompany this chapter. When you get to the Essentials home page, click on "Student Book Companion Site" in the Resource box. The Essentials website features the PRCA (Personal Report of Communication Apprehension) questionnaire described on page 25, the Speech Template and PowerPoint Speaker's Guide described in this chapter's Technology Tip for Speakers box, InfoTrac College Edition, the Suggestions for Practice and Critical Thinking activities and the InfoTrac College Edition activities that follow, a digital glossary, and review quizzes.

Key Terms

cognitive restructuring 39   situational anxiety 24
positive imagery 30   systematic desensitization 38
rhetoritherapy 39   trait anxiety 24

Suggestions for Practice and Critical Thinking

1. Have you given one of the speeches of introduction described in the Quick Start Guide yet? If so, did you have more or less anxiety than you expected? If not, were you asked to introduce yourself or a classmate the first day of class? In both of these situations, did you experience any situational or trait anxiety? Write out your plans for managing your anxiety and keep a brief weekly journal of your efforts and successes.

2. Use InfoTrac College Edition to find articles with suggestions other than positive imagery for overcoming speaking anxiety. Run PowerTrac searches using the keywords *stage fright* and *public speaking anxiety*.

3. If you haven't already done so, write out 5 to 10 positive statements that represent the speaking characteristics you wish to develop or polish. Make sure that each statement is written as if it were true right now and avoids negative images. Ask a classmate to check the wording of your statements. If necessary, make minor changes.

4. One way people indicate confidence is by using a falling pitch (downspeak)—especially when introducing themselves. If you use a rising pitch (as if you're asking a question) instead of a falling pitch (as if you're making a statement), you sound less confident. Practice saying your name until you can do so with both a rising pitch and a falling pitch. Can you hear the difference? Now, one at a time, each of you should walk confidently to the front of the room and say, "Hello, my name is _____ _____" (with a falling pitch), pause, read two positive statements about yourself (making them sound completely true), and walk confidently to your seat and sit down. Be careful not to roll your eyes or do anything else that indicates anxiety. With other class members, discuss how you felt during this activity.

5. If you are feeling as if you are the only one in your class who's really nervous about speaking, ask your classmates to respond to the following questions:

   a. *How good a speaker do you consider yourself to be?*

   Poor   Fair   Average   Good   Excellent

   b. *How much personal anxiety do you usually experience when speaking?*

   None   Little   Some   Moderate   Great

   If other sections of your course are being taught this term, ask your professor to combine the answers from all sections. How many other students answered as you did? You may wish to share your experiences with one or more of them.

6. In addition to positive imagery (a method of overcoming anxiety that you can use on your own), the Speech Communication Department on your

campus may offer a repeatable seminar or 1-hour semester course using other confidence-building methods such as systematic desensitization, cognitive restructuring, rhetoritherapy, or a combination of methods. If your PRCA scores indicate that you have moderate to high trait anxiety, you may wish to enroll in one of these programs and benefit from the help of a trained professional. Ask your professor for more information. (The PRCA is located under Student Resources for Chapter 1 at the Essentials of Public Speaking website.)

7. Check out the following websites. *You can access these sites under the Student Resources for Chapter 2* at the Essentials of Public Speaking website.

   • A 1999 study conducted by the National Communication Association found that only 24 percent of Americans are comfortable giving a speech. Check out the complete results of the study, "How Americans Communicate," at the NCA website.

   • The website for the Rhetoric Department at the College of New Jersey has a few pages on anxiety that feature some advice you might find helpful. Check it out at the department's Speech Resources page (click on the link "speech anxiety").

   • Steve Eggleston takes a humorous look at speaking anxiety, "Fear of Public Speaking," in his Public Speaking Online Tutorial. He says his problem began in the fifth grade. When did yours begin?

   • A good place to practice speaking in a nonthreatening environment is a local Toastmasters International club. There may be a club on your local college campus. Local clubs are listed on the Toastmasters website. While at their site, click on the link "10 Tips for Successful Public Speaking."

Listening: What Speakers Should Know

Flashback One way listeners avoid being persuaded is by devaluing the speaker's credibility. Even Aristotle, trained as a Greek field biologist to rationally investigate subjects, came to realize that a speaker's credibility depends less on logical proof and more on the listener's perception of the speaker (ethical proof).

WHAT DO THESE TWO SITUATIONS HAVE IN COMMON?

Situation 1: You have worked long and hard on a proposal to present to a Japanese firm. With the help of a translator, you have even prepared your visuals in Japanese. After the introductions, you and the interpreter get right to business and outline what you know to be an excellent presentation. The Japanese listeners seem to be nodding in agreement, so you feel fairly confident that things are going well. At the end of the presentation, the Japanese promise to look over the proposal and get back in touch with you. But they never do. Whenever you call, they politely give a reason for not meeting with you "at this time." (Hamilton, 2005, p. 125, Checkpoint 5.4)

Situation 2: You are the last speaker of the day. The previous speakers each took more than their allotted time. Even though there are only 20 minutes remaining before the program is scheduled to end, the director assures you that you may have your full time. As you speak, you are impressed by the fact that the audience seems to be listening so well—most of them are looking directly at you and sitting totally still. By omitting the less important items, you manage to end on time and conclude with a startling bit of information. However, you are surprised that no one acknowledges your unexpected information as they file out of the room.

Can you tell what each of these speakers failed to do? Both apparently prepared their presentations carefully and took their specific audiences into consideration. The first speaker even prepared visuals in Japanese. The second speaker ended the presentation with a startling statement designed to reestablish audience interest. Neither speaker, however, really understood audience members as listeners. In this chapter, we will discuss what successful speakers need to know about listening and listeners.

People from different cultures listen differently. Some of these differences are discussed by Kiewitz, Weaver, Brosius, and Weimann in an article called "Cultural Differences in Listening Style Preferences." To locate the article (*International Journal of Public Opinion Research,* Fall 1997), use InfoTrac College Edition to conduct an advanced search for the lead author.

Stages of Listening

To understand listeners, speakers first need to know what is involved in effective listening. As shown in Figure 3.1, the process of listening has five stages: sensing, interpreting, evaluating, responding, and, if the other steps are completed correctly, remembering the speaker's message (Steil, Barker, & Watson, 1983).

The Sensing Stage

In the **sensing stage**, listeners select or ignore one or more stimuli from the multitude of stimuli that bombard us continually. It's impossible to notice every sound, sight, and smell or to acknowledge every event or feeling. We learn to become highly selective; we pay attention to things that are of interest to us and tune out everything else. In his book *Listen for Success,* Arthur K. Robertson (1994) cites an example:

> Eugene Raudsepp of Princeton Creative Research tells the story of a zoologist walking down a busy city street with a friend amid honking horns and screeching tires. He says to his friend, "Listen to that cricket!" The friend looks at him with astonishment. "You hear a cricket in the middle of all this noise?" The zoologist takes out a coin and flips it into the air. As it clinks to the sidewalk a dozen heads turn in response. The zoologist says quietly, "We hear what we listen for." (p. 45)

In addition to needs and interests, our gender, age, cultural background, biases, and emotions, as well as environmental distractions, affect what we sense. The goal of the speaker is to get listeners to focus their senses on the message at hand. ➔ *Suggestions for how to do this are discussed later in the chapter.*

The Interpreting Stage

In the **interpreting stage**, listeners supply meaning to the messages that they have sensed—or seen, heard, and felt. In other words, they try to figure out what the speaker really means. The problem is that words can have different meanings. For example, suppose that your boss says in a staff meeting that raises are "likely" this year. What's the chance that the audience's interpretation and the boss's interpretation of

Figure 3.1

Stages of Listening

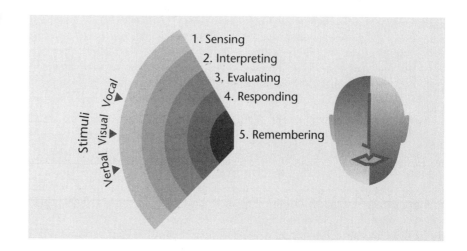

Multiple stimuli are competing for the attention of these listeners.

the word will be the same? Or when your boss gives you a "rush" assignment, how much time do you have to complete the task? One printing company had so many misunderstandings over the word *rush* that it posted the following definitions:

As soon as possible: Do within 2 or 3 days.

Rush: Do by the end of today.

Hot: Don't drop what you're doing, but do it next.

Now: Drop everything.

The same factors that cause faulty sensing can also cause faulty interpretation. Listeners often assume that they understand and don't bother to ask questions or to paraphrase (summarize the speaker's ideas in their own words). Sometimes they are so sure they understand that they stop listening. For example, suppose a group of students were given the following instructions: "In the center of your paper, draw a 1-inch square. Next, label the corners as reference points. Label the upper left-hand corner 'a.' Label the upper right-hand corner 'b.'" At this point, most audience members would stop listening and complete the labeling on their own. But which of the two labeling schemes shown in Figure 3.2 would they follow? In a class exercise, more than half of the students labeled their square according to scheme 1 even though the speaker gave clear instructions for scheme 2.

Some of the most serious listening problems occur in the interpreting stage. Many of the problems in the interpreting stage are clarified by **attribution theory**, which describes how people process informa-

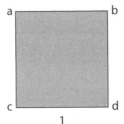

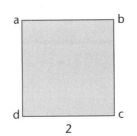

Figure 3.2

Labeling Examples

tion and use it to explain the behavior of others and themselves (Griffin, 1994; Heider, 1958; Littlejohn, 2002). Sometimes these problems occur because listeners jump to conclusions, experience fatigue or information overload, or have the mistaken belief that 100 percent understanding happens with ease. ➤ *Suggestions for how to combat these problems are discussed later in this chapter. See Chapter 12 for a more complete discussion of attribution theory.*

Attribution Theory

- **Original Theorist:** Fritz Heider, *The Psychology of Interpersonal Relations,* 1958.

- **Definition:** The process of drawing inferences or how people process information and use it to explain the behavior of others and self.

- **Involves a Three-Step Process:** (1) Perceive an action, (2) judge intent of action, (3) attribute reason for action.

- **Fundamental Attribution Error** (Ross, 1977): Our tendency to overestimate the role of the person's character and underestimate the role that the situation has on behavior (i.e., we usually assume that the things that happen to people are a result of something they did).

The Evaluating Stage

In the **evaluating stage**, listeners "think about the message, make more extensive inferences, evaluate and judge the speaker and the message" (Goss, 1982). In assigning a value judgment to what they have sensed and understood, listeners decide whether the speaker seems qualified, the information and evidence appear accurate, and the comments are relevant and worthwhile.

Listeners' evaluations are often affected by their attitude toward the speaker. Imagine yourself speaking before audience members who think you are too young or have biases about your gender or ethnic group. Listeners' evaluations are also affected by their previous experiences, their expectations, and their beliefs and emotional states. As a result, listeners sometimes make evaluations based on assumptions without waiting to make sure they have all the facts. Here is an example from a rescue squad member about a call for help from a police officer:

> A 38-year-old man had pulled off the road and hit an obstruction. [After calling the rescue squad, the] patrolman had called back: "Cancel the call. The man is not really injured. He's just complaining of chest pains and probably bumped into the steering wheel." The squad went out anyway. When they arrived they could see immediately that the man was having a heart attack. "What happened," he told them between gasps, "was that I had this chest pain and went off the road." And with that he passed out. We got to work on him right away and got him to a hospital, but it was too late. Now he had told the patrolman the same thing he had told us—"I had this chest pain and went off the road." The patrolman heard him, perhaps understood him, but despite his knowledge and experience did not evaluate what he heard and in this case not evaluating correctly was fatal. I never forgot that. (Steil, Summerfield, & deMare, 1984, pp. 27–28)

What value judgment do you think the listeners in this picture are making? They are listening to arguments for and against erecting a monument to abolitionist Frederick Douglass in a Maryland county courthouse, a space traditionally reserved for veterans' memorials.

Speakers need to be aware that listener interpretations and evaluations often depend on verbal, visual, and vocal impressions. Your words (verbal code); your appearance, gestures, and visual aids (visual code); and your speaking voice (vocal code) are as important to your listeners as your ideas. → *Suggestions for how to aid listener interpretation are discussed later in the chapter.*

The Responding Stage

Once listeners have sensed, interpreted, and evaluated you and your ideas, they respond (give feedback). The **responding stage** is very important, because without feedback, speakers can only assume that they have communicated. Listeners won't always agree with what the speaker is saying, but their responses show whether they were listening and whether they understood.

Listener response can take many forms. Listeners communicate agreement, disagreement, or confusion through obvious nonverbal expressions (such as frowning or nodding). If the situation allows, they might make comments and ask questions during or after the speech or during a question-and-answer period. All these responses are invaluable in judging the success of your presentation.

Sometimes listeners don't make such obvious responses. In this case, you must try to interpret their unintentional responses to see if they understand or are even listening. Just because everyone is staring at you doesn't mean that they are listening attentively. Speakers make a big mistake when they assume that attentive posture and intent eyes equal listening. People who are actually listening tend to shift around in their seats, doodle on their papers, cough, and glance at the clock and the floor. → *More suggestions on how to interpret listener responses are discussed later in the chapter.*

The Remembering Stage

Memory storage is accomplished in the final step of effective listening, the **remembering stage**. Once listeners have completed the sensing, interpreting, evaluating,

> ## *Remember*
>
> ### In the five stages of listening, listeners . . .
>
> - Sense—they hear what is important to them.
> - Interpret—they assign meaning to what they see, hear, and feel.
> - Evaluate—they determine speaker credibility and message importance.
> - Respond—they react to the speech, usually through nonverbal cues.
> - Remember—they retain parts of the message in memory.

and responding stages, they decide what parts, if any, of the speech to retain and then attempt to store them in memory. Unfortunately, no matter how brilliant your speech, most audience members will remember only about 10 to 25 percent of your presentation (Nichols, 1996; Wolff, Marsnik, Tracey, & Nichols, 1983). The parts they don't recall may have contributed to their favorable evaluation of your talk, but they didn't store the specific facts in their memories. Basically, each of these listeners has failed to transfer information from short-term memory into long-term memory (Hauser & Hughes, 1988; Schab & Crowder, 1989). ➡ *Suggestions for what to do to aid listener memory are discussed later in the chapter.*

Knowing the stages of effective listening is not enough. As a speaker, you also must know various techniques to improve audience attention at each listening stage. These techniques are discussed in the remaining sections of this chapter.

In Sensing Stage—Stimulate and Motivate Your Audience

When customers come into a department store, there is no guarantee they will buy anything. Similarly, just because people show up at a meeting or walk into a classroom doesn't mean that they are going to listen to the speaker. In the sensing stage, audience members must be stimulated and then motivated if careful listening is to occur.

Provide External Stimuli

A stimulus can be either internal or external. An **external stimulus** is a person or object external to the listener that triggers an idea in the listener; an **internal stimulus** is a thought generated by the listener that triggers additional thought or action. Suppose you are waiting for a speech to begin and you suddenly remember that you did not return an important phone call (internal stimulus). If you go back to your office, you will miss the speech; but if you wait until after the speech, it will be too late to return the call. You become so engrossed in your problem that you are unaware that the speech has begun.

Before a speech, most audience members are thinking about something other than the topic of the speech. Therefore, the speaker's first task is to focus listeners' attention on the chosen topic. Effective speakers often attempt to eclipse the listeners'

internal stimuli with an attention-getter such as a startling statement, two or three brief examples, a personal experience, a short demonstration, a question, or a humorous anecdote that is directly related to the speech topic. Beginning your presentation with a statement of purpose is much less effective because it works only for those few listeners who are already excited about the topic. → *Methods of stimulating audience attention are discussed in detail in Chapter 7.*

Motivate the Audience to Listen

No matter how effective they are, external stimuli won't guarantee continued audience attention; sufficient motivation is also necessary. To motivate an audience to give you their time, you must convince them that your presentation will benefit them or people they care about in some way. If they perceive that your topic has no personal value, their attention will soon drift to a more pressing topic. Table 3.1 lists possible audience motivators; add as many others as you can, and refer to this list each time you plan a speech.

Speakers who begin with nothing more than a statement of purpose (such as, "Today I'm going to talk about caring for your pets") are taking a big risk. If speakers don't provide external stimuli and motivation, most listeners' concerns (internal stimuli) will keep them from paying full attention. Outstanding presenters make effective use of stimulus and motivation at the beginning of their speeches.

Table 3.1

Needs That Motivate Listeners—*Can you think of any others?*

- Reduce stress and anxiety
- Earn more money
- Gain personal satisfaction
- Impress others and gain esteem
- Develop self-confidence
- Try something new and exciting
- Solve a pressing problem
- Achieve desired goals with less effort
- Improve prestige or power
- Improve rank/position with new skill
- Gain a feeling of pride in the job
- Reach more customers
- Increase job stability and security
- Look more attractive
- Become healthier
- Improve parenting skills
- Help others
- Make a difference in the world

In Interpreting Stage—Circumvent the 100 Percent Listening Myth

Many speakers believe that if they give a good speech and their listeners are paying attention, 100 percent communication is possible. This is unlikely, however, because of *frame of reference* differences between the speaker and listeners. Think of your frame of reference as an imaginary window. Everything you see, touch, taste, smell, and hear is filtered through your own window. With so many different life experiences, it is highly unlikely that any two people will have an identical frame of reference on any topic.

Another reason 100 percent communication is unlikely relates to *code.* Many speakers assume that the only important code is the verbal (language) code. Analyzing results from 23 studies, J. S. Philpott (1983) found that the verbal code accounted for a mere 31 percent of the variance in meanings, whereas the vocal and visual codes accounted for the remaining 69 percent (see also Burgoon & Hoobler, 2002). In other words, as Figure 3.3 shows, the visual and vocal codes carry most of the meaning.

Another hurdle to 100 percent communication is that a speaker often sends *conflicting messages.* Take, for example, a company presenter speaking to a group of hostile customers who incorrectly think the company has been overcharging them. Although the presentation is well organized and clearly justifies the company's prices, the presenter acts nervous, speaks hesitantly in a fairly high pitch, and fails to make direct eye contact with listeners. If you were a customer, would you believe the verbal code, which says that all is well; the vocal code, which indicates nervousness; or the visual code, which suggests that the presenter is lying? Combining verbal and vocal communication, one researcher found that "with initially equated signals the nonverbal messages outweighed the verbal ones at least 5 to 1, and where they were in conflict the verbal messages were virtually disregarded" (Argyle, 1973, p. 78; see also Hegstron, 1979). Therefore, even if your words are completely clear to the audience, your visual or vocal communication might not be. Moreover, if your visual or vocal communication is inconsistent with your words, the audience likely will disregard what you say and pay more attention to how you say it.

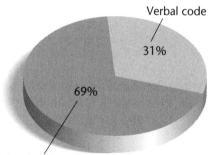

Figure 3.3

Verbal, Visual, and Vocal Codes
To interpret what speakers mean, listeners rely more heavily on the vocal code (how you speak) and the visual code (what they see) than on the verbal code (what you say).

To Maximize Listeners' Understanding

In the interpreting stage you want your listeners to supply meanings as close as possible to what you intended. Given that your chances of communicating 100 percent with an audience are highly unlikely, how can you at least improve the odds of being understood? Try the following suggestions:

- *Do your homework and carefully analyze your audience.* Try to encode your presentation in terms of the listeners' frames of reference. For example, an Army

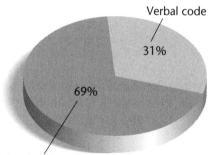 Use InfoTrac College Edition to do a keyword search for articles on listening. Use the * wildcard (*listen**) to search for all forms of the word (*listen, listening, listener,* and so on). A subject guide search on *listening* will list additional categories of interest. Find at least one listening tip that is not covered in your text. What value does this tip have for speakers?

sergeant speaking to a group of former Marines would not refer to the audience as *soldiers*. *Soldier* is an Army term; Marines refer to themselves as *Marines*. ➤ *For more on audience analysis, see Chapter 4.*

■ *Remember that the only message that counts is the one actually received.* It doesn't matter what you really said, what you thought you said, or what you meant to say; what's important is what the receivers understood you to say.

■ *Remember that what you say to an audience and how you say it may mean less to them than what they see.* Therefore, make sure that what your audience sees adds to your intended message. Obviously, visual aids can be a very powerful tool here. ➤ *See Chapter 9 for specifics on using visual aids.*

■ *Prepare for possible misunderstanding.* By anticipating potential sources of misunderstanding, you can prevent many communication breakdowns.

In Evaluating Stage—Counteract Listeners' Resistance to Persuasion

When you speak on a controversial topic, audience attitudes toward your position may range from enthusiastic agreement to absolute opposition. Listeners who disagree strongly are obviously the most difficult to persuade. In fact, even those who disagree mildly will likely do their best to avoid being persuaded. People are not willing to change without a struggle. As a result, during the evaluating stage, listeners may use a variety of methods to avoid being persuaded—or even informed. Let's examine some tactics you can use to foil the most frequently encountered listener-avoidance methods. ➤ *See Chapters 13 and 14 for a detailed examination of persuasive speaking.*

Strengthen Your Personal Credibility

A credible person is someone whom people find believable—someone who inspires their confidence. Research has found that the greater a speaker's **credibility**, the more persuasive he or she is (O'Keefe, 1990). Therefore, *one of the easiest ploys used by listeners to avoid being persuaded is to discount the speaker's credibility.* If you don't believe the speaker, there's certainly no reason to believe the message. For example, suppose Julianne is making a good, forceful argument that women are paid less than men for equal work, but John doesn't want to believe it. Her data makes him feel **cognitive dissonance** (discomfort when evidence is presented that is contrary to what we believe). But then he realizes that Julianne is at least 10 years younger than anyone in the room. Obviously, she is too young to really know how to collect first-hand information. John begins to relax. The dissonance is gone; he has avoided being persuaded.

To keep listeners from using this ploy, you need to make sure that you are perceived as trustworthy and qualified to speak on the topic. You will be considered more credible if you give a presentation that is well organized, include examples from personal experience as well as evidence from known experts, use good-quality visuals, and deliver your speech in a confident, dynamic manner. If you feel that your credibility might be in question, you can do the following:

■ *Have a highly credible expert on the topic introduce you* as a competent and trustworthy speaker.

■ *Identify your views with those of known experts* who are valued by the audience.

■ *Indicate beliefs, affiliations, or problems* that you share with your listeners.

Don't forget that if you want people to see you as confident, you must look and sound confident.

Highlight the Credibility of Your Sources

If the listener who is trying to avoid persuasion can't successfully devalue your credibility, *the next ploy will be to criticize your sources.* Most people seek information that supports their personal beliefs. If they are conservative, they read conservative newspapers; if they are liberal, they read liberal newspapers. Therefore, although listeners may know the sources on their side of an issue, they may know only hearsay about the speaker's side of the issue. Unsupported hearsay (such as, "I read somewhere that the mayor is only marginally qualified to run this city") may keep your listeners from being persuaded. Therefore, to establish the credibility of your sources, do the following:

■ Clearly describe the qualifications of your sources.

■ Refute any expected criticism of your sources.

■ Show some important quality that your sources and your listeners share.

Keep Listeners from Evading Your Message

Another listener ploy is to mentally evade persuasive messages that cause cognitive dissonance and instead hear what they want to hear (Larson, 2004, ch. 7; Littlejohn, 2002, pp. 123–126). To evade messages that might require them to change, listeners (1) deliberately misunderstand the message, (2) ignore the more discomforting parts of it, or (3) change its focus so that it doesn't personally apply. For example, if an audience were shown cartoons of prejudiced people, younger listeners might decide that the cartoons were about the prejudices of "older" people, or female listeners might tell themselves that the cartoons were about the prejudices of men and therefore exclude themselves from any need to change (Cooper & Jahoda, 1966). ➔ *See Chapter 14 for a discussion of Social Judgment Theory.*

Remember

Listener–avoidance ploys include . . .

■ Discounting the speaker's credibility.

■ Criticizing the speaker's sources.

■ Deliberately misunderstanding the speaker's message.

■ Ignoring the more uncomfortable parts of the message.

■ Deciding the message doesn't apply to them.

■ Tuning out.

To keep listeners from misinterpreting your persuasive message, first make sure that your ideas are clear and well organized. In addition, you might use one of the following tactics to make a change of opinion less threatening to listeners:

- *Make it clear that you view the "problem" as fairly common*—it isn't the fault or responsibility of only a few people or only your listeners.

- *Show that your solution won't be a strain on anyone* if everyone helps a little.

- *Show that your view is only a small distance from the listeners' current views*— a small change in opinion that has the potential to benefit all.

Keep the Listeners' Attention on the Speech

Another listener ploy is to tune out when they hear complicated information, react emotionally to an argument (claim) of the speaker, or experience an internal distraction. Sometimes listeners stop listening because it's easier to think of something else than to listen to arguments that create internal discomfort or anger. In other words, these audience members aren't taking any chances of being persuaded. The following suggestions should make it more difficult for these listeners to avoid paying attention to you:

- Use a dynamic style of delivery—including unexpected volume changes and plenty of movement and gestures. → *See Chapter 10.*

- Include powerful stories and personal experiences. → *See Chapter 6.*

- Add humor to the presentation. → *See Chapter 7.*

- Use colorful, entertaining visuals. → *See Chapter 9.*

In Responding Stage—Read Listeners' Nonverbal Cues

Because audience members do not always give obvious feedback in the responding stage, you must learn to "read" listeners' nonverbal responses. Certain nonverbal behaviors can tip you that your audience is drifting off. Before we discuss these behaviors, however, we need to caution that it is easy to misinterpret nonverbal cues. For example, a student was giving a speech in class on the mysterious stone monoliths of Easter Island. In the middle of comparing the faulty theories of the past with today's more accurate assessment, he abruptly said, "Well, if that's how you're going to act, I quit!" and sat down. His classmates looked at one another in stunned silence. The speaker had observed several classmates with their foreheads wrinkled in thought and decided that these "frowns" meant they were rejecting his speech. When the class finally convinced him that he had misinterpreted their responses, he agreed to finish his presentation.

Put Nonverbal Cues in Context

Before you assume that you know what a nonverbal behavior means, consider the specific situation, environment, and time of day, as well as the cultural background and frames of reference of the listener(s). For example, several listeners with their arms locked across their chests usually indicate disapproval, but the gesture takes on a

Technology Tip for Speakers

Adapt Internet Presentations to Receiver Frames of Reference

One reason listeners have difficulty totally comprehending a speaker's message is that they have different frames of reference. The best speakers are those who adapt their messages to the frames of reference of their listeners. In today's high-tech society, however, many business and professional speakers find that they do much of their "speaking" over the Internet, so their "listeners" are actually reading their messages. Even though their original presentation may be given "live" to a local group, it is then posted on the web or sent as an e-mail attachment to benefit customers and colleagues in other locations.

Adapting electronic presentations to receiver frames of reference is difficult because only the verbal code is operating (Crook & Booth, 1977; Giles, Coupland, & Coupland, 1991). There are no visual or vocal codes to aid receivers in accurate interpretation. Instead, electronic presentations should adapt to receivers' preferred sensory communication channels. Most people prefer one of the following communication channels for their messages: visual, auditory, or kinesthetic (touch). Researchers tell us that Internet and e-mail readers are more likely to react positively to messages whose adjectives, verbs, and adverbs mirror their preferred communication channel. For example, people who prefer the visual channel are more likely to use words such as *look, visualize, see,* and *clear.* People who prefer the verbal or auditory channel choose such words as *talk, sound, hear,* and *say.* People who prefer the kinesthetic or touch channel opt for such words as *touch, grasp, feel, run,* and *hug.* Which

one of the following three wordings would generate the most positive response from you?

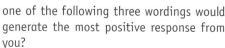

"The project *looks* like a winner."
"The project *sounds* like a winner."
"The project *feels* like a winner."

You might wonder why a speaker can't use all three sensory channels (visual, auditory, and kinesthetic) in a single presentation. This is not recommended because, although some people aren't partial to any particular approach, most of us prefer one of the sensory channels. To determine if your business associates, customers, or friends have a preference, investigate the e-mail you have sent and received during the last few months. Coe and Scharcoff (1985) suggest that a preference occurs when a count of sensory words shows one channel to make up 50 percent of the total. If needed, use your electronic thesaurus to find additional sensory words. To understand the importance of sensory channels on receiver attitudes, study the e-mail of a person (business associate, customer, or boss) whose messages you find irritating or at least lacking in rapport. Does their sensory preference differ from yours?

Since the best speakers are those who accommodate or adapt their messages to the frames of reference of their receivers, why not add preferred sensory channels to your audience analysis procedure? You never know when your presentation may have Internet "listeners" as well as "live" listeners. Even normal listeners may benefit when your presentation includes sensory words that correspond to their sensory preferences.

different meaning in a room where the air conditioner is set much too low. A puzzling lack of audience participation during a question-and-answer period might be less confusing if you see that the company president has entered the room. Nodding heads may have different meanings depending on the culture of the listeners. American listeners tend to nod when they are in agreement whereas Japanese listeners nod to indicate only that they have received the message, not that they agree. In England, audience members at formal presentations avoid nodding and instead blink their eyes—an indication of polite attention (Hall, 1992, p. 143).

Don't Generalize From Single Nonverbal Behaviors

Basing audience evaluation on a single nonverbal behavior rather than on several simultaneous responses can result in misinterpretation. For example, someone who glances at his watch during your speech might be bored with your talk, but he might also have other reasons for this gesture. He might be consulting his watch for the date in reference to something you said, or he might habitually look at his watch at this time of day because this is when school gets out. Of course, if he glances at his watch continually, looks aimlessly around the room, and shifts uncomfortably in his seat (three related behaviors), you can feel more certain that he is probably tuning you out.

Look for Telltale Signs of Nonlistening (or Listening)

Although it's risky to assign meanings to single behaviors, combinations of nonverbal behaviors can indicate whether a typical U.S. audience is listening. The following lists of nonverbal behaviors (which often occur simultaneously) should give you an idea of when listeners are probably not listening or at least not listening effectively.

Signs of Nonlistening

- Practically no movement, faces devoid of expression, unwavering eye contact or dropping eyelids, slouched posture
- Restless movement, aimless looks around the room, drumming fingers or tapping pencils, repeated glancing at watches
- Frowns, narrowed eyes or skeptical looks, arms locked across chest, raised eyebrows or rolling eyes

Signs of Listening

- Normal movement, smiles (or interested looks), occasional direct eye contact, erect or forward-leaning posture
- Occasional movement (maybe even some doodling), occasional glancing at watches—usually near the end of the presentation
- Open posture, changing facial expressions depending on speech content, occasional nods of head

In short, audience members rarely sit perfectly still unless they are daydreaming. Listening is not passive—it's active and requires conscious effort. On the other hand, too much movement is an indication of boredom and low-level listening.

Which people in this audience are showing nonverbal signs of not listening?

Effective speakers constantly monitor nonverbal feedback from their listeners. On the basis of the feedback they receive, they fine-tune their speeches as they go. If several audience members are showing similar nonlistening behaviors, it's time to take a break, switch to a more interesting point, or show a catchy visual. If your speech is almost finished, you can recapture audience attention with a statement such as, "I have one last point to make before concluding my speech" or "In conclusion . . ." The audience will visibly relax and give you a few more minutes of attention.

In Remembering Stage—Make Your Message Easier to Remember

It is up to you to make your presentations interesting and valuable enough for listeners to sense, interpret, evaluate, respond to, and remember. However, because so little of your entire presentation will be committed to audience memory, it is crucial for you to try to control what is remembered. Being organized, using good delivery, repeating important ideas, and relating the presentation to listeners' frames of reference are all important tools for improving audience memory and are discussed in detail in

various later chapters. Some additional suggestions to promote better audience listening and retention are discussed next.

Personalize Your Speeches With Narratives

One of the surest ways to guarantee that an audience will listen to you is to share something about yourself in narrative or story form (Ballard, 2003; Fisher, 1987; Robinson, 2000). In *The Elements of Great Speechmaking,* Robert Smith (2004) says that "stories represent powerful tools and materials for connecting with audiences" (p. 21). We all enjoy hearing a speaker talk about real-life experiences—it makes us feel as if we know the speaker personally, and it adds to the speaker's credibility. For example, in a speech entitled "How to Earn an MBWA Degree," James H. Lavenson (1976, p. 411) related this personal experience (MBWA stands for "management by walking around"):

> A couple of years ago, I was asked to consult with the management of the Tour Hassan Hotel in Rabat, Morocco. They had service problems and profit problems and they wanted me to help fix them. . . . I flew to Morocco not having the remotest idea how to start and just checked into the hotel like any other guest. The first morning I wanted my breakfast in the room and walked around trying to figure out how to order it. There were two buttons over the bed with a single sign over both saying "Service" in English. I pushed one button, waited five minutes and then pushed the other one. Nothing happened, so I got dressed and went downstairs for breakfast. The hotel's manager was there and again, like any guest, I was quick to tell him his buttons didn't work. He wasn't the least bit upset. "They've never worked since I've been here and that's five years. You have to call for room service on the phone," he said casually.
>
> "Can't you get them fixed?" I asked.
>
> "Cost too much," was his answer, which I've learned to expect from management in almost any business.
>
> "How much?" I wanted to know.
>
> "A lot" was his enlightening answer.
>
> Not satisfied, I went to the controller and asked if he'd seen a bid on repairing the buzzer system from the rooms. He hadn't, but he knew it would cost too much. I went to the chief engineer and asked him how much it would cost. Do you know what he said? He told me it wouldn't cost anything because there was nothing wrong with the system. It was just turned off. All that was required to make it work was to throw a switch. So why was it turned off? Because, since the two buttons were never identified as to which was which—food or maid—guests batting an even .500 would push the wrong button every other time. The maids got exasperated, the room service waiters were sick of people crying "Wolf, Wolf," or rather, "food, food," when what they really wanted was a clean towel. So the housekeeper persuaded the chief engineer to throw the switch. Nobody had told the manager, and he never asked to find out. Believe it or not, I got a citation from the King of Morocco for a stroke of sheer genius . . . putting labels over each of the two buttons, marking one "food" and one "maid" and asking the engineer to throw the switch.

If you can't think of a personal example related to the point you wish to make, tell about an experience that happened to someone you know or someone you have read about. The key is to give enough details to paint a clear and interesting picture, thus promoting listener attention and memory.

Increase Your Speaking Rate

Another way to stimulate audience listening is by speaking a little faster than you normally do. Most speakers talk at a rate of about 100 to 175 words per minute. Listeners, however, can think at a rate of 400 to 800 words per minute (Lundeen, 1993; Wolff et al., 1983). In other words, listeners can easily follow every word you speak and still have some time to think about other things. Although attentive listeners use most of that time to think about your ideas, check your evidence, and even memorize important facts, less dedicated listeners tend to use the "extra" time daydreaming. They may even become so engrossed in their own thoughts that they forget to tune back in. By delivering more than 100 to 175 words per minute, you give your listeners less time to daydream. According to researchers, "the optimal speaking rate for comprehension appears to be between 275 and 300 words per minute" (Wolvin & Coakley, 1985, p. 178).

Don't State Key Ideas in the First or Second Sentence

When a speech begins, most audience members are getting settled in their seats, yet many speakers expect them to immediately begin listening attentively. Because most listeners aren't ready to listen, they miss the first sentence or two of the speaker's introduction. Therefore, stating your central idea in your first couple of sentences is sure to catch many listeners off guard. And when listeners can't figure out the main idea fairly rapidly, they usually blame the speaker and feel justified in switching their attention to something more "important." Therefore, at the very beginning of your talk, your purpose is to capture and focus the audience's attention. This gives the typical listener time to tune in.

Use Visuals to Enhance Listening and Remembering

Have you ever seen a speaker set up a visual aid such as a poster before it was time to mention it? Was the audience listening to the speaker or reading the poster? Reading the poster, of course. For some reason, when audience members see a message in print, they immediately begin reading it. Moreover, a poorly prepared visual, such as the one shown in Figure 3.4, can throw an audience into a "reading" mode rather than a "listening" mode. Because audience members can't read and listen at the same time, they ignore the speaker for as long as it takes to read the visual. Properly prepared text and graphic visuals, such as the one shown in Figure 3.5, should allow listeners to absorb the content in one glance (around 3 to 6 seconds) and then refocus their attention on the speaker. Quality visual aids also aid listener memory (recall) of informative presentations (Hamilton, 1999) as well as persuasive presentations (Vogel, Dickson, & Lehman, 1986). You can have considerably more impact, hold the attention of your audience, and improve their retention if you use properly designed visuals, display them only when ready to speak about them, and remove them from audience view after you've referred to them. The power of visual aids cannot be overstated. ➜ *See Chapter 9 for more on the benefits of using visual aids.*

FACTS ABOUT U.S. TRANSPLANTATIONS
AS OF JULY 3, 2004, THERE WERE:
- 58,762 PATIENTS WAITING FOR A *KIDNEY* TRANSPLANT.
- 17,486 PATIENTS WAITING FOR A *LIVER* TRANSPLANT.
- 1,617 PATIENTS WAITING FOR A *PANCREAS* TRANSPLANT.
- 3,528 PATIENTS WAITING FOR A *HEART* TRANSPLANT.
- 195 PATIENTS WAITING FOR A *HEART-LUNG* TRANSPLANT
- 3,951 PATIENTS WAITING FOR A *LUNG* TRANSPLANT.
  85,539 TOTAL

TRANSPLANTS PERFORMED IN 2002:
- 14,523 *KIDNEY* TRANSPLANTS PERFORMED.
- 5,060 *LIVER* TRANSPLANTS PERFORMED.
- 376 *PANCREAS* TRANSPLANTS PERFORMED.
- 2,111 *HEART* TRANSPLANTS PERFORMED.
- 31 *HEART-LUNG* TRANSPLANTS PERFORMED.
- 1,041 *LUNG* TRANSPLANTS PERFORMED
  23,142 TOTAL

Figure 3.4
Poorly Designed Visual
Wordy, cluttered visuals like this one force listeners into a reading mode.

U.S. Transplantations

	Waiting List 2004		Transplants 2002
	58,762	kidneys	14,523
	17,486	liver	5,060
	1,617	pancreas	376
	3,528	heart	2,111
	195	heart-lung	31
	3,951	lung	1,041
	85,539	Totals	**23,142**

(United Network For Organ Sharing)

Figure 3.5
Well-Designed Visual
Although it includes the same information as in Figure 3.4, this visual is designed to encourage listening.

Summary

Think back to the two communication situations presented at the beginning of the chapter. Have you determined what listener characteristic each speaker overlooked? The first situation involved a proposal to a Japanese firm. The speaker felt sure that the Japanese executives were going to accept the proposal because they were nod-

ding in agreement. However, the speaker had misinterpreted the nonverbal clues—in Japan nodding does not mean agreement, but merely that the message has been received. In the second situation, the speaker believed that the audience was listening well because they were sitting totally still and making eye contact. The speaker was unaware that such nonverbal behavior usually means that the audience members are not listening and are someplace else mentally.

Attentive listeners progress through the stages of sensing, interpreting, evaluating, responding, and remembering. At each stage, listeners may tune out or misunderstand. Effective speakers use various methods for each of these stages to help listeners stay on track. For example, using stimulation and motivation to grab audience attention will definitely help your listeners get started, and careful analysis of your audience's frame of reference can decrease the possibility of decoding problems. Knowing the ways in which listeners may attempt to avoid being persuaded (such as criticizing your credibility) can help you develop tactics to counteract them. Similarly, knowing the telltale nonverbal signs of listening and nonlistening will help you adjust your presentation. In addition, you can make remembering easier for your audience by adding personal references, increasing your speaking speed, and using visual aids.

Essentials of Public Speaking  *Online*

Use the Essentials of Public Speaking website at **http://communication. wadsworth.com/hamiltoneps3** for quick access to the electronic study resources that accompany this chapter. When you get to the Essentials home page, click on "Student Book Companion Site" in the Resource box. The Essentials website features InfoTrac College Edition, the Suggestions for Practice and Critical Thinking activities and the InfoTrac College Edition activities that follow, a digital glossary, and review quizzes.

Key Terms

attribution theory 45
cognitive dissonance 51
credibility 51
evaluating stage 46

external stimulus 48
internal stimulus 48
interpreting stage 44
remembering stage 47

responding stage 47
sensing stage 44

Suggestions for Practice and Critical Thinking

1. Do you consider yourself a good listener? Check your general listening skills with this questionnaire adapted from Wheeless (1975).

   Directions: For each of the following statements, circle the appropriate response. Tally the results in the spaces provided at the end.

   a. I feel comfortable when listening to others on the phone.

   Yes   Sometimes   Never

b. It is often difficult for me to concentrate on what others are saying.

   Yes   Sometimes   Never

c. I feel tense when listening to new ideas.

   Yes   Sometimes   Never

d. I have difficulty concentrating on instructions others give me.

   Yes   Sometimes   Never

e. I dislike being a listener when I'm a member of an audience.

   Yes   Sometimes   Never

f. I seldom seek out the opportunity to listen to new ideas.

   Yes   Sometimes   Never

g. I find myself daydreaming when others seem to ramble on.

   Yes   Sometimes   Never

h. I often argue mentally or aloud with what someone is saying even before he or she finishes.

   Yes   Sometimes   Never

i. I find that others are always repeating things to me.

   Yes   Sometimes   Never

j. I seem to find out about important events too late.

   Yes   Sometimes   Never

Number of times I answered Yes _____

Number of times I answered Sometimes _____

Number of times I answered No _____

If you answered Yes or Sometimes to fewer than three questions, you perceive yourself to be a *good listener.* If you answered Yes or Sometimes to three to six questions, you are an *average listener.* If you answered Yes or Sometimes to seven or more questions, you are a *poor listener* and need immediate improvement of your listening skills.

2. Select a person on campus or in your community who is recognized as a good speaker. Attend one of his or her presentations and look for the answers to some of these questions:

   a. How did the speaker focus the attention and interest of the audience on his or her topic and away from distractions? Did the speaker win your attention immediately?

   b. Was there any place where the speaker's meaning was not clear? What did you do about it?

   c. Were you convinced that the speaker was qualified to speak on the subject? Did you believe what the speaker told you? What words or nonverbal behavior or visuals helped convince you?

     d. What feedback did audience members give the speaker? Did the speaker seem to respond to their reactions? How?

     e. What techniques did the speaker use to help the listeners remember his or her main points? Can you list three important ideas that were presented?

3. Use InfoTrac College Edition to run a PowerTrac search using *public speaking and listen** to narrow listening articles to those about speakers. Look for specific advice you can use to improve the listening of your audience. Share what you find with a classmate.

4. Think of a speaker to whom you recently found it difficult to listen. At what stage of the listening process did the difficulty occur? What caused the problem? Was it an internal stimulus or an external stimulus? Describe what the speaker was doing at the time.

5. Ask one of your friends to get permission from his or her instructor for you to visit the class or select another one of your classes. Observe the nonverbal reactions of the students. Record evidence of listening, and identify evidence of poor listening.

6. During the next week, watch for times when you are "tuning out" a speaker (at a meeting, lecture class, church, and so on). Record what you were thinking about when you realized that you had tuned out. Why did you stop listening? What could the speaker have done to keep you motivated to listen?

7. Check out the following websites. *You can access these sites under the Student Resources for Chapter 3 at the Essentials of Public Speaking website.*

    • The International Listening Association is the home of *The International Journal of Listening.* Check out their website. (To read their journal, you may need to download a free DejaVu plug-in available at the site.)

    • Assess your listening skills by taking the Listening Self-Assessment test at the Brandt Management Group's website.

    • To work on your listening skills, go to the International Listening Association's home page. For a summary of eight published listening tests, click on "Listening Resources" and then on "Listening Tests & Assessments."

    • For some valuable pointers on using stories (narratives) in your presentations, see the Technology for Learning Consortium's website.

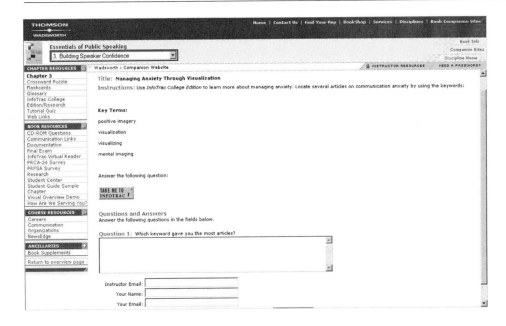

unit two

Preparing Your
Speech

What do you know about speech preparation?

The Quick Start Guide gave an overview of speech preparation. The following quiz will help you discover what more you have to learn about the process.

Directions: If you think a statement is generally accurate, mark it **T**; if you think the statement is a myth, mark it **F**. Then compare your answers with the explanations at the end of Chapter 4. You can also take this quiz online at the Essentials of Public Speaking website and, if requested, e-mail your responses to your instructor.

_____ 1. Although explanations are necessary to clarify and define, when a speaker overuses this type of supporting material, the result is a dull and boring speech.

_____ 2. Because first impressions are the most important, you should normally develop your introduction before developing the body of your speech.

_____ 3. If you are speaking to an uninterested audience, it's best to use a dynamic, theatrical tone of voice.

_____ 4. It's a good idea to rough out your thoughts in outline form before beginning to research your topic.

_____ 5. Statistics should be used as often as possible in informative speeches because listeners are impressed when you can back up your arguments with statistics.

_____ 6. A storyboard is a type of poster you can use to illustrate your speech.

_____ 7. If you're nervous, it's a good idea to tell the audience so that they will make allowances for you; also you will feel more relaxed.

_____ 8. The best speaking notes are written out in complete sentences so you won't forget what you want to say.

_____ 9. Although plagiarism should be a concern when speaking in public, it's only a minor concern to you as a classroom speaker because no one will know.

_____ 10. Plan your speech so that the body takes approximately 50 percent of your total speech time.

chapter 4

Analyzing Your Audience

Flashback

In his *Rhetoric,* Aristotle suggests that speakers may be more persuasive when they relate their proposals to things that "create or enhance" listener happiness. His list of things that made Greeks happy included prominent birth, many children, good friends, health, beauty, athletic ability, wealth, honor, power, and virtue. How many of these items still make people happy today?

B Y THIS POINT IN THE COURSE, YOU HAVE PROBABLY GIVEN AT LEAST ONE BEGINNING speech. Beginning speeches like those outlined in the Quick Start Guide (i.e., artifact speech, humorous incident speech, or speech of introduction) are fairly easy to prepare. Your next speeches will require more preparation time and more attention to detail—much like the difference between studying for a quiz and studying for a midterm or final exam. In planning your future speeches, use the Basic Steps for Preparing a Speech shown on the following page. These steps will be clarified in the chapters in this unit.

Notice that the first step in speech preparation is analyzing your audience. Audience analysis is not difficult. It simply involves knowing your listeners well enough so that you can organize your verbal, visual, and vocal messages to fit into their frames of reference. As Patricia Ward Brash (1992) explains, Christopher Columbus certainly knew the importance of audience analysis:

> Before Columbus met the King and Queen of Spain, navigational experts in both Portugal and Spain had already recommended against backing his rather unusual proposal to reach the Far East by sailing in the opposite direction—westward.
>
> But Columbus understood the art of persuasion, of tailoring the message to the audience, and he knew how to put together an effective presentation. He knew, for example, that the Queen had a fervent desire to win more converts to her religion. So he made frequent references to the teeming masses of the Orient, just waiting to be converted.
>
> Columbus learned that the Queen loved falcons and exotic birds, so he searched carefully through the accounts of Marco Polo's travels to the Orient and marked in the margin all references to those kingdoms where there were falcons and exotic birds.

> He knew the King wanted to expand Spain's commercial power, so he made frequent references to gold, spices, and other fabulous riches of the East.
>
> All these points were worked into his presentation, which won the backing that [he desired]. (pp. 83–84)

Although your ventures may not be as historic as that of Columbus, you have been analyzing your audiences since you were young. For example, think back to when you started driving the family car. When you asked to borrow it, you no doubt presented your arguments a bit differently depending on which parent you were asking—a sign of good audience analysis.

When you analyze an audience, you aren't trying to trick, manipulate, or coerce them; you are simply making sure that your message fits their frames of reference so that they will give you a fair hearing. *The number one reason that speeches fail to meet their goals is the speaker's failure to analyze the audience carefully enough* (St. John, 1995). This chapter covers additional aspects of audience analysis that will help you accurately match your message to your listeners.

Basic Steps for Preparing a Speech

1. Analyze your potential audience.
2. Determine topic, exact purpose, and main points. → *See Chapter 5.*
3. Prepare a rough-draft outline of main points and needed information. → *See Chapter 5.*
4. Research topic for material to support main points. → *See Chapter 5.*
5. Select best supporting materials. → *See Chapter 6.*
6. Determine how best to organize main points. → *See Chapter 7.*
7. Plan introduction and conclusion. → *See Chapter 7.*
8. Make preparation outline (or storyboards) and speaking notes. → *See Chapter 8.*
9. Prepare visual aids. → *See Chapter 9.*
10. Rehearse speech. → *See Chapters 10 and 11.*

Analyzing Your Audience: Situational Information

Before preparing your speech, you will want to learn as much as you can about the speaking situation. The **situational information** includes audience size, members' general expectations about the topic, and the nature of other speeches at the event. In gathering situational information for your speech, keep the following questions in mind.

First, *are audience members attending voluntarily?* Do they have a particular interest in hearing you and your topic, or are they attending because they are required to do so? Voluntary audiences tend to be *homogeneous*—that is, members have a fair amount in common. Because your classroom audience is an involuntary or "captive" audience, it is probably fairly *heterogeneous*—that is, members differ in a variety of ways, including interests, major and minor fields of study, work experience, and even age.

Use InfoTrac College Edition to locate pollster information on specific target audiences. Do an Advanced search on polling data. For additional information, do another search on audience analysis. Compare the information you find with the material in this chapter.

Second, *how many people will be attending*? The size of your audience is a crucial factor in the type of visual aids. For example, a flipchart works well for small audiences but is ineffective for audiences of 30 or more. Similarly, gestures must be larger and volume must be louder for large audiences.

Third, *how much does your audience know (or think they know) about your topic*? If the topic is discussed frequently in the mass media, your audience likely will be at least familiar with it. If so, you won't have to give much background information. However, if your topic is fairly new or is not covered much in the mass media, you will need to present background information and dispel any misconceptions about the topic. In addition, the less the audience knows about your topic, the more important it is for your introduction to stimulate interest in it. ➤ *Chapter 7 gives detailed information on attention-getters.*

Fourth, *what does your audience know about you, and what general opinions does it have of you*? If members have heard you give other speeches or know of you through other activities, they probably have already formed an opinion of you. If their opinions are positive, they are more likely to also feel positive about your speech topic. But if they don't know you or have a negative opinion of your expertise, it will be important for you to establish your credibility. Methods for doing so include citing statistics and sources that your audience considers highly credible, preparing professional visuals, and using a controlled, forceful delivery. ➤ *Chapter 14 gives additional information on establishing your credibility.*

Fifth, *what type of presentation is your audience expecting*? If your audience is expecting a multimedia presentation with color and sound but you give an intimate speech with only black-and-white transparencies, members will be disappointed no matter how excellent your speech. Likewise, if the audience is expecting a serious, scholarly speech but you present a humorous, after-dinner-type talk, members will not feel satisfied either. Knowing your audience's expectations helps you choose appropriate topics, visual aids, delivery style, and appearance.

Finally, *will anyone be speaking before you*? If so, about what? In political rallies, conventions, and college classrooms, several speeches may be given in a row. The atmosphere created by each speech (whether positive or negative) lingers into the next speech. For example, as you step up to the lectern, you may see that the audience is still amused by the previous humorous speech.

Here is an introduction to a speech given to the Institute of World Affairs by Kathy R. Fitzpatrick (2004), Director of Public Relations and Advertising at DePaul University. Do you think that her words would grab audience attention and direct it away from the mood set by a previous speaker?

> Thank you for that kind introduction. It is my honor to be with you tonight. I've entitled my remarks "Telling America's Story."
>
> We all know that America has a great story to tell. A story of democracy, freedom, peace, and opportunity.
>
> But while we have a great story to tell, is America a great storyteller?
>
> That's the question we'll explore this evening.
>
> When nations tell their stories to the people of the world, we call it "public diplomacy." Although that's a term that may not be familiar to you, I hope to change that tonight by talking with you about U.S. public diplomacy and its importance to our nation. (pp. 412–413)

When you follow another speaker, your introduction is even more important than usual. If the previous speech relates to yours, mention how. If it doesn't, mention how your speech will differ or make a startling statement to shock the audience into another mood.

Remember

Situational information includes . . .

- Voluntary or required attendance
- The number of people expected to attend
- Audience knowledge of the topic
- Audience knowledge of you (the speaker)
- The type of presentation the audience is expecting
- Other speakers and their topics

Analyzing Your Audience: Demographic Information

In addition to evaluating situational information, you will need to consider **demographic information** as you plan your speech. This includes general audience characteristics such as age, gender, marital status, education, economic status, occupations (or current jobs), major field of study, political beliefs, religion, cultural background, and group identification. If you are familiar with the audience (your classmates, for example), you can observe many of these characteristics yourself. If you are unfamiliar with the audience, ask for input from the person who invited you to speak, as well as two or three members of the prospective audience.

Identifying Specific Demographic Characteristics

It's a good idea to find out as much about each audience as possible. Although audiences are made up of individuals, members often share similar attributes or demographic characteristics. To give you an idea of what demographic information could be helpful in planning your speech, let's look at each characteristic in more detail.

Age   Because age is related to interests, knowledge of audience members' ages can guide you in selecting a topic and picking appropriate supporting materials to interest and persuade them. For example, what age group would prefer listening to Johnny Mathis, Tony Bennett, and Peter, Paul and Mary? Would they be older or younger than the age group that prefers listening to Linkin Park, Blink 182, Jessica Simpson, Metallica, or Pearl Jam? Although knowing the general age of audience members can be helpful, it may also be misleading unless you explore other demographic factors as well. For example, some high school and college students enjoy listening to "golden oldies" from the sixties (such as the Beatles and the Beach Boys) as much as their parents do.

Keep in mind that the students in your speech class probably represent a fairly wide range of ages. The mean age of students enrolled at four-year colleges and universities is around 24 (Cummins, 1995). At two-year colleges (because two-thirds are part-time students), the average age ranges from 25 to 29 (Fonte, 2003; Hankin, 2003). Now that the American population is aging (34 million Americans are now over 65) and more retired people are going back to college, these averages may increase (Challenger, 2004; Taylor, 2004). Make sure your speech is relevant to people of all ages, not just your own age group. And be careful not to draw boundaries

How might the interests of this audience differ from those of an audience of college sophomores?

© David Young-Wolff/PhotoEdit

around life stages with terms like "Generation X" or "Baby Boomers" (Reynolds, 2004a; Taylor, 2004; Williams & Giles, 1998).

Ethnic and Cultural Background Your classroom audience may be more diverse than the population of your hometown. If current trends continue, "by 2025, the term 'minority,' as it's currently used, will be virtually obsolete" (Wellner, 2003, p. 26). Non-Hispanic whites will drop to 60 percent while both the Hispanic and Asian populations will double. In addition, according to the Census 2000 (Yin, 2004), the foreign-born population in the United States is also increasing and now numbers 31 million people. As Peter Morrison (1993), researcher and senior demographer for the RAND Corporation in California, notes:

> The country we once called a great melting pot is now a racial and ethnic mosaic in which different peoples tend to keep their identities. It is made up not just of whites, blacks, and Hispanics, but a multitude of nationalities and ethnic subgroups as well.
>
> The mosaic varies from city to city. In St. Paul and Missoula, it contains Hmongs from Southeast Asia; in Atlanta and Providence, Cambodians; in Des Moines and Sioux City, Tai Dam and Vietnamese; in Arlington, Virginia, Salvadorans and other Central Americans; in Hartford, Jamaicans, Puerto Ricans, and assorted Asian populations. California's cities contain a dazzling array of nationalities and ethnic groups, including Filipinos, Koreans, Vietnamese, Hmong, Armenians, and Japanese [as well as blacks, Hispanics, and whites]. (p. 59)

Members of culturally diverse groups can have different interests and expectations of what makes a good speech. When you are speaking to a culturally diverse audience, research the different cultural groups carefully to make sure that the content of your speech and your verbal and visual delivery are appropriate. For example, some Asian cultures—such as Chinese, Thai, and Indian—generally prefer that speakers not make direct eye contact or even focus on individual faces in the audience (Hall, 1992). If you are from a culture that typically avoids looking directly at audience members,

keep in mind that many in your college audience (as well as your professor) may view lack of direct eye contact as a sign of nervousness or inexperience.

Similarly, animated facial expressions and spontaneous gestures, which are the norm in the United States, may appear brash and egotistical to some Japanese listeners. The Japanese tend to admire people who are, "for the most part, distinguished by their modest demeanor, lack of eloquence, their public modesty" (Barnlund, 1989, p. 115). At the same time, if you come from a Japanese background, you may need to add more animation to your delivery when you address your classmates.

If your audience is culturally diverse, you should also pay special attention to your visual aids. People from some cultures might be offended at the informality of writing on flipcharts during a presentation. To them, a speaker who doesn't prepare visuals ahead of time doesn't value the audience (Duleck, Fielden, & Hill, 1991).

In addition to selecting your visual messages with care, you need to ensure that your verbal messages show cultural sensitivity. In the United States, many audiences value straight talk and respond negatively to speakers who take forever to get to the point. As a result, the norm is to present the main ideas up front. In contrast, "many people (notably those in Japanese, Latin American, and Arabic cultures) consider such directness to be brash and inappropriate" (Guffey, 2003, p. 509). Thus, for audiences with a large number of people from these cultures, you should present ideas more slowly—perhaps even concluding with the main point rather than beginning with it. Also, always choose your words with care. For example, avoid referring to your audience as "you people" or beginning an example with, "I'm not prejudiced or anything, but . . ."

Obviously, the more you know about your audience, the more you will be able to relate appropriately to them. For example, at various times during his campaign and in his acceptance speech at the 2004 Republican Convention, George W. Bush spoke in Spanish.

Gender   Another demographic characteristic that can give you clues to possible audience interests is gender. Be careful, however, to avoid gender stereotyping. To assume that all men enjoy sports and women do not or that all women are interested in cooking and men are not would likely lead to some negative audience reactions. If you have both men and women in your audience, you need to relate your topic to both genders; if you can't, select a different topic (Wood, 2005).

When speaking to a mixed audience, be sure that your word choices show gender sensitivity. It's best to avoid masculine or feminine terms and expressions and to substitute more gender-sensitive words. For example, instead of "policeman" or "policewoman," say "police officer"; instead of "stewardess," say "flight attendant." → *A more detailed discussion of gender-sensitive words and phrases is included in Chapter 11.*

Group Affiliation   Most people are very proud of the groups they belong to—whether it is the Campus Crusade for Christ, the drama club, or a sorority. Knowing that your audience members belong to a particular social, religious, or political group (even though your topic isn't about their group) can help you identify what is important to them and what questions they are likely to ask. Referring to this group during your speech lets members know that you are aware of them and are speaking to them personally.

If your topic is a religious one, you need to be especially sensitive to listeners' faiths. As the United States becomes more culturally diverse, we are becoming more religiously diverse as well. In addition to the familiar Catholic and Protestant churches and Jewish synagogues, it is not uncommon to see Buddhist temples, Muslim mosques, and Hindu temples (Ostling, 1993).

Use InfoTrac College Edition to find more communication differences between men and women. Go to EasyTrac and type in *gender and nonverbal* or *gender and attitudes.* Also, using Advanced Search find one of these journals, *Sex Roles: A Journal of Research* or *American Demographics,* and read two or more interesting articles. Be sure to type in *j=* before typing the journal name.

Technology Tip for Speakers

Search for Cultural Demographic Information

The Internet makes collecting audience information amazingly easy. For example, if you know that several of your audience members are from a group demographically different from your own, you can use the Internet to research the customs and beliefs of that group. Search engines such as Yahoo and AltaVista are a good place to begin. Scroll down to the list of categories at either site and click on Regional. For specific demographic information, check the following sites. You can access all of these links at the Essentials of Public Speaking website.

- Religion: The Librarian's Index to the Internet (*www.lii.org/search/file/religion*)

- African Americans: African American Web Connection (*www.aawc.com*)

- Asian Americans: Asian American Resources (*www.mit.edu/activities/aar/aar.html*)

- Native Americans: American Indians (*www.hanksville.org/NAresources*)

- Hispanic Americans: The Library of Congress Hispanic Reading Room (*www.loc.gov/rr/hispanic/hisp.html*)

- Gender differences: GenderStats (*http://genderstats.worldbank.org*)

Also, the organization or group that has asked you to speak may have its own website, which may contain additional information about the goals, beliefs, and values of its members. To locate the site, ask the person who originally contacted you or use a search engine.

Marital Status and Children Knowing whether your listeners are predominantly single, married, divorced, or cohabiting and whether they have children can help you select examples that will relate to rather than offend them. Be careful of stereotypical statements such as "Good mothers don't work." In 2002 more than 65.9 percent of mothers with young children under the age of 6 were working, compared to 60 percent in 1992 and only 12 percent in 1950 (Chadwick & Heaton, 1992; U.S. Bureau of the Census, 2003, p. 391). Other facts of interest related to marital status and parenthood include the following (Chadwick & Heaton; Francese, 2004; Morrison, 1993; Reynolds, 2004b; Smith, 2001; U.S. Bureau of the Census, p. 77):

- Nearly half of all marriages end in divorce.

- The average length of a first marriage is 8 years.

- Divorce affects more than 1 million children each year; in 2002, 21.5 million children lived with just one parent.

- Unmarried couples living together make up 7 percent of U.S. households.

- One-third of all babies are born to unmarried women.

- Only 52 percent of children are reared by two parents in an "uninterrupted marriage."

If you wish to give a speech on a subject related to marriage, divorce, or children, don't forget your classmates who are not married or don't plan on ever marrying,

and those who have no children or don't plan on having any. If you can't relate your speech to them personally, you may be able to do so indirectly. For instance, they likely have relatives, close friends, and even neighbors who have children, so your topic can still have relevance to them.

Occupation, Education, College Major, and Economic Status Focusing on one or more of these demographic characteristics could provide you with valuable information on audience members and their interests. Do you think an audience of well-paid professionals would have different interests than an audience of blue-collar workers? The most recent U.S. Census reports that in 2003, 85 percent of adults age 25 or older had completed high school; while only 27 percent had completed college with at least a bachelor's degree (Stoops, 2004). In addition, research confirms the relationship of college to total lifetime earnings: ". . . the average high school graduate will make $1.2 million, while the average college graduate will make $2.1 million" (Brier, 2004, p. 10). If you knew that your audience members had college degrees, would your choice of topic, vocabulary, and examples be different than if your audience members were still in high school? For your college speech class, your classmates' majors and minors could be helpful. For example, if the majority of your classmates are majoring in the same subject as you, you can go into your subject in much more depth.

All the demographic characteristics discussed here can help you understand the frames of reference of your audience members and identify ways to communicate better with them. The question is, do you use all the demographic characteristics for each speech?

Remember

Demographic information includes . . .

- Age
- Ethnic and cultural background
- Gender
- Group affiliations
- Marital status and children
- Occupation, education, college major, and economic status

Choosing Which Demographic Characteristics to Use

Your topic determines which demographic characteristics are relevant for a particular speech. Suppose you want to give a speech on the importance of regular exercise. Political beliefs, religion, and cultural background would probably not be important considerations, but the age and gender of your audience members could be. For example, if your audience consisted of traditional college-age students, you might stress the value of regular exercise for maintaining a healthy, attractive body; identify the local physical fitness club as a place to socialize; and suggest that exercise breaks make long hours of study less tedious. On the other hand, an audience consisting mainly of 30- to 40-year-olds is likely to be raising children and/or establishing careers, so they have probably slacked off on exercising. For such an audience, you might want to mention

how valuable exercise is in reducing the stress associated with children and career; how athletic clubs cater to parents by offering child-care facilities; how foldaway treadmills and exercise bikes make exercise at home convenient; and how exercising with a colleague during lunch or after work makes exercise more fun. Obviously, if you were speaking to an audience of senior citizens, your focus would shift again. You might stress that walking and using weight machines add years of mobility and enjoyment to people's lives even if they rarely exercised when they were younger.

For all three of these audiences, the basic topic is the same but the focus of the speech changes to relate to their interests and needs. Of course, as with all your speeches, no matter what approach you take, you will need to cite sources and give examples to convince listeners that you know what you are talking about. ➡ *Chapter 6 discusses these supporting ideas in detail.*

Analyzing Your Audience: Psychological Information

Determining psychological information about your audience—their attitudes, beliefs, values, and needs—is also important in preparing a speech (especially a persuasive speech) that relates specifically to listeners' frames of reference. See Figure 4.1 for a pictorial view of how these characteristics relate to one another.

Attitudes

An **attitude** is a *feeling* of approval or disapproval of a person, group, idea, or event. For example, you might approve of gay rights, disapprove of women in the military, or approve of recycling programs. A poll on the American family found single-earner couples to have the most traditional attitudes, single parents to have the most modern attitudes, and dual-earner couples to have more modern attitudes than single-earner couples but to have traditional attitudes about divorce and one-parent families (McGuire, 1985).

Figure 4.1

Psychological Factors Used in Audience Analysis
Values, beliefs, attitudes, and needs build on one another; the successful speaker relates these factors to listeners' frames of reference.

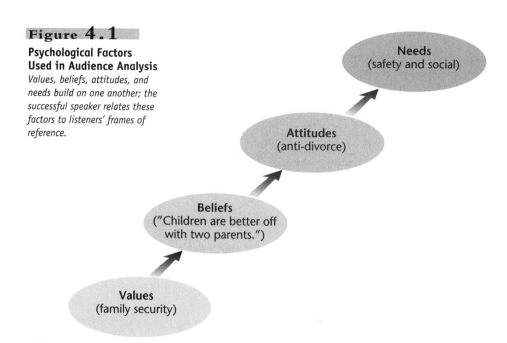

Needs
(safety and social)

Attitudes
(anti-divorce)

Beliefs
("Children are better off with two parents.")

Values
(family security)

Attitudes can influence behaviors—the stronger the attitude, the more likely the action (Perloff, 2003). Therefore, your search for psychological information about your audience should begin with your audience's attitudes. Will they approve or disapprove of your topic? Will they favor or oppose your proposal? According to the **theory of reasoned action** (Fishbein & Ajzen, 1975; Hall, Householder, & Greene, 2002), "people rationally calculate the costs and benefits of engaging in a particular action and think carefully about how others will view the behavior under consideration" (Perloff, p. 90). Effective speakers help in this thought process.

Beliefs

In your psychological analysis, discovering your audience's attitudes isn't enough; you must also know the reasons for those attitudes (beliefs). A **belief** is the mental acceptance that something is true even if we can't prove that it is true. For example, even though they may not be able to cite any definitive sources, some people believe that college is important, that women are discriminated against, that lateness shows disrespect, and that big government is bad. *Beliefs are the reasons people hold the attitudes they do* (Jowett & O'Donnell, 1999). For example, someone may hold a pro-college attitude based on the belief that education is important; or someone may have a favorable attitude toward equal rights legislation based on the belief that women are discriminated against. If you discover that a belief is based on false information or that the audience thinks they know more than they actually do, you will have a better idea of what information and arguments to present in your speech.

Values

Values are deep-seated principles that serve as personal guidelines for behavior (Rokeach, 1973; Schwartz, 1996). They are usually learned from social institutions such as the family, church, and school. *Values provide the underlying support for beliefs and attitudes.* Researcher Milton Rokeach identified two types of values, instrumental and terminal. **Instrumental values** are guides for conduct in fulfilling **terminal values**, or ideal states of being. Although we possess only a few terminal values, we possess a great many instrumental values (Warnick & Inch, 1994). For example, most of us seek an education (instrumental value) with the goal of a rewarding career (terminal value). People who work hard (instrumental value) usually have the goal of a comfortable life (terminal value) (Warnick & Inch, p. 213).

For three decades, Rokeach researched how Americans ranked 18 key terminal values (Warnick & Inch, p. 215):

1. world peace
2. family security
3. freedom
4. a comfortable life
5. happiness
6. self-respect
7. a sense of accomplishment
8. wisdom
9. equality
10. national security
11. true friendship
12. salvation
13. inner harmony
14. mature love
15. a world of beauty
16. social recognition
17. pleasure
18. an exciting life

Remember

Psychological information includes . . .

- Audience attitudes
- Audience beliefs
- Audience values
- Audience needs

He found the rankings to be highly stable across time, with only minor changes during those 30 years. Do you think that value #10 (national security) moved up in importance after the terrorist attack of September 11, 2001? If so, now that several years have passed, has national security settled back to its normal level of importance?

Not only do values appear to be stable across time, but Rokeach found only minor differences between the rankings by men and women and between those by blacks and whites. However, as you might expect, there were sizable differences between the rankings of Americans and people from other cultures (for example, Australians, Canadians, and Israelis). Thus, when you are speaking to multicultural audiences, don't automatically assume that your high-ranked values are necessarily the same as listeners' high-ranked values. Although the list of values may be the same, the importance placed on each value may differ.

Because values are so stable, they are more difficult to change than beliefs or attitudes. You should generally try to highlight (or reinforce) one or more audience values and show how your ideas or proposal fits into those values. Also, knowing your audience's values will help you determine what evidence and emotional appeals will be needed to convince them that a particular belief or attitude conflicts with their basic values. → *See Chapter 14 for information on Social Judgment Theory.*

Needs

A **need** is a state in which some sort of unsatisfied condition exists. *Needs are a result of attitudes, beliefs, and values.* We all have needs and wants that motivate us. If you can show in your introduction or supporting materials how a listener's needs will be completely or partially satisfied by information in your speech, the listener will pay close attention. Likewise, if you can show how taking a particular action will partially or completely satisfy a need, the listener likely will be persuaded to take the action. In some cases, you may have to show an audience that a need exists before you can use it to motivate behavior. For example, you won't be very successful selling a new type of lock to audience members who feel safe at home. But when you show them the police statistics on how many homes have been broken into in their community during the past 6 months and demonstrate how easy it is to pick the typical lock on a front door, they will have second thoughts about their feelings of security. And if you can anchor an unsatisfied need to audience beliefs or values (such as "It is the responsibility of parents to provide a safe home environment for children"), your audience is even more likely to listen and be persuaded.

Maslow's Hierarchy of Needs   In the early 1900s, psychologist Abraham Maslow (1954, 1973), researched and published his theory of human motivation. Maslow believed that all people have the same basic needs, which he divided into five cate-

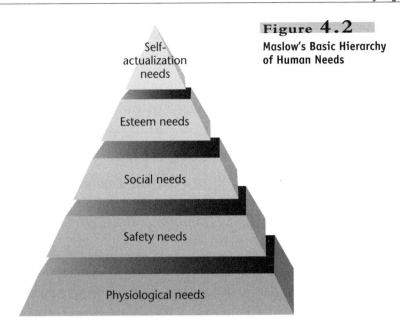

Figure 4.2

Maslow's Basic Hierarchy of Human Needs

gories: physiological, safety, social, esteem, and self-actualization (see Figure 4.2). These needs are illustrated as levels in a pyramid with lower-level needs at the bottom. Although people may be motivated by several levels at a time, usually the needs at the bottom of the pyramid must be satisfied before higher-level needs become important. Maslow's hierarchy of needs is a useful guide for adapting your speech to your audience's needs and wants.

Here are examples of needs at each level of Maslow's hierarchy (Lefton, Buzzotta, Sherberg, & Karraker, 1980):

1. Physiological needs—food, shelter, clothing, air, water, and sleep.

2. Safety needs—a job and financial security; law and order; protection from injury, poor health, harm, or death; and freedom from fear.

3. Social needs—love, companionship, friendship, and a feeling of belonging to one or more groups.

4. Esteem needs—pride, recognition from others, status and prestige, and self-recognition.

5. Self-actualization needs—becoming the best person one can, developing to one's fullest capabilities, and achieving worthwhile goals.

Applying Needs Analysis Because audience members have different frames of reference, it's unlikely that they will all be concerned and motivated by the same needs. As illustrated in Figure 4.1, needs grow out of attitudes, beliefs, and values. If you have determined these, the audience's basic needs should be fairly obvious.

Remember that before your listeners can focus on the higher needs in Maslow's model, their lower-level needs must be mostly satisfied. For example, if your audience is concerned about safety issues (perhaps a series of drive-by shootings has made everyone very nervous), appealing to the high-level ideals of self-actualization and esteem is unlikely to interest or persuade. On the other hand, a need that has already been met (the gang members were caught and the community feels safe again) is no longer a motivator. Select two or three of the lowest levels that represent your

audience's needs and use them as motivators in your speech. Fitting your message to audience needs is called **framing**. You might also keep in mind that listeners are often "more motivated by the thought of losing something than by the thought of gaining something" (Dillard & Pfau, 2002, p. 520). Therefore, framing your messages to stress potential losses that could occur if a certain action is not taken enhances persuasion. Loss framing is especially effective in situations where risk and uncertainly are prevalent (De Dreu & McCusker, 1997; Tversky & Kahneman, 1981). → *A more detailed discussion of using audience needs to persuade appears in Chapter 14.*

Hazards of Incomplete Psychological Analysis

To illustrate what can happen when the analysis of an audience's attitudes, beliefs, values, and needs is incomplete, consider the following scenario. In 1984–1985, Coca-Cola decided to change the 100-year-old formula used to make America's most popular soft drink. A blind taste-test had shown that consumers preferred the new, sweeter taste by a 6 percent margin, but according to author Mark Pendergrast (1993, p. 360), "no one had examined the psychological ramifications of withdrawing the old formula." Within a week after the change in Coke was announced, the company was receiving more than 1,000 irate calls per day, and the number eventually climbed to more than 8,000 per day. "They talk as if Coca-Cola had just killed God," reported an employee monitoring the consumer hot line (Pendergrast, p. 364). Protest letters (which numbered up to 40,000 per day) included such comments as "Changing Coke is just like breaking the American dream, like not selling hot dogs at a game" (Pendergrast, p. 363). Generations of Americans had grown up sipping Coca-Colas at Little League games, at birthday parties, and on first dates. It was an important part of their culture that they couldn't imagine changing. Reaction was so intense and sales dropped so drastically that within three months, the company reinstated the old Coke as "Coca-Cola Classic." Eventually, the new Coke was removed from the market, and the old formula again became the only Coke formula.

Coca-Cola's incomplete audience analysis (overlooking the psychological factor) led to unexpected customer reactions. As mentioned at the beginning of the chapter, if Christopher Columbus had ignored the psychological factor in his analysis of the king and queen of Spain, it's unlikely that they would have agreed to finance his expedition. Audience analysis includes more than just situational and demographic characteristics; it also includes psychological characteristics in the form of attitudes, beliefs, values, and needs of your listeners. The result of incomplete audience analysis could be nothing more than bored listeners, but it could also be angry, disbelieving listeners who are motivated to work against your position. Although inadequate audience analysis is unlikely to cause such a dramatically negative reaction in a classroom audience, treat your classroom as a laboratory setting and try to find out as much about your classmates as possible. Use them to sharpen your audience analysis skills.

Analyzing Audience Receptivity

Once you have analyzed your audience according to situational, demographic, and psychological characteristics, you need to factor in how generally receptive they will be to you. To do this, you need to determine your **audience's type**:

- **Friendly audience**—This audience has heard you speak before, has heard positive things about you, or is simply sold on your topic. These listeners are looking forward to your speech and are expecting to enjoy themselves.

- **Neutral or impartial audience**—These audience members consider themselves objective, rational, and open to new information (even though many of them have already made up their minds). They are looking for logic and facts (not emotion) and will be more receptive if you signal credibility and authority.

- **Uninterested or indifferent audience**—These listeners have a short attention span and often wish they were someplace else—therefore they're a real challenge. They will probably be polite, but will also plan to take a "mental holiday" during your presentation. A bit of razzle-dazzle may be needed to keep their interest.

- **Hostile audience**—Although you need to be careful not to stereotype any audience, this audience may be the greatest challenge of all because they are predisposed to dislike you, your topic, or both. Don't be intimidated or defensive. Stay in charge by presenting a calm, controlled appearance while citing expert data.

Table 4.1 summarizes strategies for dealing with each type of audience. → *For additional information, see also Chapter 7 (supporting materials), Chapter 8 (organization), and Chapter 11 (delivery).*

Table 4.1

Strategies for Dealing with Four Types of Audiences

Audience Type	Strategies		
	Organization	**Delivery**	**Supporting Material**
Friendly (predisposed to like you and your topic)	Any pattern. Try something new; ask for audience participation.	Warm, friendly, open. Make lots of eye contact, smile, gesture, and use vocal variety.	Humor, examples, personal experiences, quotations, statistics, comparisons, pictures, and clip art.
Neutral (consider themselves calm and rational; have minds already made up but think they are objective)	Pro-con or problem–solution patterns. Present both sides of the issue. Save time for audience questions. Use logic.	Controlled, even; nothing "showy." Use confident, small gestures; adopt look of authority and credibility.	Facts, statistics, expert opinion, comparison and contrast. Avoid humor, personal stories, flashy visuals.
Uninterested (short attention span, present against their wills, plan to tune out)	Brief—no more than three points. Avoid topical and pro-con patterns that seem long to the audience.	Dynamic and entertaining. Move around; use large gestures.	Humor, cartoons, colorful visuals, powerful quotations, startling statistics, and anecdotes.
	Do not: Darken the room, stand motionless behind the podium, pass out handouts, use boring view-graphs, or expect audience to participate.		
Hostile (looking for chances to take charge or ridicule speaker; attitude, due to bad past experiences)	Noncontroversial pattern such as topical, chronological, or geographical.	Calm and controlled. Speak slowly and evenly. Stay in charge.	Objective data and expert opinion. Avoid anecdotes and jokes.
	Avoid: Question-and-answer period if possible. Otherwise, use a moderator or accept only written questions.		

Janet E. Elsea, "Strategies for Effective Presentations," *Personnel Journal* 64 (September 1985), 31–33.

Sample Student Speech: "Our State of Health" by Lucy Tisdale Setliff

The following informative speech, "Our State of Health," was given by Lucy Tisdale Setliff to her speech class and was transcribed from the videotape. The assignment specified a 5- to 7-minute informational speech followed by a 1½- to 3-minute question-and-answer period and a 1-minute (or less) final wrap-up. Lucy's speech will be referred to throughout the text to illustrate how she went through the process of preparing her speech (see Lucy's audience analysis procedures on pages 87–88). As you read this speech, think about changes you would make if you were speaking on the same topic.

SAMPLE SPEECH

OUR STATE OF HEALTH

by Lucy Tisdale Setliff

Introduction

HIPPOCRATES ONCE SAID THAT health is the greatest of human blessings. Health— what exactly does that mean to each of us? Well, as defined in Webster's Dictionary, "Health is the absence of disease." Health became very important to me when I lost my father to heart disease. The day before he died, he said, "Lucy, I'm going to fight this thing." But, you know, he couldn't because the disease had completely taken over his heart. After he died, I became better informed about our state of health and I learned that the nation's two leading causes of death are heart disease and cancer, according to former Surgeon General C. Everett Koop. I also discovered that these and other diseases that kill us are caused partially by our own habits. Through improper diet and lack of exercise, we pay the price in the way of medical bills, plus we decrease our chances of spending our "golden years" in relatively good health.

So, this morning, I would like to look at our State of Health. I'll focus on three aspects of health: First, we'll identify major risk factors to health. **[Visual #1]** Second, we'll review cancer and heart attack warning signs. Third, we'll explore diet and exercise guidelines.

Body

1st Main Point

So let's go back to the first item and identify risk factors. **[Visual #2]**. Levy, Dignan, and Shirreffs in a text called *Life and Health* point out a number of risk factors involved in the development of disease. How many of us know them? The risk factors include heredity, genetics, improper diet, and lack of exercise. True, the risk factors of heredity and genetics remain beyond our control, but we can control the

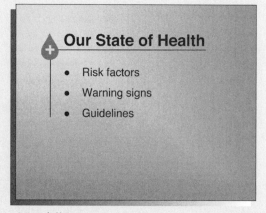

Visual #1

SAMPLE SPEECH

factors of improper diet and lack of exercise. So, how great a risk is improper diet and lack of exercise? A study by the American Heart Association shows that more than 66 million Americans, or one in four people, have some form of heart disease related to a high-fat diet and lack of exercise. Over 1 million Americans die each year from heart disease. Additionally, the American Heart Association states that cancer kills one out of every five people, and cancer experts conclude that 75 percent of these deaths could be avoided

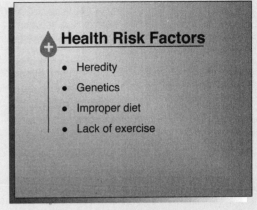

Visual #2

through a healthier lifestyle including lower intake of fat and more exercise. Yet the National Sporting Goods Association states that 45 percent of Americans do not participate in any type of physical activity. And there's high risk involved for this type of behavior because the American Heart Association states that sedentary individuals run five times the risk of developing disease compared to active individuals. So we see that cancer and heart disease are directly related to the risk factors of poor diet and lack of exercise.

2nd Main Point
We've identified risk factors; now let's review warning signs that may indicate we have a disease. **[Visual #3]** Can you list cancer's seven warning signals? They are: (1) change in bowel or bladder habits, (2) a sore that does not heal, (3) unusual bleeding or discharge, (4) thickening or lump in breast or elsewhere, (5) indigestion or difficulty in swallowing, (6) obvious change in wart or mole, and (7) nagging cough or hoarseness. According to the National Cancer Institute, "None of these symptoms is a sure sign of cancer, but if any of them last longer than 2 weeks, see a doctor."

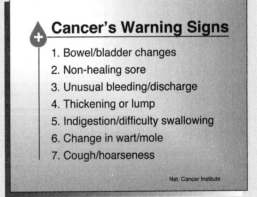

Visual #3

There are also warning signs that indicate a heart attack. Most people are less aware of these signs than they are of the cancer warning signs. According to the American Heart Association, "Sharp, stabbing twinges usually are not signals of heart attack." However, the following symptoms are definite indicators of possible heart attack: **[Visual #4]** (1) Uncomfortable pressure, fullness, squeezing, or pain in the center of the chest that lasts more than a few minutes, (2) pain that spreads to the shoulders, neck, or arms, and (3) chest discomfort with lightheadedness, fainting, sweating, nausea, or shortness of breath.

(continued)

SAMPLE SPEECH (continued)

If these symptoms occur, every minute counts. My family did not know these symptoms and waited an extra day after my father had suffered a heart attack before taking him to the hospital. He died a week later. So you see, what we do not know can hurt us.

3rd Main Point

So far we've identified major risk factors to health and reviewed cancer and heart attack warning signals. Diet and fitness guidelines are the final focus of our state of health. First, let's look at diet guidelines. If it seems like nothing's safe to eat anymore, you'll be happy to know that in 1992, the U.S. Department of Agriculture released guidelines for an improved diet called the Food Pyramid. **[Visual #5]** As we look at the diagram, we see the base of the pyramid forms the foundation of your diet consisting of breads, cereals, rice, and pasta. As we move up the pyramid, the next emphasis is on fruits and vegetables followed by lesser amounts of meats and dairy products. The tip of the pyramid shows those foods to use sparingly— those containing high levels of fats, salt, and sugar.

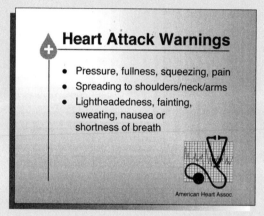

Visual #4

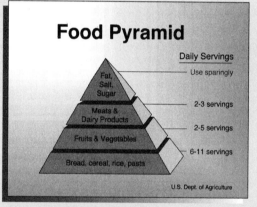

Visual #5

The tip of the pyramid needs to be our real concern, especially if you eat a lot of fast foods. The American Heart Association recommends that fats should be less than 30 percent of total calorie intake. This means for the average woman approximately 65 grams and for the average man only 80 grams of fat per day. Yet look at the fat in some of our favorite fast foods.

According to a recent issue of *Good Housekeeping,* Burger King's Double Whopper with Cheese has 63 grams of fat; Jack-in-the-Box's Colossus Burger contains 60 grams of fat; McDonald's Quarter Pounder with Cheese has 29 grams of fat; while Wendy's Big Bacon Classic contains 36 grams of fat. If you are thinking, "that's why I eat chicken and fish instead," listen to this: Jack-in-the-Box's Fish Supreme Sandwich has 32 grams of fat; Burger King's BK Big Fish Sandwich contains 43 grams of fat, and their BK Broiler has 29 grams of fat. McDonald's McChicken Sandwich also has 29 grams of fat—the same as their Quarter Pounder with Cheese.

Along with the diet guidelines are the exercise guidelines. Fortunately, exercise guidelines, as established by the American Heart Association, are fairly simple. They

recommend that a minimum of 15 minutes of exercise three times a week will help control our blood pressure and help us control our weight. To lose weight, more exercise is required—as much as 1 hour three times a week. However, jogging isn't necessary; a brisk walk can be just as effective.

Initial Conclusion

We should take a long look at the way we continue living life. Part of the great challenge of living is grasping opportunities and making the best choices we can. If we know the risk factors involved with disease, learn the warning signals that indicate disease, and discover diet and exercise guidelines, we improve our chances of preventing disease. Only then can we obtain health, the greatest of human blessings.

Questions and Answers

Are there any questions?

Question: Of all the types of exercises that are currently out there—I mean, I've heard all kinds of different things you can do. Probably most of us know all the things you can do but really don't like doing them. Is there one that's favored over others for cardiovascular health?

Answer: That's a good question, Les. As the American Medical Association states, the more exercise you do the better it is for your heart. When you do strenuous exercise such as cycling or use machines such as NordicTrack, stationary bicycles, or treadmills, you will strengthen your heart even more. However, less strenuous exercise such as brisk walking is recommended as well. Walking will help a lot in the long run.

Question: Lucy, is it important to know your family history as far as health is concerned?

Answer: Very important. Glad you asked, Leona. We need to be aware of our family health history because diseases and illnesses are passed down generation after generation. If we know that disease runs in the family, then we can be alert to that disease and start taking precautions now to prevent the problem from escalating. For example, high blood pressure runs in my family. My grandmother had it, my mother now has it. I now need to be alert to the possibility that I, too, may inherit it. So, right now I'm taking measures such as watching my salt intake and exercising to keep it down.

Question: Now I don't know if this is a myth or what, but I always thought that on the Food Pyramid that if you have too many carbohydrates . . . I mean, I could eat pasta all day long but I would gain weight.

Answer: Right, Kelly. The number of servings [refers to Visual #4] depends on how active you are. So, shoot really for the minimum because that provides the minimum nutrients. But if you are really active, if you do a lot of sports, you probably need to increase the amounts.

Final Conclusion

Thank you for your questions and your attention this morning. I think that we'll all agree that our health is what we choose to make it. How we take care of our bodies today will determine if we suffer problems later on. Health begins with awareness. Don't wait until later to get interested in your health. As it was with my father—later may be too late.

Collecting Audience Information Before and After

Remember that your purpose for analyzing your audience is to make your communication as effective as possible. Therefore, collect situational, demographic, and psychological information, as well as information on potential audience type, before your speeches so that you can adapt to audience frames of reference. After your speeches, collect information on audience reactions in order to evaluate the success of your presentation and make any needed changes in future speeches. Let's look in more detail at the collection of audience information both before and after your speeches.

Before the Speech

To gather all four types of information (situational, demographic, psychological, and receptivity) about your classroom audience, begin by observing and listening. Many demographic and situational traits become obvious through simple observation. Listening to your classmates' comments and opinions should give you a good idea of many of their beliefs and values. You might also interview a few classmates for additional information or give everyone a short questionnaire to complete at least one week before your speech. When speaking outside the classroom, a telephone interview of the person who originally asked you to speak will usually work.

Use a questionnaire including *situational questions* (the name of the organization or class and the seating arrangement), *demographic questions* (ages of audience members and any important group affiliations), *psychological questions* (basic beliefs and needs of the group), and *receptivity questions* (for example, "How would you classify your response to my topic: friendly, neutral, uninterested, or hostile?"). As the person answers your questions, jot down the responses. If you feel that you still need more information, ask for the names of two people to contact who are familiar with the expected audience.

There is one more way to obtain audience information before presenting the speech: Arrive at the site early. After checking to make sure that the lectern and equipment for visual aids are in place, greet the first few audience members as they arrive. Introduce yourself and politely ask about their interest in your speech and their motivation for attending. Not only will you have some friends in the audience, but your conversation may help you verify areas that you have in common with them. If you discover new information, you might make last-minute adjustments in your introduction. The more things you and your audience have in common, the more believable you will be.

During the hearing before the O. J. Simpson trial, prosecutor Marcia Clark used focus groups (whose members were as similar as possible to the actual jurors) to determine how her verbal, visual, and vocal communication might affect their opinions of her (Gorov, 1994; Streisand, 1994). What she found was that her hairstyle and "power" suits, as well as her hard-hitting words and vocal tone, made her come across as "aggressive," "pushy," and "aloof" instead of the friendly, caring, yet sharp attorney the focus group members said they preferred. As a result, she adopted a "softer" hairstyle, changed her wardrobe to feature soft colors and designs, altered her tone and words to be friendlier and less aggressive, and smiled and laughed in the courtroom. All of Clark's changes were an attempt to relate to the jurors' frames of reference so that they would listen to her and believe what she said.

Watch political candidates to see how they adapt their clothing and hair styles, manner of delivery, and use of examples to fit the taste of the voters to whom they

During the presidential campaign of 2004, President Bush appeared casual in khakis and blue shirt when speaking to a Republican crowd at the fairgrounds in Holland, Michigan, and formal in a dark suit, white shirt, and blue tie when addressing an audience of Air National Guard, Army National Guard, and reservists in Portsmouth, New Hampshire.

are speaking. For example, during the presidential campaign of 2004, both Senator John Kerry and President George W. Bush dressed differently depending on where they were campaigning. A sales study based on the electoral map found that Republican areas preferred khaki casual while Democratic areas preferred "dressy grays and blacks" (Bedard, 2004, p. 6).

After the Speech

Many speakers fail to recognize the importance of soliciting feedback after the speech. Assessing listener reactions is the only way you can tell if your analysis before the speech was adequate; if it wasn't, you'll want to make changes before your next speech. Of course, the most immediate feedback you will receive after a speech is the applause. If your speech ended with emotion or was particularly profound or startling, there may be a moment of silence before the applause while the audience absorbs your conclusion. You can tell the difference between an enthusiastic response and a lukewarm one.

Make yourself available after the speech so that audience members can offer their comments. Except in the classroom (where another speech begins almost immediately), audience members will tend to come up and thank the speaker, ask questions, and offer valuable feedback. If you are off in the corner talking with officials or busy putting away equipment, most people will leave without speaking to you—a missed opportunity.

Taking time to talk to audience members after your speech is a good way to get valuable feedback.

© Sepp Seits/Woodfin Camp & Associates, Inc.

A brief questionnaire similar to the one shown in Figure 4.3 is another way to get feedback after your speech. You can place the questionnaire on a table by the door for audience members to complete as they leave, or you can send a thank-you letter and copies of your questionnaire to your contact person with a request to have three or four people from the audience fill it out. Or you may simply ask specific questions of one or two people you know who attended the speech.

Once your speech is over, it's difficult to remember exactly what you said or what gestures you used, so a good way to get significant feedback is to have someone videotape your talk. If your contact person doesn't have a video camera, bring your own or rent one. Ask a friend to come along with you to tape both your speech and some audience reactions if possible. As you watch later, analyze the speech for strengths and weaknesses.

Figure 4.3

Sample Speech Evaluation Questionnaire

Directions: For each item, put a check mark in the blank that best describes your evaluation of my speech.

	1	2	3	4	5	6	7	
Dull								Exciting
Disorganized								Organized
Weakly supported								Well supported
Sources questionable								Sources believable
Poor delivery								Dynamic delivery
Unpleasant voice								Pleasant voice
Limited eye contact								Direct eye contact
Confusing visuals								Helpful visuals
Too soft								Easily heard
Poor overall								Excellent overall

Using Audience Analysis

After reading this chapter, you can see why speech preparation begins with audience analysis. Regardless of the type of speech you will be giving, before you finalize your topic selection and begin researching for information, review the situational, demographic, and psychological characteristics of your audience. For a classroom speech, you might ask yourself the following questions (Lucy's answers to these questions in relation to her speech, "Our State of Health," are in italics):

- At this point in the course, will my classmates' current opinions of me add to my credibility or take away from it? What can I do to improve my credibility?

  Lucy knew that she was well liked by most of the students in her class, but she knew that she hadn't made a very good impression with her introductory speech because she had been so nervous. She decided to add to her credibility by making her delivery more conversational and by citing several impressive sources—so research was definitely needed.

- How much do my classmates know about the general topics I am considering? (If you don't have any specific topics in mind yet, come back to this question when you do.)

  Lucy had tentatively decided to give her informational speech on the general topic of health—specifically what, she wasn't sure.

- What types of visual aids will be more likely to impress my audience? What types of attention-getters will interest them the most (for example, personal instance, startling statement, or quote)?

  When Lucy checked with the other speakers who were scheduled to speak on the same day and found that most of them were using computer visuals, she decided to use them as well. Transparencies and computer visuals create a more professional, polished presentation, which adds to the overall credibility of a speaker—something Lucy felt she needed.

- On the basis of demographic characteristics of my class (for example, age, marital status, children, major, group memberships, hobbies), how can I make my potential topics interesting and beneficial to them? (If you can't think of a way, you probably need to select a different topic.)

  Although the demographics of Lucy's class varied widely, the only ones that seemed important were age (ages ranged from 18 to 30) and group membership (several students were members of a health club). Lucy felt that audience members would be interested in maintaining their health. However, because of lack of information on health, many of them placed studying and work ahead of exercise and proper diet.

- What attitudes, beliefs, or values that are relevant to my topic already exist in the minds of my classmates? How can I use these psychological factors to communicate my ideas better?

  Before-class conversations with several of her classmates convinced Lucy that the students in her class already believed that exercise is beneficial and that health is important. She could use those beliefs to communicate her ideas about health—as soon as she decided how to narrow down the topic.

- What basic needs (physiological, safety, social, esteem, and self-actualization) do most of my classmates have that will make the need for my topic obvious?

  Lucy decided that safety, social, and esteem needs were the most closely related to the topic of health. Her classmates all wanted to avoid poor health (safety needs), would

enjoy the companionship and sense of belonging that exercising at a club or with a friend brings (social needs), and would feel a sense of pride at knowing that they had taken steps to ensure their health (esteem needs).

Most likely your classroom audience will be a friendly audience, like Lucy's. These listeners will know what you are going through and be rooting for your success. Personal examples and humor will be especially effective, as will any extra effort you put into your visual aids (such as clip art or color). You can also add to class enjoyment if you refer to a speech given by an earlier speaker or cite the behavior or statements of a student from the class as an example to support your own ideas. If, by chance, your class does not fall into the friendly audience category, review the section on types of audiences and adjust your speech accordingly.

Summary

Speech preparation involves ten basic steps that will be discussed more fully in the following chapters. This chapter covers the first step in speech preparation—analyzing your audience. You can collect four types of information to use in analyzing your audience: situational, demographic, psychological, and audience receptivity. *Situational information* (such as audience size and expectations and the possible presence of other speakers) helps you plan your speech to fit the specific situation. *Demographic information* (such as age, ethnic and cultural background, gender, group affiliation, marital status and children, occupation, and education) helps you know as much as possible about your audience and aids in selecting your topic and supporting materials. *Psychological information* is also important in planning your speech. To interest audience members in your topic or persuade them to take some action, you must identify their attitudes, beliefs, values, and needs in order to decide what information or appeals will be most effective. Once you have gathered situational, demographic, and psychological information about your audience, you are ready to determine *audience receptivity*. Audiences can be friendly, neutral, uninterested, or hostile. Each type of audience requires different verbal, visual, and vocal approaches.

All four types of audience information are gathered before your speech to allow you to adapt your presentation to listeners' frames of reference. Without this information, your chances of communicating successfully with your audience are diminished; with it, you can feel confident that your presentation will succeed. Similar information is collected after the speech to enable you to evaluate your speech and make any needed changes in future speeches.

Essentials of Public Speaking   Online

Use the Essentials of Public Speaking website at **http://communication. wadsworth.com/hamiltoneps3** for quick access to the electronic study resources that accompany this chapter. When you get to the Essentials home page, click on "Student Book Companion Site" in the Resource box. The Essentials website features the Test Your Knowledge Quiz on page 65, the web links described in the Technology Tips for Speakers box on page 72, InfoTrac College Edition, the Suggestions for Practice and Critical Thinking activities and the InfoTrac College Edition activities that follow, a digital glossary, and review quizzes.

Key Terms

attitude 74
audience type 78
belief 75
demographic informa-
    tion 69
framing 78
friendly audience 78

hostile audience 79
instrumental value 75
need 76
neutral or impartial
    audience 79
situational information
    67

terminal value 75
theory of reasoned
    action 75
uninterested or indifferent
    audience 79
value 75

Suggestions for Practice and Critical Thinking

1. Try to locate organizations in your community that have a speakers' bureau. Call one of the speakers, and ask how he or she analyzes the audience before a speech. Compare the answer with the suggestions made in this chapter.

2. Using InfoTrac College Edition, check out "Attitude Change in College Students: Examining the Effect of College Peer Groups and Faculty Groups," by Jeffery F. Milem, *Journal of Higher Education,* March–April 1998, page 117. How much influence do you think peer groups have on college student attitudes? On your attitudes? What message does the article hold for speakers?

3. Clip an advertisement out of a newspaper or magazine. What specific customer group is the ad targeting? How does the ad appeal to the needs or desires of the target group? Select a different target group and explain specifically how you would change the ad to appeal to the new group. Share your ideas with a classmate or a group of classmates.

4. Find an ad for walking shoes that targets 18- to 25-year-olds. What features of the ad made you decide that it was targeting this age group? How would you change the ad to reach people who like to travel? Senior citizens? People in organized sports? Share the ad and your interpretation of it with a group of classmates. As a group, select the best ad and prepare to present it to the class.

5. List 10 topics that you feel would interest your classmates, and ask them to select the 5 topics they would be most interested in hearing. Tabulate your results and compare them with the findings of five other students. Save this information for use in selecting speech topics to be assigned later.

6. In small groups, prepare a questionnaire to analyze the demographic characteristics of your speech class. Representatives from each group can meet to compare the questionnaires and select the best questions from each. Distribute the final questionnaire to all class members and tabulate the results for future use.

7. Are you still visualizing your positive statements once or twice a day? If not, spend the next 10 minutes going over them. Remember to read, visualize, and feel confident performing each of your statements. If you can't seem to find time to work on all of your statements, select the one that you most hope to achieve and concentrate on it for the next week. Every chance you get, visualize yourself successfully completing your statement for the week. Don't forget to feel confident and pleased while you are visualizing. When the week is over, select another positive statement and spend the next week working on it.

8. Check out the following websites. *You can access these sites under the Student Resources for Chapter 4* at the Essentials of Public Speaking website.

- At the OverViews website, three professional speech writers provide several excellent speeches. (Click on "Speech Samples.") Read two speeches and see if you can determine how each speaker adapted to the audience.

- Read about recent changes in the generation gap in "Generation Gap Narrowing on Most Attitude Areas, but Young Become More Distrustful of Society in General" at the University of Chicago News Office website.

- For poll results on the modern family, check out the article "The Emerging 21st Century American Family" by Tom W. Smith, sponsored by the University of Chicago's Opinion Research Center. You will need Adobe Acrobat Reader to access the PDF files on this site. See Adobe's website for information on how to download a free reader.

- The Gallup Organization at Princeton conducts many interesting polls. Go to the Gallup Organization's Frequently Asked Questions site and read "How Gallup Polls Are Conducted." To read about long-term poll trends, see "Long Term Gallup Poll Trends: A Portrait of American Public Opinion through the Century" at the Gallup Poll site. (You must subscribe to view this article.)

- For an excellent discussion and evaluation of Maslow and his theory of needs, visit the Personality Theories site. This article was prepared by Shippensberg University's Dr. C. George Boeree.

- To analyze your audience, adapt the worksheet prepared by Sam Walch for his *Public Speaking Workbook*. The worksheet is well suited to a telephone interview with two or three people. This excellent workbook is in the public domain and free to use, so click on "Public Speaking Workbook" for other useful information on this site. To find other audience analysis worksheets, do a Google search on "audience analysis worksheet."

Quiz Answers

Answers to Unit II Quiz: Test Your Knowledge About Speech Preparation.

1. *True.* The one thing that is most responsible for creating deadly dull speeches is the overuse of explanation. Instead of presenting statistics to illustrate the seriousness of a problem, speakers will "explain" how serious it is; instead of giving a real-life instance to show how rude drivers are today, speakers will "explain" that drivers are rude. Which of the following speeches do you think would be more interesting? → *See Chapter 6 for a discussion of overuse of explanation.*

Speech 1	Speech 2
I. First main point	I. First main point
A. Explanation	A. Personal instance
B. Explanation	B. Figurative comparison
C. Explanation	C. Statistics
II. Second main point	II. Second main point
A. Statistics	A. Explanation
B. Explanation	B. Quotation
C. Explanation	C. Humorous instance
III. etc.	III. etc.

2. *False.* An introduction that grabs the attention of your audience is very important. However, preparing the introduction before developing your main points is usually a waste of time. Speakers normally add and remove main points several times before they are satisfied. Each time you change the body of your speech, you will probably have to change the introduction as well. → *Chapter 7 covers introductions.*

3. *True.* A warm, conversational tone of voice is not likely to grab the attention of audience members. A more dynamic and entertaining approach is needed along with humor, colorful visuals, moving quotations, and startling statistics. → *See Chapter 10 for more on effective delivery.*

4. *True.* Roughing out an outline saves time because it limits and directs the amount of research needed. However, if you know nothing about your topic, you will need to do some research before making an outline. → *If you follow the advice for topic selection in Chapter 5, you will know enough about your topic to rough out an outline.*

5. *False.* Although statistics lend clarity and support to your ideas, they can confuse, bore, and overload listeners if used incorrectly. You need to relate statistics to your listeners' frames of reference. For example, telling an audience that smoke-related diseases kill half a million people a year may leave them yawning unless you also tell them that this is 50 people an hour, 1,200 a day, and 8,400 a week—every week for a year—until half a million people die (Bristow, 1994). That would be like eliminating a city the size of Fort Worth, Texas, every year! → *Chapter 6 discusses other guidelines for using statistics effectively.*

6. *False.* A storyboard is not a poster. It is a way to organize your speech that is less formal and more visual than outlining. Storyboards do not require careful use of numerals and letters, and they allow space for possible visual aids and transition statements. → *Chapter 8 discusses storyboards and how to use them.*

7. *False.* It's never good to tell your audience that you are nervous or unprepared. You may momentarily feel better by confessing, but listeners may feel anxious and uncomfortable. Your credibility in the eyes of your audience sinks as well. Also, don't forget that your feelings of anxiety rarely show—unless you confess. → *See Chapter 2 for suggestions for overcoming speaker anxiety.*

8. *False.* Although beginning speakers think notes written in complete sentences will make them feel more secure, the opposite is more often true. When you glance down at complete sentences, the words run together and you are forced to either read the notes word for word or "wing it" without using the notes at all. Key-word notes are much more helpful. Only quotations should be written word for word. If you use visual aids, you probably won't need notes at all. → *See Chapter 8 for a discussion of various types of speaking notes.*

9. *False.* An ethical speaker is always careful not to plagiarize—it doesn't matter how unlikely it is that anyone would ever know. Using other people's material without giving them credit is always unethical. → *See Chapter 5 for pointers on how to use supporting materials and avoid unintentional plagiarism.*

10. *False.* Although introductions and conclusions are important, the body of an effective speech usually takes about 70 to 80 percent of your total speech time. Therefore, in a 5-minute speech, the body should last approximately 3½ to 4 minutes; in a 7-minute speech, 5 to 5½ minutes; and in a 10-minute speech, 7 to 8 minutes. → *See Chapter 7 for suggestions on speech organization.*

chapter 5

Selecting and Researching Your Topic

Flashback
The Greek and Roman rhetoricians urged their students to research, read, and study on a daily basis. For example, in *DeOratore*, Cicero, an eminent Roman politician and famous orator, wrote: "No man can be an orator complete in all points of merit who has not attained a knowledge of all important subjects and arts. For it is from knowledge that oratory must derive its beauty and fullness, and unless there is such knowledge, well-grasped and comprehended by the speaker, there must be something empty and almost childish in the utterance" (Cicero [translated by E. W. Sutton], 1959, Book I, vi, 20).

You DON'T WANT TO SPEND DAYS SELECTING A TOPIC AND EVEN LONGER IN THE LIBRARY researching it. You won't have to if you follow the suggestions presented in this chapter. Better yet, when you finish this chapter, you will have completed steps 2, 3, and 4 of the Basic Steps for Preparing a Speech. *Step 2* is to determine topic, exact purpose, and main points. *Step 3* is to prepare a rough-draft outline of the main points and needed information. *Step 4* is to research your topic for material to support the main points. Let's turn now to the first of these steps.

Basic Steps for Preparing a Speech
1. Analyze your potential audience. → *See Chapter 4.*
2. **Determine topic, exact purpose, and main points.**
3. **Prepare a rough-draft outline of main points and needed information.**
4. **Research topic for material to support main points.**
5. Select best supporting materials. → *See Chapter 6.*
6. Determine how best to organize main points. → *See Chapter 7.*
7. Plan introduction and conclusion. → *See Chapter 7.*

8. Make preparation outline (or storyboards) and speaking notes. → *See Chapter 8.*

9. Prepare visual aids. → *See Chapter 9.*

10. Rehearse speech. → *See Chapters 10 and 11.*

Selecting Your Topic, Purpose, and Main Points

Once you have analyzed your audience, you are ready to pick a specific topic. Although sometimes you may be given a topic by the organization asking you to speak, by the manager requesting the report, or by your instructor, most of the time the selection of a topic is up to you.

Determine Your Topic

One way to make sure you always have plenty of good speech topics on hand is to carry a notepad in your purse or wallet and use it to record possible speech topics as they occur to you. Then all you have to do is decide which one(s) to use. Finding good topics isn't difficult—the following four guidelines should help. They apply regardless of the type of speech you are asked to give—demonstration, informational, persuasive, or special occasion.

Using InfoTrac College Edition, conduct a keyword search for *brainstorming*. See what advice you can find that will help you determine possible speech topics.

Select a Topic That Fits the Type of Speech   Once you have been assigned a specific type of speech, *make sure the topic you select is appropriate.* Many topics that would make ideal informational speeches would not work as demonstration or persuasive speeches. For example, "Preparing an Effective Resume" would make a good informational speech but would be difficult to make persuasive and almost impossible to demonstrate. "Lowering Your Cholesterol" could be informational or persuasive but could not be demonstrated. "Using PowerPoint to Prepare Visual Aids" would make an excellent demonstration or informational speech but would hardly be an effective after-dinner speech. On the other hand, "Lowering the Incidence of Child Abuse" would lend itself more to persuasion than to any other type of speech. Persuasive topics need to be controversial—that is, have at least two conflicting views. Although everyone agrees that child abuse is a serious problem (no controversy), we may not agree about what can be done to solve it.

Also *make sure your speech fits the allotted time.* The only way you can be certain is to practice the speech and time it. Thinking it through in your mind doesn't work, as one student found out the hard way. Layla was presenting a demonstration speech entitled "How to Wrap Attractive Gifts." She started by showing a hilarious example of how her parents wrapped her Christmas gifts when she was a child. The box looked as if it had fallen down the stairs and been rescued by a pet. Then she showed the audience a beautifully wrapped gift and suggested that listeners could wrap gifts themselves in three easy steps. Unfortunately, by this point in her speech, she had used up more than half of the allotted time and was forced to end without covering all the steps. Had she practiced her speech out loud, she would have realized that the introduction was too long and that it takes longer to actually wrap a gift than it does to talk about it.

Select a Topic That You Already Know a Lot About   You will feel more relaxed and confident giving your speech if you select a topic that is familiar—either

from personal experience or from previous research. If you don't have any specific topics in mind, brainstorm possible speech topics for each of the following categories: job (current or past), college-related topics, family, hobbies, activities that you spend most of your time doing, skills or accomplishments that you are especially proud of, and research papers you've written. As you brainstorm each topic area, list anything that comes to mind, no matter how crazy it seems. "Crazy" ideas often lead to a really good topic. Continue brainstorming until you have at least three ideas for each category.

> Stop reading at this point and brainstorm a list of possible topics.

When you have completed your list, look at the sample topics in Figure 5.1. If they stimulate you to think of additional topics, add them to your list. Now select from your revised list the topics that might be appropriate for your speech. ➜ *More detailed lists of demonstration, informational, and persuasive speech topics can be found in Chapters 12 and 13.*

Figure 5.1
Sample Speech Topics

▼ **Business**
Online sales—continue to grow?
Working in virtual teams
Business ethics

▼ **College/Education**
Who benefits most from college?
Equal funding for men's and women's sports
Cultural bias of SAT

▼ **Family**
Programming your VCR
Dealing with Alzheimer's disease
Children and bicycle helmets

▼ **Food/Beverages**
Are Atkins and South Beach diets healthy?
Fat content of fast foods
Making a great cup of coffee

▼ **Health/Exercise**
Taping ankles to prevent injury
Antidotes for household poisons
Anthrax—still a threat?

▼ **Hobbies**
How to take a good picture
Collecting baseball cards
The need for volunteers

▼ **Holiday/Gift/Home**
Save money: Make your own gift bows
Holiday safety tips

▼ **Magic/Games/Music**
Do your own magic tricks
The relaxing benefit of music

▼ **Multicultural**
Diversity training in the workplace
Illegal aliens and Constitutional rights

▼ **Miscellaneous**
Topic related to your job or major
Topic based on a research paper
The existence of angels
A vacation spot

▼ **National/Political**
Social security benefits
Preventing terrorism
America's role in Iraq

▼ **Pets/Animals**
Teach your dog a trick
Selecting a pet
Taking pets on plane trips

▼ **Personal**
Dressing professionally on a budget
Preparing an effective resume
Making a will

▼ **Social**
Neighborhood gangs
Volunteerism—on the increase?
Breakdown of the family

▼ **Sports**
Recent ethics problems in sports
Tennis tips
Violence at sports events

After Lucy (whose sample speech appeared in Chapter 4) had brainstormed possible topics and crossed out the inappropriate ones, she was left with five topics that fit her assignment.

1. *"Vacationing in Germany" (she had lived in Germany for 7 years).*
2. *"Basic health maintenance" (she had done a report on health the previous semester; also, several years earlier, she had seen her father die of heart disease and her uncle struggle with diabetes).*
3. *"The logistics of taking televised courses" (she had taken several ITV courses).*
4. *"The adult with braces" (she had gotten braces placed only days before the course began).*
5. *"Cross-stitching as a hobby" (she had found cross-stitching to be a relaxing hobby).*

Select a Topic That Interests You Use this criterion to narrow your list of possible speech topics. Cross out topics that you know a lot about but that do not interest you. It's difficult to interest your audience in a topic that you don't care about. Select a topic that you are enthusiastic about, and your enthusiasm will carry over to your audience.

By eliminating the topics that interested her the least, Lucy narrowed her possible speech topics to two: basic health maintenance and the logistics of taking televised courses. She had personal experience with both and had done some research on each.

Select a Topic That You Can Make Interesting and Valuable to Your Audience Audience members don't have to be interested in your topic before you begin speaking, but they should be by the time you finish. The audience analysis you do in step 1 of the ten Basic Steps for Preparing a Speech will help you select a topic that will interest your listeners and benefit them in some way as well. Ask yourself, Will my speech make my listeners healthier, happier, or more aware? Will it show them how to save money? Save lives? Communicate better with dates or parents? Study more productively for exams? Learn something new? Will it dispel a myth or add more excitement to their lives? In other words, a good speech topic should not only interest both you and your audience but also benefit your listeners in some way.

Although both health and ITV courses interested Lucy, she realized that few of her classmates had taken televised courses. However, everyone in her class was interested in maintaining their health. By questioning a few of the students in her class, she also confirmed her sense that a talk on health would benefit her audience more than one on televised instruction. She was now ready to determine her exact purpose and possible main points.

In spite of all these suggestions, don't worry too much about finding the "perfect" topic. Just find a topic you enjoy that fits the criteria and go with it.

Define Your Exact Purpose

After you have analyzed your audience and decided on a general topic, you are ready to narrow your topic so that it will fit the time limit and the specific needs and interests of your audience. It is better to cover fewer points and to thoroughly illustrate and support them than it is to skim over a larger number of points in an attempt to "say it all." Audiences tend to daydream when the speaker tries to cover too much material. Narrowing your topic to an exact purpose is one of the most difficult tasks a speaker faces, no matter how experienced you may be. An **exact purpose** is a

clear, simple sentence that specifies exactly what you want your audience to gain (know, perceive, understand) from the speech. An exact purpose begins with, "After hearing my speech, the audience will be able to . . ."

To illustrate the importance of narrowing your topic, let's assume that you are a fan of professional football and have selected football as your general speech topic. You have 5 minutes in which to present an informative speech. You start by making a list of possible speeches about football, writing each in the form of an exact purpose. Which of the following purposes are too broad for a 5-minute speech? How will you narrow the topic?

Exact purpose: After hearing my speech, the audience will be able to . . .

1. Explain the divisions and conferences that make up the NFL.
2. Understand the steps required for a team to make it to the Super Bowl.
3. Understand the role of the Competition Committee in making game rules.
4. Realize why the instant replay rule has caused so much controversy.
5. Contrast and compare the roles of referee, umpire, and linesman.
6. Explain the job of coaching.
7. Realize how much power the commissioner of the NFL really has.
8. Identify the qualities needed in a winning quarterback.
9. Understand the size, speed, and psychological requirements of each football position.
10. Perceive football as a money-maker.
11. Associate football players with their commercial endorsements.
12. Explain the argument over artificial versus natural turf.
13. Describe the personality of football fans in several cities.
14. Understand three facts that viewers need to know to watch football intelligently.
15. Perceive football cheerleaders as goodwill ambassadors.
16. Know the history of LaDainian Tomlinson (or some other well-known player).
17. Demonstrate how the football is held when thrown versus when it is caught.
18. Understand the history of the National Football League.

Although several of these purposes could be narrowed down if the speaker so desired, purposes 6, 9, and 18 are definitely too broad. For example, with regard to purpose 6, there are several types of football coaches so the exact purpose for a 5-minute speech should be one type of coach (such as the head coach or the offensive coordinator). To narrow purpose 9, two positions (such as tight end and wide receiver) could be compared and contrasted. Purpose 18 could be narrowed to "How the NFL got started" or "The early years of the NFL." Of course, exactly how you narrow down your topic will depend on your own interests and the interests of your audience.

> *Once Lucy decided to speak about the basics of health maintenance, she knew that she would need to narrow the topic somewhat. After listing several exact purposes, she decided on the following: "After hearing my speech, the audience will be more aware of health risk factors, warning signs, and fitness guidelines."*

EXPRESS/CONNECT

You can use Speech Builder Express, a web-based speech outlining and development tool, to help you create your exact purpose. To access Speech Builder Express, use the passcode included in your new copy of *The Essentials of Public Speaking*. When you log on, you'll be prompted to set up an account, and then you can start on a speech outline by choosing a speech type. To work on your exact purpose, select "Speech Goal" from the left-hand menu and follow the instructions. For short reminders from this chapter about exact purposes, click on the "Tutor" button.

Determine Your Main Points

Once you have selected a topic that you already know quite a bit about, this is the time to decide on your main points. You'll be able to complete your research much faster because you're more focused. Of course, in your research you may uncover additional information that you wish to include in the speech, or you may discover that one of your points should be discarded.

If you are assigned a topic that you know little about, you'll need to do some initial research just to discover what main points will work best. You might also try the brainstorming method suggested earlier. In 5 minutes or less, make a list of every possible content idea that comes to mind. Then consider each one, combining and eliminating until you settle on the three to five main points that will be most beneficial to your audience. → *Refer to the Quick Start Guide for more on the selection of main points.*

> *Since Lucy had previously researched her topic of health maintenance for a paper in another class, she already knew that she wanted to include (1) health risk factors, (2) cancer and heart attack warning signs, and (3) diet and fitness guidelines. Although her instructor pointed out that any one of these main points could be developed into a complete speech, Lucy felt that for her listeners to get a clear picture of health maintenance, they needed information from all three areas. She was now ready to rough out an outline of her main points and possible supporting materials to help her determine what research needed updating and what supporting materials were lacking.*

EXPRESS CONNECT

You can use Speech Builder Express to help you create your main points. Select "Main Points" from the left-hand menu and follow the instructions. For short reminders from this chapter about main points, click on the "Tutor" button.

Prepare a Rough-Draft Outline

Before beginning your research, make a rough outline of the main points and supporting information that you think you might use. With a rough outline as a guide, you can avoid researching areas that won't be included in your speech. Keep in mind

Preparing a rough-draft outline before you begin your research (as this student is doing) will save you valuable research time.

© Hangarter/The Picture Cube, Inc.

Figure 5.2

Lucy's Rough-Draft Outline

Notice how it indicates where research is needed.

Our State of Health

I. <u>Risk factors</u> to health
   A. Beyond our control—heredity & genetics ⎞
   B. In our control—diet & exercise   ⎬ [Health Textbook]
   C. How great a risk?   ⎠
   [need expert quote] 1. % of people with heart disease [Am. Heart Assoc. Pamphlet]
                       2. % who die with cancer [Am. Cancer Society]
                       3. % of people who don't exercise [source?]

II. Cancer and heart attack <u>warning signs</u>
   A. Warning signs for cancer [Encyclopedia or Am. Heart Assoc.]
   B. Warning signs for heart attack [Ask father's doctor; look for pamphlet]

III. Diet and exercise <u>guidelines</u>
   A. Diet guidelines
      ▪ Food Pyramid [Source?]
      ▪ Example ?
   B. Exercise guidelines
   [Interview Trainer from health club]
      ▪ How often to exercise? [Source?]
      ▪ What type exercise? [Health Textbook]
      ▪ Personal example?
                    [need expert quote]

---

that a **rough-draft outline** is exactly as it sounds—rough. Don't worry about following the rules for outlining. Later, when you are ready to expand your rough draft into a more detailed outline or into storyboards, you will need to be more aware of procedure. Figure 5.2 shows Lucy's rough-draft outline.

If formal outlines make you break out in a cold sweat, you may want to use a storyboard instead. A storyboard doesn't require the structure of a formal outline; moreover, it allows for a rough sketch of visual aids and provides space for transitions between main points. ➝ *Outlines and storyboards are discussed more completely in Chapter 8.*

Researching Your Topic

Analyzing your audience, selecting an interesting and beneficial topic, and roughing out an outline are preliminary steps in speech preparation. However, without the in-

formation from the next step—researching your topic for verbal and visual supporting materials—your speech won't make much of an impression. Although it's a good idea to keep your eyes open for usable visual material such as pictures, maps, and graphs, most of your research will concentrate on verbal information that you can use to clarify and prove the main ideas in your speech. Ideally, some of your supporting materials should come from your own experiences, but it's also important to gather supporting materials (such as explanations, illustrations, statistics, quotations, and examples) from books, magazines, encyclopedias, journal articles, and the Internet. Using information from respected sources adds to your credibility as a speaker. The remainder of this chapter will cover where and how to research for information.

Avoid Research Mistakes

In researching their topics, beginning speakers often make one of two mistakes: (1) they do too little research because they plan to rely primarily or completely on their personal experience, or (2) they use only the Internet to do their research.

First, even if you are speaking as an expert on your topic, it's a good idea to have a minimum of two additional sources. Using information from other respected sources shows that you are an objective and informed speaker and adds to your credibility.

Second, although the Internet can be a wonderful research tool, it is best used to supplement information from more traditional sources. Much of the information found on the web is superficial, biased, or out of date. Moreover, many of the best websites are difficult to find with standard search engines (Knowlton, 1997). Also, many valuable sources are not yet available electronically or charge a substantial fee. Therefore, your college library is still an important part of any quality research—librarians can help you find print materials, give you access to electronic databases, and direct you to reliable websites.

Begin With Printed Materials

If you are relatively unfamiliar with your topic, it's a good idea to begin your search for information with an overview from one or two current books on the topic. Then check your library for other printed materials.

- *Books.* To save time, check the *Library of Congress Subject Headings* for terms that your topic is likely to be indexed under before checking your college's online catalog of books. Also, don't forget to look in your college bookstore for textbooks on your topic—not only are they current, but additional sources are listed in footnotes and/or references. You can also search for current books by author, title, or topic on Amazon.com, eBooks.com, and NetLibrary.com websites.

- *Brochures and pamphlets.* These can give you a useful thumbnail sketch of your topic. Check your library's *Vertical File Index* for pamphlets on your topic. You might also want to contact local or national organizations (like the American Cancer Society)—check phone book listings.

- *Magazines/journals.* Most of the magazines or journals you will want to use are located in the reference section of the library and indexed in the *Readers' Guide to Periodical Literature* or in one of the more specialized print indexes such as *Business Periodicals Index, Cumulative Index to Nursing and Allied Health, Education Index,* or *Index to Journals in Communication Studies.* Expect to

search using more than one word—it may take several tries before you find the exact term to locate the information you want. Most libraries also have several electronic databases (like InfoTrac College Edition) that offer the complete text of many magazine and journal articles. → *See the following section on using electronic databases.*

- *Newspapers.* Although newspaper articles may not tell the complete story, they are more current than books and contain personal details and quotations that can serve as good supporting materials. Check your library for national, large-city, and local newspapers. Many libraries also have electronic indexes of major newspapers, such as *Lexis-Nexis,* the *National Newspaper Index,* and InfoTrac's *National Newspaper Index,* which include complete articles, not just the references.
- *Specialized dictionaries and encyclopedias.* If you aren't very familiar with your topic, you might begin your research with a specialized dictionary such as the *Dictionary of American History* or an encyclopedia such as *Encyclopedia of Sociology, Encyclopedia of Science and Technology,* or the *Physician's Desk Reference.* These reference books contain overviews of basic information in the field—for example, the *Physician's Desk Reference* contains pictures and explanations on the Heimlich maneuver.
- *Quotation books.* Libraries contain many books of quotations such as *Bartlett's Familiar Quotations,* the *Oxford Dictionary of Quotations,* the *Speaker's and Toastmaster's Handbook,* and *A Treasury of Jewish Quotations.* Most quotation books include not only quotations but also humorous stories, sayings, and proverbs—excellent supporting materials for your ideas. You will also find many quotation books now online. Yahoo, for example, links to Quotations on CD, which references over 100,000 quotations.
- *Yearbooks.* For facts or little-known statistics, look in such yearbooks as *The Book of Lists, The Guinness Book of World Records,* the *World Almanac, Facts on File Yearbook* (which includes national and international events from the previous year), and the *Statistical Abstract of the United States* (which contains general statistical data on a wide variety of topics from the U.S. Census Bureau). Most colleges now provide many of these yearbooks online for student use.
- *Other library resources.* Check with your librarian for government documents, special collections, and films or videotapes that are relevant to your topic. Also, you may be able to obtain additional materials through interlibrary loan services.

Use Electronic Databases When Possible

As already mentioned, college libraries provide commercial electronic databases that contain books, magazines, journal articles, and government documents. These databases have been screened to include only reliable information from business, education, government, and international sources and contain complete text of most articles. Some databases that might be helpful for researching your speeches are *AltaVista, Comm Index, Communication and Mass Media Complete, EBSCOhost, Education Index, Ethnic Newswatch, InfoTrac, InfoTrac College Edition, Opposing Viewpoints Resource Center, OVID,* and *ProQuest.* Your librarian will give you the CD-ROM or the Internet password for these databases.

INFOTRAC® COLLEGE EDITION
From Gale Group and Thomson Learning

Keyword search

Click in the entry box and enter search term(s)

search engines   [Search] [Clear Form]

Search for words ⊙ in title, citation, abstract ○ in entire article content
Type words to search for. You can use AND, OR, NOT. Results are sorted by date.

Limit the current search (optional)
☑ to refereed publications
by date ⊙ all dates ○ before ○ on ○ after
○ between [   ] [   ] [   ] and
[   ] [   ] [   ]

InfoTrac College Edition has 19,340,953 articles and was last updated on Jan 5, 2005.

THOMSON
GALE
Copyright and Terms of Use

Commercial databases like InfoTrac College Edition are especially helpful in researching magazines, journals, and newspapers. More than 19 million full-text articles are available for your use. Use the free InfoTrac passcode (included in your new copy of Essentials of Public Speaking) to access the InfoTrac College Edition database.

INFOTRAC® COLLEGE EDITION
From Gale Group and Thomson Learning

Keyword search (in title, citation, abstract): search engines
Limited by: refereed publications

──── **Citations 1 to 20 (of 77)** ──── ⊙ ⊙

☐ Mark all items on this page

☐ 📄 **With specialty search engines.** (searching the web) Holly Gunn.
Mark   *Teacher Librarian* Dec 2004 v32 i2 p50(1) (636 words)

☐ 📄 **Search engines essential to internet, study finds.** (tech briefs)(Brief Article) Ronald Roach.
Mark   *Black Issues in Higher Education* Sept 23, 2004 v21 i16 p37(1) (214 words)

☐ 📄 **THIS WAY APP.** (Search Engines) NOAH RUBIN BRIER.
Mark   *American Demographics* Sept 1, 2004 v26 i7 pNA (2616 words)

☐ 📄 **Top dog on the Web: how personal trainers have found a back door to top-10 status on**
Mark   **Internet search engines.** (Technology) Joe Dysart.
      IDEA Fitness Journal June 2004 v1 i1 pS8(4) (1777 words)

☐ 📄 **With free visual search engines.** (searching the web) Holly Gunn.
Mark   *Teacher Librarian* June 2004 v31 i5 p51(1) (648 words)

Use the Internet With Care

Most people don't realize what a recent creation the Internet is: It has been in common use only since 1992. In 2000 there were over 10 million new users signing onto the Internet each month (Bufton, 2000); by December 2002, there were 665.9 million Internet users worldwide (Juliussen, 2002). The growth of websites is also staggering: 19,000 in 1995, 5 million in 2000, and 47 million in February 2004 ("February," 2004; Saunders 2000).

Although the Internet offers access to seemingly limitless information, you need to keep three facts in mind:

1. Much of the information on the web lacks authority. Some of it is outdated, fallacious, and basically worthless. Evaluate what you find on the Internet very carefully. → *See pages 104–106 for "Evaluating Internet Sources."*

2. Unless you know where to look, you can waste many hours on the Internet. "Surfing" the web and researching the web are not the same. → *See page 106 for "Finding Quality Websites."*

3. Many valuable sources are not available on the web. Much of the reference and circulating collections in your college library are not yet available electronically, and they probably never will be available for free. For example, you can't access the following resources from your computer for free: specialty encyclopedias, index and abstract services (such as *EBSCOhost,* which searches over 25 databases including Academic Search Premier and Communication and Mass Media Complete, which together provide over 4,000 scholarly publications, 8,000 magazines, and 26 journals in communication studies), books under copyright, most scholarly journals, full-text books on scholarly topics, current magazine articles, and most newspaper articles (Drake, 2005).

Preparing for Online Searches To save the time and frustration of an inadequate search, do your homework before going online. First, *take a look at your rough-draft outline* of the main points and supporting information to see what information (such as a fact, statistic, quote, or example) you still need.

Second, when you visit the library looking for print materials and electronic databases, *make a list of keywords and phrases* to use when searching the Internet. The information you want may be on the Internet, but if you don't have the right keywords, you may never find it. For example, some important documents on positive imagery and speaking can be found only under the keyword *visualization;* other documents appear only with a search for *mental imaging.* To narrow a search of "positive imagery" to speaking situations, would you use the keyword *speech, presentation,* or *public speaking*? Consulting print materials on the subject first will help you to identify appropriate keywords.

Now you are ready to go online to look for specific information to supplement your library and electronic database research. To maximize your database searches, always look at each database's Help icon for tips.

Selecting a Search Engine You can use a variety of **search engines** (utilities or tools that search the Internet and download requested information) with your Internet browser. Keep in mind that no one search engine will find all available sites. Also, be aware that although most search engines rank the matched documents for relevancy, several of them (like Yahoo) allow businesses to pay to be ranked as one of your top 10 matches. → *See this chapter's Technology Tip for Speakers for search engine specifics.*

Conducting Effective Searches You can search the Internet by keywords or browse subject directories. A **keyword search** looks for websites that contain a specific word or phrase. Whether you are using an electronic database or a search engine, keyword searches on some search engines will be more effective if you know how to link your search terms with **Boolean operators** such as OR, AND, and NOT (see Figure 5.3).

Figure 5.3

Boolean Operators*
(such as AND, OR,
NOT, +, –, " ")

OR   *motorcycle OR motorbike*—searches for documents with either *motorcycle* or *motorbike* in them as well as documents containing both words. Result: maximum number of hits.

AND   *motorcycle AND racing*—documents must include both words to be selected.

" "   *"motorcycle racing"*—searches for documents that include *motorcycle racing* as a single word or phrase. Without the quotation marks, most search engines will search for each word separately.

NOT   *women AND "motorcycle racing" NOT "dirt bike"*—narrows search to documents about women and motorcycle racing but will not include documents using the phrase *dirt bike*.

+   *motorcycle + racing*—includes *racing* as well as *motorcycle* in the search.

–   *motorcycle – racing*—excludes documents that contain the term *racing*.

---

*Not all databases and search engines use all these operators; some, however, use additional operators as well. To save time and mistakes, always check the Help screen before beginning your search. (Note: Boolean operators can be in lowercase or in all caps.)

Although the number of hits a search produces is important, the *quality of hits* is much more important. Usually if the first two pages of hits don't contain what you want, the wrong term or wrong search engine was used.

To narrow the number of hits, try the following suggestions:

- Use phrases (enclose titles, common phrases, or specific diseases or procedures with quotation marks). For example, a search for *motorcycle racing* in Google returned 1,510,000 hits, whereas *"motorcycle racing"* returned only 308,000 hits.

- Avoid the Boolean operator OR. For example, *motorcycle OR racing* returned 1,550,000 hits on Google.

- Specify additional words using + or AND. For example, *"motorcycle racing" AND women* returned 75,100 hits on Google.

- Exclude words or phrases using – (hyphen) or NOT. For example, *"motorcycle racing" NOT "dirt bike racing"* returned 261 hits on Google.

To increase the number of hits, try these suggestions:

- Check that spelling and keywords are correct.

- Use the wildcard (*) to search for all forms of a word. (Note: This is not used on all search engines.) For example, *listen** will find *listen, listener, listening,* and so on; *legisl** will search for *legislature, legislation, legislator,* and so on.

- Use fewer search words.

- Connect similar search words with OR.

- Use alternative keywords—for example, *automobile* instead of *car.*

- Change full name to initials or initials to full name.

- Avoid using "s," "ing," or "ed" on search words.

Technology Tip for Speakers

Select the Proper Search Engine

Selecting a search engine to use with your Internet browser becomes more important as the Internet continues to grow by millions of pages a day. Obviously, no single search engine can find all available sites. Saunders (2000) notes that "search engines cover no more than 16 percent of those pages, down sharply from 34 percent in 1997" (p. 31). Therefore, to maximize your searches, know which search engines to use and use more than one. Note the following information about search engines (Berkman, 2000; Sullivan, 2004). You can access all of these links at the Essentials of Public Speaking website.

■ For broad or complex subjects, pick a search engine that uses a **hierarchical index** in which websites are organized into categories. You will find fewer sites (because real people organized these sites, so only a small part of the web is included), but you are more likely to find relevant items. The most popular hierarchical search engine is Yahoo (*www.yahoo.com*).

■ For specific subjects, use a standard or an alternate search engine. With a **standard search engine**, more of the web is searched. This is because computer "robots" search the web, index the pages found, and determine the relevance of the pages by mathematical calculation. Popular standard search engines include:

AltaVista (*www.altavista.com*)— now powered by Yahoo

Go Network (*www.infoseek.go.com*)

Excite (*www.excite.com*)

HotBot (*www.hotbot.lycos.com*)

Yahoo (which uses both hierarchical and standard search engines)

Alternate search engines have different ways of sorting or ranking the pages located in the search. Popular examples include:

AskJeeves (*www.askjeeves.com*)—lets you input sentences instead of keywords and gives you a list of sites that are likely to have an answer to your question.

In some cases, a **subject search** can locate needed information faster than a keyword search—especially if you aren't sure of the exact keyword to use or just want a general topic. On their home pages, many search engines provide a subject directory of general topics that contain links to several layers of subtopics. Be sure to evaluate these sources carefully.

Evaluating Internet Sources The Internet is a blend of many interests: educational (such websites are identified with the suffix .edu or .cc), commercial (identified by .com), governmental (.gov), organizational (.org), military (.mil), and personal. You can't assume that all the information you find on the Internet is authoritative. Internet searches are as likely to include outdated, inaccurate, and biased information as they are to turn up valuable information. It's up to you to evaluate the credibility of your information by asking the following questions (Drake, 2005):

■ *Is the author a qualified expert in the field?* Along with the author's name should be an indication of his or her occupation, position, education, experience,

Google (*www.google.com*)—ranks results by the number of websites that link to that page.

NorthernLight (*www.northernlight.com*)—sorts the results into folders and subfolders; charges a fee.

■ To search as many sites as possible, use a **metasearch engine**—a search engine that searches other search engines. Popular metasearch engines include:

AllTheWeb (*www.alltheweb.com*)—now powered by Yahoo, searches in 36 languages.

Dogpile (*http://dogpile.com*)—uses Boolean operators (covered in this chapter).

Ixquick (*www.ixquick.com*)—searches multiple engines simultaneously and gives a star to a site each time a search engine places it in its top 10 list.

MetaCrawler (*www.metacrawler.com*)—searches AltaVista, Excite, Infoseek, Lycos, WebCrawler, and Yahoo.

Search (*www.search.com*)—claims to search 700 search engines including Direct Hit, Yahoo, Lycos, and Inktomi.

TheBigHub (*www.thebighub.com*)—identifies and searches "free" databases with a slant toward education and software.

Vivisimo (*http://vivisimo.com*)—organizes results by category.

New search engines are appearing regularly—for example see Wisenut.com, Searchlaw.com, and AskScott.com. A new search engine called VisIT is under development at the Beckman Institute of Advanced Science and Technology at the University of Illinois. VisIT will organize hits by website, include a diagram indicating related pages, provide a text summary of pages, and even highlight inactive sites (Rae-Dupree, 2001, p. 58). The next time you conduct a search, try using several search engines and compare the results. Remember, using only one search engine won't even scratch the surface of the available information on the web.

and organizational affiliations. If no author is given, is the website clearly attributed to a reliable source such as a university or agency?

■ *Is the information objective?* Are conclusions based on facts? Are sources cited? Are opinions and personal bias clearly stated? Is the purpose of the publication clear—to inform, persuade, sell? Is the author affiliated with an organization or group that might indicate a bias? For example, an article on animal testing of cosmetics on the website Beautysupply.com or Savetheanimals.org might indicate the possibility of bias.

■ *Is the information accurate?* websites with grammatical and typographical errors should usually be avoided—content may be faulty as well. Can you verify the facts and conclusions in this publication with other sources you have read?

■ *Is the information current?* When was the information written? Has it been updated? Some websites will include the date of last revision. If not, Netscape

allows you to check the date—go to the File menu, select Document Info, and select Last Modified. Are the sources used by the author up to date? If no date is given, the information may be completely outdated.

As a speaker, you will be expected to use information that is current, accurate, objective, and attributed to a qualified expert. Always verify the credibility of documents obtained on the Internet by comparing them to information you find in the library's print materials and electronic databases.

 Finding Quality Websites Check to see if your college or university has completed some initial leg work for you by creating a gateway to valuable links and websites. If not, try some of the gateways described below. *You can access these sites under the Student Resources for Chapter 5* at the Essentials of Public Speaking website.

Try the Librarian's Index to the Internet, the Internet Public Library, or other gateways created by colleges. For example, Wesleyan University maintains the Social Psychology Network, which includes more than 5,000 links to social psychology sources. Be sure to check out the social psychology and the psychology subject areas for valuable speech information. Also, the librarians at Tarrant County College (a multicampus community college in Texas) have produced a marvelous Internet gateway. For example, the following sites listed there contain links to information on hundreds of topics—your speech topic is probably included:

- *Research the Issues* from Project Vote Smart

- *Issues Library* from SpeakOut.com

It is amazing how little time it takes to locate materials through online library catalogs, electronic indexes and databases, and the Internet. Of course, reading and analyzing the information will take time, but since you will have picked a topic that you enjoy, this part of your speech preparation should be pleasurable.

Conduct Personal Interviews

It is possible that not even your personal knowledge and library and Internet research will provide all the information you want. When this occurs, you may want to find more information by conducting some interviews. In many ways, conducting an interview is similar to presenting a speech. After you decide on likely candidates for your interviews, you should plan your questions.

Decide Who to Interview and Contact Them The research you have done on your topic should have given you some ideas about whom to interview. For example, if you are doing a speech on drunk driving, you might decide to interview a local member of MADD (Mothers Against Drunk Driving), a police officer assigned to DWI (driving while intoxicated) cases, a local politician with the power to help change the state's DWI laws, an ambulance driver who sees DWI accidents, or a local doctor who might be able to tell you why drunk drivers often seem to escape serious injury. Once you have selected the appropriate people, contact them and arrange for a meeting in a convenient, quiet place. When you call, be sure to tell the interviewees who you are, what course you are taking, why you want to interview them, and how much of their time you will need.

Plan the Interview Carefully Even though the interview should take only 15 or 20 minutes, its success will depend on how carefully you plan your interview. It should include the following steps:

There are many ways to obtain information for a speech. This student is conducting a personal interview.

1. *Introduction:* Thank the interviewee for his or her time and establish rapport by talking about your assignment or the reason you especially wanted to speak with him or her. Be relaxed and friendly, and make good eye contact. Next, state why you are there (unless already mentioned), how long you expect the interview to take, exactly what information you are looking for (if there are several points, list them), and how the responses will be used.

2. *Body:* Here is where you ask your questions, which you have already planned. Be sure to write out your questions and bring them with you. Most people will be more open and relaxed if you do not record the interview. Just listen carefully and take an occasional note to record an important fact, figure, or idea. Try to use mainly open-ended questions—you will get more information that way. An open-ended request (such as "Tell me about the accident") allows for any response. Specific questions (such as "Was he speeding?" or "How fast was he driving?") should be kept to a minimum. Use probing comments such as "Tell me more" or "What happened next?" to keep the interviewee talking. To make sure you haven't missed valuable information, end your questioning with, "Is there anything else you think I should know?"

3. *Conclusion:* Use this step to verify information and give closure to the interview. Briefly summarize the main areas you covered in the interview (this allows both you and the interviewee to see if anything important was omitted). If you are planning to quote the interviewee directly, now is the time to review the quotation for accuracy and ask for permission to use it in your speech. End by thanking the interviewee, shaking hands, and making a timely exit.

4. *Follow-up:* As soon as you can, send the interviewee a thank-you note expressing the value of the information to you and your speech.

Review Your Interview Notes Use the results of the interview carefully. When you get back from the interview, expand your notes immediately so that you won't forget or misrepresent the interviewee's information. In deciding what, if anything, to use in your speech, be sure to keep all matters confidential that you agreed not to reveal.

Record Your Research Information

Although some instructors may prefer that you write your research notes on 4-by-6-inch note cards, any organized method will work. Instead of taking notes, some students prefer to photocopy information and articles, and keep everything in a special folder. If you use this method, circle or highlight important information, and use Post-it notes for summaries, messages, and ideas. What's important is to find a procedure that works for you. Of course, note cards have some definite advantages. For one thing, they are all the same size, so they are easy to handle and store. Also, because each card contains only one idea, it is easy to move a card from one main point to another until you have decided where it belongs (if at all) in your speech. On the other hand, a disadvantage of note cards is the length of time it takes to hand-write quotations and summaries of the ideas you might want to use. Another disadvantage is that you may later decide to use more information from the source and have to locate it again; or the summary that seemed so clear when you wrote it may be confusing when you get ready to prepare your speech (see Figure 5.4).

Avoid Unintentional Plagiarism No matter how you decide to record your research information, make sure to avoid unintentional plagiarism by using a method that does the following:

- *Provides ready access to researched information.*

- *Makes clear which passages you have paraphrased and which ones you quoted.* **Paraphrasing** is putting another person's ideas into your own words. If you use cards or Post-its, always put quotation marks around any material that is taken word-for-word from the source.

Figure 5.4

Sample Note Card

Male/Female Style Differences

Tannen, <u>Talking from 9 to 5</u>, p. 37

    Researchers found that when women freshmen were asked to <u>publicly</u> predict their grades for the coming year, they "predicted lower grades for themselves than men did."

    However, when their predictions were made <u>privately</u>, neither their predictions nor their actual grades were lower than the men's.

- *Includes complete source citations* (such as complete name of author, source, date, publisher, and page numbers). For books from your college library, you may want to add a call number.

- *Includes a bibliography.* Many experienced speakers prefer to have a separate note card for each source because the cards are so easy to manage, but you can also use a sheet of paper. When your bibliography record (card or page) includes the complete source information for each reference, each individual note card need include only the last name of the author, title of source, and page number.

Supporting Materials to Look for as You Research

Now that you know where to find research materials for your speech, let's discuss what type of information you should be looking for as you research. Obviously, you will want to find the information that best supports your main ideas. These **supporting materials** are any type of verbal or visual information used to clarify, prove, or add interest to the ideas presented in your speech. → *Chapter 6 will provide more specific suggestions for selecting valuable supporting materials from your research information.*

When looking for supporting materials, keep the following points in mind:

- *Look for supporting materials that clarify.* Just because an idea is clear to you doesn't mean it will be equally clear to your audience—their frames of reference may differ. Therefore, it is important for speakers to clarify concepts and terms with both visual supports (such as graphs, charts, and pictures) and verbal supports (such as explanations, specific instances, and comparisons).

- *Look for supporting materials that prove.* Rarely will listeners accept your statements without some kind of proof. Verbal supporting materials (such as quotations from experts, statistics, or personal instances) serve as evidence for the ideas presented in a speech. Although supporting materials that prove your points are essential in persuasive speeches, they are also important in informative speeches.

- *Look for supporting materials that add interest.* Using a variety of supports is one of the best ways to keep your audience listening. For example, some listeners may find statistics and expert opinion interesting. Others may tune out statistics but listen carefully to personal or humorous anecdotes. It's very unlikely that all of your listeners will respond to the same type of support.

Summary

This chapter covered steps 2–4 of the Basic Steps for Preparing a Speech—determine topic, prepare a rough-draft outline, and research for desired information. You will find that your research is more meaningful and will take less time if you prepare a rough-draft outline before starting your research. When researching your speech topic, you should look for information in several types of sources: (1) printed materials (such as books, magazines, newspapers, specialized dictionaries and encyclopedias, books of quotations, and yearbooks), (2) electronic databases, (3) the Internet, and (4) personal interviews. As you research, look for specific materials that will clarify your ideas, prove your points, and add interest to your speech.

Essentials of Public Speaking  *Online*

Use the Essentials of Public Speaking website at **http://communication. wadsworth.com/hamiltoneps3** for quick access to the electronic study resources that accompany this chapter. When you get to the Essentials home page, click on "Student Book Companion Site" in the Resource box. The Essentials website features the links found in the Technology Tips for Speakers box on pages 104–105, the links in the discussion about finding quality websites on page 106, InfoTrac College Edition, the Suggestions for Practice and Critical Thinking activities and the Info-Trac College Edition activities that follow, a digital glossary, and review quizzes.

Key Terms

alternate search engine
   104
Boolean operator 102
exact purpose 95
hierarchical index 104

keyword search 102
metasearch engine 105
paraphrasing 108
rough-draft outline 98
search engine 102

standard search engine
   104
subject search 104
supporting materials 109

Suggestions for Practice and Critical Thinking

1. Using InfoTrac College Edition, click on the Help Index and read "Searching in PowerTrac," "Search Expressions," and "Search Operators." This information will help you find the exact information you need for your speeches faster. To practice, select a topic and conduct an advanced search using several complex search expressions. If you are not sure what keywords to use, begin with a Subject Guide search. What do the following search expressions mean?
   (Professional ethic★) and education
   R1 and da since January 1 1999
   R1 and R2

2. Using your college library's online catalog, find a book that appears to contain helpful information on your next speech topic. List the title, call number, and campus location of this book. (If no books are listed under the term you chose, check the *Library of Congress Subject Headings* to see if your topic is listed under a different term.)

3. In the reference section of the library, locate a specialized dictionary or encyclopedia that relates to the subject area of your topic (such as *Encyclopedia of Sociology, Encyclopedia of Science and Technology, Dictionary of American History,* and *Physicians Desk Reference*). Photocopy at least one page from this source.

4. Also from the reference shelves, choose a quotation book and find a quotation or humorous anecdote that relates to your topic and photocopy it.

5. Using an Internet search engine, conduct a search on your speech topic. Find a web page that meets this chapter's guidelines on quality websites and one that does not. Share your results with the class.

6. Using a specialized index to magazines and journals (for example, *Business Periodicals Index, Education Index,* or *Cumulative Index to Nursing and Allied Health*), locate an article related to your topic. Write down the title, author, name of magazine, volume number, issue date, and page numbers.

7. Using an electronic database (such as *InfoTrac College Edition, EBSCOhost,* or *ERIC*), locate an article related to your topic. Print out the abstract (summary) of this article (or the complete article if you wish), including the title, author, name of magazine, volume number, issue date, and page numbers.

8. Check out the following websites. *You can access these sites under the Student Resources for Chapter 5* at the Essentials of Public Speaking website.

    • If you need some topic ideas, take a look at a subject-based search engine like Yahoo, the Librarian's Index to the Internet, an electronic news-magazine like the *Washington Times,* or an Idea Generator like the one produced by Old Dominion University.

    • Try several of the following websites for printed materials:

        For links to web-accessible libraries worldwide, try the University of California's LibWeb, library servers via the World Wide Web.

        For newspapers, try Newspapers.com or Newslink.org.

        For quotations, see Bartlett's Familiar Quotations website; for other links to quotations see Yahoo's quotations directory.

        For statistics, see the Statistical Abstract of the United States website. For other statistics sites, see the U.S. Department of Labor's statistics site; FedStats, the gateway to statistics from over 100 U.S. Federal agencies; RobertNiles.com, a guide to hundreds of data links; or the National Center for Education Statistics website.

        For online encyclopedias, see the online version of the Encyclopedia Britannica or Encyclopedia.com.

    • If neither InfoTrac College Edition nor your library's databases includes what you need, try CARL.org and click on "Search CARL," or try Northern Light.org. For a reasonable fee, these services will e-mail you the article you need.

    • Read the site Evaluation Criteria by Susan E. Beck, Head of the Reference and Research Services Department at the New Mexico State University Library. Do her suggestions agree or disagree with the advice in this text? For an online exercise to test your ability to evaluate materials on the Internet, take the *Evaluating Sources Competence Test* at the California State University Competence Information Project's website.

chapter 6

Supporting Your Ideas

Flashback The ancient Greek writer Aesop is credited with writing numerous fables (a type of supporting material)—such as "The Tortoise and the Hare" and "The Boy Who Cried Wolf"—that are still enjoyed today.

E FFECTIVE SPEAKERS SEARCH FOR SUPPORTING MATERIALS THAT WILL CLARIFY THEIR IDEAS, prove their points, and add interest to their speeches. Once you have completed your research, you are ready to select the best of the supporting information you have found. This process, step 5 of the Basic Steps for Preparing a Speech, makes the difference between a good speech and an excellent one.

Try to use several types of material to support the main points of your speech, including (1) explanations, (2) statistics, (3) brief or detailed instances (examples and illustrations), (4) comparisons, (5) expert opinion, (6) fables, sayings, poems, and rhymes, and (7) simple demonstrations. Note, however, that explanations and statistics tend to be used too often, whereas the remaining types are not used often enough.

Basic Steps for Preparing a Speech

1. Analyze your potential audience. → *See Chapter 4.*
2. Determine topic, exact purpose, and main points.
   → *See Chapter 5.*
3. Prepare a rough-draft outline of main points and needed information. → *See Chapter 5.*
4. Research topic for material to support main points.
   → *See Chapter 5.*
5. **Select best supporting materials.**
6. Determine how best to organize main points. → *See Chapter 7.*
7. Plan introduction and conclusion. → *See Chapter 7.*
8. Make preparation outline (or storyboards) and speaking notes. → *See Chapter 8.*
9. Prepare visual aids. → *See Chapter 9.*
10. Rehearse speech. → *See Chapters 10 and 11.*

Each of these types of support will be described and illustrated in the sections that follow. As you read, note the types of support that you feel would be most appropriate for your topic.

Overused Supports—Use Them With Care!

Speakers, especially beginning speakers, tend to overuse explanations and statistics. Too many of these types of supports can make a speech terribly dull, but when used correctly, they can add to listener understanding and enjoyment.

Explanations

An **explanation** defines or gives more information about a term or topic, gives instructions on how to do something, or describes how something works or the relationship between certain items.

> *Refer to Lucy's sample speech in Chapter 4. In the introduction, Lucy defined* health *as the "absence of disease." This explanation clarified the meaning of* health *and prepared the way for her three main points: major risk factors, cancer and heart attack warning signs, and diet and fitness guidelines.*

Louis Platt (2004), Chairman of Boeing and former CEO and Chairman of Hewlett-Packard, used a definition to clarify his meaning of *entrepreneur* in a speech titled, "Accepting Risk—Daring Greatness":

> The word entrepreneur comes from the French *entreprenre* which means "to undertake" or to set out on a new mission or venture. In a business sense, an entrepreneur is someone who starts a business, or who reinvents or revolutionizes an existing business. The entrepreneur launches new products, opens new markets, discovers new forms of organization, or acts in other ways to change the status quo. (p. 541)

In a speech on fishing, the speaker explained how worms are gathered using a technique called "grunting":

> A popular method employed by fishermen and others to collect earthworms is the "grunting" technique, in which a stake is violently pounded into the soil and then vibrated. For reasons not fully understood, the vibrations produced drive worms to the surface where they can be collected. ("Stomping Turtles," 1987, p. 77)

Although explanations and definitions are important to successful speeches, nothing is more deadly than too much explanation. Think of a really boring lecture you've heard lately. Chances are, this lecture included no comparisons, quotations, short or detailed instances, visual aids or statistics—just explanations.

Statistics

Another often overused support is **statistics**, or numbers used to show relationships between items. When used correctly, statistics (which both clarify and prove your ideas) can have a powerful impact on listeners (Allen & Preiss, 1997). Too many statistics, however, create a confusing and boring speech. To make sure your statistics are a positive addition to your speeches, follow five simple rules (Hamilton, 2005).

Remember

Explanations . . .

■ Should be used sparingly because they tend to be dull.

■ When used, should be brief but specific.

■ Are more effective when followed by one or two "for instances"—discussed further on page 118.

■ Are used for clarification, not proof.

■ Can be replaced by other types of support, such as quotations, that clarify the same ideas as the explanations you planned to use.

Rule 1: *Make your statistics meaningful by relating them to your listeners' frames of reference.* Even audience members who don't like statistics will listen if you know how to use this rule. For example, a student who was giving a speech on the meteorite crater in Arizona couldn't understand why the audience seemed unimpressed when she said, "This meteorite crater is two miles wide." During the Q&A after her speech, she discovered that very few in the audience could picture a 2-mile-wide hole. In exasperation, she said, "Well, this meteorite crater is large enough to hold our entire college campus with room left over for at least one football field!" Finally, the audience was impressed.

Instead of just telling his Indiana University audience that tobacco kills nearly half a million Americans each year, Lonnie Bristow (1994), M.D. and chair of the Board of Trustees of the American Medical Association, made the statistic more meaningful in the following way:

> I ask you to check your watches. Because in this hour, by the time I'm done speaking, 50 Americans will die from smoke-related diseases. By the time you sit down to breakfast in the morning, 600 more will have joined them; 8,400 by the end of the week—every week, every month, every year—until it kills nearly half a million Americans, year in, year out. (p. 333)

Rule 2: *Eliminate any statistics that are not absolutely necessary.* Even people who generally relate well to statistics can experience overload when too many statistics are presented. John A. Challenger (2004), CEO of the global outplacement firm Challenger, Gray & Christmas, Inc., gave an informative speech on "Boomers at a Crossroads." If you had been in the audience, how would you have reacted to the following interesting but statistic-laden words?

> According to the latest available data from the Department of Education, the number of people 55 and older enrolled in adult education courses increased by 27 percent from 10.8 million in 1995 to 13.7 million in 1999. Of the 13.7 million, 40 percent or 5.5 million were taking job-related courses, up from 3.8 million in 1995. (p. 363)

When you cannot avoid using a large number of statistics, present some of them in graphic form. ➜ *See rule 5.*

Rule 3: *Round off the numbers to make them easy for your listeners to recall.* The audience is less likely to remember 8,211 than they are to remember 8,200 or, better yet,

8,000. Unless the audience expects it or your topic demands it, exact numbers normally are used only in handout materials and occasionally on graphic visuals. However, when you *discuss* the data on a graphic visual (even exact-number data), round off the numbers.

Rule 4: *Demonstrate the credibility of your statistics* by citing the source, the reason the source is considered expert (if the audience doesn't already know), and the size of the population from which the statistics were compiled. Since sophisticated audiences know how easy it is to distort or falsify statistics, you want your listeners to feel confident that the statistics you are presenting are accurate. For example, "Four out of five dentists recommend Gleam-on toothpaste" sounds good until we realize that only five dentists had to be interviewed to make that claim. However, if we knew that 300,000 dentists were surveyed and four out of five of them (240,000) recommend Gleam-on, we could feel more confidence in the results. In a speech about Detroit and global competition, Richard E. Dauch (2004), Chairman of the National Association of Manufacturers, demonstrated the credibility of his statistics as follows:

> . . . as a part of my role as chairman of the National Association of Manufacturers (NAM) . . . [I] addressed the NAM's recent study entitled "How Structural Costs Imposed on U. S. Manufacturers Harm Workers and Threaten Competitiveness." . . . The study concludes that external overhead costs, costs out of the control of manufacturers, conservatively add 22.4 percent to the price of production for U.S. manufacturers relative to our foreign competition.
>
> These overhead costs include:
> - Corporate tax rate and tax code (5.6 percent).
> - Employee benefits including health care and pension costs (5.2 percent).
> - Rising energy prices (3.8 percent).
> - Tort litigation ($1 per hour of expense).
> - Excessive government regulations (the equivalent of a 12 percent excise tax). (p 539)

Rule 5: *Whenever possible, present your statistics in graphic form*—your audience will comprehend them faster and remember them longer. For example, Figure 6.1 is a graphic visual of the statistics on Boomers and adult education courses that John Challenger could have used in his speech, "Boomers at a Crossroads." → *For more on graphic visuals, see Chapter 9.*

Remember

Statistics . . .

- Are numbers used to show relationships between items.
- Are more effective when related to listeners' frames of reference.
- Should be used sparingly.
- Should be rounded off.
- Are more credible when the source and the source's qualifications are given.
- Are easier to understand and remember when shown in graphic form.

Figure 6.1
Graph of Statistics

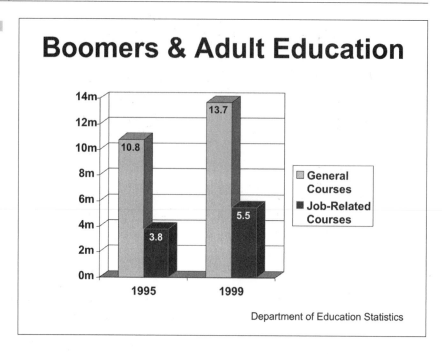

Figure 6.1
Graph of Statistics

Underused Supports—Use Them More Often

Among the effective types of support that are underused are factual and hypothetical instances; literal and figurative comparisons; expert opinions; and even fables, sayings, poems, and rhymes. All of these supports can clarify ideas and add interest; in addition, some of them (factual instances, literal comparisons, and expert opinions) also add proof to your arguments. Let's take a more detailed look at these useful types of support.

Instances

An **instance** is an example or illustration that is used to clarify, add interest, and (in some cases) prove a point. One of the surest ways to grab the attention of your audience and keep them listening is to use a variety of instances.

Types of Instances An instance can be any of the following:

- Factual (actually happened)

- Hypothetical (made up but could happen)

- Brief (basic facts only)—usually called an *example*

- Detailed (vivid picture or narrative)—usually
  called an *illustration*

Most effective instances are illustrations that are both factual and detailed (describing things, people, or events that actually happened with enough detail that your listeners can picture events exactly). For example, if you were describing an accident, you would set the stage by telling what the weather was like on that day and what emo-

tions the participant(s) were feeling prior to the accident. Kenneth A. Haseley (2004) included the following factual illustration in a speech on "Dealing With Public Anger":

> Some years ago, the plant manager of a chemical plant asked me to observe a public meeting for residents who lived near his facility. At one point, a woman stood up and angrily stated that she had three miscarriages, and was certain that they were caused by the plant's chemical emissions. The plant manager responded by citing a Johns Hopkins University study that showed no connection between the emissions and any ill human health effects. Think of how much better it would have been if he had first said to the woman, "I'm sorry to hear that. I have two children of my own, so I know how precious a life is." Then he could have mentioned the research study. (p. 243)

Detailed hypothetical illustrations can also work well. Since the speaker creates the hypothetical instance, it's very important to cue the audience to the fact that it is not "real." Begin hypothetical instances with such words as "Suppose . . . ," "Imagine . . . ," or "What would you do if . . . ?" For example, Joseph N. Hankin (2003), President of Westchester Community College, used this hypothetical illustration in a presentation:

> Picture this: the scene is a seaside hotel breakfast room. Enter a resident. He summons the headwaiter and, to that gentleman's growing consternation, says, "I want two boiled eggs, one of them so undercooked it's runny, and the other so overcooked it's about as easy to eat as rubber; grilled bacon that has been left on the plate to get cold; burnt toast that crumbles away as soon as you touch it with a knife; butter straight from the deep freeze so that it is impossible to spread; and a pot of very weak coffee, lukewarm." The headwaiter rallied slightly and said, "That's a complicated order, sir. It might be a bit difficult." "Oh?" said the guest. "You didn't find it difficult yesterday." (p. 126)

One of the advantages of using hypothetical instances is that audience members can relate the instance to their own experiences and become more involved in your speech. For example, a speech on class attendance might include the following hypothetical illustration:

> Imagine that it's a school day and your alarm has just gone off. You reach over and after several tries finally get that awful noise to quit. You pull the cover from your head, force your eyes open, yawn, and roll over. You're thinking, "Should I get up and go to class, or should I skip the class and sleep in a bit longer. After all, the weather is bad today and I do have a cold . . ."

You'll probably see some sheepish looks on your listeners' faces because they've done a similar thing more than once—maybe even this morning.

Another type of instance is the example. *Examples, which are always brief and usually factual, are more effective when used in groups of two or more* because one by itself is easy to overlook. In a speech to the City Club of Cleveland, Dr. Randolph D. Smoak, Jr. (2001), President of the American Medical Association, used instances to add impact to his assertion that many working Americans can't afford insurance:

> The uninsured are all around us—average working Americans like the man who hands you your cleaning when you pick it up—the woman behind the cash register at your local diner—and Nancy, who works in the barbershop where I get my hair cut. (p. 443)

Details aren't needed in these instances because they are part of the everyday life of the audience. But using only one of them would not have had nearly the same impact, would it?

Instances are also used by speakers after an explanation to add clarification. Speaking to the V.A. Veterans Service, Michael P. Sullivan (2004) used an explanation followed by several examples to make his point that health care will need to make some changes to meet Boomer expectations:

> Boomers have never lost the need to be in control. They are less likely to accept the word of authority than their parents. [For example] Tell them they have to do things your way because those are the rules of the institution and they will choose another institution. "Take a number and wait" means they don't have control. In fact, most healthcare processes that devalue the patient's time and individualism run smack up against the Boomer need for control. (p. 444)

Using Instances to Prove   Although you can't prove an idea by using only instances, factual instances (whether examples or illustrations) can add some proof to your arguments. Suppose you are trying to prove that the lakes in your state are polluted. You describe in detail the pollution that you and other people who live near a local lake have experienced. You tell about the broken glass on the beach and the bottles and cans on the bottom of the lake, the soap scum and trash floating on the surface, the awful smell in the summer, the sign the city posted on the beach last summer that warned parents not to let their children come into contact with the water, and the disbelief of the community when two teenage boys died after diving in the polluted water. Would describing this one lake be enough to convince your audience that the state's other lakes were polluted? Of course not.

But imagine that you presented two detailed factual illustrations of polluted lakes—one in your community and another one elsewhere in the state. Then you showed a visual aid listing 10 other lakes and their pollution indexes and said, "Each lake on this list is as polluted or more polluted than the two I have described to you." Now your audience would likely be convinced. Presenting one or two detailed instances (illustrations) followed by several brief instances (examples) is a very powerful proof package. Add some statistics and a quotation from a water pollution expert, and your proof would be complete.

Proof is more likely when two or more types of supporting material are used (for example, an explanation, a factual illustration, and several examples). Even statistics, when used alone, are unlikely to prove a point.

Using Varied Topics for Your Instances   As indicated previously, the more variety of instances, the better. Although there is no limit to the topics you can choose for your instances, the following topic areas are very effective in speeches: personal and/or family, famous, business, and humorous. Let's look at each of these topic areas in more detail.

Personal and/or family topics (experiences or events that you observed firsthand, often involving family life) are of special interest to your listeners because they get to know you better. Personalizing your speeches is an effective way to aid audience listening and memory. Everyone listens to personal and family instances—even the daydreamer—and as a result are more likely to recall the point the instance was supporting. ➤ *See Chapter 3 for more on the importance of personalizing speeches.*

> *Lucy used a personal instance in the introduction of her speech when she told about the conversation she had with her father the day before he died of heart disease.*

In an informative speech on drunk drivers, Ken gave the following detailed personal instance of DWI to his speech classmates:

> On July 4th last year I was 18 years old. I got out of work early. A friend of mine bought a case of beer. We went to his house and drank three six-packs in an hour. Then we got this stupid idea to go to the beach. I had to go to my house, about three miles away, to change clothes. There are only three things I remember about that time. I remember turning the key; I remember putting in a hard rock tape; and I remember hitting a tree, head-on. Apparently the police were following me. I was told that I was driving through parking lots screaming with my beer out the window. I don't remember anything about it.

In a speech about her years in the communication business, Susan Peterson (2003) used an illustration that was both personal and family:

> When I was a CBS correspondent, my father used to track every time I was on the air reporting from London. He would get up early in the morning and stay up at night to see if he could catch my reports. . . . He was my biggest fan. And he especially loved to go to the post office every morning in our small town in Michigan where he'd wait to hear, "Hey Harold, I saw your daughter on television last night."
>
> So it was with some trepidation that I came home to tell my dad that I was leaving the television news business to start my own business. At first, he was stunned. "You're going into business?" he asked. "Yes," I said tentatively.
>
> And then I saw a look I've never seen in my dad—he just puffed up his chest and beamed! He couldn't have been prouder. Later he took me aside and of all the things I know he wanted to say to me, he gave me only one piece of advice: "Learn by your mistakes."
>
> That was probably the best advice ever given to me by anyone. From my father, it was golden because it said I could and would make mistakes. He gave me permission to make them and then learn from them. So every time I'd make a mistake—and believe me, there have been plenty—I'd think of my dad, pick myself up and go on. (p. 766)

Take a few minutes to think of personal or family experiences that are related to your speech topic. Remember, you are looking for instances that will clarify, add interest, or provide proof for your main points. Ask family members and close friends if they can remember an instance involving you or your family that you may have forgotten. Make notes on these topics.

Famous topics (involving famous or well-known people) can also capture audience attention and add support for your ideas. In a speech on the importance of keeping a positive attitude, Richard L. Weaver (1993), author and communication expert, gave a series of brief examples involving Abraham Lincoln's win–loss record to make his point:

> Probably the most dramatic example in history of what attitude can accomplish occurred in the track record of Abraham Lincoln. Look at his professional accomplishments. He lost his job in 1832. He was defeated for the legislature, also in 1832. He failed in business in 1833. He was elected to the legislature in 1834. His sweetheart died in 1835. He suffered a nervous breakdown in 1836. He was defeated for speaker of the House in 1838. He was defeated for nomination for Congress in 1843. He was elected to Congress in 1846. He lost his renomination for Congress in 1848. He was rejected for land officer in 1849. Lincoln was defeated for Senate in 1854. He was defeated for

A humorous instance is an excellent way to add interest and enjoyment to your speech.

© Davis Barber/Photo Edit

the nomination for vice-president of the United States in 1856. He was again defeated for Senate in 1858. And Abraham Lincoln was elected president of the United States in 1860. (p. 479)

Business topics (including business experiences and advice of your own and from others) are also used to clarify, add interest to, and help prove your main points. In a speech on "Succeeding in Business," Jean L. Farinelli (1994), CEO of Creamer Dickson Basford, used the following illustration:

[When I joined Carl Byoir and Associates], Byoir was the second-largest public relations firm in the world. Most of the role models above me were men. Only one vice president was a woman. Moreover, I noticed that the men did not line up at my office door, taking bakery numbers, for the chance to become my mentor.

So I used guerrilla tactics. Every time I went to lunch, I sat next to a different vice president. I asked each VP how he succeeded, or, in Byoir terms, how they all got to the eighth floor. After a few weeks of lunches, a pattern emerged. I had broken the code. To get to the eighth floor, you managed a large account. Then you had enough work to spread around the firm, helping many of your colleagues fill up their time sheets. . . .

If you have a mentor, that's wonderful and lucky. But even if you don't, you can still get people to help you break the code. (p. 533)

Humorous topics can also include personal, family, famous, or business topics that are humorous. Of course, before selecting a humorous instance, analyze your audience carefully, because what is humorous to some people may be offensive to others. James Whitworth (2003) used the following humorous and famous instance in a speech to the Miami Township Fire and Emergency Medical Services:

Of course, this is the same Winston Churchill that, during a visit with the Astor family at his cousin's palace, and after arguing most of the day with Lady

Nancy Astor, had the following exchange. Lady Astor said, "Winston, if I were your wife I'd put poison in your coffee." To which Winston Churchill replied, "Nancy, if I were your husband, I'd drink it." (p. 26)

A good place to look for humorous instances is the *Reader's Digest*. For example, Frank Scott (1994) sent the following humorous instance for the "Life in These United States" section:

When we got married, my wife kept her maiden name. Although it is pronounced exactly as it's spelled—Verderosa—it frequently presents a stumbling block to telephone salesmen and others who don't know her.

On one such call I was addressed as "Mr. Verdonga." Sensing my displeasure, the salesman asked, "Did I pronounce your last name correctly?"

"No," I replied.

"How do you pronounce it?" he asked.

"Scott," I told him.

After a moment of silence, he said, "Boy! It's sure not pronounced like it's spelled, is it?" (pp. 83–84)

This humorous instance would work well in a speech about local words that visitors typically mispronounce or in the introduction of any speech if your own name is often mispronounced. Can you think of other uses for this instance?

Remember

Instances . . .

- Are factual, hypothetical, brief, or detailed examples or illustrations used to clarify ideas, add interest, or prove points.

- When brief, are more effective when two or more are used at a time.

- When detailed, should paint a vivid picture for listeners.

- Can be of personal or family, famous, business, or humorous events.

- Will add spice to a speech and help ensure continued audience attention.

Comparisons: Literal and Figurative

Comparisons are another type of underused supporting material that are effective in adding interest and clarifying points for your listeners. You do this by comparing (or contrasting) something your listeners know a lot about with something they know little about in order to make the unfamiliar clear.

There are two types of comparisons: literal and figurative. A **literal comparison** shows similarities or differences between two or more items in the same class or category. Examples are comparisons of two species of saltwater fish, three well-known diets, or the way the people of two countries view the importance of product packaging. For example, M. George Allen (1994), senior vice president of research and development for the 3M Corporation, used the following literal comparison in a speech entitled "Succeeding in Japan":

In Japan, perfection is the baseline expectation from which you begin—not where you end. For example, many Americans wouldn't care if a package is printed poorly—as long as the product inside is a good one. To the Japanese,

Technology Tip for Speakers

Cite Electronic Sources Correctly

Don't make the mistake of thinking that plagiarism does not apply to information you obtain on the Internet. Plagiarism occurs anytime you use the ideas of another person (whether paraphrased or word for word) without giving him or her credit. Even if the information on a specific website gives no author, you still are obligated to give as much information as possible, including title, date (of copyright, electronic publication, last update, or posting), URL, and date of access. The *Publication Manual of the American Psychological Association* (APA)* and the *MLA Handbook for Writers of Research Papers*† differ on the details of form but agree on the basic rule: electronic citations should include the same information as required for a printed source with web information added at the end. Some of the differences in the details of MLA and APA style are illustrated below:

■ *Personal site (MLA style):*
  Lancashire, Ian. Home page. 10 April 2004. 29 June 2004 <http://www.chass.utoronto.ca:8080/~ian/>.

■ *Personal site (APA style):*
  Lancashire, I. (2004, April 10). Home page. Retrieved June 29, 2004, from http://www.chass.utoronto.ca:8080/~ian/index.html

■ *InfoTrac College Edition article (MLA style):*
  Cyphert, Dale. "The Problem of PowerPoint: Visual Aid or Visual Rhetoric?" *Business Communication Quarterly* 67 (2004): 80–85. InfoTrac College Edition. 15 August 2004 <http://www.infotrac.thomson learning.com>.

■ *InfoTrac College Edition article (APA style):*
  Cyphert, D. (2004). The problem of PowerPoint: Visual aid or visual rhetoric? *Business Communication Quarterly,* 67, 80–85. Retrieved August 15, 2004, from InfoTrac College Edition, http://www.infotrac.thomson learning.com/

---

*Publication Manual of the American Psychological Association, 5th ed. (Washington, D.C.: American Psychological Association, 2001).

†Joseph Gibaldi, *MLA Handbook for Writers of Research Papers,* 5th ed. (New York: Modern Language Association, 1999).

---

a less than perfect package is a matter of concern. They ask: "How can you make a good product if you can't get the packaging right?" (p. 432)

In an address on "Business Ethics in the Current Environment of Fraud and Corruption," Archie B. Carroll (2003) used statistics and comparisons to show how CEO earnings have gotten out of hand:

In 1973, the average CEO earned 45 times the average worker. By 1991, this had grown to 145 times the average worker. And, in 2001, the average CEO earned 500 times the average worker. (By contrast, some European countries set a cap at 20x the earnings of the least paid worker.) (p. 531)

Whereas a literal comparison is used for two or more items that are basically alike, a **figurative comparison** is used for two or more items from different classes or categories. Examples include comparing individual differences to snowflakes, which are never alike, or the mayor of a city to the skipper of a boat. Figurative comparisons cannot be used for proof, but they do add interest and clarify ideas. For example, in a speech delivered at George Washington University, the Japanese ambas-

sador to the United States, Takakazu Kuriyama (1994), used a figurative comparison to clarify the state of Japanese-American relations:

> Conceptually, the Japanese-U.S. relationship has been compared to the three legs of a stool. The three legs are security, global cooperation, and economic relations. The first two legs are strong. Our security ties remain close. We cooperate on a number of global issues. . . . It is the third leg of economic relations that makes the whole stool seem a little wobbly right now. (p. 422)

If you aren't sure that a concept or main point will be clear to your audience, consider using a literal or figurative comparison. If no literal comparison comes to mind, creating a figurative comparison is as simple as saying, "This concept is just like . . ." For example, in a speech about overcoming speaker nervousness, you might use this figurative comparison:

> The fear of giving a speech is similar to the fear you had as a child when you first learned to ride a bike. Remember how nervous you were, waiting for your dad to put you on the bike? But as soon as you began to ride, your fear was replaced by excitement, and by the time the lesson was over, the excitement had turned to a feeling of accomplishment and of being in control. And you wondered why you had been so nervous at all. Well, speaking is much the same. Once you start speaking, nervousness turns into excitement and then into a feeling of accomplishment. You will wonder why you bothered being nervous at all.

Remember

Comparisons . . .

- Compare or contrast an unfamiliar idea with one that is familiar to the audience.

- Are especially good for clarifying the unfamiliar.

- Are an excellent way to add interest and variety to your speech.

- Can be either literal (comparing items of the same type or category) or figurative (comparing items of different types or categories).

Expert Opinions

When you refer to the ideas of an expert on your topic, you are using a type of support known as **expert opinion**. This is an excellent way to clarify an idea or prove a point, whether you paraphrase the expert or quote him or her directly. When using expert opinion as proof, be sure to (1) state the name of the expert, (2) briefly describe his or her qualifications (unless you are sure that your audience is familiar with the person), and (3) briefly cite when and where the expert reported the information (such as the last issue of *U.S. News and World Report* or a personal interview you conducted last week).

When paraphrasing the expert's ideas, make sure you don't misrepresent them as your own. Here is an example of a paraphrase:

> In his new book [*RE-imagine! Business Excellence in a Disruptive Age*], Tom Peters quantifies that American women constitute—are you ready?—the largest

economy in the world; followed by the entire nation of Japan, and then American men. (Nelson, 2004, p. 339)

Next is an example of a paraphrase followed by a personal opinion:

> David Lawrence, the retiring CEO of Kaiser Permanente, noted that in the $1.5 trillion that Americans spend on healthcare, close to $300 billion of that in his estimation is due to medical mistakes and errors in medicine, and we [the California Endowment for Unequal Healthcare Treatment] think that some significant percentage of that $300 billion is due to mistakes as a result of language services and appropriate interpretation and medical translation in the clinical setting. (Ross, 2003, p. 53)

Lastly, here is an example of a direct quotation:

> Many years ago, 21 years before he published the *Wealth of Nations* in 1776, Adam Smith was lecturing to his students and, according to notes taken, was asked if he could tell them what was necessary for a country to be prosperous. And he replied: "Little else is required to carry a state to the highest degree of opulence from the lowest barbarism—but peace, easy taxes, and a tolerable administration of justice; all the rest being brought about by the natural course of things." (Anderson, 2002, p. 799)

When you read direct quotations aloud, make sure that your delivery is lively and convincing—avoid a dull or monotone presentation.

When your audience is unfamiliar with your experts, you will need to introduce them thoroughly, as student and oratory winner Jenny Clanton (1989) did in a speech entitled "Plutonium 238: NASA's Fuel of Choice." In her attempt to inform the audience of the danger of Plutonium 238, she used the following paraphrase:

> Last July, *Common Cause* magazine contacted Dr. Gofman at Berkeley and asked him to place Plutonium 238 in perspective. Before I share Dr. Gofman's assessment, please understand he's no poster-carrying "anti-nuke." Dr. Gofman was co-discoverer of Uranium 233, and he isolated the isotope first used in nuclear bombs. Dr. Gofman told Karl Grossman, author of the article "Red-tape and Radioactivity," that Plutonium 238 is 300 times more radioactive than Plutonium 239, which is the isotope used in atomic bombs. (p. 375)

Remember

Expert opinions . . .

- May be paraphrased or quoted directly.
- Should be kept brief to maintain listener interest.
- Can be used for both clarification and proof.
- Should be quoted as though the expert were actually speaking—not read in a dull or monotone voice.
- Should usually include the name and qualifications of the expert and the source and date of the information.
- In many cases, should be followed by a brief summary or explanation.

If an expert is well known to your audience, it is not necessary to cite his or her qualifications. For example, when speaking to the Nebraska YWCA Women of Distinction Annual Dinner, Janice Thayer (2001), president of Excel Corporation, used the following quotation needing no detailed introduction:

> Barbara Bush must have been heartened when, in his acceptance speech her son said, "I believe in grace, because I have seen it. . . . In peace, because I have felt it. . . . In forgiveness, because I have needed it." (p. 408)

Whether you are paraphrasing or using a direct quotation, try to make sure that your audience understands what the expert is saying. If you feel that there is any chance of confusion, follow the paraphrase or quotation with a comment such as "In this quotation, _____ is making the same argument I made earlier," or "What is _____ saying? He or she is telling us . . . ," or "I cited _____ because . . ."

Fables, Sayings, Poems, and Rhymes

Fables (fictitious stories, usually with animal characters, meant to teach moral lessons), *sayings* (pithy expressions of truth or wisdom), *poems* (words written in meter or free verse that express ideas, experiences, and emotions in an imaginative style), and *rhymes* (verses that regularly repeat sounds) deserve to be used more often. Although these supporting materials are usually used in the introduction and conclusion, they can be effective at any point in your speech where clarification and variety are needed. They do not, however, provide proof. The impact of these supports depends on your delivery (enthusiasm and vocal variety are important) and on whether the audience can relate to them. Fables, sayings, poems, and rhymes that are well known to your audience are most effective.

Fables Jane Goodall (2003), naturalist and UN Messenger of Peace, used the following fable in a speech entitled "Dangers to the Environment: The Challenge Lies in All of Us" to show the importance of working together:

> It makes me think of a fable my mother used to read to me and my sister when we were little, about the birds coming together to have a competition: who could fly the highest? The mighty eagle is sure he will win, and majestically with those great, strong wings he flies higher and higher, and gradually the other birds get tired and start drifting back to the ground. Finally, even the eagle can go no higher, but that's all right, because he looks down and sees all the other birds below him. That's what he thinks, but hiding in the feathers on his back is a little wren and she takes off and flies highest of all.
>
> The reason I love this story is because . . . if we think of our life as an effort to fly always just a little bit higher and reach a goal that's just a little bit beyond our reach, how high can any of us go by ourselves? We all need our eagle. . . . (p. 71)

Use InfoTrac College Edition to find examples of quotations, comparisons, fables, sayings, poems, rhymes, and humorous instances. Take each of these words and conduct subject guide and keyword searches for them. Compare the results with similar searches using a search engine like Ixquick.

Sayings Farah M. Walters (1993), president and CEO of University Hospitals of Cleveland, clarified the federal government's attitude toward health-care reform with these words: "It's like that old saying: 'Success has many parents, but failure is an orphan'" (p. 687). Theodore J. Forstmann (1991), senior partner of Forstmann Little, used another saying in a speech entitled "The Spirit of Enterprise":

> An old Middle Eastern saying runs as follows: "Lease a man a garden and in time he will leave you a patch of sand. Make a man a full owner of a patch of sand, and in time he will grow there a garden on the land." (p. 122)

Poems   In a speech on "Make a Difference, Have No Regrets," Joseph N. Hankin (2002) read a poem that a student had written as an assignment during the Vietnam War. The poem was called "Things You Didn't Do." ➙ *See Chapter 13 for another poem used by a student speaker.*

> Remember the day I borrowed your brand new car and scratched it— I thought you'd "kill" me, but you didn't.
>
> And the time I nagged you to take me to the beach and you said it would rain and it did. I thought you'd say, "I told you so," but you didn't.
>
> And the time I flirted with all the guys to make you jealous—and you were. I thought you'd leave me, but you didn't.
>
> And the time I spilled pie all over your brand new strawberry rug. I thought you'd yell at me, but you didn't.
>
> And the time I forgot to tell you that the dance was formal and you showed up in jeans. I thought you'd drop me, but you didn't.
>
> There were lots of things you didn't do. You put up with me and you loved me and you protected me. There were lots of things I wanted to make up to you when you returned from Vietnam.
>
> But you didn't. (p. 507)

Rhymes   The following children's rhyme was used in the introduction of a speech on sexist fairy tales to clarify the speaker's position that children are introduced to male and female stereotypes while they are very young:

> What are little boys made of, made of?
> What are little boys made of?
> Frogs and snails and puppy-dogs' tails,
> That's what little boys are made of.
>
> What are little girls made of, made of?
> What are little girls made of?
> Sugar and spice and all things nice,
> That's what little girls are made of. (dePaolo, 1985)

Remember

Fables, sayings, poems, and rhymes . . .

- Add interest and clarify meanings.
- Should be read with enthusiasm and good vocal variety.
- Are especially effective when they are familiar to your audience.

Demonstrations

"A picture is worth a thousand words" is a saying that expresses the importance of visual demonstrations. A **demonstration** uses objects or people to explain or clarify an idea. Telling about the efficiency of a vacuum cleaner may impress a client, but the client's seeing the vacuum suck up a pile of dust makes the sale. One of the reasons

To keep your listeners from displaying the skepticism you see here, make sure you use supporting materials that prove as well as clarify.

© Bob Daemmrich

that TV infomercials are so successful is that we see demonstrations of the products. We see a lady with ordinary hair use the amazing hand-dryer with curling attachment to create a stunning hairstyle; we see a knife whack through a frozen block of ice and two soft drink cans and still shave thin slices off a tomato.

Whether your demonstration involves objects or people or both, you should follow these guidelines:

■ If your objects are not large enough to be seen by the entire audience, *show pictures of the objects* on transparencies, computer visuals, or posters.

■ *Practice the demonstration* until you can perform it smoothly. One student meant to demonstrate that common drain cleaners are highly caustic, but she didn't practice. She filled a clear bowl with water and placed it in a large, shallow pan of water, and then placed a Styrofoam cup full of water in the bowl. She planned to show how drain cleaner would eat a hole through the cup. But instead of carefully measuring the drain cleaner crystals, she dumped too much in. When the drain cleaner hit the water in the Styrofoam cup, it began to bubble and fizz, devouring the cup and forming a mushroom cloud that reached the ceiling. At the same time, foam bubbled up and over the edge of the bowl of water, over the side of the desk, and onto the carpet. The fumes were so potent that the room had to be cleared.

■ Unless you are giving a demonstration speech, *keep the demonstration extremely brief*—30 seconds or less. Showing the correct way to hold a racquet or swing a golf club adds clarity and interest to a speech while taking only a few seconds. Be sure to clear all demonstrations with your instructor ahead of time. ➡ *See Chapter 12 for more on demonstration speeches.*

■ While doing the demonstration, *maintain direct eye contact with your audience* and continue speaking as you demonstrate.

Supporting Materials: Clarification or Proof

At the beginning of the chapter, we stated that supporting materials are used to clarify ideas, prove points, or add interest to your speech. Selecting supports to keep listeners interested is easy—select ones that relate to your audience and use a variety of them. Selecting supports to clarify and to prove is more complicated because some supports are used only for clarification and don't work for proof. As a speaker, it's important to know what different supporting materials can do. For example, if you were presenting a new procedure to a skeptical audience, you would need to use supports that could prove the accuracy of your information. Here is a handy chart categorizing the types of supporting materials discussed in this chapter:

Supports Used Only for Clarification	Supports Used for Both Clarification and Proof
Explanations	Statistics
Hypothetical instances	Factual instances (detailed or brief)
Figurative comparisons	Literal comparisons (very weak proof)
Fables, sayings, poems, and rhymes	Expert opinions
Demonstrations	

Remember to use two or more types of supporting material per point for more effective proof.

Summary

Supporting materials can clarify ideas, prove points, and add interest. Although explanations and statistics can be effective, they are often overused. The following types of supports are also effective and need to be used more often: instances (brief, called examples; detailed, called illustrations; factual; and hypothetical); literal and figurative comparisons; expert opinions (either paraphrased or direct quotes); and fables, sayings, poems, and rhymes. Demonstrations can also be used to clarify information.

Essentials of Public Speaking   Online

Use the Essentials of Public Speaking website at **http://communication. wadsworth.com/hamiltoneps3** for quick access to the electronic study resources that accompany this chapter. When you get to the Essentials home page, click on "Student Book Companion Site" in the Resource box. The Essentials website features InfoTrac College Edition, the Suggestions for Practice and Critical Thinking activities and the InfoTrac College Edition activities that follow, a digital glossary, and review quizzes.

Key Terms

comparison 121
demonstration 126
expert opinion 123

explanation 113
figurative comparison
   122

instance 116
literal comparison 121
statistics 113

Suggestions for Practice and Critical Thinking

1. To see how difficult it is to listen to a speech containing nothing but explanations, select a paragraph from Additional Speeches for Analysis at the Essentials of Public Speaking website, or from *Vital Speeches* that is nothing but explanation. Read your paragraph aloud to the class trying to make the explanation sound as interesting as possible. When the reading is completed, discuss whether the selection held your attention or whether you kept drifting off. How could the original speaker have made this information more interesting?

2. Talk to family members and come up with at least two favorite family or personal instances. If possible, conclude each instance with a moral. Write down the instances and exchange them with several classmates. Save them for possible use in future speeches.

3. Select one detailed family instance and prepare to present it to the class. Begin your presentation with a simple sentence of explanation, present the instance, and end with a moral or brief comment on the instance. Each presentation should take no longer than 1 minute.

    If you and your instructor prefer, have a "family instance talk-down" in which two students simultaneously present their family instance, each trying to capture and hold the audience's attention. This activity could include all members of the class or just volunteers. Not only is this activity a lot of fun, but it will demonstrate what types of instances tend to be the most effective. Let the student on the left be speaker A and the student on the right be speaker B. At the end of 1 minute, ask each audience member to hold up either the letter A or the letter B to indicate which speaker held their attention more of the time. Have an assistant quickly count and record the votes.

4. Use InfoTrac College Edition to locate several interesting speeches from *Vital Speeches*. (Or locate a speech in the Additional Speeches for Analysis at the Essentials of Public Speaking website.) You may wish to use advanced search operators and expressions to locate speeches on a specific topic. Read the speeches looking for at least two examples of each type of supporting material covered in this chapter. Present the best examples to your class or share your list with a classmate or your instructor.

5. Check out the following websites. *You can access these sites under the Student Resources for Chapter 6 at the Essentials of Public Speaking website.*

    • For a website on statistics—what they are and where to find them—check out the site RobertNiles.com, developed by Robert Niles, writer for the *Los Angeles Times.*

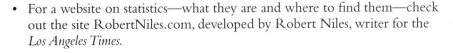

- Having problems finding specific information for a speech? Try the LibrarySpot, a free virtual library resource center that includes video and sound.

- For advice on using anecdotes, quotations, and excerpts, see "Ways to Improve Your Presentations" at Idea-Bank.com. For use of their idea bank, membership is required.

- Galaxy Directories is a good place to look for quotations on a specific topic. It also contains links to many other quotation sites.

- Check out the APA Electronic References web page, the MLA website (click on "MLA Style," then "Frequently Asked Questions," and then the question, "How do I document sources?"), or Documenting Electronic Sources at Purdue University's Online Writing Lab.

- Looking for fables? Look at Aesop Fables Online Collection and a list of Aesop's fables at Siberia, a website full of interesting links.

chapter 7

Organizing Your Speech: Introduction, Body, and Conclusion

Flashback Ancient Greek and Roman rhetoricians generally divided speech-making into five parts or canons:
- Invention—researching the topic and the audience
- Disposition—organizing materials in an orderly fashion
- Elocution—choosing effective language and style
- Memory—remembering the ideas to be presented
- Delivery—presenting the speech (verbal, vocal, and visual aspects)

Into which canon does this chapter of the text fit?

YOU ARE ALREADY FAMILIAR WITH THE BASIC STRUCTURE OF A SPEECH—INTRODUCTION, body, and conclusion. As your speeches become longer, their organization becomes more complex. This chapter will cover steps 6 and 7 of the Basic Steps for Preparing a Speech: step 6—determine how best to organize your main points—and step 7—plan your introduction and conclusion.

Basic Steps for Preparing a Speech

1. Analyze your potential audience. → *See Chapter 4.*
2. Determine topic, exact purpose, and main points. → *See Chapter 5.*
3. Prepare a rough-draft outline of main points and needed information. → *See Chapter 5.*
4. Research topic for material to support main points. → *See Chapter 5.*
5. Select best supporting materials. → *See Chapter 6.*
6. **Determine how best to organize main points.**
7. **Plan introduction and conclusion.**
8. Make preparation outline (or storyboards) and speaking notes. → *See Chapter 8.*
9. Prepare visual aids. → *See Chapter 9.*
10. Rehearse speech. → *See Chapters 10 and 11.*

When you plan a speech, it is usually better to plan the body before the introduction or conclusion. Otherwise, you may find it necessary to change the introduction and conclusion if you make changes in your main points.

Organizing the Body of Your Speech

The body of your speech includes your main ideas and the material to support them. This section will describe some common approaches to organizing main points, present some organizational tips, and suggest types of transitions to move from one main point to the next.

Whether the speech is a demonstration, informational, persuasive, or special occasion speech, it can be organized in a variety of patterns (see Figure 7.1). Some patterns work best for informational speeches, some for persuasive speeches, and some can be used for any type of speech. Regardless of which organizational pattern you choose, *the body of your speech should take approximately 70 to 80 percent of your total speech time—3½ to 4 minutes in a 5-minute speech, 5 to 5½ minutes in a 7-minute speech.*

Instead of settling on the first pattern you think of, try out several to see which one will make your speech the most interesting. For example, in her informative speech on health, Lucy experimented with four patterns before deciding on the topical pattern, which seemed the most appropriate for her topic, purpose, and audience:

Topical Pattern	Chronological Pattern	Geographic Pattern	Causal Pattern
Risk factors	Risk factors for youth	Health of eastern U.S.	Cause: Poor health habits of Americans
Warning signs	Risk factors for adults	Health of middle U.S.	Effect: These habits lead to cancer and heart disease
Guidelines	Risk factors for elderly	Health of western U.S.	

Select an Informative Pattern of Organization

As you see in Figure 7.1, there are four basic organizational patterns for informative speeches: (1) topical, (2) chronological, (3) spatial or geographic, and (4) causal. Let's look briefly at each one.

Topical Pattern The **topical pattern** is often used for informative speeches when each main point is one of several aspects of the topic. The best arrangement is the following:

- Your most important or interesting point first

- Your least compelling points in the middle

- An important or interesting point last

It's important that the beginning and end of your speech have an impact. Listeners tend to remember better the information covered at the beginning and at the end of a speech. However, if you are speaking to a business or professional audience, you

Figure 7.1

Organizational Patterns

Basic INFORMATIVE Speech Patterns*

▼ **Topical Pattern**
  I. Point 1
  II. Point 2
  III. Point 3

▼ **Chronological Pattern**
  I. First   I. Past
  II. Second (or) II. Present
  III. Final   III. Future

▼ **Spatial or Geographic Pattern**
  I. North   I. Bottom
  II. East   (or)   II. Middle
  III. South   III. Top
  IV. West

▼ **Causal Pattern**
  I. Cause   I. Effect
  II. Effect (or) II. Cause

* (also used for special occasion and demonstration speeches)

Basic PERSUASIVE Speech Patterns

▼ **Claim Pattern**
  I. Claim 1
  II. Claim 2
  III. Claim 3

▼ **Causal Pattern**
  I. Cause   I. Cause
  II. Effect   (or)   II. Effect
  III. Solution   III. Action

▼ **Problem–Solution Pattern**
  I. Problem   I. Problem
  II. Solution (or)   II. Solution
  III. Benefits   III. Action

▼ **Criteria Satisfaction Pattern**
  I. Any plan must meet the following necessary criteria
  II. Solution X does (or does not) meet the criteria

▼ **Comparative Advantages Pattern**
  I. Plan X is ineffective
  II. Plan Y is superior
     (or)
  I. Plan X is average
  II. Plan Y is far better

could organize your main points from the most to the least important, since some members of the audience may have to leave before the speech is finished.

In a speech to health-care administrators on "How Boomer Generational DNA Will Change Healthcare," Michael P. Sullivan (2004), president of 50-Plus Communications Consulting, used the following topical arrangement:

  I. Boomer Attitude #1: Live Young

  II. Boomer Attitude #2: Take Control

  III. Boomer Attitude #3: Change the World

Chronological Pattern When you arrange your main points in a step-by-step order or by dates, you are using a **chronological pattern** of organization. For example, a talk about what to do in case of a fire could be presented from first step

Boomer Attitudes

Include . . .

● Live young

● Take control

● Change world

to last. Or you could discuss the history of your favorite sport from the time it first became popular to the present. The chronological pattern is also used in demonstration and special occasion speeches.

In a speech titled "Successful Strategies for Achieving Your Career Goals," Virgis Colbert (1993), vice president of plant operations for Miller Brewing Company, organized his goal-setting advice in a chronological pattern:

Achieving Your Career Goals

① Set specific goals

② Put them in writing

③ Review them daily

   I. First, set very specific goals.

   II. Second, write down those goals.

   III. Third, review them and work toward their accomplishment every day.

Spatial (or Geographic) Pattern When you arrange your main points according to location in space, such as front to back, left to right, first floor to third floor, or north to south, you are using a **spatial (or geographic) pattern**.

For example, a speech about a new Super Playground built entirely with community donations of time and money would lend itself to a spatial pattern:

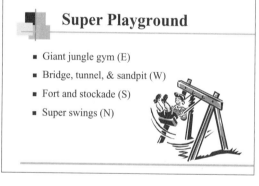

Super Playground

- Giant jungle gym (E)
- Bridge, tunnel, & sandpit (W)
- Fort and stockade (S)
- Super swings (N)

   I. The giant jungle gym at the east entrance

   II. The swinging bridge, tunnels, and sandpit at the west entrance

   III. The fort and stockade at the south entrance

   IV. The super swings at the north entrance

Causal Pattern When your main points have a cause–effect or effect–cause relationship, you are using the **causal pattern** of arrangement. If you decide to use a causal pattern, you must do more than simply assert that a causal relationship exists. You will still need to cite evidence and use a variety of supporting materials. An informative speech can be either cause–effect or effect–cause (although persuasive speeches are normally cause–effect). In a cause–effect speech, you discuss a problem or condition and then follow with the result or effects of the condition.

For example, an informative cause–effect speech about the negative effects of spanking might be organized as follows (Chadwick & Heaton, 1992; Sears & Sears, 1995):

Spanking

- Used by many parents
- Can have negative results

I. Many parents use spanking to discipline their children.

    A. Over 44 percent of all parents discipline by spanking.

    B. Spanking takes many forms.

II. Spanking can have negative consequences for the child.

    A. Spanking lowers a child's self-esteem.

    B. Spanking teaches that violence is acceptable.

The same speech arranged in effect–cause pattern would be organized as follows:

I. Spanking can have negative consequences for the child.

    A. Spanking lowers a child's self-esteem.

    B. Spanking teaches that violence is acceptable.

II. Even so, many parents use spanking to discipline their children.

    A. Over 44 percent of all parents discipline by spanking.

    B. Spanking takes many forms.

Notice that the speaker is not trying to persuade the audience to stop spanking children. The speaker is merely informing the audience about the causal relationship between spanking and certain characteristics of children.

Select a Persuasive Pattern of Organization

As you see in Figure 7.1, there are five basic organizational patterns for persuasive speeches: (1) claim, (2) causal, (3) problem–solution, (4) criteria satisfaction, and (5) comparative advantages. ➤ *Another persuasive pattern, the motivated sequence, is a method for organizing the complete speech rather than just the body; it will be discussed in Chapter 13.*

Claim Pattern Persuasive speeches use a variation of the topical pattern called the **claim pattern**. In this variation, the main points are the reasons (or claims) for believing a particular fact, holding a particular value, or advocating a particular plan. Although the claim pattern is similar to the topical pattern, the language is definitely persuasive.

    Susan Peterson (2003), founder and president of Susan Peterson Productions, Inc., used the claim pattern in her speech, "Top Secrets From an Expert." ➤ *The complete text of Peterson's speech is located under Additional Speeches for Analysis at the Essentials of Public Speaking website.*

I. Live by one mantra—it can get done tomorrow. [*claim 1*]

II. Find creative and unique ways to communicate. [*claim 2*]

III. Make room on your calendar for a crisis—every day. [*claim 3*]

IV. Turn yourself and your organization into a lean, mean, learning machine. [*claim 4*]

In the student speech, "Drug Legalization," Tricia Seeley Lewis presents

the following main claims. → *The complete transcript and a video clip of Tricia's speech is located under Additional Speeches for Analysis at the Essentials of Public Speaking website.*

I. Unless you listen carefully to the pro-legalization advocates, you may miss the fallacies in their reasoning. [*claim 1*]

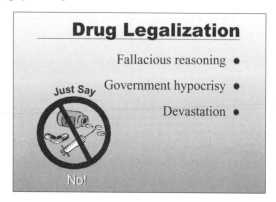

II. If the government does accept these fallacies and legalizes drugs, they would be acting hypocritically. [*claim 2*]

III. When drugs are used, they devastate the user and the user's family. [*claim 3*]

The claim pattern can be ordered inductively or deductively. In **inductive reasoning**, the supporting evidence is presented first and leads up to the conclusion; in **deductive reasoning**, the conclusion is presented first and then the supporting evidence is provided. → *See Chapter 14 for a complete discussion.*

Causal Pattern Persuasive speeches normally use only cause–effect (not the effect–cause that is also used in informative speeches), and the effect is usually followed by a solution or action step (see Figure 7.1). When you use the cause–effect–action or cause–effect–solution pattern to prove a point, it's important that the relationship truly be cause and effect and not just a chance connection. → *See Chapter 14, page 315, for a list of questions that will help ensure that the causal link is a real one.*

If you decide to use the causal pattern in a persuasive speech, it may be similar to the causal pattern used by Jeff Davidson (1993) in a speech titled "Overworked Americans or Overwhelmed Americans? You Cannot Handle Everything":

I. The overwhelmed, pressured feeling that Americans have is caused by the complexity of our society. [*cause*]

A. Population growth

B. Expanding volume of knowledge

C. Growth of electronic and mass media

D. Paper trail culture

E. Overabundance of choices

II. As complexity increases, these pressured feelings will turn into feelings of overwork and total exhaustion. [*effect*]

III. It's not too late to take control of your life. [*action*]

A. Make choices about what to ignore.

B. Avoid engaging in low-level decisions.

C. Learn to enjoy yourself.

Problem–Solution Pattern   The **problem–solution pattern** used in persuasive speeches takes a variety of forms. The two most popular forms are the problem–solution–benefits and problem–solution–action patterns. In both, you begin with a detailed discussion of the problem, its seriousness, and its effect on the audience. Next, you present ways to solve or lessen the problem. Finally, you describe benefits resulting from your solution or recommend a particular course of action. → *See Chapter 14 for suggestions on using persuasive appeals.*

Janet Napolitano (2003), lawyer and governor of Arizona, used a problem–solution pattern in a commencement address titled "Law Is a Public Service":

I. Fundamental changes will affect the entire legal profession through this new century. Problems include: [*problem*]

   A. Changes in American criminal justice.

   B. Changes in technology.

   C. Changes in community growth.

II. Lawyers will be needed to solve these problems. Specifically, [*solution*]

   A. Stay in Arizona to practice law.

   B. Wherever you practice law, be sure to use your profession to improve your community and those who live in it.

The Legal Profession

Changes are occurring in . . .

■ American criminal justice

■ Community growth

■ Technology

Lorna McElaney's persuasive speech "Drinking and Driving" uses a problem–solution–action pattern. → *See Figure 13.5 for a complete outline. To watch a video clip of Lorna's complete speech, look under Additional Speeches for Analysis at the Essentials of Public Speaking website.*

I. The high number of alcohol-related automobile accidents (DWI) indicates a serious problem. [*problem*]

   A. Nationally, 2 of 5 accidents involve DWI.

   B. Nationally, 17,000 killed in such accidents.

   C. In Texas, 1,800 killed in these accidents.

II. There are several workable solutions to the DWI problem. [*solutions*]

   A. Year-round sobriety checkpoints.

   B. Legal blood-alcohol level lowered from .1 to .08.

   C. Stronger penalties for drunk driving.

III. Action must be taken now. [*action*]

   A. "Lights-on-for-Life" promotion on December 16.

   B. Letter to senator.

Comparative Advantages Pattern   The **comparative advantages pattern** is a persuasive pattern that is normally used when your audience agrees with you on the problem but may not agree on the solution. Only a brief mention of the problem is needed during the introduction. The body of the speech compares courses of action.

Usually you will want to show that one course of action is superior or has more advantages than the others. In a speech titled "Aid to Russia," Lawrence M. Lesser (1993) used the comparative advantages pattern to show that his plan was superior to current practice:

Russian Defaults

◆ U. S. guaranteed loans - $180 million

◆ U. S. government - $600 million

◆ U. S. companies - $200 million

I. The current method of giving aid to Russia in the form of cash grants, loans, and credit guarantees isn't working. [*current practice is ineffective*]

A. Russia has defaulted on payments on $4.5 billion it borrowed from international lenders, forcing the United States to pay $180 million in loan loss claims.

B. Russia is in default on $600 million of interest payments on $4.2 billion of U.S. agricultural credit guarantees used to purchase American grain.

C. Russia has failed to pay $200 million in debts that it owes to 57 American companies.

II. Bartering, a concept very familiar to Russians, is a much better way of providing aid to Russia. [*new plan is superior*]

Criteria Satisfaction Pattern   Whether you are dealing with products, services, or ideas, the **criteria satisfaction pattern** is a persuasive tool that works well even when audience members may oppose your position. First, you establish criteria (guidelines or rules) that should be followed when evaluating proposals ("We all want our professors to be knowledgeable and fair"). Second, you show how your proposal meets or exceeds the criteria ("Not only is Professor X knowledgeable and fair, she is also a dynamic speaker"). Of course, it's important to carefully consider your audience's values and needs when selecting and explaining your criteria. If you can get your listeners to agree with your criteria, the chances are good that they will also agree with your proposal.

Using the criteria satisfaction pattern, Farah M. Walters (1993), president and CEO of University Hospitals of Cleveland and a member of the National Health Care Reform Task Force, gave a speech called "If It's Broke, Fix It: The Significance of Health Care Reform in America":

I. Any health-care plan should be measured against six fundamental principles: [*necessary criteria*]

A. Provide security for all Americans.

B. Provide choice of physician.

C. Provide continuity of care.

Health Care Criteria

▷ Security for all

▷ Choice of physicians

▷ Continuity of care

▷ Affordable to all

▷ Comprehensive coverage

▷ "User friendly"

D. Be affordable to the individual, to business, and to the country.

E. Be comprehensive in terms of coverage.

F. Be "user friendly" for both consumers and providers.

II. The health-care plan designed by the National Health Care Reform Task Force meets all six of these fundamental principles. [*plan meets criteria*]

Using More Than One Pattern   The supporting materials for each of your main points may be organized in different patterns, but the main points themselves can be organized in only one pattern. For example, in a speech about racquetball, John organized his three main points (equipment, court, and history) in a topical pattern. However, the supporting points for each main point were organized in a variety of patterns—topical, spatial, and chronological:

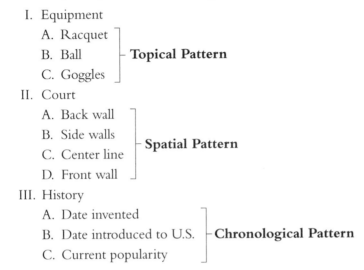

I. Equipment
   A. Racquet
   B. Ball   **Topical Pattern**
   C. Goggles

II. Court
   A. Back wall
   B. Side walls
   C. Center line   **Spatial Pattern**
   D. Front wall

III. History
   A. Date invented
   B. Date introduced to U.S.   **Chronological Pattern**
   C. Current popularity

Highlight Your Main Points

When you highlight **main points** (making the important ideas in your speeches stand out), it's much easier for listeners to follow and remember your messages. Also, if listeners drift off for a moment, they have a better chance of reorienting themselves if your speeches include highlighting techniques. There are four effective ways to highlight your points: transitions, signposts, internal summaries, and repetition and restatement. Let's look briefly at each of them.

Transitions   A **transition** is a word, phrase, or brief sentence used to link ideas, main points, or major parts of a speech. Transitions help listeners follow the development of the speaker's ideas and keep them from getting lost. Examples of transitions are words such as *also, although, but, because,* and *however;* phrases such as *in addition, on the other hand, for example,* and *in other words;* and brief sentences like the following:

"If you don't remember anything else from this speech, be sure to remember this."

"This next point will be of special interest to all parents."

"No mistake can be more costly than this last one."

"Although my third point sounds complicated, in reality it's the easiest process of all."

You should also make your points parallel. **Parallel points** use similar phrasing and sentence structure and use the same voice (either active or passive). For example, "Many remedies have been tried," "Modern therapy is best," and "Curing the cold with vitamin C" are not parallel. The first two items are complete sentences (one in passive voice and one in active voice), and the third one is a sentence fragment. "Ancient remedies, Modern therapy, and Vitamin C cure" are parallel—they are all noun phrases, and they are much easier to remember. One way to check whether your points are brief and parallel is to create an outline or storyboards. ➡ *See Chapter 8 for details on various types of outlines and storyboards.*

Create a Rhyme or Acronym Your **acronym** could be a word formed by the first letter of each of your main points. For example, in a speech on "Tips for Communicating With Your Roommate," the following acronym would add interest and make the main points easier to remember:

T   Tell each other when you are unhappy.

I   Identify potential problem areas needing discussion.

P   Participate equally in all discussions.

S   Schedule regular discussion sessions.

Check your understanding of how to make your speech memorable by taking the following quiz.

> Stop reading at this point and take the quiz below.

Test Your Knowledge Quiz

Memorable Main Points*

Directions: Choose the statement that best describes each of the following mini-outlines: (a) the main points are wordy, (b) the main points are not phrased in parallel form, (c) the main points are both wordy and not parallel, or (d) the main points represent an effective outline (for use on a visual aid, or for a verbal summary in the speech introduction or conclusion). You can also take this quiz online under the Student Resources for Chapter 7 at the Essentials of Public Speaking website and, if requested, e-mail your responses to your instructor.

_____ 1. "Aspirin: One Tablet a Day"
- ▶ Prevents heart attacks.
- ▶ Makes major heart attacks minor.
- ▶ Minimizes strokes.

_____ 2. "Aspirin: One Tablet a Day"
- ▶ Aspirin (one tablet a day) helps prevent heart attacks from occurring.
- ▶ Aspirin helps reduce the seriousness of a heart attack once it has begun.
- ▶ Aspirin helps prevent death and disability from cerebral thrombosis (stroke).

*Based on Castleman, 1994.

Left column (partially cut off)

Peter M. (
speech titled "
tion of it were

If the leg
prominen
rather po
boy as the
become a
as animals
tied, rathe

Humor A jok
in mind, howe
speaker telling
when the speak
funerals." How
cause the speak
They think this
incident related
pared for the s
humor in poor
ilarly, self-dispar
backfire, causin;
(Hackman, 1988

When used
example, in a sp
drew B. Wilson
and establish rap
under Additional

Dear fellov
bulent tim
sissippi, Juc
It won inst

I'm sur
Judge Swe;
or against v

"If whe
poison scou
lambasting
declared, he
you mean t
was equally
fits of mod
mean, the j
not retreat

Inspired
that is not l
ric itself. Pl;
bate over rh

Taking
(p. 734)

Right column / main area

____ 3. "Aspirin: One Tablet a Day"
- Prevents heart attacks.
- Major heart attacks will be turned into minor ones.
- Less likelihood of death and disability from strokes.

____ 4. "Aspirin: One Tablet a Day"
- For people who have never had a heart attack, one tablet a day prevents heart attacks from ever occurring.
- If you have an attack, its seriousness will be diminished if you will chew one or two tablets immediately.
- Death and disability from strokes were greatly decreased for stroke victims who had taken an aspirin a day.

Answers

1. (d) Of the four speech outlines, this one is by far the best. The points are brief and parallel—easy for an audience to comprehend and remember.

2. (a) Although these main points are parallel (each begins with "Aspirin helps . . ."), they include too many words. The wordiness would make them more difficult to grasp and certainly more difficult to remember.

3. (b) The main points are relatively brief, but they are not parallel. The first and third points are phrases but are not parallel; the second point is in sentence form. Also, the first point is in the present, whereas the second point is in the future.

4. (c) The main points in this outline are neither brief nor parallel. The tense changes from present to future to past; the voice changes from "people" to "you." This would be the most difficult outline to remember.

Using InfoTrac College Edition or a database like AltaVista or Communication and Mass Media Complete, run a keyword search with *oral presentations* or *public speaking* to find the most current suggestions for preparing and presenting a speech. Try out one of these suggestions in your next speech.

Now that we have examined the organization of your main points (step 6 in the Basic Steps for Preparing a Speech), let's move to step 7—developing your introduction and conclusion. First, we'll discuss how to prepare the introduction.

Organizing the Introduction of Your Speech

Many good speeches fail because their introductions are confusing and dull. Just because people show up at your speech doesn't mean they plan to listen—unless you make it impossible for them not to. Which of the following speech introductions do you think is more effective?

Today, I want to talk to you about a hobby of mine—using a metal detector to search for metal objects in yards, parks, and around deserted buildings.

It's three days until the end of the month. How many of you could use a little extra money right about now? I certainly could, and I've got some. In my hand is a check for $92 made out in my name. Last month about this time, I received a check for $34. Where did I get this money? No, it wasn't from the lottery. I found it! I found the money represented by these checks by using an inexpensive metal detector. Today, I'm going to tell you about this hobby of mine that pays me money instead of costing money.

EXPRESS/CO

You can use Speech
Express to help you
your introduction t
speech. Select "Int
tion" from the left-
menu and follow th
structions. For shor
minders from this c
about introductions
on the "Tutor" butt

In deciding whether to use jokes or humorous instances, make sure that humor is appropriate for your topic and that you are good at using it. Although anyone can tell a humorous instance, not everyone can tell a joke. Nothing is worse in the beginning of a speech than a joke that falls flat.

Quotation   A quotation or paraphrase from a well-known source can grab the interest of your audience if you read it with good vocal variety and eye contact and if the expert has something of real interest to say. Quotations are more effective when the audience is familiar with the source. Steve Rogel (2003), chairman, president, and CEO of Weyerhaeuser Company and a scouting enthusiast for more that 48 years, successfully introduced his speech "Business Ethics and the Boy Scout Code" by using expert opinion, as follows:

> Mahatma Gandhi, the great Indian leader, once said, "There are seven things that will destroy us: wealth without work; pleasure without conscience; knowledge without character; religion without sacrifice; politics without principle; science without humanity; business without ethics."
>
> While each of these topics is deserving of attention in its own right, I'm going to focus on the last of Gandhi's concerns—business without ethics—in relation to the values imbedded in the Boy Scout code. Specifically, does being a good scout help one become a good business leader? And can we apply the ethics of scouting to the business of business? (p. 403)

Startling Fact   Revealing one or more startling facts is another good way to grab listeners' attention. When your facts involve statistics, make them meaningful by relating them to your listeners' frames of reference. If you were speaking on smoking, for example, you might begin your speech with the following startling statistics (Bristow, 1994):

> Approximately 3,000 children (average age 12½ years old) start smoking every day. That's over 1 million children a year!
>
> To show you how successful the tobacco industry is in targeting these children, look at the success of their Joe Camel Campaign. Before the campaign, sales were approximately $6 million. After the campaign, sales reached $500 million! Before the campaign, ads reached approximately one-half of 1 percent of children under 18 years of age; after the campaign, the ads were reaching 33 percent! (p. 334)

Question   Asking a rhetorical or an actual question is a good way to get listeners involved. A **rhetorical question** is designed to make the audience think—no real answer is expected. Asking your audience, "If I could prove that every penny would be spent purchasing items of clothing for the needy, would you be willing to donate from $1 to $5?" is a rhetorical question. But asking your audience, "How many of you had breakfast before coming to class this morning?" is an actual question for which a response is expected. To make sure your audience realizes that you want a show of hands, raise your own hand as you ask the question, or say, "I would like a show of hands on this question: How many of you had breakfast before coming to class this morning?"

Reference to the Occasion   Referring to the event in the introduction is essential if you are speaking at a special occasion (such as the company's 20th anniversary). For regular classroom speeches, however, there is no need to mention how thrilled you are to be here for the first day of informative presentations.

Fable, Saying, Poem, and Rhyme   Opening with a piece of folklore—a fable, saying, poem, or rhyme—can also stimulate listener attention. Speaking on medical ethics, Richard D. Lamm (1993) used a **parable** (a fable that illustrates a moral or religious principle) to grab the attention of his audience:

> I would like to start with a parable. In the Christian tradition, there is the story about Saint Martin of Tours who in the Medieval Ages was riding his horse, alone and cold, through the deepening night toward the walled city which was his destination. Right outside the gate to the city, Saint Martin of Tours met a cold and starving beggar. In an act of charity that lives in Christian tradition, Saint Martin of Tours divided his cloak in half and gave it with half of his dinner to the cold and starving beggar. It was clearly the ethical and moral course to take. It has served as an example of Christian charity for centuries.
>
> Yet Brecht, in his play *Mother Courage,* raises the issue of what if, instead of one cold and starving beggar, there were 40. Or, if you like, 100. What then is the duty of an ethical and moral person? It obviously does not make any sense to divide one's cloak into 40 or 100 painfully inadequate pieces. There is no reason to choose one among the many cold and starving beggars, and it is hard to solve this dilemma other than perhaps saying a prayer for them all as you ride past them into the city.
>
> It is my passionate belief that this parable applies to the dilemma we are faced with in health care. There is a new set of realities with which we are confronted; and we must develop a new set of values and a new way of looking at health care if we are to resolve the implications of this brave new world of health care. (p. 549)

Demonstration   A brief demonstration of a procedure or skill is another method for getting the attention of your audience. Any demonstration needs to be brief yet impressive. For example, a demonstration speech about how to tie gift bows might begin with the following brief demonstration:

> [On the table in front of the speaker are two beautifully wrapped packages. The speaker points to the one on the left.] The bow on this package can be purchased at most specialty stores for $5. However, the bow on this package [the speaker points to the package on the right] cost only 50 cents because I made it myself. Not only is this bow inexpensive, it is easy to make. [The speaker then picks up ribbon and a wire and in only a few seconds produces a beautiful, professional-looking bow. She looks at the audience.] Look at the money you could save on birthday and Christmas gifts by making your own bows.

An informational speech about types of dead-bolt locks might use the following brief demonstration as an attention-getter:

> [Two miniature door frames are placed on a table by the speaker. One frame is labeled "A"; the other is labeled "B."] The lock on door A is the same lock that 85 percent of you have on your doors. Anyone can pick this type of lock. [The speaker then reaches into his pocket and pulls out a common bobby pin, straightens it, places it in the lock, and in less than two seconds has door A swinging open.] However, the lock on door B has a special dead-bolt lock that no one can pick. In fact, the only way a person could get in this door without a key would be to kick in the door frame. [He then takes out another bobby pin and tries to open door B with no success. He looks directly at his audience.] Which door would you feel safer sleeping behind at night?

Remember

Attention-getters include . . .

- A narrative (detailed factual or hypothetical instance)
- Two or more brief instances (examples)
- A joke or humorous instance
- A quote or paraphrase
- One or more startling facts
- A rhetorical or actual question
- A reference to the occasion or event
- A fable, saying, poem, or rhyme
- A brief demonstration of a procedure or skill

The type of attention-getter that will work best depends on the type of audience—friendly, neutral, uninterested, or hostile. Humor works especially well for a **friendly** audience; well-supported statistics or a detailed factual instance are ideal for a **neutral** audience; a colorful yet professional visual aid or startling facts may surprise an **uninterested** audience into listening; and a powerful quotation by a well-known authority or by a member of their own group will work best for a **hostile** audience.

Goal 2: Motivate Your Audience to Listen

Unfortunately, just because your listeners laugh at your opening joke or pay attention to your personal instance doesn't mean they will continue to listen. They must be made to feel that there is some advantage in it for them. In other words, what will your speech do for your listeners? Will it show them how to reduce stress, lose weight, have more interesting dates, improve their health, or what? When you answer the "So what? Why should I care?" question that goes through listeners' minds, you are motivating them to listen. To determine how best to relate your topic to your audience, refer to the demographic and psychological information you discovered earlier when you analyzed your audience. → *Refer to Chapter 3, Table 3.1, for a list of additional motivators.*

Depending on your topic, it is possible to combine attention-getting and motivation. For example, the gift-wrapping and door-lock demonstrations described in the preceding section not only grabbed attention but also included a reason for listening (saving money and increasing personal safety). Persuasive speakers commonly combine the attention and motivation steps, as Jenny Clanton (1989) did in her award-winning speech "Plutonium 238." → *To read Jenny's complete speech, look under Additional Speeches for Analysis at the Essentials of Public Speaking website.*

As you read the following excerpt from Jenny's speech, think about which basic needs she is appealing to. If you had been in the audience, would you have been motivated to listen to her speech?

On January 28, 1986, the American Space Program suffered the worst disaster in its more than 30-year history. The entire world was shocked when the space

shuttle Challenger exploded seconds after lift-off, claiming the lives of seven brave astronauts and crippling our entire space agenda. I suppose the oldest cliché in our culture, spoken on battlegrounds and indeed virtually anywhere Americans die, is "We must press forward, so we can say they did not die in vain." Rest assured. They didn't. The deaths of our seven astronauts probably saved the lives of untold thousands of Americans.

For, you see, if the O-rings had not failed on January 28, 1986, but rather on May 20, 1987, the next scheduled shuttle launch, in the words of Dr. John Gofman, Professor Emeritus at the University of California at Berkeley, you could have "kissed Florida goodbye."

Because the next shuttle, the one that was to have explored the atmosphere of Jupiter, was to carry 47 lbs. of Plutonium 238, which, is, again according to Dr. Gofman, the most toxic substance on the face of the earth. Dr. Helen Caldicott corroborates Dr. Gofman's claim in her book, *Nuclear Madness,* when she cites studies estimating one ounce of widely dispersed Plutonium 238 particles as having the toxicity to induce lung cancer in every person on earth. (p. 375)

Goal 3: Establish Credibility and Rapport

The third goal of an effective introduction is to establish your credibility (believability) as a speaker and develop rapport (feelings of respect and liking) with your audience. If you have personal experience with your topic, this is the time to mention it ("I have taught CPR for the last five years" or "I have played racquetball since I was old enough to hold a racquet"). There's no need to wear all of your medals or bring in your trophies, but it is important to let your audience know of your expertise.

If you don't have personal experience with your topic, your audience will want to know why you selected it. Did you write a paper on it in another course and find that the subject really mattered to you? Are you interested in it because of something that happened to a family member or a friend? Unless it's too personal, sharing this kind of information with your audience will add to your credibility and help establish rapport with your audience.

Another way of establishing credibility is to mention the expert sources you have consulted. If your listeners are unfamiliar with your experts, you will need to establish their qualifications. The number of sources you will need in order to establish your credibility often depends on your topic. If you are discussing the advantages of joining a fraternity or sorority and have been a member of such a group for 2 years, you can depend largely on your own personal credibility. But if you have never been a member, your personal opinion on this topic will not carry much weight. You will need to strengthen your credibility by using outside experts.

Goal 4: Present Your Thesis Statement

It is amazing how many speakers fail to present a thesis statement. Their introduction may make the general topic they are discussing clear, but their exact purpose and the main points to be covered may not be clear until the speech is completed, if then. A good **thesis statement**—built from the exact purpose you determined while narrowing your topic—includes identification of the topic, any conclusions you may have reached, and a preview of the main points you plan to present.

EXPRESS/CONNECT

You can use Speech Builder Express to help you create your thesis statement. Select "Thesis Statement" from the left-hand menu and follow the instructions. For short reminders from this chapter about thesis statements, click on the "Tutor" button.

Using InfoTrac College Edition, conduct a keyword search for *thesis statement** and *position statement* and see what advice you can find on making a clear and powerful thesis statement.

State Purpose (If Informative) or Position (If Persuasive) Remember, audience members are not always skilled listeners. If they have to do too much work to figure out your purpose, they will probably take a mental holiday. Unless you need to build suspense or your audience is hostile, you will want to quickly make your purpose or position as clear as possible.

For example, Robert McDermott stated the following purpose in his speech "The Electoral College": "Today we are going to look at three aspects of the Electoral College." ➡ *The complete speech appears in Chapter 8. To watch a video clip of Robert's speech, look under student resources for Chapter 8 at the Essentials of Public Speaking website.*

In his speech, "What You Don't Get Out of a College Education," author and communications professor Richard L. Weaver II (2003) stated his purpose as follows:

> What I would like to do today is share with you some of those things that you don't get out of a college education—personal success skills necessary to exceed in school and in life. (p. 604)

Jenny Clanton (1989) began her speech "Plutonium 238" with the following statement of purpose. ➡ *To read Jenny's complete speech, look under Additional Speeches for Analysis at the Essentials of Public Speaking website.*

> Today, when you leave this room, I want you to fully understand just what impact NASA's plans could have on this planet. I want you to become cynical. I want you to be a little scared. I want you to become angry. But most of all, I want you to begin to demand some answers. (p. 375)

Preview Main Points Listing your main points after you state your specific purpose will improve the chances that your audience will recall your main ideas. If you are using visual aids during your speech, this is an excellent time to present one because audience members are more likely to remember information that they can both see and hear. A high-quality visual aid that lists your main points could be used in both your introduction and your conclusion. ➡ *Guidelines for creating visual aids are covered in Chapter 9.*

We've already read Jenny Clanton's attention-getter and her position statement. Now let's see how she previewed her main points:

> To move you in this direction I would first like to explore with you just what plutonium is and what could happen if it were released in our atmosphere. Second, let's consider NASA's argument for the safety of the plutonium as used in the shuttle program. And finally, I want to convince you that NASA's conclusions are flawed. (p. 375)

Optional Introduction Information

We've discussed the four basic goals of an introduction. The following are some optional elements that you may occasionally wish to include.

Background Information If you need to include some clarifying information but don't wish to spend enough time on it to make it a main point, cover it in the introduction. For example, in a speech about the causes, effects, and cures of anorexia, you probably would want to explain what anorexia is and briefly compare it to other types of eating disorders. You might also include some statistics on how many young

women are afflicted with anorexia (unless you used these statistics as your attention-getter). Such background information would clarify your topic and prepare the audience to get the most from your three main points.

Persuasive speeches often need background information about a problem. Before others will accept your solution or plan of action, they must agree that the problem is serious enough to warrant change. If you are using a problem–solution pattern to organize your main arguments (discussed earlier in the chapter), you will cover the problem in the body of the speech. However, when using most other organizational patterns, you will need to present the seriousness of the problem and its potential effects on your audience during the introduction.

If your audience is already familiar with the problem, a brief reminder is all that is needed. In a speech entitled "Business and School Reform," Vern Loucks, Jr. (1993), chairman and CEO of Baxter International, didn't need to spend much time explaining the problem:

> The last thing that any of us in business can afford is the existence of a permanent and largely ignored or forgotten underclass. Yet in nearly every big city of our nation, that underclass seems entrenched in our society. That is an absolute tragedy. It's also a grim and dangerous waste. All of us in this room know and understand the correlation between academic failure and crime. All of us fully understand the negative potential of a society where a very large minority does not participate in the successes of society as a whole. (p. 466)

On the other hand, if the problem is relatively unknown or is based on listener misconceptions, a more thorough discussion will be needed.

Definition of Unfamiliar Terms For some speech topics, you may need to define unfamiliar terms right at the start. For example, it would be a mistake to assume that everyone in your audience knows that *STD* stands for "sexually transmitted disease," that *MBWA* stands for "management by wandering around," or that plutonium is a radioactive element manufactured in uranium chain reactors. In the introduction to a speech titled "U.S. Public Diplomacy," Kathy R. Fitzpatrick (2004) defined what she meant by *public diplomacy:*

> In official government jargon, public diplomacy is a nation's efforts to understand, inform, and influence the people of other nations. Many—including myself—view it as international public relations. The goal of U.S. public diplomacy is—or at least the goal should be—to develop and sustain positive relationships between the United States and foreign publics. (p. 413)

Mention of Handouts You should only distribute handouts rarely during your speech—it's usually better to wait until the end. But let your audience know that they are available. For example, if you had a computer visual or transparency showing contact information for organizations providing free information, many listeners would want to take notes, and the shuffle to find paper and pencil would be distracting. But if you mentioned in your introduction that you would pass out a handout listing the organizations and their phone numbers at the conclusion of your speech, audience members could relax and spend their time listening.

Earlier we saw a good example of an informative speech, "Our State of Health," by Lucy Tisdale Setliff. The introduction to Lucy's 7-minute speech lasted a total of 50 seconds. Let's take a look at Lucy's introduction in more detail. ➔ *See Chapter 4 for Lucy's complete speech.*

SAMPLE INTRODUCTION

Analysis

Lucy uses a paraphrase of a well-known quote by Hippocrates and a definition of *health* as her attention-getter.

The brief family instance not only serves as an attention-getter but shows why Lucy is so interested in health and helps establish her credibility. She furthers her credibility by telling us that she has researched the topic of health.

Lucy identifies "looking at our state of health" as her specific purpose and lists three main points. Her computer visual listing her main points adds interest and should make it easier for the listeners to identify and recall her points.

Speech

Hippocrates once said that health is the greatest of human blessings. Health—what exactly does that mean to each of us? Well, as defined in Webster's Dictionary, "Health is the absence of disease." Health became very important to me when I lost my father to heart disease. The day before he died, he said, "Lucy I'm going to fight this thing." But, you know, he couldn't because the disease had completely taken over his heart. After he died, I became better informed about our state of health and I learned that the nation's two leading causes of death are heart disease and cancer, according to former Surgeon General C. Everett Koop. I also discovered that these and other diseases that kill us are caused partially by our own habits. Through improper diet and lack of exercise, we pay the price in the way of medical bills, plus we decrease our chances of spending our "golden years" in relatively good health.

So, this morning, I would like to look at our State of Health. I'll focus on three aspects of health: First, we'll identify major risk factors to health. [Visual #1]. Second, we'll review cancer and heart attack warning signs. Third, we'll explore diet and exercise guidelines.

Now that we have thoroughly examined the organization of the introduction and body of your speech, let's discuss how to create a conclusion that will leave your audience feeling satisfied and pleased.

Organizing the Conclusion of Your Speech

No speech is complete without a conclusion, because the conclusion helps make sure your audience understood and will remember all points, and it provides closure. It's possible that some of your listeners missed, misunderstood, or simply forgot one of your points. A conclusion lets you remind them. A conclusion is especially important if you have a question-and-answer (Q & A) session at the end of your speech. Provide a brief summary before the Q & A and another one after it to redirect audience attention back to the central ideas of your speech and to provide closure.

A conclusion includes at least a summary and a final refocusing thought. Persuasive speakers may refocus the audience by visualizing the future or challenging the audience to change a behavior or belief. *An effective conclusion should take no more than 10 to 15 percent of your total speaking time*—approximately 30 to 45 seconds in a 5-minute speech, 45 to 60 seconds in a 7-minute speech.

Summarize Main Ideas

In an informative speech, the goal of the summary is to reclarify the purpose of your talk or your main points. A summary can be general (referring to the topic of the

EXPRESS CONNECT

You can use Speech Builder Express to help you create your conclusion for your speech. Select "Conclusion" from the left-hand menu and follow the instructions. For short reminders from this chapter about conclusions, click on the "Tutor" button.

speech) or specific (listing the main points). Your choice depends on how important it is for listeners to remember specific points. If you want them to recall your main points or remember specific details from your speech, use a visual aid during your summary. The visual used to summarize your main points in the introduction could be used again here.

In her classroom speech "Outdoor Oklahoma," Christina used the following summary:

> So the next time you're looking to escape into a corner of wilderness for a moment of solitude—go to Oklahoma and check out four of nature lovers' dream spots: Quartz Mountain State Park, Lake Tenkiller, Talimena Drive, and Arbuckle Wilderness.

In a persuasive speech, the purpose of the summary is to remind your listeners of your position or your specific arguments and recommendations. To conclude her persuasive speech, Jane Goodall (2003) summarized what her audience should do about the "Dangers to the Environment":

> So my message to you tonight is that we look around the world and we see many problems. But equally we look around the world and we find many solutions, and our job is to replicate the solutions and to live with courage and not to live in fear and to live with determination that we will create a more healthy and a better world for our children and for theirs, and to know that there is hope. But the hope really lies in the hands of all of us in this room. It's *we* who can make the difference. It's *we* who can put the right people in power to make the right decisions that must be made. If we can die knowing that we've done our best to create a world that will be a safer, healthier and more beautiful world for our great grandchildren—it's up to us. (p. 78)

Refocus Audience Attention

You don't want your listeners to forget your message the minute they leave the room. Try to make your final thought so memorable that they continue to think and talk about your speech long after it's over. Any of the supporting materials used to gain attention in the introduction of your speech (detailed factual or hypothetical narratives; two or more brief instances; a joke or humorous instance; a pithy quote or paraphrase; a startling fact; a rhetorical question; a fable, saying, poem, or rhyme; or a brief demonstration) can also be used effectively to end your speech.

Offer a Closing Thought   Speaking to the Institute of World Affairs about "U. S. Public Diplomacy," Kathy R. Fitzpatrick (2004) refocused her audience's attention with the following quote and closing thought:

> In closing, I'd like to share with you a quote by novelist Ursula LeGuin, who said: "There have been great societies that did not use the wheel, but there have been no societies that did not tell stories."
>
> As a nation, we can have the mightiest military and the most sophisticated technology. But such strengths ultimately will not matter if we fail to capture the minds and hearts of people around the world with the enduring story of freedom and democracy.
>
> America must tell its story—and must tell it well. The security and prosperity of the citizens of the United States of America depend on it. (p.416)

Refer to the Introduction Another effective way to refocus audience attention is to refer to your introduction. The delightful and compelling speech titled "Light the Fire: Communicate With Your Child" is an excellent example of tying the introduction and conclusion together. Speaking at a parents workshop sponsored by the Heart of America Suzuki Teachers Association, Joan E. Aitken (1993), an assistant professor at the University of Missouri-Kansas City, used the following introduction and conclusion:

Introduction

As I light these four candles, I want to share some things I've heard my five year old child say . . .

CANDLE 1: "Whoops."

CANDLE 2: "Why do elephants put dirt on their backs?"

CANDLE 3: "Knock, knock" ("Who's there?") "Bananas." ("Bananas who?") "Bananas are something monkeys like to eat. Ha, ha, ha, tee-he, ho."

CANDLE 4: "Your lap is my favorite place, Mom."

As I blow out these four candles, I want to share some things I've said to my son . . .

CANDLE 1: "What's the matter with you?"

CANDLE 2: "I don't know why elephants do things."

CANDLE 3: "I don't get it. Is that joke supposed to be funny?"

CANDLE 4: "Ow. You're getting so big. Get off me."

Conclusion

[After a 30-minute speech on how to communicate with your child:]

In closing, I want to light these four candles again, saying other words I try to use.

CANDLE 1: My child said: "Whoops."

And I said: "That's okay. What do you need to do to fix it, Wade?"

CANDLE 2: "Why do elephants put dirt on their backs?"

"You ask the most interesting questions. I've noticed the elephants in the zoo do that. Do you suppose it makes them cool? Maybe it's their sunscreen. What do you think?"

CANDLE 3: "Knock, knock" ("Who's there?") "Bananas." ("Bananas who?") "Bananas are something monkeys like to eat. Ha, ha, ha, tee-he, ho."

"Darlin', I love to hear you laugh."

CANDLE 4: "Your lap is my favorite place, Mom."

"Then, come sit. You are the light of my life!" (p. 477)

Issue a Challenge In a persuasive speech titled "The Dynamics of Discovery: Creating Your Own Opportunities," Catherine B. Ahles (1993) issued this challenge:

As you go forward to discover your world of possibilities, I challenge you to think about the seven questions I've posed tonight:

- Are you creating your own opportunities?
- Can you make more informed choices?
- How keenly are you paying attention?
- How daring are you?
- What are your convictions?
- How strong is your confidence?
- What is your personal philosophy? (p. 352)

John J. Ring (1992), chair, president, and CEO of Unocal Corporation, ended his speech with a detailed factual instance and a challenge. It's too long for most speeches, so as you read the following selection from Ring's speech, think about how it could be shortened and still retain its effect.

> Let me end my comments today with a true story. It was told to me by a senior Soviet official who visited the United States last year.
>
> This was the first time he'd ever been outside his country. He was amazed by almost everything he saw in the United States—especially our personal freedom and our material abundance. They went beyond the wildest rumors he'd heard about America in his home country.
>
> But what really caught his eye was a visit to a local supermarket. To him, the shelves were chock full of an incredible variety of food, beverages, and other products. He assumed that this market was reserved for high government officials and wealthy businessmen.
>
> No, his hosts told him, anybody could just walk right in and buy whatever they liked. He did not believe them.
>
> That night, after dinner, he decided to check it out for himself. He found a supermarket, went up to the front entrance, and just walked right in. No one stopped him, no one questioned him, no one asked to see his credentials. There were no long lines and no one was hoarding food.
>
> He returned to his hotel room, lay down on the bed and cried. He realized that his whole life had been based on a lie.
>
> "Your system of free enterprise works," this official said to me. "My system must change. I will never see such a high quality of life, but perhaps my children or grandchildren will live to enjoy it," he concluded.
>
> Ladies and gentlemen, we live in a great country. Somehow, in recent years, we've begun to lose our way. To get back on track, we must ask ourselves some hard questions and squarely face our responsibilities. We must learn to value our economic rights as well as our political rights. Together, they made America the envy of the world.
>
> Thank you for inviting me to join you today. (p. 367)

Visualize the Future   Because your audience may not be good at doing it themselves, in persuasive speeches you need to visualize the future for them—the future with or without your proposal. Kim, a student speaking on drunk driving, visualized a future with year-round sobriety checkpoints in this way:

> Take a moment and picture a world where we could all feel safer on our roads again. We could all go out on New Year's Eve, because, quite frankly, those of us who do drink responsibly won't go out on this night because we are afraid of the other people on the road. Families wouldn't have to be as fearful of going on a vacation over a long holiday weekend such as Memorial Day, Labor Day, or the Fourth of July; they wouldn't feel as threatened by the other drivers on the road. Wouldn't this safety be worth the inconvenience of stopping at sobriety checkpoints?

Look your listeners in the eye, use forceful and dynamic language, and speak with emotion and sincerity while you paint a vivid mental picture of the future. You want to encourage listeners who are almost persuaded—they just want to see how your topic relates to them one more time—without, of course, using faulty reasoning or unethical emotional appeals. ➡ *For a discussion of faulty or fallacious reasoning, see Chapter 14.*

Don't forget as you conclude your persuasive speech to visualize the future for your audience—look them right in the eye, use forceful and dynamic delivery, and speak with emotion and sincerity.

© Richard Hutchings/PhotoEdit

Using Q & A

The key to successful Q & A sessions is to know your topic really well and to antic-ipate audience questions. Make a note card or two listing important sources, experts, and organizations to refer to if needed. As you come up with possible questions, pre-pare one or two visual aids to use when answering them. All you may need is one or two overlays (for example, a bar graph containing new information) or a new com-puter visual of a chart to add to visuals that you plan to use in your speech. Of course, it's always possible that none of these questions will be asked, but if they are, your audience can't help being impressed. → *See Lucy's Q & A in Chapter 4 and in-formation on overlays in Chapter 9, page 189.*

Here are some additional suggestions to help you with your Q & A session:

■ Repeat each question before answering it to make sure everyone heard the question.

■ Rephrase any confusing or negative questions in a clear and positive manner.

■ Think a moment before answering each question. If you don't know the an-swer, say so and refer the questioner to someone in the audience who does know, or tell the person that it's a good question and that you will find the answer and let him or her know at the next meeting.

■ If you think a question is irrelevant or will take too long to answer, thank the person for the question and mention that you will talk with him or her personally about it after the session.

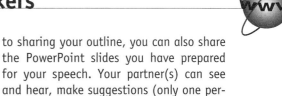

Technology Tip for Speakers

Critique Your Speech Online

Convincing a friend or classmate to give you advice on a speech isn't easy—unless you make it fun. One way to do this is to do it online. You'll be amazed how many needed changes will show up when the outline appears in a different medium. You can use e-mail, or the Online Collaboration Tool in Microsoft's Office 2000 (if your campus supports it). Or you can critique a speech through Centra, a voice-enabled web service (www.centranow.com).

Centra offers a virtual conference room that is free as long as you include no more than five people. One of you will need to be the "meeting planner" and set up the meeting. Then you send an e-mail invitation with the meeting ID number to your partner(s), who simply click the "Attend a meeting" button, type in the ID, and join the meeting. The meeting planner can broadcast any application running on his or her desktop. This means that in addition to sharing your outline, you can also share the PowerPoint slides you have prepared for your speech. Your partner(s) can see and hear, make suggestions (only one person can speak at a time), and even send information during the meeting. Once received by the planner, the new information can be added to the outline and then broadcast back for additional revision. (The easiest way to prepare PowerPoint slides is to use the Speech Template available under Student Resources for Chapter 2 on the Essentials of Public Speaking website.)

If your professor does not assign partners, find your own partner and check the organization of your speech online. You'll find that you get more helpful advice than the usual, "Oh, it looks nice!" And, of course, you don't have to get dressed up or meet your partner face-to-face—anytime you are both available online (day or night) will work.

- Don't argue or get angry or defensive while answering questions. What you say during the Q & A session will affect the audience's overall judgment of your credibility and your speech.

- Mention in your introduction that there will be a short Q & A period at the end of your speech, and ask audience members to write out questions during the speech. After your initial conclusion, collect the questions, select three or four good ones, and answer them—ignoring the less desirable ones.

- Watch your time, and end the session with a final conclusion that refocuses audience attention and puts a pleasing closure on your speech.

As you can see, the conclusion of a speech is essential. If you see that time is running out, don't eliminate your conclusion. It is better to abbreviate your final point (or even skip it entirely) than to leave out your conclusion. Of course, if you time your speech while practicing, you won't have to worry about leaving anything out. Let's end this chapter by taking a detailed look at Lucy's conclusion.

SAMPLE CONCLUSION

Analysis

In the first two sentences, Lucy is challenging the listeners to make the best choices possible.

She summarizes her main points and ends the initial conclusion by referring to her opening paraphrase of Hippocrates.

Since Lucy planned a question-and-answer period immediately after her speech, a detailed initial conclusion is not necessary.

After the Q & A, Lucy brings closure by including a final summary. Her sincerity, direct eye contact, and reference to her father's death (which ties the introduction and the conclusion together) leave the audience thinking.

Speech

We should take a long look at the way we continue living life. Part of the great challenge of living is grasping opportunities and making the best choices we can. If we know the risk factors involved with disease, learn the warning signals that indicate disease, and discover diet and exercise guidelines, we improve our chances of preventing disease. Only then can we obtain health, the greatest of human blessings.

[Q & A session]

Thank you for your questions and your attention this morning. I think that we'll all agree that our health is what we choose to make it. How we take care of our bodies today will determine if we suffer problems later on. Health begins with awareness. Don't wait until later to get interested in your health. As it was with my father—later may be too late.

Summary

Great ideas and outstanding supporting materials will be lost on the audience if your speech is not well organized. Clear and memorable presentations that flow smoothly are the result of three important steps.

First, organize the main points that make up the body of the speech. You can use a chronological, spatial (or geographic), topical (or claim), causal, problem–solution, comparative advantages, or criteria satisfaction pattern. Main points should be stated clearly and backed up with a variety of supporting materials designed to hold the audience's attention as well as clarify and prove your ideas.

Next, organize the introduction. Include an attention-getter, motivate the audience to listen, establish credibility and rapport, clearly state your purpose, and preview the main points of the speech. If your main points are brief and parallel (and are presented on a transparency or other visual aid), it will be easier for the audience to remember them. In the introduction, it may also be necessary to include background information, define unfamiliar terms, or briefly mention handouts.

Finally, organize the conclusion of your speech. The conclusion includes a summary of the main points and refocuses audience attention so that listeners will remember your speech long after it is finished. In persuasive speeches, the refocus step may also include a visualization of the future and a challenge to action. Any type of supporting materials that can be used to get attention at the beginning of the speech can be used to refocus attention at the end. Be sure to leave the audience satisfied, with a feeling of closure, especially after a Q & A session.

Essentials of Public Speaking *Online*

Use the Essentials of Public Speaking website at **http://communication.wadsworth.com/hamiltoneps3** for quick access to the electronic study resources that accompany this chapter. When you get to the Essentials home page, click on "Student Book Companion Site" in the Resource box. The Essentials website features video clips of Tricia Seeley Lewis's speech "Drug Legalization" (pages 135–136), Lorna McElaney's speech "Drinking and Driving" (page 137), and Robert McDermott's speech "The Electoral College" (page 150); InfoTrac College Edition; the Suggestions for Practice and Critical Thinking activities and the InfoTrac College Edition activities that follow; a digital glossary; and review quizzes.

Key Terms

acronym 142

causal pattern 134

chronological pattern
   133

claim pattern 135

comparative advantages
   pattern 137

criteria satisfaction
   pattern 138

deductive reasoning
   136

highlight main points
   139

inductive reasoning 136

parable 147

parallel points 142

repetition 140

restatement 140

problem–solution pattern
   137

rhetorical question 146

signpost 140

spatial or geographic
   pattern 134

thesis statement 149

topical pattern 132

transition 139

Suggestions for Practice and Critical Thinking

1. Select at least two of the following speech topics (make one persuasive and one informative) and write four mini-outlines for each using a different organization pattern for each outline:

   a. Teen curfew

   b. Children and discipline

   c. Recreational activities (in your state)

   d. Exercise and health

   e. Recycling

   f. Year-round schooling

   g. Fraternity–sorority hazing

   h. Buying a car

   As you phrase the main points, make sure they are brief and parallel. Compare answers with a classmate.

2. Using InfoTrac College Edition, analyze the introductions and conclusions in at least four speeches found in current issues of *Vital Speeches* (run an Advanced Search using *jn=Vital Speeches*). How effective do you think they were? Why do you think they used some techniques and not others?

3. Take a careful look at the organizational pattern you have selected for the speech you are currently working on. Is it possible that another pattern could create more audience interest? If you aren't sure, prepare outlines using other patterns and ask classmates or friends which one they like best.

4. Take another look at the factual instance from John J. Ring's conclusion on page 155. How would you shorten this instance so that it could be used in a 7- to 10-minute speech? Compare your revision with that of a classmate. Do the two of you basically agree?

5. Select a written speech (student or professional) from the Essentials of Public Speaking website and see if you can identify the exact line on which the introduction ends and the body and the conclusion begin. What pattern of organization is used for the main points? Use the evaluation form in Figure 12.7 (on page 269) or Figure 13.6 (on page 305) to critique the speech. Compare the grade you gave with that given by a classmate.

6. Select a videotaped speech from the Essentials of Public Speaking website or view the sample videotaped speech that your instructor plays for the class. Evaluate the speaker using the appropriate evaluation form (Figure 12.7 or 13.6). Compare the grade you gave with that given by your classmates.

7. After giving an informative or persuasive speech in class, offer a Q & A session in which classmates ask four to seven questions. Don't forget to include a final conclusion at the end of the Q & A.

8. Check out the following websites. *You can access these sites under the Student Resources for Chapter 7* at the Essentials of Public Speaking website.

   - To practice writing a quality thesis statement, read and apply the suggestions on the following websites: (1) "Developing a Thesis Statement" by the University of Wisconsin–Madison Writing Center and (2) "Introductions and Thesis Statements" by the Hamilton Writing Center at Hamilton College.

   - Look at several introductions and conclusions from current or historical speeches. See the OverViews website (click on "Speech Samples" link) or the Douglass Archives of American Public Address.

   - For tips on question-and-answer sessions, see the article "How to Handle That Dreaded Question-and-Answer Period," at professional speaker Lenny Laskowski's website.

8

Outlines, Storyboards, and Speaking Notes

Flashback Ancient Roman orators such as Quintilian and Cicero didn't use note cards to aid their memories. Instead, they used a technique that is still taught in memory courses today: they mentally associated each point they wanted to make with a physical item at the speaking location (or in a room familiar to them). For example, the door on the left of the room might represent point one; the chairs at the front, point two; the statue on the right, point three; and the window at the back, point four; and so on. Quintilian's *De Institutione Oratoria* includes specific information on memory (Quintilian [translated by J. S. Watson], 1856).

OW DO YOU REACT WHEN YOU HEAR THE WORD *OUTLINE*? IF YOUR IMMEDIATE REACtion is a negative one, you aren't alone—many people dislike outlining. This dislike is unfortunate, because outlines can be valuable tools. Professional speakers consider making outlines or storyboards an essential step in speech preparation—a step that not only improves their final product, but saves them time. In the Basic Steps for Preparing a Speech, you make outlines and notes in both steps 3 and 8.

Basic Steps for Preparing a Speech

1. Analyze your potential audience. → *See Chapter 4*.
2. Determine topic, exact purpose, and main points. → *See Chapter 5*.
3. Prepare a rough-draft outline of main points and needed information. → *See Chapter 5*.
4. Research topic for material to support main points. → *See Chapter 5*.
5. Select best supporting materials. → *See Chapter 6*.
6. Determine how best to organize main points. → *See Chapter 7*.
7. Plan introduction and conclusion. → *See Chapter 7*.
8. **Make preparation outline (or storyboards) and speaking notes.**
9. Prepare visual aids. → *See Chapter 9*.
10. Rehearse speech. → *See Chapters 10 and 11*.

A variety of speaking aids will be discussed in this chapter: rough-draft outlines, which are used to aid research; preparation outlines and storyboards, which are used to aid planning and organization; and speaking notes, which are used to aid speaking.

Outlining

An outline is especially helpful at three stages of your speech. The first is after topic selection, to help you narrow your main points and research your topic. A rough-draft outline (or a list of points) can save time by pinpointing what research you will need to do.

The second time an outline is needed is after your research is finished. At this point, a preparation outline or several storyboards become tools to fine-tune the organization of your speech. Preparation outlines and storyboards are expanded versions of your rough-draft outline. They are planning tools, not speaking tools. Neither is recommended for use while speaking.

The third time you might use an outline is while rehearsing and presenting your speech. Speaking notes, which are always brief, are made from your preparation outline or storyboards. These notes can be in outline form or whatever brief form works best for you.

Remember

To aid in . . .

- **Research:** Use a rough-draft outline.
- **Planning/organizing:** Use a preparation outline or storyboards.
- **Speaking:** Use speaking notes.

Advantages of Outlining

Many inexperienced speakers fail to use outlines. In fact, if they prepare an outline at all, it's done after the speech is completed and only because the instructor insists. Does this sound like you? If you don't organize your initial thoughts with a brief, rough-draft outline and revise this rough draft into a more detailed preparation outline, you must be writing your speech out word for word. Let's look at the reasons why outlining is better than writing out your speeches.

It's Easier to Detect Problems When you look at a speech written out word for word, can you tell at a glance how the main points are organized? Can you tell which of the main points may have too much supporting material and which ones may not have enough? Can you tell whether a variety of supporting materials has been used? Reading a speech in manuscript form is like trying to do research in a book without a table of contents or section headings in the chapters. Without an overview to show what it contains and how the contents are organized you would have to read every page of the book. With an outline of your speech, you can easily see the big picture and determine what changes are needed.

It's Easier to Solicit Worthwhile Critiques Have you ever handed a speech manuscript to friends or classmates and asked them to look it over and make some suggestions? If so, they probably said, "Looks good to me." It would be an unusual friend who carefully read the entire speech. However, if you hand them an outline, they can read it without too much effort and will likely make some valuable suggestions.

There Is Less Temptation to Memorize When a speech is written out word for word, the tendency to memorize it is great. Inexperienced speakers will often say, "I'll make an outline to speak from later; right now, I'm just practicing with the manuscript until I get familiar with it." The problem is that after you get used to reading your speech (a comfortable crutch), it's difficult to change to a speaking outline. When you speak from an outline, on the other hand, your speech will be slightly different each time you give it—this is positive, not negative. A spontaneous delivery is much more interesting for an audience than a memorized speech. ➤ *Refer to Chapter 10 for some of the problems involved in memorized speaking.*

It Increases Your Flexibility Not knowing how to create and use a speech outline limits your speaking flexibility. For example, what if your boss says, "We have a team coming from our plant in Akron. They'll be here in thirty minutes and I would like you to present . . ." There is no time to write out the speech word for word. All you have time to do is jot down the main points you want to cover, decide on some supporting facts (you may have to make a couple of phone calls to get the most recent data or statistics), and think of an attention-getter to focus the team on your topic. Learning to use an outline adds to your flexibility as a speaker.

The only way you can see the true value of outlining is to use it. It won't be easy if you are used to writing your speeches word for word, but the rewards can be great.

Tips for Creating Outlines

Five simple suggestions will help you create readable and useful outlines.

Tip 1: Use Standard Outline Numbering Since the main parts of a speech—introduction, body, and conclusion—don't need to be preceded by any number or letter, you can use Roman numerals (representing the highest level in an outline) for your main points. Use capital letters for the first-level subpoints or supporting material, and use Arabic numerals for second-level supporting materials. The three levels are these:

    I. First main point
       A. Subpoint or supporting material
          1. Supporting material

Tip 2: Indent for Faster Comprehension When the supporting points are indented under their main point (which is left-aligned), you can see the organization more quickly. Compare three alignments of point II in a speech by Beverley on ADHD (Attention Deficit Hyperactive Disorder):

All points centered

        II. The real trouble begins when the child starts kindergarten.
             A. First conference
               B. Testing
          1. Stanford Binet (IQ test)

2. Attention Deficit Rating Scale
3. Oppositional Defiant Scale
4. Physical exam
C. Recommended treatment
1. Ritalin
2. Clonidine

All points left-aligned

II. The real trouble begins when the child starts kindergarten.
A. First conference
B. Testing
1. Stanford Binet (IQ test)
2. Attention Deficit Rating Scale
3. Oppositional Defiant Scale
4. Physical exam
C. Recommended treatment
1. Ritalin
2. Clonidine

Main points left-aligned with subpoints indented

II. The real trouble begins when the child starts kindergarten.
    A. First conference
    B. Testing
        1. Stanford Binet (IQ test)
        2. Attention Deficit Rating Scale
        3. Oppositional Defiant Scale
        4. Physical exam
    C. Recommended treatment
        1. Ritalin
        2. Clonidine

Tip 3: Include at Least Two Subpoints Per Level In general, each point should have two or more supporting points; that is, if you have an A, you need a B; if you have a 1, you need at least a 2 (for an example, see Figure 8.1). However, don't force an unnatural division just to have two items per level. On rare occasions, you might use a single support.

Tip 4: Make Items in Each Level Parallel If A is a sentence, then B should also be a sentence (for example, see Figure 8.1, A, B, and C). Or the items could be phrases (for example, see Figure 8.1, A1 and A2). Normally, it is best to state your main points in sentence form in your preparation outline (even if the subpoints are in phrases) because sentences contain more information. Notice that Lucy's preparation outline in Figure 8.3 uses complete sentences for all except the third-level supporting information. William's preparation outline in Figure 8.4 uses phrases for everything except main points. ➤ *John's outline in Chapter 7 (page 139) uses key words for everything.*

Figure 8.1

Sample From Lucy's
Preparation Outline
(First Draft)

I. There are several health risk factors.
  A. Two factors are linked to heart disease and cancer.
    1. Improper diet
    2. Lack of exercise
  B. Foods high in saturated fats place us at risk.
  C. Lack of physical exertion places us at risk.
    1. Less than 45 percent of Americans participate in any kind of regular physical activity.
    2. Sedentary people run five times the risk of developing heart disease.
II. Cancer and heart attack warning signs are important to know.

Tip 5: Capitalize the First Word in Each Level When the first word in each level is capitalized, it takes only a glance to know where a new level begins (see Figure 8.1).

Although your rough-draft outline may not follow all these guidelines, you will need to adhere to them carefully when you polish and expand your rough draft into a preparation outline. In addition, check with your instructor to see if there are additional guidelines. With these general tips in mind, let's discuss rough-draft outlines and preparation outlines in more detail.

Rough-Draft Outlines

After you analyze your audience (step 1) and determine your topic and exact purpose (step 2), you are ready to rough out an outline (or list) of main points and possible supporting information. You should prepare this rough-draft outline before beginning your research because it can help you narrow the points you will be discussing and identify the supporting materials you'll need to research. Although you will need to research until you have a complete understanding of your topic, your rough outline can focus your research and save valuable time. ➔ *Refer to Lucy's rough-draft outline in Chapter 5, Figure 5.2. Notice that it does not include an introduction or conclusion but only the information and supporting materials she thought she might want to use in the body of her speech. Not all of it ended up in her speech, and the speech included some information not in her rough-draft outline.*

Once your research is completed, you are ready to turn your rough-draft outline into a more detailed and polished preparation outline (or storyboards, which will be discussed shortly).

Preparation Outlines

Whereas your rough draft contained only main points and supporting information, your **preparation outline** should also include your introduction and conclusion. Figure 8.2a shows a preparation outline format to use in finalizing your speeches. Use the following guidelines to develop your preparation outline:

■ Write the introduction and conclusion in complete sentences, partial sentences, or phrases. Normally these steps are not outlined, but you may outline them if you wish.

■ Outline the body of your speech. Main points are normally written in complete sentences; the subpoints and supporting material may be complete

Figure 8.2a

Use This Outline Format As a Model for Your Own Speeches

Preparation Outline Format

Topic or Title:
Exact Purpose or Position Statement:

	Type of Source
INTRODUCTION • **Attention-getter:** • **Audience motivation:** • **Credibility:** • **Purpose or position statement:** • **Preview:** • **Background** (optional) • **Handout information** (if any)	(personal observation, interview, media, or reference)

BODY
   I. **Main Point (or Claim) 1:**
     A. Subpoint or supporting material
       1. Supporting material
       2. Supporting material
     B. Subpoint or supporting material
 	
   [Transition]
 	
   II. **Main Point (or Claim) 2:**
     A. Supporting material
     B. Supporting material
 	
   [Transition]
 	
   III. **Main Point (or Claim) 3:**
     A. Subpoint or supporting material
     B. Subpoint or supporting material
       1. Supporting material
       2. Supporting material
 	
CONCLUSION
• **Summary:**
• **Refocus:**	

References:
(Books, magazines, newspapers, etc.)

Figure 8.2b

How to Create the Outline Format in Figure 8.2a Using Microsoft Word

1. Go to File/Page Setup and change the right and left margins to 1 inch. Go to View and turn on the Ruler and the Drawing toolbar.
2. Begin by typing your outline title and exact purpose.
3. Click on the Line tool in the Drawing toolbar and draw the following lines:
   • A horizontal line separating the exact purpose from the body of your speech
   • A vertical line downward at approximately the 5-inch mark on the ruler
   • Another horizontal line near the bottom of the page
4. Type your outline on the left side of the vertical line, your sources on the right side of the vertical line, and your complete references below the bottom line.

sentences, phrases, or key words although complete sentences are not recommended. Whichever you choose, make sure the items in each level are parallel.

- Write out transitions between main points in sentence form.
- Include a list of references at the end of the outline.
- In a column down the right side of the outline, list the types of sources you used, including references (books, magazines, newspapers, and so on), personal observations, interviews, and media (radio or television programs). For print sources, include the exact page numbers. (See Figure 8.2b for help in creating the column format.)
- Identify types of supporting materials in brackets: for example, [statistics]. This allows you to tell at a glance whether you are using a variety of supporting materials for each of your main points. → *Review Chapter 6 for the various types of supporting materials.*
- Identify the locations of visual aids in your speech with boldface and brackets: for example, **[Visual #1]**.

Preparation outlines containing the features described above are illustrated in Figures 8.3 and 8.4 (pages 168–171). Figure 8.3 is Lucy's preparation outline for her speech "Our State of Health" (which appeared in Chapter 4). Figure 8.4 is the preparation outline from another student speech titled "Career Choice: Airline Pilot" by William Weiss, a sophomore planning on a career as a pilot. You will be surprised (as both these students were) at how easy it is to expand your rough draft simply by following the preparation outline format in Figure 8.2a. *See practice suggestion 2 on page 181 for practice in making a preparation outline.*

Storyboarding

A **storyboard** is an informal visual and verbal representation of your ideas. When you use storyboards to plan your speech, you make a page of notes with supporting information and sketches for each of your main points.

Advantages of Storyboards

Storyboarding is an effective way to prepare a speech and offers some advantages over the traditional method of outlining. Storyboards have these benefits:

They Can Be Prepared Quickly Storyboards generally can be prepared more quickly than traditional outlines because you don't have to worry as much about structure. There is no standard structure; you can use anything you want—bullets, dashes, numbers—for your lists of supporting points.

They Encourage Simultaneous Verbal and Visual Planning When you are developing a storyboard, you are writing down ideas and sketching possible graphic and text visuals at the same time. With traditional outlining, visuals usually come later. Storyboards are an excellent tool for planning visuals as you develop your speech.

Figure 8.3

Lucy's Preparation Outline

Lucy's Preparation Outline

Title: "Our State of Health" by Lucy Tisdale Setliff
Exact Purpose: After listening to my speech, the audience will be more aware of health risk factors, cancer and heart attack warning signs, and diet and exercise guidelines.

	Type of Source
INTRODUCTION	
• **Attention-getter:** Hippocrates—"Health is the greatest of human blessings." Webster's definition: "Health is the absence of disease." *[Explanation]*	Ref. #6, p. 9
• **Audience motivation:** Surgeon General C. Everett Koop—two main causes of death (cancer and heart disease) are caused by our own habits.	Ref. #5, p. 112
• **Credibility:** Health important after my father's death from heart disease; personal research. *[Family instance]*	Personal
• **Purpose:** To become more aware of our state of health	
• **Preview:** Focus on three aspects of health: [Transparency #1] —major risk factors —cancer and heart attack warning signs —diet and exercise guidelines	
BODY	
I. **There are several major risk factors to health.**	
A. There are four basic risk factors to health. [Transparency #2]	
1. Two of these risk factors (heredity and genetics) remain beyond our control.	
2. Two of these risk factors (diet and exercise) we can control.	
B. Statistics indicate that the health risk from poor diet and lack of exercise is great.	Ref. #5, p. 321

	Type of Source
1. One in four (or 66 million) Americans have some form of heart disease related to a high fat diet and lack of exercise. *[Statistics]*	Ref. #3, p. 3 and Ref. #5, p. 287
2. Cancer kills one out of every five persons, yet experts conclude that 75% of cancer deaths could be avoided through a healthier lifestyle. *[Statistics]*	Ref. #1, p. 3 and Ref. #5, p. 318
3. Physical activity is avoided by 45 percent of Americans even though sedentary people run five times the risk of developing heart disease. *[Expert opinion and statistics]*	Ref. #7, p. 37 and Ref. #5, p. 85
[Transition]: We've identified risk factors; now let's review warning signs that may indicate we have a disease.	
II. **There are specific warning signs for cancer and heart attacks.**	
A. Most people are aware of some of the warning signs for cancer.	
1. Cancer's seven warning signs are: [Transparency #3]	Ref. #1, p. 13
a. Change in bowel or bladder habits	
b. A sore that does not heal	
c. Unusual bleeding or discharge	
d. Thickening or lump in breast or elsewhere	
e. Indigestion or difficulty in swallowing	
f. Obvious change in wart or mole	
g. Nagging cough or hoarseness	
2. According to the National Cancer Institute, "None of these symptoms is a sure sign of cancer, but if any of them lasts longer than two weeks, see a doctor." *[Expert opinion]*	Ref. #1, p. 14
B. Fewer people are aware of the warning signs for heart attack.	

Figure 8.3

Lucy's Preparation Outline *(continued)*

Outline	Type of Source
1. According to the American Heart Association, "Sharp, stabbing twinges usually are not signals of heart attack." *[Expert opinion]*	Ref. #2, p. 1
2. There are three indicators of possible heart attack: **[Transparency #4]**	Ref. #3, p. 3
a. Uncomfortable pressure, fullness, squeezing, or pain in the center of the chest that lasts more than a few minutes	
b. Pain that spreads to the shoulders, neck, or arms	
c. Chest discomfort with lightheadedness, fainting, sweating, nausea, or shortness of breath	
3. My family did not know these symptoms and waited an extra day before taking my father to the hospital.	

[Transition]: So far we have identified major risk factors to health and reviewed cancer and heart attack warning signs. Diet and exercise guidelines are the final focus of our state of health.

III. **Fortunately, diet and exercise guidelines are fairly simple.**

Outline	Type of Source
A. The 1992 Food Pyramid provides healthy diet guidelines. **[Transparency #5]**	
1. Each level of the pyramid includes suggested daily servings. *[Explanation]*	Ref. #4, p. 62
2. The tip of the pyramid (fat) should be our real concern. *[Explanation]*	
a. Fats should be less than 30 percent of our total calorie intake—65 grams for an average woman, 80 grams for an average man. *[Statistics]*	Ref. #5, p. 117
b. Many fast-food items contain too much fat. *[Instances/statistics]*	Ref. #8

Outline	Type of Source
B. The American Heart Association suggests simple exercise guidelines.	Ref. #5, pp. 86 and 103.
1. To control blood pressure, exercise 15 minutes a day, 3 times a week. *[Expert opinion]*	
2. To lose weight, exercise for 1 hour, 3 times a week is required. *[Expert opinion]*	
3. A brisk walk can be as effective as jogging.	

CONCLUSION

- **Summary:** The challenge of living is grasping our opportunities. If we know the risk factors, learn the warning signs, and discover diet and exercise guidelines, we can improve our chances of preventing disease.
- **Refocus:** Our health is what we choose to make it. How we take care of our bodies today will determine if we suffer problems later on. Health begins with awareness. Don't wait until later to get interested in your health. As it was with my father—later may be too late.

References:

1. American Cancer Society. *Cancer Facts and Figures—1990.* Atlanta: American Cancer Society, 1990.
2. American Heart Association. *Fact Sheet on Heart Attack, Stroke and Risk Factors.* Dallas: American Heart Assoc., 1994.
3. American Heart Association. *1990 Heart and Stroke Facts.* Dallas: American Heart Assoc., 1989.
4. Brownlee, Shannon, and Barnett, Robert. "A Loaf of Bread, a Glass of Wine." *U.S. News & World Report* 117 (July 1994), pp. 62–63.
5. Levy, Marvin R., Dignan, Mark, and Shirreffs, Janet H. *Life and Health: Targeting Wellness.* New York: McGraw-Hill, 1993.
6. Richards, Donna Beck. *Here's to Your Health,* 2nd ed. Dubuque, Iowa: Kendall/Hunt, 1992.
7. Smith, Charles, and Jones, Don. *Exercise Just for the Health of It.* Dubuque, Iowa: Kendall/Hunt, 1981.
8. "The Fast Food Survival Guide." *Good Housekeeping* 220 (May 1995), pp. 118 and 120.

Figure 8.4

William's Preparation Outline

Sample Informative Presentation

Title: "Career Choice: Airline Pilot" by William Weiss
Exact Purpose: After listening to my presentation, the audience will know the advantages of choosing the career of airline pilot.

INTRODUCTION

- **Attention-getter:** What do you think when you hear the word airline pilot? According to Wallace R. Maples, author of *Opportunities in Aerospace Careers*, 2002, the career of airline pilot is "perhaps the most exciting and romantic position to which one may aspire today ...."   Ref. #1, p. 9
- **Qualifications:** I am currently aspiring to become an airline pilot even after 9/11 and have researched the topic thoroughly.
- **Audience motivation:** Imagine the thrill of 140,000 lbs. of thrust at your finger tips; traveling at mach .82, and cruising 6 miles above the earth!   *[slide 1]*
- **Thesis:** The career of airline pilot has many advantages:
  --Adventure
  --Travel
  --Salary
  --Time off
  --Job opportunities

BODY

   I. Airline pilots experience adventure   *[slide 2]*
     A. Never stuck in the same office.
     B. Every flight different.
     C. Always a window with a view.   *[slide 3]*

    Transition: If adventure isn't enough, airline pilots also get to see the world.

   II. Airline pilots travel extensively   *[slide 4]*
     A. Opportunity to see the world.
     B. Begin by flying domestic routes, then international.
     C. Travel to interesting and popular destinations.

    Transition: Not only do airline pilots experience adventure and travel, their salary is outstanding also.

They Stimulate Right–Brain Thinking and Creativity   Whereas traditional outlining is basically a left-brain activity (the left hemisphere seems to specialize in step-by-step, analytic processing of information and pays close attention to details), storyboarding takes advantage of right-brain intuition and often inspires creativity. Seeing your ideas in visual form often clarifies your thinking and stimulates new ideas.

They Are Easy to Read and Evaluate   Because a storyboard includes a simplified verbal account of the speech as well as a visual representation, it is easy to identify organizational problems. Exchanging storyboards with a classmate is a good way to get helpful feedback on your planned speech. If you are involved in a team presentation, storyboards are especially effective. Pin or tape all the storyboards to a wall in the order in which they will be presented. Seeing a written list of ideas with sketches of the accompanying visual aids helps the team quickly grasp each member's part of the speech and identify weaknesses in the overall presentation.   → *For information on team speaking, see Team Presentations in Chapter 13.*

They Encourage the Use of Transitions   Speakers soon discover that transitions don't flow easily off the tongue during a speech unless they are consciously planned

Figure 8.4

William's Preparation Outline *(continued)*

III. Airline pilots are very well paid   *[slide 5]*
   A.   Starting salary—$36,000.   Ref. #4
   B.   Average salary—$115,000.   Ref. #4
   C.   Average pilot earns more than the average lawyer.   Ref. #1, pp. 13–14

   Transition: For these salaries you would expect long hours, but airline pilots
   have a relaxed working schedule.

IV. Airline pilots have extensive time off each month   *[slide 6]*
   A.   Maximum hours flown per month—100.   Ref. #1, p. 12
   B.   Maximum hours flown per year—1000.   Ref. #1, p. 12
   C.   Average hours flown per month—75–80.   Ref. #3, p. 17

   Transition: Even after 9/11, jobs are still available.

V. Airline pilots can still find jobs after 9/11.   *[slide 7]*
   A.   In 2000, 20,000 pilots hired.   Ref. #2, p. 53
   B.   In 2003 (after 9/11), 4,743 pilots hired.   Ref. #5, p. 70
   C.   Hiring projections for 2004: 6,000–7,000   Ref. #5, p. 70

CONCLUSION
   Due to adventure, travel, salary, time off, and job opportunities, becoming
• an airline pilot is one of the best professions available today.
   Maybe you or someone you know will join me in pursuing this career.
• See you in the sky!

REFERENCES:

1. Maples, W. R. (2002). *Opportunities in aerospace careers* (Rev. ed.). Chicago:
    McGraw-Hill/VGM Opportunities Series.

2. Pilot hiring for '99 breaks record. (2000, March). *Flying*, 127, 53.

3. Griffin, J. (1990). *Becoming an airline pilot*. New York: TAB Books.

4. Air Inc. (2002–2003). *December 2003 pilot hiring summary*. [Online]. Accessed
    March 26, 2004 at http://jet-jobs.com/pres%20releases.01.12.04.html.

5. Fowler, R. (2003). Career update: The field of aviation is slowly recovering
    from 9/11 with new jobs emerging. *Plane & Pilot Magazine*, June, 70.

and practiced. Storyboards have a special section at the bottom for transition sentences, allowing your arguments to flow smoothly from one point to another.

Guidelines for Storyboards

Storyboards, like preparation outlines, are planning tools that grow out of your rough-draft outline. Figure 8.5 shows a storyboard format to use in finalizing your informative speech (Holcomb & Stein, 1996). Follow these guidelines for effective storyboards:

■ Create separate storyboards for the introduction and conclusion, and usually for each main point in the body of the speech. Keep everything as brief as possible. You can use key words, phrases, sentences, or a combination of all three.

■ Include a transition sentence at the bottom of each storyboard that leads to the next point.

■ Sketch text and graphic visuals on the right side the storyboards. Once you are satisfied with your visuals, you can turn them into polished slides,

Figure 8.5

Suggested Storyboard
Format

Storyboard Format

Topic or Title:
Exact Purpose or Position Statement:

Step or Main Point:

Supporting Statements or Arguments:	Type of Source	Data, Charts, Tables, etc.

Transition Sentence:

References:

---

transparencies, or flipcharts. ➤ *See Chapter 9 for more about preparing visual aids.*

■ Make a list of supporting points for each main point. Again, you can use key words, phrases, sentences, or a combination of all three.

Figure 8.6 shows a sample storyboard for Christina's speech on "Outdoor Oklahoma." Think about which format you like best—a preparation outline or storyboards.

Speaking Notes

Once you have read through your preparation outline or your storyboards several times and feel comfortable with the main points and supporting materials, you are ready to prepare your **speaking notes**—brief key words or phrases written on note cards or paper.

Figure 8.6

**Sample Storyboard
From Christina's
Speech**

Storyboard 1
Title: "Outdoor Oklahoma"
Exact Purpose: After listening to my speech, the audience
will realize that Oklahoma has a lot to offer in the way of
outdoor recreation.

Step or Main Point: Introduction

Supporting Statements:
- Ellenbrook "The trail is a   Ref.#1
  beginning—a first step on the   p. 103
  way to self-discovery. A sought-
  for exhilarating experience is
  self-discovery of one's senses, Personal
  instincts, and the use of only
  your own mind and body to co-
  exist with nature."
- I am a native Oklahoman and
  have spent 2/3 of my life there.
- Escape concrete jungle
- Nature lover's dream spots
  – Quartz Mtn. State Park
  – Lake Tenkiller
  – Talimena Drive
  – Arbuckle Wilderness

Outdoor Oklahoma

Recreational
facilities

32 state pks
100 natural lakes
200 artif. creat.
  lakes
28 St. Rec. areas
48 Wildlife mgmt
  areas

Transition Sentence: I will speak about one of each
of the facilities listed here.

References: Ellenbrook, Edward Charles.
Outdoor + Trail Guide to the Wichita Mountains.
Lawton, OK: The Valley of the Wichitas House, 1988.

Don't be tempted to speak from your preparation outline or storyboards. Beginning speakers often want to use a manuscript with complete sentences while speaking because they think it will make them feel more secure. *Experienced speakers will tell you that complete sentences usually are no help while speaking.* Your eyes can't grasp more than three or four words at a time. As a result, speakers whose notes are written in complete sentences (or even long phrases) usually either (1) end up reading the notes word for word, which means they can't make eye contact with the audience and have a stilted speaking voice, or (2) they forget the notes and try to "wing it" and leave out much of the interesting detail they intended to include.

Effective *speaking notes* are brief, include key words or phrases, use color and underlining so that important words will stand out, and include notes (such as *pause* and *louder*) in the margins. Your speaking notes may be in outline form if you wish, but it's not necessary. Many speakers prefer to use note cards (one 4-by-6-inch card is usually enough) because they are easy to hold and easy to see, especially when reading a quotation. Some speakers prefer a single 8½-by-11-inch sheet of paper so they can see the entire speech at one time (see Lucy's notes in Figure 8.7). However, using a sheet of paper for your notes has disadvantages. If you place your notes on a lectern, chances are the lectern will not be tall enough for easy reading. If you decide to hold your notes, a sheet of paper is large enough to be distracting and it may shake, making you look nervous. If you use transparencies, you can jot notes on the cardboard frames and won't need to use cards or other types of notes. In fact, after

Technology Tip for Speakers

Don't Fall Into the Plagiarism Trap: Write Your Own Speeches

The Internet can be a wonderful place to find valuable help and information for your speeches. For example, a brief search of speech writing using the search engine Ixquick found over 4 million hits; Google returned over 7.5 million hits! The first hits included:

- Websites that give advice on finding topics, making speeches, finding quotes, or overcoming anxiety.

- Websites (such as Great American Speeches and the History Channel) that include text, audio, or video of speeches by famous people.

You can access links to some of these sites under the Student Resources for Chapter 8 at the Essentials of Public Speaking website.

Unfortunately, the hits also included many websites willing to sell both canned and custom speeches for the classroom (as well as for weddings, birthdays, graduations, campaigns, after dinner, and business meetings). As a result, and as your professor knows, beginning speakers are often tempted to go online and buy their speeches from a site. Unless you plan to purchase a speech as a model only (this text and its website contain many sample speeches to give you ideas), you are on dangerous ethical ground—plagiarism is a serious offense. If your professor has a doubt about your speech, there are several online sites he or she can use to check your work for plagiarism. For example, Turnitin .com reports plagiarism from both print and Internet sources.

Therefore, if you are tempted to buy your speeches from online speech writers (or even fraternity/sorority files or friends), don't! You already know the reasons:

- It's unethical to pass off someone else's work as your own.

- The consequences of plagiarism can be severe (as discussed in Chapter 1) and may haunt you later in life as well.

- You won't learn the necessary skills for successful speech preparation— although the chances are better than 90 percent that you will need these skills in the future. In fact, your educational and business success may depend on your knowledge of these skills.

- Delivering a speech you didn't write is very difficult—especially if you are already nervous. Your professor is no fool! In fact, your professor has already heard many of these speeches and will recognize them for what they are.

- You will be wasting money and taking a great risk—when the skills necessary to write your own quality speeches are in your text, in your professor's lectures, and in your own mind and experience.

The most useful speaking notes are brief and include key words or phrases rather than sentences.

© David Young-Wolff/PhotoEdit

you rehearse your speech a few times with computer visuals or transparencies, you will probably discover that you really don't need any notes at all.

Another type of speaker notes is a **mind map**—a visual aid for the mind (Buzan, 1991; Buzan & Buzan, 1996). We've talked about how audience recall is greatly improved with effective visual aids. A speaker's memory can be improved with visual aids as well. Psychologist Peter Russell (1979) describes it this way:

> To make a mind map, one starts in the center of the paper, with the major idea, and works outward in all directions, producing a growing and organized structure composed of key words and key images.

Russell also recommends using color, printed lowercase letters (all caps should be used sparingly), three-dimensional shapes, and arrows to make the maps more visual. In other words, you can turn your speaking notes into a visual map designed to stimulate recall of the main points and supporting information. Figure 8.8 shows a mind map that Lucy could have used as her speaking notes.

If you decide to use speaking notes—regardless of the type—keep them brief and practice until you can use them comfortably or have no need for them.

Figure 8.7

Lucy's One-Page
Speaking Notes

"Our State of Health"

Introduction Hippocrates—*"Greatest of human blessings"*
Def—*"absence of disease"*
Example of father/Surgeon General C. Everett Koop
Look at 3 aspects: **Risk factors**
                             Warning signs (trans. #1)
                             Guidelines

Body

I.   **Risk factors** (trans. #2)
    A. 4 risk factors
    B. Statistics indicate high risk
        • 1 in 4 (heart disease) = 99 million
        • 1 in 5 (cancer); 75% deaths avoidable
        • 45% Americans = no exercise; 5 times risk
  [Transition]

II. **Warning signs**
(trans. #3)   A. *Cancer's* 7 warning signs [2 weeks = see Dr.]
    B. *Heart attack* warning signs [sharp twinge *not* sign]
(trans. #4)   • Family did not know signs
  [Transition]

III. **Guidelines**
    A. Diet — Food Pyramid [fat = 30% total / w = 60g; m = 80g]
(trans. #5)   — Fast food: Dbl Whopper w C = 63g /
                      C Burger = 60g / 1/4 lb w C = 29g
                      Fish supreme = 32g / BK fish = 43g
                      BK Broiler = 29g / McChicken = 29g
    B. Exercise — 15 min, 3 times a week = healthy
                 1 hour, 3 times a week = weight loss

Conclusion

The challenge of living . . . (Q & A) *"questions?"*
**Don't wait to get interested in health. As with my father,
later may be too late!**

Figure 8.8

Lucy's Speaking Notes
in Mind-Map Form

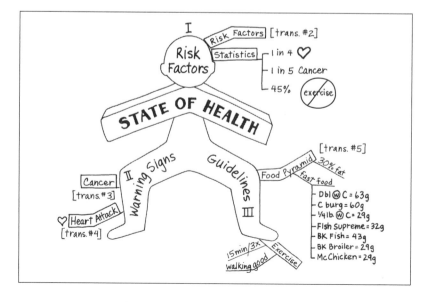

Sample Student Speech: "The Electoral College" by Robert McDermott

The following informative speech, "The Electoral College," by Robert McDermott, concludes this chapter and this unit on speech preparation. Robert's speech was updated to reflect the 2000 presidential election, which occurred after his original speech was given. The speech was transcribed from the videotape. Robert's assignment specified a 4- to 6-minute informational speech. As you read his speech, think about changes you might make if you were speaking on the same topic. Pay particular attention to Robert's visual aids. He created and designed all of his visuals from scratch except for the final one, a map of the United States showing a candidate's view of the importance of each state. Although two of Robert's visuals contain more than six lines of text, he felt that the topic justified the text-heavy visuals. To watch and analyze a video clip of Robert's original speech, look under Student Resources for Chapter 8 at the Essentials of Public Speaking website.
→ *Chapter 9 discusses the "no more than six lines of type" guideline.*

SAMPLE SPEECH

THE ELECTORAL COLLEGE

by Robert McDermott

IMAGINE, IF YOU WILL, that we are coming up on a presidential election. To make things simpler, let's pretend that each state has 100 voters, plus Washington D.C. That's another 100 voters, so a total across the United States would be 5100 votes. When you go to the polls on Tuesday morning, you vote for the candidate of your choice. Well, you are really interested in the election, so Wednesday morning you pick up the paper because you'd like to see who won this election. When you open it up, **[Visual #1]** the headline reads, "Candidate A received 561 popular votes and Candidate B received 4539 popular votes." Well, you would think to yourself that Candidate B won this election by a large margin, but actually in this scenario Candidate A won the presidential election. And he won it because of an entity in the Constitution called the Electoral College.

Visual #1

Presidential Election in 2000
Final results

Candidate "A"   561 Popular Votes

Candidate "B"   4539 Popular Votes

(continued)

SAMPLE SPEECH (continued)

Since I began studying the Constitution, I have found out that not many people know about the Electoral College. Less than 10 percent can actually tell you how it works. **[Visual #2]** When you ask people about the Electoral College, they give answers like, "Isn't it that college in New Hampshire?" or "How's its football team?" or "Where is it?" Actually, it's not an institution of higher learning. It's the way that our government votes and elects the president of the United States.

Visual #2

Today we are going to look at three aspects of the Electoral College: First, we are going to look at where the Electoral College came from; second, what is it; and third, how does this thing work.

First of all, where did it come from? In 1787 during our Constitutional Convention our forefathers weren't really sure how to elect a president of the United States. A lot of them really didn't trust the public; they felt that they weren't educated enough to elect the president of the United States. So they wanted Congress to vote for him. But the other half thought that, no, the people really need to vote for our president. But they didn't have the transportation or the technology available to gather all the votes across the country and take them to the nation's capital without people tampering with the ballot boxes. So they came up with an indirect way of electing the president that's called the Electoral College.

Now that you know where the Electoral College came from, what is it exactly? The Electoral College by definition is a system of electing the president by a set number of electoral votes. Each state has electors equal to the number of members it has in Congress **[Visual #3].** There are 535 total people in Congress—100 senators and 435 members in the House of Representatives. Each state automatically has two senators and at least one member in the House of Representatives. The rest of the members in the House of Representatives are based on the state's population. And these same numbers in Congress equal the number of electoral votes they each have. As you can see, a state like California has 54 electoral votes because they have 52 members in the House of Representatives and 2 senators,

Visual #3

Electoral Votes Per State

State	# Of Votes	State	# Of Votes
California	54	Colorado	8
New York	33	Arizona	8
Texas	32	Connecticut	8
Florida	25	Iowa	7
Pennsylvania	23	Mississippi	7
Illinois	22	Oregon	7
Ohio	21	Arkansas	6
Michigan	18	Kansas	6
New Jersey	15	Nebraska	5
North Carolina	14	West Virginia	5
Virginia	13	New Mexico	5
Georgia	13	Utah	5
Indiana	12	Maine	4
Massachusetts	12	New Hampshire	4
Wisconsin	11	Idaho	4
Missouri	11	Hawaii	4
Tennessee	11	Nevada	4
Washington	11	Rhode Island	4
Minnesota	10	Vermont	3
Maryland	10	North Dakota	3
Alabama	9	South Dakota	3
Louisiana	9	Delaware	3
Oklahoma	8	Montana	3
Kentucky	8	Wyoming	3
South Carolina	8	Alaska	3
		Washington D.C.	3

Total Votes.............................538
Total Votes Needed To Win...270

SAMPLE SPEECH

where a state like Montana only has 3 electoral votes. Washington, D.C., which has no senators or voting representatives, is still represented in the Electoral College; it has 3 electoral votes.

Our last topic to discuss is really the most interesting to me—how does it work? Well, when you go to the polls to vote for a president, you are not exactly voting for that candidate. You are voting for an elector that you hope votes for that candidate. That sounds—you know it's kind of confusing, so let's take a quick example. New York, for instance, has 33 electoral votes because they have, again, 31 members in the House of Representatives and 2 members in the Senate. Well, let's say I'm running against Candidate C. OK. And once again there are 100 voters in the state of New York. I receive 51 of the votes and Candidate C receives 49 of the votes. Well, even though I won this election by two votes only, I still receive all 33 electoral votes that New York has. You see, the Electoral College is a winner-take-all system. Whoever wins by whatever margin, they receive all that state's electoral votes. Why is this important? Well, all a candidate has to do is concentrate on the largest states, because those are the ones that contain most of the electoral votes. So, all a candidate has to do is win a majority of the Electoral College. There are 538 electoral votes, so that means all a candidate has to do is win 270 of the votes to win the election.

Let's go back and look at the results we looked at at the beginning of the speech and see how this actually came about **[Visual #4]**. As you can see, Candidate A concentrated on the top 11 most populated states. Even though he only won each one of those states by 2 votes, he still received all the electoral votes from those states. And the bottom states, they just hated him because all he did was concentrate on the large states—and they didn't even give him one vote. He lost every one of those states 100 to zero. So he came up with 561 popular votes compared to 4539 for Candidate B, but the electoral vote is what counts and he received 270 compared to Candidate B's 268. Thus the winner of the presidential election in the year 2000 is Candidate A.

You might ask yourself, well, has this ever happened? Actually, it's happened three times in the history of the United States. It happened in 1876 when Rutherford Hayes lost the popular vote but he won the electoral vote. He lost the popular vote by about 250,000 votes. Now that may not seem like a lot today when you have over 100 million voters, but that would be like 2 or 3 million votes nowadays. And it also happened in 1888 with Benjamin Harrison. He lost (the popular vote) by about a thousand or two thousand votes, but he still won the Electoral College. More recently, it happened in the Bush/Gore election in 2000. Because the popular vote was so close in Florida and questions about the punch-card balloting machines in Leon County

Visual #4

Hypothetical Election in 2000

State	A	B	State	A	B
California	51	49	Colorado	0	100
New York	51	49	Arizona	0	100
Texas	51	49	Connecticut	0	100
Florida	51	49	Iowa	0	100
Pennsylvania	51	49	Mississippi	0	100
Illinois	51	49	Oregon	0	100
Ohio	51	49	Arkansas	0	100
Michigan	51	49	Kansas	0	100
New Jersey	51	49	Nebraska	0	100
North Carolina	51	49	West Virginia	0	100
Virginia	51	49	New Mexico	0	100
Georgia	0	100	Utah	0	100
Indiana	0	100	Maine	0	100
Massachusetts	0	100	New Hampshire	0	100
Wisconsin	0	100	Idaho	0	100
Missouri	0	100	Hawaii	0	100
Tennessee	0	100	Nevada	0	100
Washington	0	100	Rhode Island	0	100
Minnesota	0	100	Vermont	0	100
Maryland	0	100	North Dakota	0	100
Alabama	0	100	South Dakota	0	100
Louisiana	0	100	Delaware	0	100
Oklahoma	0	100	Montana	0	100
Kentucky	0	100	Wyoming	0	100
South Carolina	0	100	Alaska	0	100
			Washington D.C.	0	100

Total:

Popular Votes		Electoral Votes	
"A"	561	"A"	270
"B"	4539	"B"	268

Winner Is Candidate "A"

(continued)

existed, and lawsuits were filed by both sides, a hand count of certain ballots was ordered by the Supreme Court of Florida. Out of approximately 6 million votes, the difference between them was only 537 votes in favor of Bush. More lawsuits were filed demanding that additional hand counts be made. At this point, the U.S. Supreme Court ruled that all counting would cease and that Florida's 25 electoral votes would go to Bush. As a result, Bush became the 43rd President of the United States winning by 5 electoral votes; Gore won the popular vote by approximately 530,000 votes.

Visual #5

Candidate View of U.S.

Well, you can see when a candidate embarks on a presidential election, **[Visual #5]** he (or she) doesn't view the United States the same way as you and I do. Presidential candidates view the United States with a distorted view because they have to concentrate on the states that have more electoral votes if they want to win the presidency of the United States. They see states such as New York and California and Texas and Ohio as bigger than all these smaller states like Montana and Wyoming, North Dakota and South Dakota. That's why during a presidential election, on the newscasts you will never see candidates appearing in Wyoming or any place like that because they don't need any of those states to win the presidency.

Summary

Outlines are beneficial at three stages of preparing a speech. In step 3 of the Basic Steps for Preparing a Speech, you prepare a rough-draft outline (or list) to aid you in researching your topic. The rough-draft outline helps you narrow your main points and determine areas needing research. Since it is "rough," the format does not need to be perfect.

A preparation outline or storyboards are aids in planning and organizing your speech (step 8 of the Basic Steps for Preparing a Speech). The preparation outline is a polished and expanded version of the rough-draft outline and follows these guidelines: (1) use standard outline numbering, (2) indent the levels for faster comprehension, (3) include at least two points per level, (4) make points parallel, and (5) capitalize the first word of each point. Storyboards are less structured than traditional outlines. The introduction, conclusion, and each main point usually have their own separate storyboards with a list of supporting points, sketches of visual aids, and a transition to the next point. Storyboards can be prepared quickly, encourage simultaneous verbal and visual planning, stimulate right-brain thinking and creativity, are easy for others to read and evaluate, and encourage use of transitions.

Speaking notes aid you while rehearsing and presenting your speech and are also prepared in step 8 of the Basic Steps for Preparing a Speech. As long as they are brief, speaking notes can be free style, outlines, or mind maps. Some speakers use one or two note cards; some prefer a single sheet of paper; and others make notes on transparencies. After rehearsing a few times with transparencies or electronic slides, many speakers find they don't need notes at all.

Essentials of Public Speaking www *Online*

Use the Essentials of Public Speaking website at **http://communication. wadsworth.com/hamiltoneps3** for quick access to the electronic study resources that accompany this chapter. When you get to the Essentials home page, click on "Student Book Companion Site" in the Resource box. The Essentials website features a video clip of Robert McDermott's speech "The Electoral College" (pages 177–180), the web links featured in the Technology Tip for Speakers box on page 174, InfoTrac College Edition, the Suggestions for Practice and Critical Thinking activities and the InfoTrac College Edition activities that follow, a digital glossary, and review quizzes.

Key Terms

mind map 175   speaking notes 172
preparation outline 165   storyboard 167

Suggestions for Practice and Critical Thinking

1. Using InfoTrac College Edition, identify at least five businesses or professions that use storyboards. Use the wildcard (*storyboard*★) to find all forms of the word, including *storyboard, storyboarding,* and *storyboards.* Read several articles. Compare the uses of storyboards contained in these articles with the advice given in this chapter.

2. Reread the speech on the Electoral College by Robert McDermott. What organizational pattern (topical, chronological, spatial, or causal) does Robert use to structure his main points? Make a preparation outline of his speech and compare with other classmates. If you had been giving this speech, what would you have done differently? Why? Share your opinions with a classmate.

3. Use the evaluation form from Chapter 12 (Figure 12.7) to evaluate Robert's speech. How did you rate Robert's speech? How does your rating compare with those of your classmates?

4. Check your understanding of outlining by organizing a scrambled outline prepared by a classmate or your instructor. Or fix the scrambled outline located under Student Resources for Chapter 8 at the Essentials of Public Speaking website.

5. Check out the following websites. *You can access these sites under the Student Resources for Chapter 8* at the Essentials of Public Speaking website.

   • For guidelines on how to develop an outline, check out Purdue University's Online Writing Lab.

   • Go to Boeing's website of speeches given by company representatives. (From the company's home page, click on the "News" link, then on "News Home," then the "Speeches" link.) Select one of the recent speeches given by a Boeing official and see if you can put it into outline form.

   • Take a look at what Stephen Eggleston has to say about storyboards in his "The Key Steps to an Effective Presentation." Scroll down to number 6 (Prepare a Storyboard).

   • As you decide what type of notes or whether to use notes, read Robert Gwynne's advice. Access his home page, click on "Class Stuff," and then on "Reading or Memorizing a Speech."

   • Discover more about the ancient Roman memory technique described in the Flashback on page 161. See "The Roman Room Mnemonic" at MindTools.com.

   • "Concept mapping," as described on the University of Victoria website, is similar to mind mapping. Check out this site to see if concept mapping might be useful to you as you prepare your speech outline.

unit three

Presenting Your Speech

What do you know about verbal, visual, and vocal delivery?

Some of the following statements about presenting a speech are true; others are common misconceptions that research has proven false.

Directions: If you think the statement is generally accurate, mark it T; if you think the statement is a misconception, mark it F. Then compare your answers with those at the end of Chapter 9. You can also take this quiz online at the Essentials of Public Speaking website under Student Resources for Chapter 9 and, if requested, e-mail your responses to your instructor.

_____ 1. The main reason for using visual aids is to entertain your audience.

_____ 2. If you can use words to create mental pictures in the minds of your listeners, it isn't necessary to use visual aids.

_____ 3. An audience typically waits until after you have completed the introduction to decide whether your speech will be interesting enough to listen to.

_____ 4. When you are speaking, you should either look just over your listeners' heads or find one or two people who seem interested and talk to them.

_____ 5. Using a markerboard or chalkboard as a visual aid is good because you already know how to use it—practice is seldom necessary.

_____ 6. To make your visual aids more interesting, use several colors and several typefaces.

_____ 7. You should avoid using sexist language because some of your audience members may be turned off by it and not listen to your message.

_____ 8. If practicing your speech out loud is embarrassing or inconvenient, going over it mentally will be just as good.

_____ 9. In order to make the text easy to read, you should use all capital letters on your visuals.

_____ 10. If you have a good memory, it is better to memorize your speech than to take a chance on forgetting part of it.

chapter 9

Preparing Effective Visual Aids

*Flash*back Although ancient orators weren't aware of our current research on picture memory, they did know the importance of vividness. They knew that audiences were more likely to pay attention to and be persuaded by visual images painted by the speaker. In his *Rhetoric* (Book III, Chapters 10–11), Aristotle describes the importance of words and graphic metaphors that should "set the scene before our eyes." He defines *graphic* as "making your hearers see things" (Aristotle [translated by W. R. Roberts], 1971, pp. 663–664).

ONE OF THE EASIEST WAYS YOU CAN HELP ENSURE THE SUCCESS OF A SPEECH IS TO PREPARE interesting and powerful visual aids. Unfortunately, many speakers (including instructors) either don't use visual aids or use ones that are overcrowded and difficult to read. Poorly designed visual aids force audience members to choose between listening to the speaker or reading the visual aid. When listeners must spend much longer than 6 seconds to grasp the content, they are likely to slip into a reading mode and hear almost nothing the speaker says (Scoville, 1988). Preparing effective visual aids is step 9 of the Basic Steps for Preparing a Speech. (See Figure 9.1 for the basic steps presented in visual-aid form.)

Figure **9.1**

The Basic Steps for Preparing a Speech as Shown on Two Computer Slides

Speech Preparation Steps

1. Audience analysis.
2. Select topic, purpose & main points.
3. Prepare rough draft.
4. Research topic.
5. Select best supports.

Speech Preparation Steps (cont.)

6. Organize main points.
7. Plan introduction & conclusion.
8. Make outline & speaking notes.
9. **Prepare visual aids.**
10. Rehearse speech.

Benefits of Using Visual Aids

We have all heard of great speakers who were riveting without the help of visuals. Winston Churchill and Martin Luther King, Jr. come to mind. These speakers created pictures in the minds of their audiences through vivid words, narratives, analogies, and other supporting materials. Such techniques are very important, but they don't replace visual aids, especially in speeches containing complex, technical information. You may be one of those rare people who can hold an audience spellbound without visual aids, but why take the chance? Speakers who know the power of visual aids are usually reluctant to give presentations without them. Let's examine the many ways in which properly designed visual aids can enhance your presentation.

Visual Aids Speed Comprehension and Add Interest

The saying "A picture is worth a thousand words" is usually true. A single visual aid may save you many words and, therefore, time. A look at right brain/left brain theory explains why visuals speed listener comprehension. While the left hemisphere of the brain specializes in analytical processing, the right hemisphere specializes in simultaneous processing of information and pays little attention to details (Bryden & Ley, 1983; Russell, 1979). Speakers who use no visual aids or only charts loaded with statistics are asking the listeners' left brains to do all the work. After a while, even a good left-brain thinker suffers from information overload, begins to make mistakes in reasoning, and loses interest. In computer terminology, "the system shuts down." The right brain, however, can quickly grasp complex ideas presented in graphic form (Thompson & Paivio, 1994).

  To illustrate this point, let's look at two different versions of the same data. First, look at the statistical data on advertising expenditures in Table 9.1. In 6 seconds, can you tell which advertising expenditure is now the number one businesses expenditure?

Table 9.1

	Advertising Expenditures in Millions (106,725 represents $106,725,000,000)		
Statistical Data in Table Form Can Often Be Difficult to Grasp			
Medium	**1990**	**1998**	**2002**
Broadcast TV	$26,616	$39,173	$41,830
Direct mail	23,370	39,620	45,860
Magazines	6,806	10,518	10,990
Newspapers	32,281	44,292	44,380
Radio	8,726	15,073	18,940
Yellow pages	8,926	11,990	13,720
Total	**106,725**	**160,666**	**175,720**

SOURCE: U.S. Bureau of the Census, 2003. Statistical Abstract of the United States, Washington, D.C.: GPO, p. 794.

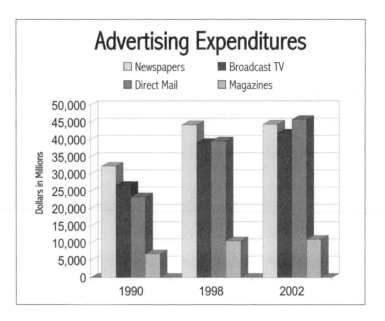

Figure 9.2

Statistical Data in Graph Form on Advertising Expenditures (Much Easier to Grasp)

SOURCE: U.S. Bureau of the Census, 2003. *Statistical Abstract of the United States*, Washington, D.C.: GPO, p. 794.

Probably not. In fact, some people simply give up when they see a statistical table. Now look at the data presented in the form of a graph in Figure 9.2. At a glance, you can tell that although direct mail was the second lowest expenditure in 1990, by 2002 it had moved to the highest expenditure. Therefore, when you need to include complicated data in a speech, comprehension will be quicker and more complete if you present the data in visual form.

Visual Aids Improve Audience Memory

Ralph Nichols, the father of research on listening, maintains that a few days after a verbal presentation, listeners have forgotten most of what they heard. He theorized that good listeners might remember no more than 25 percent—and probably much less (Wolff, Marsnik, Tracey, & Nichols, 1983). In fact, as shown in Figure 9.3, "less" is a more accurate assessment of listener recall—10 percent recall is all you can expect from listeners when no visual aids are used (Zayas-Baya, 1977–1978). But recall improves dramatically when speakers use high-quality visual aids. Research by the University of Minnesota and 3M Corporation found that speeches using visual aids (especially in color) improved immediate recall 8.5 percent and delayed recall (after 3 days) 10.1 percent (Vogel, Dickson, & Lehman, 1986, 1990). Summarizing research in instructional media, E. P. Zayas-Baya presents statistics showing that when verbal and visual information are presented together, they are more effective than either verbal or visual information alone (see Figure 9.3). In a more recent study, C. Hamilton (1999) found that audience recall of an informative presentation was 18 percent better when visual aids were used than when they were not. High-quality color visuals produced the greatest increase in recall (19.5 percent), and poor-quality color visuals produced the least (13 percent). There was little recall difference between high-quality and low-quality black-and-white visuals, although both improved recall more than the poor-quality color visuals did. The message of all the studies is the same: *Presenters should consider visual aids as absolute necessities!*

To understand why visual aids cause such an improvement in listener recall, let's look at the research on memory. As indicated by the statistics in Figure 9.3, *visual images are easier to remember than either spoken or printed words* (Perecman, 1983, p. 222; see

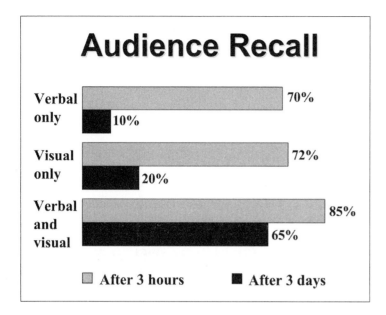

Figure 9.3
Audience Recall Rates
Are Greater When
Speakers Use Visual
Aids

also Katz & Paivio, 1975). In one of the first studies of the power of picture memory, subjects were shown 2,560 slides—one slide every 10 seconds for a total of 7 hours over several days. One hour after the last slide was shown, the subjects were shown 280 pairs of slides, with each pair containing one picture they had seen and one they had not (although it was similar to one they had seen). Subjects were able to pick out the previously viewed picture 85 to 95 percent of the time. Even when they viewed the pictures for only 1 second, and with some of the pictures reversed so the left-hand side became the right-hand side, recognition rates were the same. The researcher concluded that "these experiments with pictorial stimuli suggest that recognition of pictures is essentially perfect. The results would probably have been the same if we had used 25,000 pictures instead of 2,500" (Haber, 1970, p. 105).

Recall is especially good when vivid pictures are used. This may be because vivid pictures, like vivid mental images, are coded in both hemispheres, making them easier to store and retrieve (Perecman, 1983, p. 122). A Canadian researcher showed subjects 10,000 pictures, some of which were "vivid" and others were "normal." The vivid pictures contained especially interesting subject matter. For example, a picture of a dog would be a normal picture, but a picture of a dog with a pipe in its mouth would be a vivid picture. This study found that subjects were able to correctly identify 99.6 percent of the vivid pictures as ones they had already seen (Nickerson, 1980).

Not only is our recognition of pictures almost perfect, but it is also long-lasting. In one study (Babrick, Babrick, & Wittlinger, 1975), subjects were shown yearbook pictures of their former high school classmates. Each picture was grouped with three pictures of nonclassmates. Even up to 35 years after high school graduation, recognition rates were more than 90 percent accurate.

Researchers have also discovered that vivid (concrete) words—especially ones that stimulate mental images in listeners' minds—are also easier to remember (Bryden & Ley, 1983; Hishitani, 1991). Therefore, we should describe pictures and graphics when using them. For example, words like *friend, snake,* and *corpse* are high-imagery words and are easier to remember than words like *devotion, greed,* and *cost,* which are low-imagery (abstract) words. Adding some vivid adjectives to the concrete words will enhance the imagery even further (for example, a *long, slimy snake*).

In summary, research on memory has given us three clues for making memorable visual aids:

- Use graphics such as maps, charts, and graphs to present complex data.

- Use vivid, image-creating words.

- Include a picture or piece of clip art to illustrate (anchor) important ideas (Alesandrini, 1982).

Visual Aids Decrease Presentation Time

One of the biggest complaints heard in most organizations is, "I can't get anything done because I spend so much of my time in meetings." One researcher estimates that the average supervisor spends as much as 40 percent of the workweek in meetings and conferences (Tortoriello, Blatt, & DeWine, 1978). Because people can comprehend information faster and more completely when visual aids accompany the verbal explanation, meetings take less time if visuals are used, even if they are nothing more than a list of options to be considered. A study by the University of Minnesota and the 3M Corporation, mentioned previously, found that the use of visuals could reduce the length of the average business meeting by 28 percent (Vogel et al., 1990).

Visual Aids Add to Speaker Credibility

If you are in a situation in which you have fairly low credibility, visuals can be important. One study found that low-credibility speakers who use visual aids can overcome an audience's view of them as untrustworthy and nonauthoritative, and can elicit the same level of audience retention as high-credibility speakers (Seiler, 1971). The study conducted by the University of Minnesota and the 3M Corporation also found that an "average" presenter who uses visuals can be as effective as an "expert" presenter who uses no visuals (Vogel et al., 1990). The minute the audience sees the first visual aid they will be surprised; by the second visual aid, they likely will decide that the speaker is obviously prepared and will settle back to enjoy the speech.

Types of Visual Aids

Before discussing how to design an effective visual aid, let's take a brief look at the types of visual aids you might use. Although the options for visual aids are limited only by your imagination and the speaking situation, the following types are used most often: overhead transparencies; slides; flipcharts and posters; objects, models, and handouts; markerboards and chalkboards; and projected computer visuals. Each type has advantages and disadvantages. Whatever kinds of visuals you use, make sure that the audience can see them. Here is a handy way to check: Letters on a screen should be approximately 1 inch high for each 10 feet of viewing distance, and screens should be 1⅔ feet high for each 10 feet of distance (Kaufmann, 1987).

Electronic/Multimedia Presentations

In many professions, computer-generated presentations are now the most popular visual aids (even more popular than transparencies). Affordable computer hardware and software make it possible to produce sophisticated electronic and multimedia shows

with color, graphics, animation, sound, and video clips. One of the most popular software programs is Microsoft's PowerPoint. Many of the visuals in this text, such as those in Chapter 7 and the student visuals in the color insert in this chapter, were produced with PowerPoint. → *If you aren't familiar with PowerPoint, see the PowerPoint Speaker's Guide under Student Resources for Chapter 9 at the Hamilton Essentials of Public Speaking website.*

When using computer-generated visuals (Hamilton, 2005):

- *Remember that the main point of using visuals is to aid listener understanding.* Using too many slides, too much text, too many colors, typefaces, or sounds only distracts from your message. Everything must work together to *simplify meaning* and *direct audience attention.* → *See the design rules and general design principles for slide preparation on pp. 197–202. Also, problems with electronic presentations are discussed in Chapter 13's Technology Tip for Speakers, "Make PowerPoint Your Ally, Not Your Enemy."*

- *Make sure that the audience can see you when the lights are turned off.* If possible, select a room with appropriate lighting over the speaker's stand. If the listeners are likely to make notes, a room with soft lights on a dimmer switch can light both the audience and the speaker.

- *Make sure the visuals can be seen by all.* For a small group (probably not more than eight), your computer visuals can be viewed directly on the computer screen. For larger groups, you will need to project the images onto a larger screen using a portable LCD flat-panel (which sits on top of a regular overhead projector) or an all-contained video or data projector.

- *Try using a cordless mouse or remote* such as Logitech's TrackMan Live so you can advance slides from anywhere in the room.

- *Look at your computer screen and your audience* instead of turning away from the audience to look at the projection screen behind you.

- *Come prepared with a backup plan in case of equipment failure.* Having a copy of your PowerPoint slides to use as notes, three or four transparencies of the most important slides, and a second copy of your disk or CD is always a good idea.

Using InfoTrac College Edition, run a keyword search using *multimedia presentations.* Read several articles looking for valuable advice to use for your own presentations. Share what you find with a classmate.

Overhead Transparencies

A transparency is a piece of transparent acetate with text and/or pictures that can be projected onto a screen from an overhead projector. Transparencies lend a polish that can greatly enhance the impact of your speech. They are popular for several reasons:

- *They can be projected in normal room light* so you can maintain eye contact with the audience and still glance down at the transparency on the overhead projector. Don't turn to look at the screen, turning your back to the audience. If you wish to point to the screen, back up within a few inches of it. This way, you can point to an item on the screen and still maintain eye contact with your audience.

- *Notes and personal reminders can be placed on the frames around each transparency.* Frames are also good for overlays. An **overlay** is a piece of clear or colored acetate with text material that is taped to the frame and folded back until needed. Another reason for using frames is that they keep light from glaring in audience members' eyes and add a professional touch to your presentation.

Technology Tip for Speakers

Customize Your Presentation Visuals

Whether you are using transparencies or computer slides, nothing is worse than having the audience think, "Oh, I've seen those visuals before." When you use the design templates that come with software programs, you run that risk. This will never happen to you if you customize your visuals. **Customizing** means that you take a basic idea or template and change and adapt it so it becomes your own. To customize Microsoft's PowerPoint, follow these simple steps:

1. **Type your speech outline into the Speech Template or AutoContent Wizard.** The Speech Template will open to Outline view. To view your outline in slide form, click on the **Slide Sorter View** button (bottom left of screen). *Note:* Any changes you make to individual slides will update the outline; also, any changes you make to the outline will update your slides. → *If you haven't used the Speech Template yet, go back to Chapter 2 and reread the Technology Tip for Speakers. The Speech Template can be found under Student Resources for Chapter 2 at the Hamilton Essentials of Public Speaking website.*

2. **Turn on the ruler and guides** from the **View menu** if they are not already visible. Drag the vertical guide (dashed line) to where you want your left margin to be. *Note:* Although the guides will not print or show during your presentation, they are a great help with alignment. Titles and text are left-aligned in the speech template. To change alignment, click on the text; when a text box appears, click on the edge of the highlighted box and use the up, down, left, or right arrow keys to move the text box.

3. **Turn off the "snap to grid" feature** by clicking the **Draw** button in the

- *They can be made with minimal effort.* With software (such as WordPerfect, Word, PowerPoint, PageMaker, or Harvard Graphics) and clip art, you can create professional-looking transparencies. With the appropriate acetate film, transparencies can be photocopied at home, the office, or the local copy shop.

- *They can be shown effectively to an audience of any size.*

35-Millimeter Slides

Since computer presentations are so popular, slides are used less often. Nevertheless, slides continue to be popular because they can use intense colors, are easy to transport, and can be shown to an audience of any size. However, there are several disadvantages:

- *They require substantial time to produce.* Once you have created your visual aids, you still must photograph them and send the film out for processing.

- As a result, *it is almost impossible to make last-minute changes.*

- *The room must be darkened for projection,* which makes interaction with your audience difficult and reference to your notes impossible.

Drawing toolbar, choosing **Snap**, and **Snap to grid**.

4. **Open the PowerPoint Speaker's Guide** and download or print a copy to use while creating and customizing your visuals. The guide includes both basic and advanced suggestions (including PowerPoint 2003). Basic Suggestions include how to customize text, lines, bullets, background, design, clip art, and color. Advanced Suggestions include customizing titles with boxes; customizing clip art, scanned images, and video; adding animation, transitions, and sound; building custom bullets; and adding recorded narration. ➤ *The Power-Point Speaker's Guide can be found under Student Resources for Chapter 9 at the Hamilton Essentials of Public Speaking website.*

5. **Begin customizing** titles, text, bullets, clip art, color, sound, movement, etc. Even if you decide to use one of Power-Point's design templates instead of the Speech Template (choose **Format/Apply Design**, and select a template), you should always customize it to fit your specific presentation and audience. And of course, for the best results, be sure to follow the text and graphic design suggestions in this chapter.

6. **Save your presentation to a disk or CD.** Test your disk by trying it on a different computer. *Note:* PowerPoint 2003 has a feature under **File/Package for CD** that lets you save your entire presentation to a CD—much better than previous versions. It includes a new Viewer that allows your presentation (created in PowerPoint 2000 or later) to run on any computer operating Windows 98 Second Edition or later, even when PowerPoint is not installed on the computer. The viewer is available free on Microsoft's website at www.microsoft.com—type *Power-Point 2003 Viewer* in the search box.

Be sure to practice using the remote control and coping with a dark room. Unless the remote control is cordless, bring a long cord for it so you can control the slide projector from the front of the room. You may wish to bring a pencil flashlight to place on the lectern so you can see your notes.

Flipcharts and Posters

No doubt you have seen posters and flipcharts used during class reports or lectures. The advantages of using posters and charts are that they tend to set an informal mood, are simple to prepare (but make sure the print is large enough to be seen easily), and can add a feeling of spontaneity to your speech if you write on them as you speak. They do have disadvantages, however:

- *They are awkward to transport and store.*
- *Markers tend to bleed through newsprint.* To avoid this, leave a blank page between each page or use water-based markers that will not bleed.
- *They can be used only with small groups* (fewer than 30 people).

To use posters and flipcharts effectively, learn to write on them without blocking the audience's view and to talk and write at the same time—both of these take

Notice how the speaker is standing next to the easel to keep from blocking the audience's view.

practice. Alternatives are to write them ahead of time or to lightly pencil in guidelines to trace over during your talk. These pencil markings will be invisible to the audience but will free you from worry about misspelled words or forgotten points.

Markerboards and Chalkboards

Markerboards usually are preferable to chalkboards because the glossy white of the markerboard is more attractive and there's no messy chalk residue. Also, small markerboards can be placed on easels and moved closer for a personal feel. However, both markerboards and chalkboards have several drawbacks:

- *It takes more practice to use them effectively* than most other types of visuals. Practice is vital. Without practice, you might write either so small that the audience can't see the words or so large that you run out of space; or you might have to erase a sketch or repeat it several times to get the proportions correct; or you might forget the spelling of a key word.

- *You must be able to speak and draw at the same time,* which also takes a great deal of practice. You can't afford to use up valuable speaking time drawing on the board.

- *While writing on the board, your back is toward the audience.* This not only affects audience interest and denies you valuable audience feedback but also makes it difficult for you to project your voice to the back of the room. A markerboard is better because you can stand beside it and still look at your audience occasionally.

- *Using a chalkboard makes you look less prepared* and less professional than using other, more state-of-the-art types of visuals.

Because of these disadvantages, markerboards and chalkboards should be used only as a last resort. If you must use a chalkboard, have your information on note cards ready to transfer to the board.

Objects, Models, and Handouts

Objects can be effective visual aids as long as they are large enough to be seen yet small enough to be transported and displayed easily. For example, in a speech about computer graphics, you might bring in a small computer terminal and printer and let the audience watch the entire process from input to final printed graphic. Or in a speech on women and self-defense, you might use a live model to show the proper self-defense techniques.

If an object is too small, too large, or too dangerous to be used as a visual aid, you might use a **model** instead. For example, a model car, a model office layout, or a model of an atom would all serve as effective visual aids.

Handouts can be both a blessing and a curse. Although handouts reduce the necessity for listeners to take notes, the typical audience member will read the handout instead of listening to you. So, unless you need listeners to actually do something with the material while you are speaking (such as fill out a checklist), it's better to pass out handouts at the end of your speech. But don't forget to tell your audience in the introduction to your speech that a handout will be provided.

Audiovisual Aids

Audiovisual aids, if used with care, can also add interest to a speech. If a VCR or DVD player is available, you could show, for example, a brief segment of a rafting trip down the Colorado River. To point out something of special interest, you could use slow motion or pause, or you could replay a segment. Normally, the sound should be turned off so that you can talk while showing the segment as you do with other visuals. Of course, PowerPoint allows you to insert video (such as mpeg or avi) into a computer presentation—choose Insert/Movies and Sounds/Movie from File or Movie from Clip Organizer. ➜ *For specifics, see the PowerPoint Speaker's Guide (Advanced Suggestions) under Student Resources for Chapter 9 at the Essentials of Public Speaking website.*

Audiotapes and CDs can also enhance your speech. For example, a speech about types of jazz would be much more informative if the audience could hear brief cuts from well-known jazz performers.

Selecting Your Visual Aids

Now that you understand the benefits of using visuals and are familiar with some of the most popular types, you are ready to discover how much fun it is to create them. In fact, it's so much fun that some speakers use too many visuals, too many different typefaces, and the wrong type sizes.

Text or Graphic Visuals?

Visual aids can be divided into text visuals and graphic visuals. **Text visuals** (see Color Figures C–G in the color insert) include mainly words with an occasional clip art drawing or picture. The majority of visual aids used in speeches are text visuals. Text visuals are especially helpful during the introduction of your speech as you list your main points, during the conclusion of your speech as you summarize the main points, and at any other time you want to list information. You can use clip art or pictures in your text visuals to anchor the audience to the concept you are presenting

(Paivio, 1971). For example (Color Figure G), in a speech about the steps that realtors follow in selling homes, you could use a picture of a house with a "For Sale" sign in front. Later, when audience members try to remember the steps in your speech, they will recall the house with the "For Sale" sign (the anchor).

Graphic visuals (see Color Figures H–N in the color insert) include organizational charts and flowcharts, diagrams and schematic drawings, maps, pictures, and graphs with just enough words to clarify the visual. **Graphs** depict numerical data in visual form. *Line graphs* show changes in relationships over time; *bar graphs* compare countable data at a specific moment in time; *pie charts* and *stacked bar graphs* show parts of the whole or percentages; and *pictographs* replace bars with graphic symbols or icons.

Whether you use text or graphic visuals, be sure to follow the design guidelines that follow. Sample text and graphic visuals are shown in the color insert in this book. These visuals can also be found under Student Resources for Chapter 9 at the Essentials of Public Speaking website.

How Many Visuals?

Creating visuals is so enjoyable that some speakers use too many visuals in their speeches. To decide how many visuals to use without causing your audience to experience visual overload, try the following formula on a speech you are preparing:

$$\frac{\text{Length of speech}}{2} + 1 = \text{Maximum number of visuals}$$

For example, for a 6-minute speech, you would want a maximum of four visuals (6 divided by 2 plus 1); for a 10-minute speech, you would want a maximum of six visuals (10 divided by 2 plus 1). Of course, fewer visuals could certainly be used, but more visuals should be used only with caution.

Designing Your Visual Aids

To produce professional-looking visual aids, all you have to do is follow the general and specific design principles covered in this section.

Use the Correct Type Size

One of the most common mistakes that even experienced speakers make in preparing visuals is to use text that is too small for easy audience viewing. For *posters, flipcharts, chalkboards,* and *markerboards,* these are the guidelines:

- Titles should be approximately 3 inches high.

- Subtitles, if used, should be 2 to 2½ inches high.

- Text should be 1½ inches high.

Although these size recommendations may seem too large at first, they will ensure that even the people in the back row can see your message clearly.

For *slides, transparencies,* and *projected computer visuals,* type size is measured in points, not inches. (A point is about ½₂ inch.) Your listeners will have no problems if you use type that is no smaller than the following point sizes (see Figure 9.4):

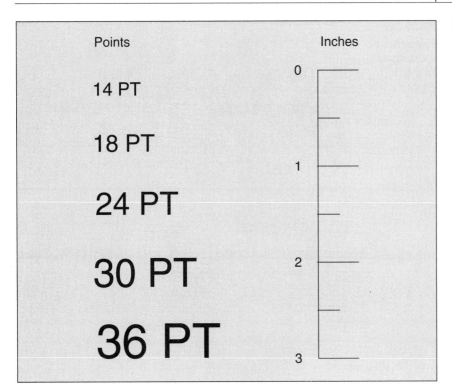

Figure 9.4

Determining Type Sizes in Points or Inches (measure only capital letters)

	Title	**Subtitle**	**Text**
Transparencies	30–36 pt.	24 pt.	18 pt. (24 pt. if no subtitle)
Computer visuals	30–36 pt.	24 pt.	18 pt. (24 pt. if no subtitle)
Slides	24 pt.	18 pt.	14 pt. (18 pt. if no subtitle)

Use larger type sizes when possible, but never use smaller sizes than those listed here. Obviously, the size of type used for class papers (12 point) will not work!

Use the Correct Typeface

For slides, transparencies, and projected computer visuals, you will also need to select a typeface or font. More than 10,000 typefaces are in existence and more than 1,000 are readily available for personal computer users (Bergsland, 2003; Byers, 1992). Typefaces are divided into two types, sans serif and serif. A **sans serif typeface** (a geometric-looking typeface) is recommended for titles or emphasis. Sans serif typefaces include Helvetica (or Arial), Futura, and Optima. A **serif typeface** (a typeface with small lines, or finishing strokes, that extend from letter stems) is especially good for text and small labels on charts. Serif typefaces include Times Roman, Palatino, Bodoni, and Century.

Typefaces can affect the readability of your visuals and will either reinforce or distract from the tone of your speech. Figure 9.5 shows some sample typefaces and the images they tend to convey. If you were giving a speech on a serious topic, you probably wouldn't want to use Poster Bodoni, a playful typeface, for your visuals. Sometimes the typeface you choose depends as much on your audience as on the topic. For example, if you were speaking to a group of skeptical parents about the educational values of a day-care facility, a Times Roman typeface would give your

Figure 9.5

Each Typeface Has an Image or Connotation It Suggests to Audiences

Official
Times Roman

Sophisticated
Garamond

Playful
Poster Bodoni

Friendly
Century

Trendy
Bodoni

Elegant
Optima

Upbeat
Palatino

Urban
Helvetica

Modern
Futura

visuals an official, confidence-inspiring look. If you were emphasizing the personal, loving attention that the day-care facility gives to each child, Century would be a good choice because it conveys a friendly tone. Sometimes the only way to be sure that your visuals are sending the message you desire is to see them projected on a screen—once they are enlarged, the tone is more obvious. Use special care in combining typefaces. As mentioned previously, sans serif typefaces are usually used for titles, and serif typefaces for text. Generally, *use no more than two different typefaces per visual, and use the same typefaces for all the visuals in a speech*—consistency projects professionalism. Figure 9.6 shows some successful typeface combinations and the images they project (Buchanan, 1993; Dewsnap, 1992).

Figure 9.6

Successful Typeface Combinations and Projected Connotations

Title Text	Image
Helvetica with Times Roman	Classical business look
Helvetica with Century	Traditional, nostalgic look
Helvetica with Garamond	Bold, direct look
Helvetica with Helvetica	Modern, urban look
Times Roman with Times Roman	Official, confidence-inspiring look
Century with Century	Reassuring, friendly, lively look
Futura with Bodoni	Collegiate or athletic look
Futura with Garamond	Corporate look
Futura with Times Roman	High fashion, "tabloid" look
Poster Bodoni with Times Roman	Sophisticated, trendy look
Poster Bodoni with Futura	Light, artistic look
Optima with *Garamond Italic*	Glamorous, elegant look
Optima with Palatino	Soft, gentle look
Optima with Optima	Restrained, formal look
Palatino Italic with Palatino	Fresh, modern, upbeat look
Helvetica Extended with **Bodoni Bold**	**Fitness club look**
Helvetica Extended with Futura	Modern, clean look

General Design Principles

Before we discuss specific principles for text and graphic visuals, let's look at general design principles that apply to all visuals, whether text or graphic. In *The Non-Designer's Design Book,* Robin Williams (2004, p. 13) discusses the four **general design principles**—guidelines used in constructing the visual elements of all well-designed visuals:

- ■ *Contrast*—If the elements are not to be the same, then make them very different. Contrast is often the most important attraction on a visual.

- ■ *Repetition*—Repeat visual elements of the design. This helps develop the organization and strengthens the unity of the whole presentation.

- ■ *Alignment*—Every element should have some visual connection with another element on the visual. This creates a clean, sophisticated look.

- ■ *Proximity*—Items relating to each other should be grouped together so that they are one visual unit. This helps organize information and reduces clutter.

Analyzing Figure 9.7 Let's illustrate how these four design principles can make a difference in the quality of a visual aid by applying them to a visual from a speech on choosing a day-care center. Look at the visual aid in Figure 9.7. What's right about it? The speaker has chosen Century as the typeface (a typeface that gives a friendly impression), which seems appropriate for the topic. The type is large enough for easy audience viewing (the title is in 36-point type and the main ideas in 30-point type), and only necessary words have been used. Also, an underline separates the title from the main points, which helps the audience grasp the organization of the visual. This visual, then, is basically good.

But it's bland, isn't it? Nothing attracts the eye. This visual aid does not follow the four general design principles presented by Williams:

1. There isn't enough *contrast.* Even though the title is in boldface, the type sizes of the main points and the title are too similar. The bullets (squares in front of the main points) do repeat, but they are too light to be noticed.

2. There isn't enough *repetition.* The boldface of the title needs to be repeated somewhere—maybe the bullets could be filled in or the underline could be made bold.

3. The main points are in *alignment,* but they don't line up with anything else on the page. If the main points were centered (normally not a good idea), they would align with the title and underline, which are already centered. According to Williams, "Every item should have a visual connection with something else on the page" (p. 27). Right now, neither the title nor the underline have such a connection.

4. *Proximity* is weak. There is equal space between the title and each of the main points so it seems as if there are five separate items on the page. Closer proximity between the bulleted points would make them a visual unit.

Figure 9.7

How Would You Improve This Visual?

Choosing a Day Care

□ Location

□ Outside appearance

□ Interior

□ Directors and teachers

Choosing a Day Care

- Location

- Outside appearance

- Interior

- Directors and teachers

Figure 9.8

One Approach to Redesigning Figure 9.7.

Redesigning Figure 9.7 How can we redesign the day-care visual to incorporate the four design principles? Figure 9.8 shows one approach:

1. For *contrast,* the type size of the title (40 point) is larger than the type size of the list (24 point).

2. For *repetition,* the boldface of the title is repeated in the solid bullets (the black squares), the black line under the title, and the black line at the bottom of the visual.

3. For *alignment,* the title and underline span the visual from left to right, the bullets are left-aligned under them, and the graphic and bottom line are right aligned.

4. For *proximity,* the main points in the list are grouped closer to one another than they are to the title.

5. Finally, the addition of the graphic creates warmth and visual interest.

This is only one of many possible ways to redesign the visual. For example, adding contrast with an Optima bold (36 point) typeface for the title and a Garamond italic (24 point) typeface for the main points would suggest a classier day-care environment. Color would also add power to the visual.

Redesigning the Business Card in Figure 9.9 Let's take one more try at using Williams's design principles. The business card in Figure 9.9 has problems with all four principles. What changes would you recommend? → *For a redesigned business card, see the color insert section in this chapter.*

Design Principles for Text Visuals

Used Cars   (817) 555-1212

Connor Blake

6195 Del Lane   Mansfield, TX

Figure 9.9

How Would You Improve This Business Card?

The rules for text visuals are summarized in Figure 9.10 (revised from Holcombe & Stein, 1983, 1996). Before reading further, look at the figure and try to identify which rules listed in the visual are violated in it. Then continue reading the text and see if you were correct. Remember, *if it takes too much effort to read visual aids, the audience is forced into a reading mode rather than a listening mode.*

Use No More Than Four to Six Lines of Text Not counting the title and subtitle(s), a visual should contain no more than six lines of text. An exception is a list of single words, in which case seven or eight lines might be fine. If you need more than six lines of text, you probably should either split the information into two visuals or narrow and simplify your text.

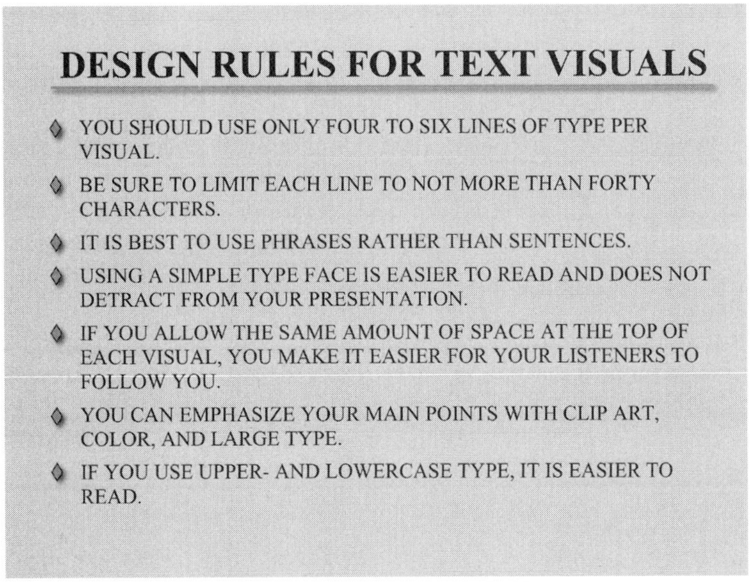

DESIGN RULES FOR TEXT VISUALS

◊ YOU SHOULD USE ONLY FOUR TO SIX LINES OF TYPE PER VISUAL.

◊ BE SURE TO LIMIT EACH LINE TO NOT MORE THAN FORTY CHARACTERS.

◊ IT IS BEST TO USE PHRASES RATHER THAN SENTENCES.

◊ USING A SIMPLE TYPE FACE IS EASIER TO READ AND DOES NOT DETRACT FROM YOUR PRESENTATION.

◊ IF YOU ALLOW THE SAME AMOUNT OF SPACE AT THE TOP OF EACH VISUAL, YOU MAKE IT EASIER FOR YOUR LISTENERS TO FOLLOW YOU.

◊ YOU CAN EMPHASIZE YOUR MAIN POINTS WITH CLIP ART, COLOR, AND LARGE TYPE.

◊ IF YOU USE UPPER- AND LOWERCASE TYPE, IT IS EASIER TO READ.

Figure 9.10

Effective Visuals Can Be Read in 6 Seconds or Less. Can You Read This Visual in 6 Seconds?

Limit Each Line to 40 Characters If your text contains more than 40 characters per line (including letters and spaces), you aren't leaving enough **white space** (space that contains no text or graphics). White space is essential for fast comprehension and helps your visual look organized. Use white space between visual units and on all four sides of your visual. Keep in mind, however, that too much white space between the lines of text makes them look unrelated.

Use Phrases Rather Than Sentences Eliminate unnecessary words so that your listeners can grasp the content of your visual in 6 seconds or less. In Figure 9.10, note how full sentences slow down comprehension. Figure 9.11 presents the same key information using easy-to-comprehend phrases. Which visual would you rather have an instructor use in a lecture? If you feel the audience needs more information than you can place on your visuals, put it in a handout to give them at the end of the speech.

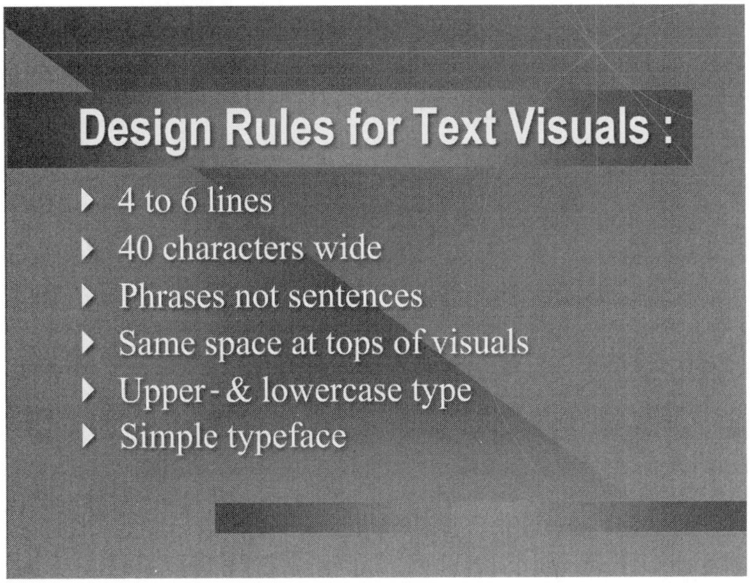

Design Rules for Text Visuals :

▶ 4 to 6 lines

▶ 40 characters wide

▶ Phrases not sentences

▶ Same space at tops of visuals

▶ Upper- & lowercase type

▶ Simple typeface

Figure 9.11

Which Computer Visual Would You Rather Have an Instructor Use in Class—This One or the One in Figure 9.10?

Use Upper- and Lowercase Type ONE OF THE EASIEST WAYS TO ENSURE AUDI-ENCE COMPREHENSION OF YOUR VISUALS IS TO USE UPPERCASE AND LOWERCASE LETTERS RATHER THAN ALL CAPITALS. If you need a larger title, use a larger type size—don't use all caps. Research has shown that text in all caps is more difficult to read and comprehend. To see why this is true, try a brief experiment using Figure 9.12. The word *official* has been divided into upper and lower parts. Hold your hand over the top part and ask at least four people to read the bottom part. Now hold your hand over the bottom part and ask four other people to read the top part. Which part were more people able to read correctly? The reason the top part was easier to read is that *word recognition comes mainly from the upper half of lowercase letters.* But when a word is put in all caps, it becomes a shapeless box that cannot be instantly recognized (Baskette, Sissors, & Brooks, 1992).

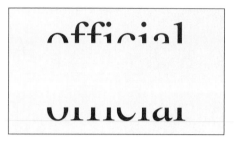

Figure 9.12

Word Recognition Experiment

Word recognition comes mainly from the upper half of lowercase letters, which is why all caps are difficult to read.

SOURCE: Adams, Faux, & Rieber, 1988.

Use a Simple Typeface Many of the typefaces available for use on personal computers are completely inappropriate and basically illegible except when used for special emphasis. Simple typefaces are always easier to read than script or fancy fonts. Begin with the typefaces suggested earlier in the chapter—they have stood the test of time and are known to work for visual aids.

Leave the Same Amount of Space at the Top of Each Visual Many speakers incorrectly center the content on each visual—that is, they leave an equal amount of white space above and below the text. This means that some visual aids have only a few lines in the middle, whereas others are filled with text. As a result, each time a transparency or computer visual is projected onto the screen, the audience has to search for the title. Your visuals will look more professional and be easier to comprehend if the text begins at the same depth on each one. In general, for transparencies, the title should be about 2 inches from the top of the page; for computer visuals, 1½ inches from the top; and for posters and flipcharts, 3 inches from the top.

Use Clip Art, Larger Type, and Color for Emphasis One of the general design principles is contrast. Clip art, larger type, and color all add contrast and emphasis. Like the children in Figure 9.8, clip art or a picture, photo, or freehand drawing will anchor the content of your visual in the minds of the audience.

Large type and color are other ways to direct the eye to points you wish to emphasize. The largest and boldest type will always be read first unless you have also used color. If you want to direct your audience's attention to a portion of a complicated diagram, color is the way to do it. Even on a color visual, a bright, contrasting color will focus your audience's attention. ➤ *We discuss the use of color in the last section of this chapter.*

Design Principles for Graphic Visuals

In order for graphic visuals to trigger the right brain and allow for rapid comprehension of complicated data, you must design the visuals carefully. In addition to the general design principles of contrast, repetition, alignment, and proximity discussed earlier, some specific principles apply to graphic visuals (revised from Holcombe & Stein, 1983, 1996).

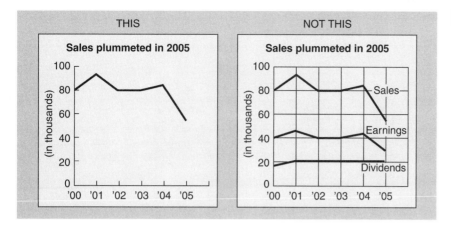

Figure 9.13

Limiting Data
Limit data to what is needed to support your verbal point and eliminate distracting grid lines.

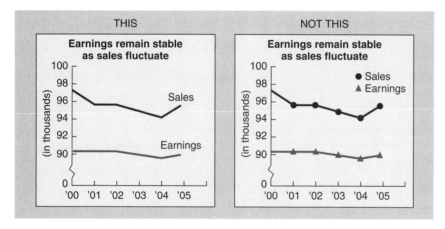

Figure 9.14

Eliminating Data Points
Use more than one line graph when necessary, but for viewing ease, eliminate data points.

Limit Data to What Is Absolutely Necessary   Figure 9.13 illustrates the importance of using only the data needed to support your points. If the speech deals only with sales, the data lines for earnings and dividends (as well as the distracting grid lines) are not necessary and actually obscure the seriousness of the sales decline. You could have an overlay showing the data lines for earnings and dividends to use while answering questions. When you use more than one data line, be sure to label each one.   ➥ *See page 189 for more on transparency overlays.*

Keep Background Lines and Data Points to a Minimum   In most cases, grid lines (such those in Figure 9.13) and data points (like those in Figure 9.14) should be eliminated. They are distracting, take too much time to interpret, and are not usually necessary for understanding. Use them only if you know that your audience (say, a group of engineering students) expects grid lines and data points, but include only essential data points and make the grid lines lighter than the data lines.

Group Data When Possible   Even after you have limited the data to only what is necessary, see if there are any small categories of data that you can group into one larger category. Figure 9.15 illustrates this principle. When seven small categories of costs were grouped under the general heading of "Other expenses," the pie chart became much easier to grasp. If necessary, you could follow this pie chart with a visual that lists the contents of "Other expenses."

Figure 9.15

Grouping Data
Group distracting data under a general heading.

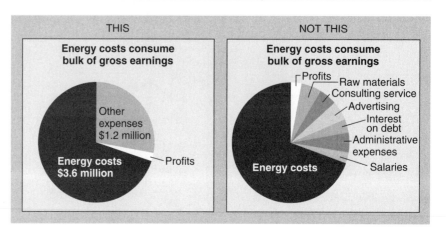

Figure 9.16

Limiting White Space
For viewing ease, make the space between bars narrower than the bars.

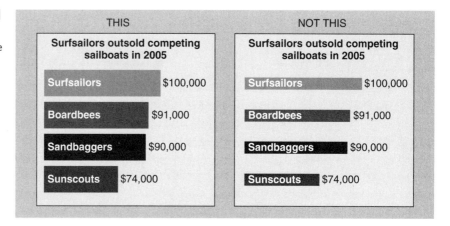

Make Bars Wider Than the Spaces Between Them When the white space between the bars in a bar graph is wider than the bars, as in the graph on the right in Figure 9.16, the "trapped" white space visually pushes the bars apart, making them seem unrelated (Williams, 2004). Therefore, for easier comparison, make the bars wider than the spaces between them, whether the bars are horizontal or vertical.

Always Use Headings Whether your graphic visual is a chart, graph, map, or picture, always use a title or heading for clarity. For example, it might seem obvious to you that your drawing shows the correct position to begin water skiing, but without a title or heading, it wouldn't be immediately clear to everyone in your audience.

Using Color Effectively

Using color in your visuals is so much fun that it's easy to go overboard. But if it is used to highlight, organize, or add interest, color has real benefits:

- *Color visuals are more persuasive* (Vogel et al., 1986, 1990).

- *Color advertisements are more likely to be read and produce higher sales.* The Bureau of Advertising found that readers are 80 percent more likely to read a color ad than a black-and-white ad and that sales from color ads are 50 to 80 percent greater than sales from noncolor ads (Johnson, 1990).

Color Wheel and Color Visuals

I. Twelve-Hue Color Wheel

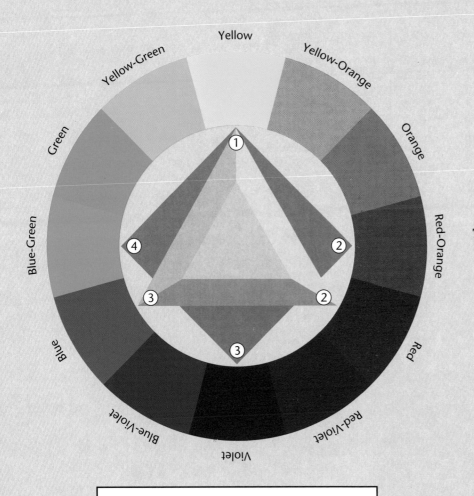

**Color Figure A
Twelve-Hue Color Wheel
Used in Picking Colors
for Visual Aids**

The triangle is used to find colors that harmonize; the square is used to find pairs of opposite colors that complement each other. (See pages 203–204 for more details.)

Connor Blake

Used Cars

6195 Del Lane
Mansfield, Texas
(817) 555-1212

Color Figure B
Redesigned Business Card
from Figure 9.9.

II. Student-Prepared Visuals

Color Figure C

Color from the clip art repeats in the title and bullets of this **text visual.**

Color Figure D

The Network Blitz design template used in this **text visual** was an excellent
background choice for a famous television show like "I Love Lucy."

5 Basic Food Groups

Bread & grains   Rice & legumes   Fruits & nuts   Milk & cheese

Meat, poultry, & fish

U.S.D.A.

Daniel Pineda

Color Figure E
Pictures from Microsoft's Clipart Gallery add color and
interest to this **text visual**.

Idiot's Guide to Swimming

- Swimming Basics

- Swimming Equipment

- Swimming Lingo

Sara Allen

Color Figure F
In this **text visual**, a picture and boxes highlight the topic and text.

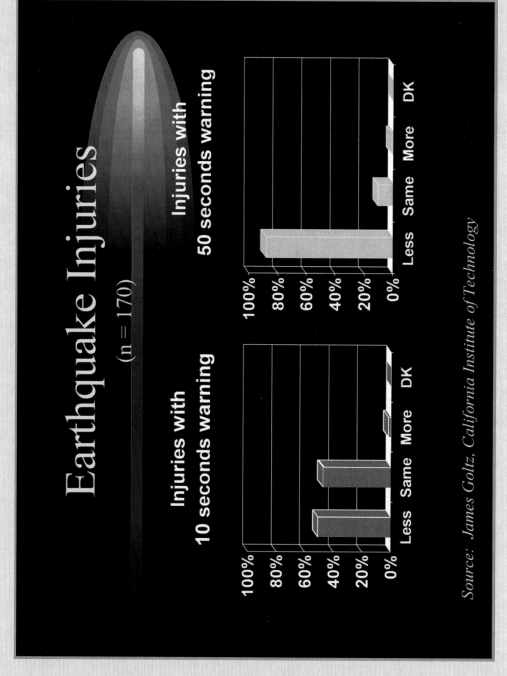

Color Figure N
Professionally produced **graphic visual** with 3D bar graphs.

- *Color visuals produce better recall.* The Bureau of Advertising found that recall of ad content is 55 to 78 percent greater for color ads than for black-and-white ads (Johnson, p. 7). And, as reported earlier in this chapter (Hamilton, 1999), high-quality color transparencies produce better recall than poor-quality color transparencies or than black-and-white transparencies (regardless of their quality). In fact, poor-quality color is the least effective. Vogel et al. (1990) also found color transparencies to produce better recall than black-and-white transparencies. Therefore, if you have time to produce them, quality color visuals can significantly increase recall of your presentation; if preparation time is limited, use black-and-white visuals instead.

- *Colors add spatial dimensions.* "Warm" colors (such as orange and red) are more active and seem to jump forward from a neutral background such as gray. "Cool" colors (such as green and blue) are more passive and stationary. Dark colors appear farther away, while light colors appear nearer (Marcus, 1982).

- *Colors produce an emotional response.* Cool colors generally have a calming effect; warm colors generally have a stimulating, invigorating, and sometimes anger-producing effect (Gardano, 1986).

Using the 12-Hue Color Wheel Selecting effective color combinations is difficult. One of the safest ways to pick color combinations is by using a color wheel such as the 12-hue wheel (Itten, 1973) shown in Color Figure A in the color insert in this chapter. Colors can be described by their hue and saturation. **Hue** refers to the actual color—each color on the color wheel is a different hue. **Saturation** is the amount of color used in the hue. Fully saturated colors are vivid; low-saturated colors appear dull and show less color.

Use the color wheel in three different ways:

- Use the color wheel to pick **harmonizing hues** (colors that tend to relax and calm when used together). To determine which colors harmonize, use the following method: Make a triangle the same size as the one shown in the color wheel and number the corners from 1 to 3. Place the triangle in the center of the color wheel and turn it so that number 1 is pointing to a color you would like to use (say, green). The colors that numbers 2 and 3 are pointing to (violet and orange) are the harmonizing colors. If you selected yellow-orange, the harmonizing colors would be red-violet and blue-green.

- Use the color wheel to find pairs of **complementary hues** (colors that are opposites on the color wheel—such as blue and orange—and are less relaxing pairs than harmonizing colors). Complementary colors are especially good when you need emphasis. Although complementary colors should not be placed side by side because they appear to vibrate, they can create eye-catching visuals when used with two other complementary colors. To find two pairs of complementary colors, use the following method: Make a square like the one shown in the color wheel and number the corners from 1 to 4. Put the square in the center of the color wheel and point the number 1 toward a color you like. The other corners of the square will identify the three colors that complement the selected color. For example, if you selected yellow, the other three colors would be red-orange, violet, and blue-green (colors 1 and 3 and colors 2 and 4 are opposites).

- Use the color wheel to select **spectral hues** (colors that are next to each other on the color wheel). Spectral hues have low contrast so they are

perfect for the subtle effect needed for shadowing or suggesting three dimensions (Rabb, 1993).

To be sure that your color choices are effective, project them onto a screen and check them. The wrong color combinations can make your visuals difficult to read. In 1993, for example, American Airlines put up signs (each listing 15 to 20 cities) along the entrance roads to the Dallas–Fort Worth Airport to aid drivers in determining which terminal and gate they wanted. In the daylight the signs were fairly legible. At night, however, the dark-blue capital letters on the blue background were so difficult to read that several accidents occurred as drivers slowed down to locate their destination city. The million-dollar signs were removed (Lunsford, 1994). Also, be aware that the colors you see on your computer monitor may not be the exact colors that the audience sees projected on the screen—video projectors vary in the set of color chips they use and even the way they are adjusted.

Additional Thoughts on Color   As you add colors to your visuals, keep these additional suggestions in mind (Baird, Turnbull, & McDonald, 1987; Conway, 1988; Johnson, 1995; Pastoor, 1990; Vogel et al., 1990):

- *Use the same color scheme for all visuals in any one speech.* Don't be tempted to use a different color background for each visual or for each title. Consistency projects professionalism and organization.

- *Use different hues for unrelated items; use a single hue with different saturation levels for related items.*

- *For graphs and charts, use fully saturated hues* to make them easier to read. Also, research has found that blue, cyan (greenish blue), and red are the favored colors for highlighting important items on graphs and charts.

- *For backgrounds and texts, select hues low in saturation.* In a recent study, adults aged 20 to 56 were asked to select text and background color preferences from over 800 color combinations shown on video monitors. Low-saturated colors were preferred in almost all cases.

- *Contrast text and figures with the background.* For legibility, dark backgrounds require light letters, bullets, and figures; light backgrounds should have the opposite. When light colors (such as pastels) are used for figures, bullets, or letters against a light background, they should have a darker color outline or shadow. For example, blue letters on a dark blue or black background would be almost impossible to read; white or yellow letters on a dark background would be easy to read. Contrast also can be created by varying the saturation of color (such as a fully saturated figure on a partially saturated background). The contrast between lightness and darkness is the most important factor of visibility.

- *Avoid using colors that can look the same at a distance,* such as red and brown; red-orange, and orange; and yellow and yellow-green. On the other hand, colors such as black, white, red, yellow, blue, green, purple, and pink are easy to distinguish.

- *Be especially careful about using red and green together,* because some people have red–green color blindness.

- *Limit the number of colors you use.* Using more than four colors usually makes visuals look cluttered and slows down audience comprehension.

Summary

The benefits of using visual aids in speeches cannot be overemphasized. Visual aids have so much power because they (1) speed listener comprehension, (2) improve audience memory, (3) decrease the time needed to present a message, and (4) add to speaker credibility. In short, speakers should not consider visual aids as optional.

As you were reading the section on types of visuals, was there one type in which you were especially interested? Computer visuals and transparencies are the most commonly used types of visual aids today. You will certainly want to practice designing and using a variety of visuals until you are comfortable with them.

When designing your text and graphic visuals, remember to select typefaces with care and to use a type size that is large enough for everyone in the audience to read with ease. Also keep in mind the four design principles—contrast, repetition, alignment, and proximity—as well as the specific design principles for text and graphic visuals. Have fun with color, but use it with caution.

Essentials of Public Speaking  Online

Use the Essentials of Public Speaking website at **http://communication. wadsworth.com/hamiltoneps3** for quick access to the electronic study resources that accompany this chapter. When you get to the Essentials home page, click on "Student Book Companion Site" in the Resource box. The Essentials website features the PowerPoint Speaker's Guide: Basic and Advanced Suggestions, the visuals featured in the color insert in this chapter, the Speech Template described in the Technology Tip for Speakers box on pages 190–191, InfoTrac College Edition, the Suggestions for Practice and Critical Thinking activities and the InfoTrac College Edition activities that follow, a digital glossary, and review quizzes.

Key Terms

complementary hues 203
customize 190
general design principles 197
graph 194

graphic visual 194
harmonizing hues 203
hue 203
overlay 189
sans serif typeface 195
saturation 203

serif typeface 195
spectral hues 203
text visual 193
white space 199

Suggestions for Practice and Critical Thinking

1. What do we mean when we say, "Quality visual aids anchor your audience to the concept you are presenting"? Share your interpretation with a classmate.

2. Do you know how to take your speech outline and easily turn it into Power-Point presentation slides? Using InfoTrac College Edition, run a keyword

search on *PowerPoint presentations* to locate the following article: "Turn Word Outlines into PowerPoint Presentations," *PC/Computing,* July 1997, page A22. Once you have read the article, take one of your speech outlines and create at least two visual aids.

3. If your instructor has a stack of visual aids (transparencies) from past student speeches, try the following impromptu speaking exercise: Student names are placed in a hat. The instructor draws a name from the hat, reads it out loud, and hands the student two unrelated visual aids. The student walks to the front of the class and presents an impromptu speech of approximately 1 minute using the two visuals. The speech may be humorous or serious. This assignment is fun and offers practice in using visual aids.

4. Select a manuscript of a speech on a topic that you can speak about with enthusiasm. For speech ideas, look in *Vital Speeches* (in your college library or via InfoTrac College Edition) or check out one of the videotaped speeches on the Essentials of Public Speaking website. Prepare two visuals that the speaker could have used with the speech. ➔ *You will use this manuscript and these visuals again in Chapter 10, activity 4.*

5. On the basis of this chapter, prepare a list of the 10 most important do's and don'ts for designing visual aids. Compare your list with one or two classmates' lists and justify your choices.

6. Prepare a chart or graph using the information in the following paragraph (Davidson, 1993):

> From the beginning of creation to 1850 A.D. world population grew to one billion. It grew to two billion by 1930, three billion by 1960, four billion by 1979, and five billion by 1987, with six billion en route. Every 33 months, the current population of America, 257,000,000 people, is added to the planet.

Ask two or three friends to help you think of ways in which your chart or graph might be improved.

7. Practice the design rules covered in this chapter by redesigning one or more of the visual aids in the chapter. Color Figures C–L in the color insert would be especially interesting to redesign. If your instructor is willing, why not have everyone in the class redesign the same two or three visuals. Ask three people from the community or the department to serve as judges and select the three best visual aids.

8. Check out the following websites. *You can access these sites under the Student Resources for Chapter 9 at the Essentials of Public Speaking website.*

• Go to Microsoft's website and download the viewer described in this chapter's Technology Tip for Speakers. Type *PowerPoint 2003 Viewer* in the search box.

• The Virtual Presentation Assistant at the University of Kansas website has good advice on visual aids. Click on the "Using visual aids" link.

• Are you trying to choose a media screen? Check out the article "Carefully Consider Ambient Light When Selecting a Screen" by Dave Dicklich at the Presentations.com website. For other interesting articles, go to the Presentations.com home page and type *ambient light* or *projection screen* in the search box.

- For valuable technical articles and critiques of presentation equipment, see Presentations.com, publishers of *Presentation* magazine, and ZDNet.com.

- For free downloads, see the following sites:

    Microsoft.com for PowerPoint templates. From the Microsoft home page, click on "Office" under Product Families in the menu bar at left. On the Office Online page, choose "Templates" from the left-hand menu.

    Microsoft.com for clip tips, photos, clips, and animations. From the Microsoft home page, click on "Office" under Product Families in the menu bar at left. On the Office Online page, choose "Clip Art and Media" from the left-hand menu.

    AnimationFactory.com for animated clip art.

    WebPlaces.com for sound clips.

    Macromedia.com to download free Flash Player and Shockwave Player. From the Macromedia home page, click on "Downloads" from the menu bar at the top of the page.

- For additional PowerPoint guides, use Google to search for *PowerPoint Manual.* For product documentation for PowerPoint 2003 (and other versions of PowerPoint), go to the Microsoft home page and click on "Office" under Product Families in the menu bar on the left. On the Office Online page, choose "PowerPoint" under Products in the left-hand menu. The PowerPoint page features a section called Browse PowerPoint, which includes "assistance" links.

- Microsoft's Office Online offers an excellent page titled "Other Sites Offering Additional Information for PowerPoint Users." This page provides links to companies that offer services, tips, or additional information to help you get the most out of Microsoft Office.

- For an excellent example of what can be done with electronic visuals, see the virtual slide show produced by the Archaeology Department at the University of Calgary. From the Department of Archaeology home page, click on "Virtual Slide Show."

- For several links to popular 3D and animation websites, check out the Computer Graphics links at the University of California, Santa Cruz, Perpetual Science Lab (click on "Links," then "Computer Graphics").

Quiz Answers

Answers to Unit III Quiz: Test Your Knowledge of Verbal, Visual, and Vocal Delivery.

1. *False.* Although visual aids do add to the interest and enjoyment of the audience, that is only one of the reasons effective speakers use them. A more important reason is to help listeners remember the main points of the message. You may be surprised to learn in Chapter 9 that average listeners remember only 10 percent of what they hear but as much as 65 percent of what they hear and see.

2. *False.* Certainly your audience will listen more attentively and, therefore, remember your ideas better when you paint vivid mental pictures of scenes

and events. But some well-designed visuals will make your presentation even more powerful. → *See page 187 for a discussion of use of vivid words.*

3. *False.* Listeners assess visual messages (whether intentional or not) before they even hear any verbal messages. This means that preparation is critical. → *Chapter 10 will give you the information you need to have your audience eagerly waiting to hear what you have to say.*

4. *False.* Besides being a valuable source of feedback from your audience, making eye contact with listeners throughout the audience makes them feel that you are one of them and that you care about them. When an audience feels friendly toward you, they listen more attentively and are more likely to believe what you are saying. → *For effective delivery, see Chapters 10 and 11.*

5. *False.* Regardless of the types of visuals you use, practice is essential if you want to feel confident and give an effective speech. Markerboards and chalkboards have their uses, but for most speaking occasions, a more polished visual aid is recommended. → *See Chapter 9 for types of visual aids and Chapter 10 for how to use them effectively.*

6. *False.* With the possibilities offered by computer software, it is tempting to fill your visuals with lots of typefaces, colors, and pieces of clip art. Although you may have created a lovely piece of art, it will not be as effective as a visual if it doesn't emphasize main points and group related data. → *Chapter 9 will give you the information needed to produce visual aids that are the envy of your classmates and colleagues.*

7. *True.* You don't want to alienate your listeners by using sexist language. → *Figure 10.3 suggests gender-neutral alternatives for some common terms.*

8. *False.* Thinking through your speech does not help you make the connection between the brain and the mouth. There is no substitute for practicing your speech aloud while using your notes and visuals. Oral practice will make you feel confident and allow you to give a speech that both you and your audience will enjoy. → *Review Chapter 2 for confidence suggestions.*

9. *False.* Although some textbooks favor using only capital letters on your visuals, and media departments in many organizations use them, research shows that words written in all caps are more difficult to read than those written in both uppercase and lowercase letters. → *See Figure 9.12 for more on the drawbacks of using all capital letters.*

10. *False.* Although memorizing your opening and closing statements is all right if it makes you feel more comfortable, memorizing the entire speech has several drawbacks. Speaking from keyword notes is preferable because it allows you to speak in a relaxed, conversational way. → *Chapter 10 covers the drawbacks of speaking from memory.*

Delivering Your Message

F l a s h b a c k Quintilian, a noted Roman rhetorician, gave his students detailed suggestions on gestures and facial expressions in *De Institutione Oratoria*. Some of his suggestions included:

- Use the head to indicate humility or haughtiness.
- Use the face to show sadness, cheerfulness, or pride.
- Strike the thigh to show indignation.
- Use the fingers to indicate specific ideas.

HAT DO LEE IACOCCA, OPRAH WINFREY, AND COLIN POWELL HAVE IN COMMON? THEY are public speakers who really know how to connect with an audience (Decker & Denney, 1993). They are enthusiastic, interesting, powerful, persuasive, caring, and— most important of all—believable.

Lee Iacocca took over Chrysler Corporation when the company was several billion dollars in debt. He was able to convince Congress to approve a $1.5-billion loan guarantee. He was also able to convince Chrysler workers who had received huge wage cuts and Chrysler dealers who were being wooed by Japanese franchises to pull together to get the company back on its feet. And finally, he was able to persuade the American public to buy Chrysler cars through his personal appearances in advertisements. Chrysler was able to pay back the federal loan seven years before it was due (Iacocca & Novak, 1984). What made Iacocca so effective? "Iacocca was able to get people to cooperate because they believed in him," MaryAnn N. Keller, a Wall Street auto industry analyst, told the *New York Times* (*New York Times,* 1980).

Oprah Winfrey became a popular talk-show host at a time when it seemed that no one could compete with Phil Donahue. One month after she arrived in Chicago, her show, "A.M. Chicago," drew even with "Donahue," and after three months it nosed ahead ("Oprah Winfrey," 1987). Oprah's national TV show continues to lead the talk-show ratings. How does she do it? She makes it seem as if she is speaking directly to each of her listeners; she is real, and she is believable.

Colin Powell, born in New York City of Jamaican immigrant parents, has had a varied career in the military, the government, and the volunteer sector. In all these areas he has inspired confidence and trust. During his 35-year military career, Powell served in many capacities, beginning in Vietnam and ending as a four-star general and Chairman of the Joint Chiefs of Staff, where he oversaw Operation Desert Storm. As a diplomat, Powell is best known in his role as 65th Secretary of State,

---

Basic Steps for Preparing a Speech

1. Analyze your potential audience. → *See Chapter 4.*
2. Determine topic, exact purpose, and main points. → *See Chapter 5.*
3. Prepare a rough-draft outline of main points and needed information. → *See Chapter 5.*
4. Research topic for material to support main points. → *See Chapter 5.*
5. Select best supporting materials. → *See Chapter 6.*
6. Determine how best to organize main points. → *See Chapter 7.*
7. Plan introduction and conclusion. → *See Chapter 7.*
8. Make preparation outline (or storyboards) and speaking notes. → *See Chapter 8.*
9. Prepare visual aids. → *See Chapter 9.*
10. Rehearse speech.

---

which required him to present numerous speeches both at home and abroad. He holds an MBA degree and serves on the boards of the Boys and Girls Clubs of America, the Children's Health Fund, and the United Negro College Fund. When Powell speaks, he is warm and dynamic and makes emotional contact with his listeners—listeners feel that he really cares about them (and he does). (For more on Powell, see Powell, 1995 and Harari, 2002.)

These three speakers do more than just prepare convincing and well-organized ideas; they present their ideas in a believable manner. They communicate verbally, visually, and vocally with their audiences. And so can you. As Iacocca said in his autobiography, "You can have brilliant ideas, but if you can't get them across, your brains won't get you anywhere" (Iacocca & Novak, p. 16). Your delivery isn't more important than what you have to say, *but without good delivery, your audience may never hear what you have to say.* To make your presentation believable, you must rehearse, which is the final but very important step in the Basic Steps for Preparing a Speech (listed above). This chapter will give you suggestions for improving your visual, vocal, and verbal delivery, ending with specific rehearsal suggestions. → *Chapter 11 covers specific pointers on how to perfect your use of language.*

Visual Delivery

Since the audience's first impression comes more from what they see than from what they hear, visual delivery will be discussed first—specifically, how you appear to your listeners and how you handle your visual aids. As a speaker, your overall appearance, facial expressions, eye contact, posture, and gestures all affect how you are perceived by the audience.

Appearance

Right or wrong, audience members use your appearance as their first clue to your status and credibility (Knapp & Hall, 2002). Unless you are certain that some other

---

Using InfoTrac College Edition, run a keyword search for *Republican Convention* and look for Laura Bush's addresses to the 2000 and 2004 conventions in *Vital Speeches.* What differences do you see between the two speeches? Also type in *Democratic Convention* as a keyword search for speeches given at the 2004 Democratic Convention. Read Senator Barack Obama's speech. How was it similar to Laura Bush's 2004 convention speech? How was it different?

Effective speakers (such as Illinois Senator Barack Obama) communicate verbally, visually, and vocally with their audiences.

© Gary Hershorn/Reuters/Corbis

style of dress is more appropriate for the audience and the occasion, dress on the conservative side. For women, this means a suit or dress in a classic style with a simple hairstyle and minimal jewelry (Damhorst & Fiore, 2000). For men, this means dress slacks and a sports coat or a suit and tie with dark shoes (Greenleaf, 1998; Molloy, 1988, 1996). Dark clothes generally communicate authority, rank, and even competence (Damhorst & Reed, 1980, 1986; Molloy, 1996).

Facial Expressions and Eye Contact

We all enjoy listening to speakers who smile appropriately, look at us while speaking, and seem to enjoy giving the speech. With speakers who appear tense, don't smile, and only rarely make eye contract, listeners will probably interpret their behavior in one of two ways:

1. *Observation:* The speaker is nervous.
   Reason: The speaker is not prepared, is inexperienced, or is uncertain.
   Conclusion: Listening is not worth my time.

2. *Observation:* The speaker won't look us in the eye.
   Reason: The speaker is lying, is trying to manipulate us, or doesn't respect us.
   Conclusion: Listening is not worth my time.

In either case, your audience will tune out.

When you make eye contact, hold your gaze for 3 to 5 seconds before moving on to someone else; if your eyes dart too quickly, you will appear nervous. Also be sure to look at people in all parts of the room—some speakers inadvertently favor one side or the other.

Posture, Movement, and Gestures

A relaxed yet straight *posture* makes you look confident, friendly, and energetic. Avoid slumping and hunching your shoulders or putting your weight on one hip; both pos-

tures make you look less confident, less interested, and less believable. In addition, the confidence indicated by straight upper-body posture can be sabotaged by nervous foot tapping. For the best posture, take a comfortable, open stance with one foot slightly ahead of the other, and lean slightly forward without locking your knees. This posture gets you ready to move in any direction yet makes it almost impossible to sway or rock as some speakers do. Also, leaning slightly forward indicates that you have a positive feeling toward the audience.

Don't be afraid to move around occasionally. *Movement* can add interest, energy, and confidence to your presentation. Move at the beginning of an idea to add emphasis, or move as a transition between ideas. If you are using transparencies, be sure you are back at the overhead projector when it's time to put on the next transparency.

The best *gestures* are natural ones. If you don't worry about them, appropriate gestures will usually occur naturally. When speaking to a group of friends about an exciting event, you don't worry about when or how to gesture. In the same way, if you concentrate on getting your meaning across while speaking, your gestures will come naturally. However, the larger the audience, the bigger your gestures must be. For example, imagine it's the seventh-inning stretch at a baseball game and you're talking about the game to a group of friends seated several rows away. Not only will you automatically speak louder, you will also exaggerate your gestures. Do the same when speaking before an audience.

If possible, videotape yourself while practicing your speech or have a friend observe you and make suggestions. Make sure that your gestures are noticeable, and look out for any distracting ones. If you notice a nervous gesture (such as playing with your hair or rubbing your nose), make a concerted effort to stop it or to replace it with a more appropriate gesture. Check your awareness of which gestures stimulate or hinder listening by answering the questions in Figure 10.1. When not gesturing,

Figure 10.1

Nonverbal Awareness Check

Check your awareness of a speaker's nonverbal behaviors by completing the scale below.

*Based on an exercise in Burley-Allen, 1982, p. 113.

Directions: Put an S by those behaviors you think would stimulate listening. Put an H by those behaviors you think would hinder listening.* You can also complete this quiz online under Student Resources for Chapter 10 at the Essentials of Public Speaking website.

____ 1. Constantly moving eyes	____ 16. Looking delighted
____ 2. Smiling	____ 17. Puffing cheeks
____ 3. Nodding	____ 18. Looking straight at listeners
____ 4. Leaning forward	____ 19. Drumming fingers
____ 5. Pausing	____ 20. Shuffling papers
____ 6. Frowning	____ 21. Showing enthusiasm
____ 7. Looking at upper corner of room	____ 22. Hanging head down
____ 8. Rolling eyes	____ 23. Tilting head down
____ 9. Having relaxed body posture	____ 24. Narrowing eyes
____ 10. Folding arms across chest	____ 25. Scowling
____ 11. Pacing	____ 26. Playing with pointer
____ 12. Making eye contact	____ 27. Clearing throat often
____ 13. Jingling coins	____ 28. Moving about calmly
____ 14. Gesturing	____ 29. Sighing
____ 15. Looking out window	____ 30. Walking to side of podium

Answers

Behaviors 2–5, 9, 12, 14, 16, 18, 21, 23, 28, and 30 would stimulate listening.

The remaining behaviors would most likely hinder listening.

rest a hand on the lectern or let your hands fall naturally at your sides. Using visual aids will keep your hands so busy that you won't have time to worry about them.

Handling Visual Aids

When you practice your speech, practice using your visual aids. Let's look at the do's and don'ts of handling each type of visual aid.

Using Electronic/Multimedia Presentations Whether you are showing your electronic visuals on a computer or on a screen in front of the room, you should keep several do's and don'ts in mind:

- *Do limit the number of slides you use*—your visuals should add to your speech, not replace it. ➜ *See Chapter 9, p. 194 for the formula to help you determine the appropriate number of slides.*

- *Do use a cordless mouse or remote* so that you can advance your slides from anyplace in the room.

- *Don't turn your back to the audience while you look at the screen.* If you need to look or point to the screen, step back beside it.

- *Do make sure the audience can see you when the lights are turned off.* Determine this well before the speech begins. If the listeners will need to take notes, see if you can use a room with soft can-lights on a dimmer switch. (Newer data projectors are bright enough that the overhead lights can remain on.)

Using Transparencies Speakers have two main problems with transparencies. The first is *turning their backs to the audience* to check the position of the transparency on the screen. The first time you practice using transparencies, you will discover how strong the urge is to turn and look at the screen. However, turning to check the placement not only looks unprofessional but also keeps you from observing audience reactions to the visual.

The second problem is *leaving transparencies on the screen too long.* If a transparency about one point is still on when you move to another point, it distracts the audience. Therefore, as soon as you have finished discussing a transparency, immediately replace it with another or cover the projector light. To replace transparencies use both hands—one to remove the current transparency and the other to position the new one. To block the projector light, lower the light shield that comes with newer projectors or attach a small piece of cardboard (that you can flip up or down) to the light frame.

Other do's and don'ts for using transparencies:

- *Do align the transparency with the top and left side of the glass.* If your projector has an indentation designed to hold a pointer, place a pencil in it and align your transparencies to that edge.

- *Don't turn on the projector until the first transparency is in place.*

- *Don't use paper to cover lists of items*—the projector fan may blow it onto the floor. Instead, *use a sheet of lightweight cardboard* to cover all but the first item and move the sheet down to uncover each subsequent item as you discuss it.

- *Don't stand in front of the screen*—you may block the view of some audience members. When pointing to the screen, take a couple of steps back so that you are beside the screen rather than in front of it.

- *Do bring an extra bulb*—they tend to burn out at inconvenient moments.

Using 35-Millimeter Slides More practice is required to use slides effectively than to use many other types of visuals. Consequently, keep in mind the following do's and don'ts:

- *Do practice using the remote control in the dark*—it's easy to mistakenly push the reverse button instead of the advance button. If someone else is going to advance slides for you, you must practice together so the helper knows when to advance to the next slide without your having to say, "Next slide, please."

- *Do check lighting options beforehand*—slides don't project well unless the room is dark. In most speaking environments, there are two choices. Either the room can be put in total darkness (which is best for slide clarity), or the dimmers can be set so that some light is on the speaker (which usually means that the screen is also bathed in light). If your slides have dark-colored or black backgrounds, a dark room is a must for legibility.

- *Do exaggerate your verbal and vocal delivery* slightly when speaking in a darkened room—this is important when the audience can't see your facial expressions or gestures.

- *Do make sure your slide carousel fits the projector* (there's no uniform standard) and project two or three slides to make sure that the slides are positioned in the tray correctly. After your speech has begun, it's embarrassing to discover that your slides are upside down or sideways.

- *Don't get caught in the dark*—bring a pencil flashlight to place on the lectern so you can see your notes even if the lectern doesn't have a light.

Using Flipcharts and Posters Although most speaking environments have some type of easel to hold posters, they might not have an easel with a **T-bar** (the horizontal bar to which most flipchart pads attach). People who do a lot of public speaking often purchase their own inexpensive, lightweight easel with a detachable T-bar (most easels have collapsible legs so they can also be used on a table). Or speakers may purchase a flipchart pad with a rigid backing board that folds into a self-standing easel that can be set on a table. In any case, make sure you have a way to display your posters and flipcharts in clear view of your audience. If at all possible, avoid setting posters in the tray of a wall-mounted chalkboard or markerboard—both you and your posters will likely be too far from the audience. Following are some more do's and don'ts:

- For flipcharts, *do prepare lightly penciled guidelines ahead of time* to trace during the speech—you'll appear spontaneous while avoiding misspellings and illegible writing.

- *Don't use white poster boards*—light green or pale blue is easier for your audience to read.

- For posters, *do use dark or black marker pens for text and contrasting colors for emphasis.* Avoid pastel colors like yellow, pink, or light blue, which the audience will be unable to read.

- For flipcharts, *do use watercolor markers*—they won't bleed through the paper onto the next sheet the way permanent markers do.

- *Do try self-stick adhesive* on the back of each flipchart sheet when speaking to a small group. The completed sheets can be placed on the wall (in clear view

of the audience) and referred to later in the speech or during the question-and-answer period.

- *Don't block the visual from audience view* when referring to a poster or flipchart. Stand to the side of the easel and near it. If you will be using a lectern, position the easel so that only a step or two is required to reach your posters or to draw on the flipchart.

Using Markerboards and Chalkboards   These visual aids should be used only as a last resort. Of the two, portable markerboards are preferable because you can position them just as you would an easel—at an angle and close to the lectern. Since your markerboard is at an angle, you can still make occasional eye contact with your audience as you write. By contrast, since your back is toward the audience when you are writing on a chalkboard, it should be avoided, if possible.

Using Objects, Models, and Handouts   The value of using objects to clarify points and add interest can easily be seen by watching a painting, cooking, or sewing program on television. One student, inspired by the way people on these programs use objects, used four jogging shoes as well as a cutaway model of the inside of a shoe to illustrate his points in a speech on selecting jogging shoes. Note the following do's and don'ts:

- *Don't use objects or models that are too small for the audience to see clearly*—frustrated audiences will stop listening. If needed for clarity, use a drawing or an enlarged model of the object, but when possible have the real object on hand for the audience to view after your speech is finished.

- *Do practice using objects and models*—when poorly handled they can distract from your speech and your credibility. For example, one student who was giving a speech about bowling dropped his bowling ball on the floor—the audience was not impressed. Another speaker brought in a kitchen knife

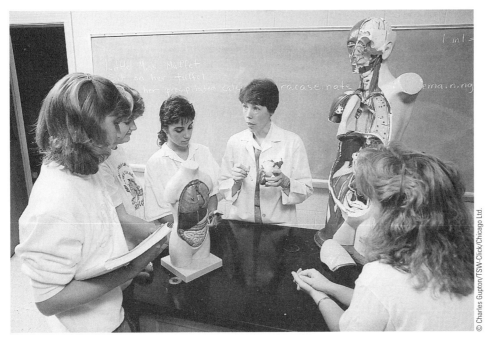

Models clarify and add interest to your presentation.

© Charles Gupton/TSW-Click/Chicago Ltd.

designed to cut through anything, but when he tried to slice through an aluminum can, he failed.

Handouts can also cause distractions if they are not used correctly. Consider the following:

- *Don't distribute handouts before or during the speech*—audience members will likely read them instead of listening to you. If a handout is needed during the speech, be prepared for a loss of attention as it is distributed.

- In some professions, speakers are expected to hand out paper copies of their transparencies or computer slides to audience members. If so, *do reduce the size of the original visuals by 20 percent* (Rabb, 1993). If you want your handout to include both a reproduction of a visual and some explanatory text, reduce the originals even more, as illustrated in Figure 10.2, so that there is room for the additional text.

Figure 10.2

Simple Handout Using Visuals and Text (see actual speech in Chapter 4)

"Our State of Health" by Lucy Tisdale Setliff

#3

Cancer's Warning Signs

1. Bowel/bladder changes
2. Non-healing sore
3. Unusual bleeding/discharge
4. Thickening or lump
5. Indigestion/difficulty swallowing
6. Change in wart/mole
7. Cough/hoarseness

Nat. Cancer Institute

#4

Heart Attack Warnings

- Pressure, fullness, squeezing, pain
- Spreading to shoulders/neck/arms
- Lightheadedness, fainting, sweating, nausea or shortness of breath

American Heart Assoc.

#5

Blood Pressure Warnings

- Systolic pressure above 140
- Diastolic pressure above 90
- Frequent headaches, feelings of tension and irritability, dizziness, and fatigue

Life & Health,
Levy, Dignan, & Shirreffs

Can you list cancer's 7 warning signals without looking? According to the National Cancer Institute, "None of these symptoms is a sure sign of cancer, but if any of them last longer than two weeks, see a doctor."

Don't wait for your symptoms to become painful. The National Cancer Institute warns that "pain is not an early cancer sign." By the time you feel serious pain, it may be too late.

According to the American Heart Association, "Sharp, stabbing twinges usually are *not* signals of heart attack." However, if you feel uncomfortable pressure, fullness, squeezing, or pain in the center of the chest that lasts more than a few minutes, take immediate action. Call 911 and tell them you suspect a heart attack or, if you are near a hospital with a cardiac unit, have someone drive you. Every minute counts. Some experts also recommend that you immediately chew and swallow an aspirin tablet as well.

Blood pressure is measured in two numbers. Systolic pressure (the top number) measures the force of the blood as it travels from the heart into the arteries. Diastolic pressure (the lower number) indicates your blood pressure in between beats.

If you suspect high blood pressure, have your pressure checked regularly and see a physician.

Using Audiovisual Aids Professional or home-prepared video clips and sound bites, whether on VCR, DVD, CD, or audiotape, can add interest to a presentation as long as they are short and run without a hitch. If you are using sound (with or without images), here are a couple of important do's:

- *Do make sure the volume is turned up loud enough* for the people at the back of the room to hear.

- For DVDs or videotapes, *do try turning off the sound*—talk during the tape as you would with other visuals.

- For audiotapes or CDs, *do cue it to the exact place where you want to start*—set the volume and practice smoothly integrating it into your speech.

Final Thoughts on Using Visual Aids As you add visuals to your presentation, keep the following do's in mind:

- *Make sure your visuals add to your presentation,* not distract from it.

- *Conduct a technological rehearsal* if you are using electronic equipment. → *See the Technology Tip for Speakers in this chapter for details.*

- *Arrive early* to check that the equipment works and is located where you want it.

- *Show your visuals only when you are ready to use them.* When you are finished referring to them, remove them from audience view. Even objects and models should be covered or removed from view until you are ready for them.

- *Make sure your back does not face a window,* because the glare from the window will make it difficult for the audience to see your facial expressions.

- If possible, *arrange the chairs so the door is at the back of the room.* This way, late-comers can enter without causing a disturbance.

- *Practice using your pointer.* Lay the pointer down between visuals so it won't be distracting. Some speakers will tap it on the desk or, if it is a telescoping pointer, nervously move it in and out. Even laser pointers require practice for effective use.

- Finally, *practice giving your speech without visuals.* There's always a slight possibility that you will forget to bring them, that the equipment won't be there or will quit working, or that the power will go off. If you have practiced without your visuals at least once, you'll feel more confident should a problem occur.

Vocal Delivery

An audience is more likely to listen closely to your speech and understand your ideas better if you speak in a voice that is conversational, natural, and enthusiastic. **Vocal variety**, the key to a conversational voice, is achieved by varying volume, pitch, emphasis, rate, and pauses in a natural manner, as well as articulating and pronouncing words clearly.

Using InfoTrac College Edition, run a keyword search for speaking tips. Try using *public speaking techniques* and *public speaker*.

Volume and Pitch

For your first speeches, don't strive for perfect delivery. Concentrate on using enough volume and pitch changes to sound conversational and interesting.

Volume, the loudness and softness of your voice, is important in several ways. First, you need to speak loudly enough to be heard all over the room. Second, you need to vary your volume in order to make the speech interesting. Third, you need to increase and decrease your volume to emphasize certain words or phrases.

If your volume (which depends on the amount and force of the air you expel while speaking) is generally too soft, practice saying the word *stop*, emphasizing the *ah* sound while rapidly expelling as much air as possible. Say the word *stop* loudly enough that a person passing by the room could hear you. Don't yell; just speak loudly and project your voice. Practice speaking at this louder volume until it feels comfortable.

Pitch, the highness and lowness of vocal tones, is also important to vocal variety. Effective speakers use two types of pitch changes: (1) steps in pitch (changes between high, medium, and low pitch) and (2) pitch inflection (gradually rising or falling pitch). Together, these pitch changes add interest and energy to speakers' voices and communicate subtle meanings.

First, let's look at *steps in pitch*. Read the sentences below aloud, following the indicated step changes in pitch, and decide which one sounds best:

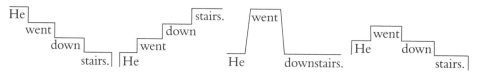

Now, let's look at *pitch inflection*. A rising pitch at the end of a sentence usually signals a question (*She stole the money* ⤴), whereas a falling pitch indicates a statement or understanding (*She stole the money* ⤵). A drawn-out rising pitch implies doubt (*Really* ⤴); a drawn-out high falling pitch implies a light-bulb understanding (*Oh* ⤸, *now I understand*); and a low falling pitch indicates boredom (*Sure* ⤸).

Some speakers (especially during a question-and-answer session) use an upward pitch inflection (called **upspeak**) at the end of declarative sentences and phrases. When overused, the audience will likely perceive this as a sign of insecurity or a desire to gain approval. Say the following sentences, ending each with a downward inflection:

Hello, my name is _____ _____ ⤵. I am a confident speaker ⤵.

Now say the same two sentences, ending each with an upward inflection:

Hello, my name is _____ _____ ⤴. I am a confident speaker ⤴.

Could you hear the difference? With downward inflections, the sentences sound confident; with upward inflections, they sound as if you are asking for approval. Therefore, if you want to sound more interesting and authoritative, use more pitch step and inflection, but limit your use of upspeak.

Emphasis, Rate, and Pauses

Good vocal variety requires more than just effective use of volume and pitch. To make your voice as expressive as possible, you also need to develop your use of emphasis, rate, and pauses.

Emphasis, stressing a word in order to give it significance, is an important ingredient of vocal variety. When you emphasize a word, (1) your pitch goes up (usually followed immediately by a downward inflection), and (2) your volume increases. For a demonstration of this point, say the sentence below five times, each time emphasizing a different word as shown. Listen to your pitch and volume as you speak. You should be able to give five different meanings to the sentence.

Why did you fire him?

Why *did* you fire him?

Why did *you* fire him?

Why did you *fire* him?

Why did you fire *him*?

Rate, how fast or slowly you speak, is especially important in maintaining listeners' attention. Constantly speaking at the same rate can lull your listeners to sleep. Work on varying your speaking rate. Try speaking faster to show excitement or enthusiasm and to emphasize key points; speak more slowly to indicate importance, to build suspense, or to indicate boredom.

Pauses, or "live silence," and **phrases**, groups of words preceded and followed by pauses, also add to listener interest and understanding. Pauses and phrases can be short, medium, or long. If you have ever been told that you speak too fast, it probably means that you don't pause long enough or often enough for your listeners to absorb your ideas. Pauses not only make phrases easier to understand but can also add suspense and dramatic effect. Read the following sentence, each time pausing where indicated with a slash:

That / outfit / looks great / on / you.	(Too many pauses for effective phrasing.)
That outfit looks great on you.	(No pauses needed; the speaker sounds sincere.)
That outfit looks great / on you.	(Pause after *great* makes it sound as if you may like it, but no one else would consider wearing it.)

Try not to fill the "live silence" of a pause with distracting vocalizations such as *ah, uh, um, OK, and uh, well uh,* or *you know.* The silence may seem awkward at first, but pauses give your listeners time to absorb your ideas.

Articulation and Pronunciation

Both articulation and pronunciation are important for maximum audience understanding. Although they are often used synonymously, they are really very different.

Articulation, the production of clear and distinct speech sounds, is vital for audience understanding. Many speakers tend to run words together or leave off some word endings. For example, *Whadayamean* instead of *What do you mean, Seeya* instead of *See you,* and *goin'* instead of *going.* Practice making your articulation crisp and clear by exaggerating all the sounds as you read aloud a rhyme like "Peter Piper picked a peck of pickled peppers" or "To sit in solemn silence in a dull, dark dock."

Pronunciation, saying words according to standard usage, is not always easy. Words that a speaker pronounces "incorrectly" are difficult for listeners to ignore. If your speech includes several mispronounced words, the audience may begin to

doubt your credibility. For example, the chancellor of a large college continually mispronounced the word *registration* when speaking to the faculty. Instead of *rej-i-stra'-shun* the chancellor always said *red-ster-a'-shun,* which made him sound uneducated. Take a look at the following list of commonly mispronounced words to see if you need to work on any of them:

Word	Correct	Incorrect
arctic	arc'-tic	ar'-tic
ask	ask	aks
athlete	ath'-lete	ath'-a-lete
February	Feb'-ru-ary	Feb'-yu-ary
get	get	git
library	ly'-brery	ly'-berry
picture	pic'-ture	pitch'-er
secretary	sek'-ra-terry	sek'-a-terry
with	with	wit or wid
nuclear	nu'-kle-er	nu'-ku-lur

Now that you have read this section on vocal delivery, which two or three areas do you think you need to polish the most? Each time you speak, try to work on an additional vocal skill.

Verbal Delivery

In addition to being aware of your *visual delivery* (your appearance and your visual aids) and your *vocal delivery* (your style of speaking), listeners will pay attention to your *verbal delivery* (the words you choose and the way you construct sentences). Listeners expect speakers to use a more informal language style than is typical for written reports. For example, in oral communication it is best to use short, simple sentences, and it isn't always necessary to use complete sentences. Also, it is perfectly all right to use personal pronouns such as *I, we, you,* and *us* and contractions such as *I've* and *won't*—forms that are often avoided in formal written English. The best language is *vivid* (paints a picture for the listener), *specific* (gives details), and *simple* (easy to understand).

One of the most serious mistakes a speaker can make is to use extremely technical words or *jargon* in an attempt to impress listeners. Even if you are speaking in a professional setting, don't assume that everyone in your audience uses or understands the same technical terms that you do. To drive home this point, one professor who was training people to write government forms and regulations created a sample of the worst kind of bureaucratic writing:

> We respectfully petition, request, and entreat that due and adequate provision be made, this day and date herein under subscribed, for the satisfying of these petitioners' nutritional requirements and for the organizing of such methods of allocation and distribution as may be deemed necessary and proper to assure the reception by and for said petitioners of such quantities of cereal products as shall, in the judgment of the aforementioned petitioners, constitute a sufficient supply thereof (Hensley, 1992, p. 117).

Technology Tip for Speakers

Conduct a Technological Rehearsal

By now you may have learned to effectively use a presentation software program such as PowerPoint or Harvard Graphics. If so, you know how much fun it can be to design and use electronic visuals. However, nothing is worse than clicking to what you thought was a beautiful visual and seeing a blank screen or a missing-picture icon. Just because your presentation looked great on your own computer doesn't mean it will transfer to another computer system. Some computers are not compatible with certain LCD or video projectors. Therefore, it is very important to conduct a technological rehearsal well before your scheduled presentation.

■ Unless you are planning to use your own computer, test your disk/CD by trying it on two or three different computers. If certain sounds, clip art, or pictures don't appear, locate the original files on your computer and save them onto your disk. *Note:* PowerPoint 2003 has a feature under File / Package for CD that lets you save your entire presentation to a CD. It includes a new Viewer that allows your presentation (created in PowerPoint 2000 or later) to run on any computer operating Windows 98 Second Edition or later, *even when PowerPoint is not installed on the computer.* The Viewer is available free on Microsoft's website.

■ If you can't see the slides on your laptop screen at the same time the audience sees them on the wall screen, press Ctrl+F7. Once PowerPoint has loaded, click F5 to open your slides to a full-screen presentation. For an even more professional way to load PowerPoint, save your presentation as a PowerPoint show (.pps)—go to File / Save As, select PowerPoint Show, and click Save. Now a simple double-click on your presentation icon will immediately show a full-screen view of your opening slide without any indication that PowerPoint is running.

■ Talk through your presentation, clicking your visuals when needed. To make sure your speech fits within the required time, you can practice with PowerPoint's Rehearse Timings feature. It will show you both the total time spent and the time spent on each slide. Don't forget to turn off the Timings feature before giving the actual speech.

■ Practice using a remote control if possible—it frees you from the keyboard so you can advance slides from any place in the room.

■ To move back and forth between slides, press the number of the slide and then the Enter key. For example, if you are on slide 6 when someone asks a question about slide 3, simply press 3 and Enter to switch to slide 3. To return to the beginning of your presentation, use Ctrl+Home; to return to the end of the presentation, use Ctrl+End.

■ Print a paper copy of your slides by selecting Handouts (four to six slides per page) and Frame Slides. Number your slides for easy reference in case you need to move back and forth between slides.

■ Regardless of the success of the technological rehearsal, if the presentation is really important, have a backup (transparencies or handouts) in case of equipment or power failure.

Were you able to interpret this paragraph? According to the professor, it illustrates how most bureaucrats would write "Give us this day our daily bread."

A recent postcard sent to customers by SBC was intended to communicate that if the customer changed service plans, all remaining funds would transfer to the new plan; but if customers cancelled their service, they would "only get half their remaining money back" (Lazarus, 2004). Here is part of the actual card. Does it make sense to you?

> If the Customer moves between Business Optional Calling Plans a UUF may be assessed. If the remaining unpaid portion of the original plan's Total Revenue Commitment is greater that the Total Revenue Commitment of the new plan, the UUF is equal to the lesser of:
> a. the difference between the dollar value of the unpaid portion of the Customer's Total Revenue Commitment on the Customer's current term plan and the dollar value of the Customer's Total Commitment for its new term plan agreement, or
> b. 50% of the unpaid portion of the Customer's Total Revenue Commitment on the Customer's current plan that is being canceled by the Customer.

Another mistake that many speakers make is using language that risks offending audience members due to gender, race, age, or disabilities. For example, avoid using gender-specific terms (such as *he* used as a generic term to refer to both males and females), and replace them with gender-neutral alternatives (such as *humanity* instead of *mankind*). Figure 10.3 lists additional words and their suggested alternatives.

Putting your ideas into simple, easy-to-understand language that fits the frames of reference of your listeners and is vivid, specific, and bias-free can be hard at first. But as you work on the basics of delivery and keep the principles discussed here in mind, your language and speaking style will improve. → *Additional language tips are included in Chapter 11.*

Figure 10.3

Alternatives to Gender-Specific Terms

SOURCE: Ivy & Backlund, 2003; Online Writing Lab, 2004.

▼ Biased Words and Phrases	▼ Gender-Neutral Alternatives
anchorman	anchor; newscaster
actress	actor
chairman	chair; chairperson; coordinator
comedienne	comedian
congressman	congressional representative
fellow classmates	classmates
fireman	firefighter
lady, girl, gal, or doll	woman
mailman/postman	mail carrier; postal worker
man-eating	flesh-eating; carnivorous
mankind	humankind; humanity; people
man-made	artificial; synthetic; manufactured
modern man	modern people; modern civilization
mother earth	earth
mother hen	nurturer
policeman or policewoman	police officer
signing your John Hancock	signing your name
stewardess or steward	flight attendant

Immediacy Behaviors

Researchers use the term **immediacy behaviors** for the verbal, visual, and vocal behaviors that instructors use to promote a sense of closeness and personal interaction with students. Studies show that students learn significantly more and have a better attitude toward the classroom experience when instructors use these behaviors (Baringer & McCroskey, 2000: Gorham, 1988; Kelsey, Kearney, Plax, Allen, & Ritter, 2004; Menzel & Carrell, 1999)—even when the class is a web course (Arbaugh, 2001; LaRose & Whitten, 2000). As the size of the class increases, so does the importance of immediacy behaviors (Gorham). Although research on immediacy behavior has focused on teachers and students, public-speaking environments have similar characteristics.

The three speakers mentioned at the beginning of the chapter (Lee Iacocca, Oprah Winfrey, and Colin Powell) use immediacy behaviors. What are these behaviors?

Verbal and vocal immediacy behaviors include:

- Using humor sensitively

- Citing personal instances and experience

- Referring to the group as *we* and *our*

- Praising individuals for their work, actions, or comments

- Referring to people by name (especially when giving praise)

- Occasionally asking for opinions and questions

- Conversing with the audience before and after the presentation

- Being vocally expressive—that is, using good volume, pitch, emphasis, and rate

Visual immediacy behaviors include:

- Making eye contact

- Smiling at appropriate times at individuals as well as at the group as a whole

- Keeping a relaxed posture

- Gesturing naturally

- Moving around rather than staying behind the lectern

To decrease the psychological distance between you and your listeners and replace it with a feeling of closeness, make your verbal, visual, and vocal immediacy behaviors work for you.

Methods of Delivery

Often the success of your presentation depends on your method of delivery: extemporaneous speaking from brief notes, extemporaneous speaking from visual aids, impromptu speaking (without prior knowledge of a specific topic), speaking from a written manuscript, or speaking from memory.

Using InfoTrac College Edition, you can find several interesting articles on extemporaneous speaking. Run a subject search for *extemporaneous speaking*.

Speaking From Brief Notes (Extemporaneous Speaking)

For most speeches, you will be most effective and connect best with your audience if you speak extemporaneously. An **extemporaneous speech** is not memorized or written out word for word; it is developed and presented from brief notes. In planning an extemporaneous speech, you follow the Basic Steps for Preparing a Speech that we have been discussing in the preceding chapters. Each time you give an extemporaneous presentation, it will be a little different because you have not memorized it.

To prepare notes, turn your preparation outline into key-word notes and copy them onto one or two note cards. Write each quotation on a separate card. If you are using transparencies, notes can go on the transparency frames. With computer visuals, you probably won't need any additional notes, but be sure to have a hard copy with you in case of equipment failure.

Speaking from brief key-word notes allows you to sound conversational, maintain good eye contact with listeners, and alter your speech if feedback indicates that some listeners may be confused. ➡ *See more on speaking notes in Chapter 8.*

Speaking From Visual Aids (Also Extemporaneous Speaking)

Many business and professional speakers use another form of extemporaneous speaking—speaking from visual aids (Smith, 2004). Like the outlined extemporaneous presentation, the visual aid method is not memorized or written out word for word. Instead of note cards, however, speakers use their PowerPoint slides as a memory device or refer to printed copies of their slides (nine per page works well).

If you plan to use animation so that each point comes in at the click of the mouse, consider building your own bullets, which allows them to remain stationary with the title. This helps you recall exactly how many points you planned for each slide. In contrast, PowerPoint Bullets, which fly in with each point, make it difficult to remember how many points a slide has—especially if you are a bit nervous.

 ➡ *For specifics, see the PowerPoint Speaker's Guide under Student Resources for Chapter 9 at the Essentials of Public Speaking website.*

Speaking Impromptu

An **impromptu speech** is one given without prior knowledge of the specific topic and without detailed notes or manuscript—obviously a hazardous way to give a major speech. However, anytime you are unexpectedly asked a question (in class, at a PTA meeting, or on your job), your response is an impromptu speech. Ideally, even though you have no time to prepare for the specific question, you will sound intelligent, authoritative, and confident because you have practiced answering questions. Wiles (2001) recommends that you set up a video camera and tape yourself answering some difficult questions asked by a friend. The more you practice, the more confident you will become.

When asked to do impromptu speaking, try the following (Stone & Bachner, 1994):

- *Appear confident* (even if you must pretend).

- *Decide on your conclusion or objective first* so that everything you say can lead up to it in an organized manner.

- *Begin with a general statement or background information* to give yourself time to think of one or more supporting reasons for your conclusion.

- *Introduce your supporting reasons with the word "because"* to give yourself time to think. For example:

    Q: Do you think speech training should be a requirement for all college students?

    A: *Because* most college students have to give presentations in upper-level courses, and *because* many college students will be getting jobs that demand speaking skills, I see speech training as an important requirement for all college students.

Another technique for answering impromptu questions is a simple *three-step method* recommended by Dr. Susan Huxman of Wichita State University: (1) Make a single point, (2) support that point, and (3) restate that point.

Question-and-answer sessions are another type of impromptu speaking. Even though you should plan for possible questions, many questions will be unexpected and require an impromptu response. Answer these questions directly and honestly. Exceptions are questions that you don't wish to answer or for which you don't have an answer (and feel it would be unacceptable to say, "I don't know"). In such cases, it may be justifiable to change the topic. Politicians are very good at changing the subject, using such comments as

"That's an important question—almost as important as . . ."

"I was hoping someone would ask me that question, because it gives me an opportunity to talk about . . ."

"Could I come back to that question? I've been wanting to reply to the remark this gentleman made earlier. He said . . ."

"I think we need to look at the problem from a different angle . . ."

If you don't have figures and sources at your fingertips, you can use a personal, family, or humorous instance to clarify and support your point. For example, in an impromptu speech on "What types of animals make the best pets?" a student supported her point that the best pets are dogs by telling the audience about her three dogs. She told them what kinds of dogs she had, gave their names, and described an instance that showed what good companions they were. The instance was both humorous and heartwarming. The audience loved her speech. ➞ *Chapter 6 gives more examples of instances.*

There's no telling when your next impromptu speaking opportunity may occur, but it could be one of the most important and successful short speeches you give. You will probably have several opportunities to give impromptu speeches in class. Try the techniques suggested here until you find the one technique or variety of techniques that work best for you.

Speaking From a Manuscript

Although it might seem that reading your speech would be easy, speaking from a manuscript is much harder than speaking from notes. It's difficult to use good vocal variety and maintain direct eye contact while reading a speech word for word. Also, unless you occasionally deviate from the manuscript, you can't respond to verbal or nonverbal listener feedback, so your talk will likely seem somewhat stiff and remote.

Manuscript speeches are usually given by politicians and top-level business and professional people who must give copies of their speeches ahead of time to the media. These public figures need to make sure that what they say is exact enough to avoid misinterpretations, especially in an emergency or unexpected situation (such as the briefing to the press after the capture of Saddam Hussein in Iraq), and to guard against saying something unintentionally.

If you must use a manuscript, be sure that the manuscript is double- or triple-spaced in 14- or 16-point type. Use a hole punch and place manuscript pages into a stiff binder. Practice holding the binder high enough that you can glance down at the manuscript without having to bob your head. Be sure to practice reading it until your pitch, rate, volume, and emphasis make you sound authoritative yet conversational and you are able to glance up and make eye contact with listeners often enough to look natural. ➞ *To see how difficult it is to speak effectively from a manuscript and why speech teachers don't want you to give speeches this way, try Practice Suggestion 4 at the end of the chapter.*

Speaking From Memory

Speaking from memory has even more drawbacks than reading from a manuscript. First, it takes a great deal of time and effort to memorize a speech. Second, speaking from memory makes it difficult to react to listener feedback. A question from a listener can make you forget the next sentence or maybe even the rest of your speech. Or if facial expressions indicate audience confusion, you can hardly risk deviating from your practiced speech to add another example. Also, it's difficult to make your delivery relaxed, spontaneous, and believable if you are trying to recall memorized text. There's one more drawback to depending exclusively on memorized speeches: They won't work on occasions when there's only enough time to decide on your main points and find the necessary supporting materials. Always memorizing your speeches is a crutch that could easily work against you in the future.

Some speakers do feel more comfortable memorizing their opening and closing remarks and, sometimes, the transitions between main points. Memorizing small segments such as these shouldn't cause a problem; just don't memorize the entire speech.

Rehearsing Your Speech

There is a big difference between reading about delivering a speech effectively and actually doing it. The only way to transfer what you have read in this chapter into what you can do is to practice. Remember that your goal is to sound confident and natural—just the way you do when talking to friends. If you have been visualizing yourself giving an effective speech since reading Chapter 2, you have taken an important first step toward confident delivery. If you haven't been visualizing, find the positive statements you wrote about yourself as a speaker and read them several times. As you read each one (for example, "It's easy for me to make direct eye contact with my audience while speaking"), picture yourself in front of the class, looking directly at the audience and feeling good about it.

Feeling confident while speaking is one of the benefits of rehearsing. The following suggestions will help you as you practice:

■ At least in the beginning you will probably want some type of speaking notes. However, the fewer the notes, the better!

Before rehearsing in front of others, practice alone (as this speaker is doing). Once you feel comfortable, ask a friend or family member to listen and give you suggestions.

© Dwayne E. Newton/PhotoEdit

- Practice your speech out loud—thinking through it silently does not count as practice. It may help you check for problems of organization and familiarize yourself with the content, but it won't help at all with your vocal or visual delivery and will help only a little with your verbal delivery. There is no substitute for standing on your feet, using your notes and visual aids, practicing your gestures and eye contact, and speaking aloud.

- Practice alone at first. Tape-record yourself in order to get feedback on your vocal delivery, or practice in front of a mirror. If possible, practice in a room similar to the one in which you will be speaking. If your practice room does not have the equipment necessary for using your visuals, simulate handling them.

- After you begin to feel comfortable with your speech, practice it in front of a friend or family member. Ask them for specific comments on your verbal, visual, and vocal delivery. Practice making direct eye contact and using gestures. If you have a video camera, let a friend film you so that you can observe yourself. If you discover any awkward spots in your talk, decide how to alter the speech to smooth them out.

- At least once before the actual speech (two or three times would be better), practice using your visual aids with all the equipment. Videotape yourself if possible, or ask a friend to observe one of your final practices.

- Try to get plenty of sleep the night before your speech. On the day of the speech, get to class early so that you can compose yourself, check to see that your notes and visuals are in the proper order, and read through your outline one last time.

■ Plan for the unexpected. Laura Bush certainly didn't expect the confetti dropping from the ceiling of the 2000 Republican Convention to cause problems with the two teleprompters as she began her speech. Fortunately, a large screen was mounted on the back wall and she was able to read her speech from there.

Remember, no one expects perfection. If you make a mistake, correct it if necessary and go on. Then forget it. If you have practiced until you feel comfortable with your speech and have visualized yourself giving a successful speech, you should feel excited and confident.

Summary

Successfully delivering your message depends on three important aspects of delivery—visual, vocal, and verbal codes. Effective visual delivery entails paying close attention to your appearance, facial expressions, eye contact, posture, movement, and gestures, as well as the content and handling of your visual aids. Effective vocal delivery is achieved by varying volume, pitch, emphasis, rate, and pauses, as well as making sure your articulation is clear and your pronunciation is correct. The best speaking voice is one that sounds conversational, natural, and enthusiastic. Rarely do people achieve their best speaking voice without practice. Effective verbal delivery results from the use of vivid, specific, simple, and bias-free language. It is also important that your verbal message fit the frames of reference of your listeners.

Your delivery can be enhanced by using immediacy behaviors such as making direct eye contact, smiling, being vocally expressive, using humor, and referring to your audience as *we*. These behaviors reduce the psychological distance between speaker and audience.

In addition to your visual, vocal, and verbal delivery, your method of delivery can affect the success of your speech. In most cases, speaking from a manuscript or memorizing your speech should be avoided. Impromptu speaking is a good way to gain confidence in speaking. If you can add a personal or humorous instance, not only will your audience enjoy your speech, but you will feel more relaxed as well. The preferred method of delivery for major classroom speeches is extemporaneous speaking, which involves careful preparation and speaking from brief notes or visual aids.

The only way to transfer what you have learned from this chapter into a dynamic, believable delivery is to practice. First, visualize yourself giving a successful speech. Then practice your speech aloud using visual aids. You will soon find yourself getting compliments on the way you deliver your speeches.

Essentials of Public Speaking   Online

Use the Essentials of Public Speaking website at **http://communication. wadsworth.com/hamiltoneps3** for quick access to the electronic study resources that accompany this chapter. When you get to the Essentials home page, click on "Student Book Companion Site" in the Resource box. The Essentials website features the Nonverbal Awareness Check on page 212, the PowerPoint Speaker's Guide mentioned on page 224, InfoTrac College Edition, the Suggestions for Practice and

Critical Thinking activities and the InfoTrac College Edition activities that follow, a digital glossary, and review quizzes.

Key Terms

articulation 219
emphasis 219
extemporaneous speech 224
immediacy behavior 223

impromptu speech 224
pause 219
phrase 219
pitch 218
pronunciation 219

rate 219
T-bar 214
upspeak 218
vocal variety 217
volume 218

Suggestions for Practice and Critical Thinking

1. To get an idea of how your voice sounds to others, leave a detailed message on your answering machine or voice mail system. Do this regularly until your vocal variety and tone project the warmth, enthusiasm, or authority you desire (Decker & Denney, 1993).

2. Using InfoTrac College Edition, conduct a keyword or subject-guide search for the term *gestures*. How many articles did you locate? Read at least two of the articles and share any speaking tips that you find.

3. Keep a brief log of any particularly good speeches you see live or on TV. What specific visual, vocal, and verbal techniques made the speeches so effective?

4. For Practice Suggestion 4 in Chapter 9, you prepared at least two visual aids that you thought would clarify and add power to a speech given previously by someone else. Read the manuscript (or at least a 2-minute portion of it) to the class using the visuals you prepared. Follow the guidelines in this chapter for reading from a manuscript. As you read, make your delivery as effective as possible. Not only will this assignment show you how difficult it is to speak from a manuscript and why your instructor requires extemporaneous speeches, but it will give you a chance to polish your visual, vocal, and verbal delivery without having to worry about speech content.

5. With a group of classmates, select a scene from a play, a short story, or a children's storybook such as a Dr. Seuss book. Assign characters or parts to each and practice presenting it as a readers' theater. (In a readers' theater, participants sit on stools and speak directly to the audience, not to each other—thereby creating the action in the minds of the audience.) Be sure to make your vocal and visual cues fit the story.

6. Practice reading to a small group of classmates the following excerpt from Michael Warder's (1993) speech, "The Politics of Cultural War." Try to present the speech as you think he would have delivered it at the 1993 Chicago Conservative Conference. Then discuss with classmates how you could read this excerpt so that an audience would realize that you do not believe what you are saying. Take turns reading it aloud before the class.

Foolish? I'll tell you what's foolish. Foolish is setting up another federal program to fix the family, fix education, fix race relations, fix out-of-wedlock births, fix urban housing, or any other federal program that's supposed to fix a personal or social problem. I can't think of any institution more ill-suited to solve these kinds of problems. Seeking to involve the federal government in our social lives is a little like an ant inviting an elephant over to its home for dinner. The federal government tends to crush whatever small things with which it comes in contact.

7. Using a humorous instance speech and the delivery suggestions covered in this chapter, have a "talkdown" with a classmate to see who is more successful at capturing and holding audience attention. At the end of 1 or 2 minutes, have the audience vote on which speaker held their attention more of the time. This activity could include all members of the class or only four to six volunteers—always with two people speaking at once. ➡ *Read more about humorous incident speeches in the Quick Start Guide at the beginning of this book.*

8. With a partner, select a 1-minute segment from a speech that uses effective language style. (Use InfoTrac College Edition to find a current issue of *Vital Speeches,* or look under the student resources for Chapters 1, 4, 8, and 12–14 at the Essentials of Public Speaking website for sample student speeches.) On the appointed day, each pair should have a "read-down"—both students reading the same selection at the same time, each student using good visual and vocal delivery. At the end of each reading, have the audience vote on which speaker held their attention more of the time. This activity is fun and shows the importance of good delivery when reading quotes during a speech.

9. Check out the following websites. *You can access these sites under the Student Resources for Chapter 10 at the Essentials of Public Speaking website.*

   • What did classical orators say about emphasis? For more information on classical rhetoric, see Robert Gwynne's website, Classical Rhetoric.

   • Having problems with *uh* and *um*? Read "Throwing Away Your Verbal Crutches: Avoiding the Uhhh Factor" at speaker Stephen Eggleston's website, The Egg-Man.com. Click on "Presentations & Communications," then on "Throw Away Your Verbal Crutches." Worried about speaker anxiety? Read "How to Conquer Public Speaking Fear" by Morton C. Orman, M.D.

   • Read the interesting article on teleprompters, "New Prompters Open New Presentation Opportunities," by Lorin Fisk at PresentersUniversity.com. Click on "Courses" at the top of the page, then on "Visual Aids." Under "Choosing the Appropriate Vehicle," click on the article link.

Perfecting Language Style

Flashback In his *Orator,* Cicero describes three kinds of rhetorical styles—Plain, Middle, and Grand. Skilled rhetoricians were advised to vary their use of styles:

- **The Plain style**, used to prove or inform, was an "easy" style subdued in delivery, language, and ornamentation.
- **The Middle style**, used to gain attention or entertain, was a polished style that included humor, wit, and ornamentation of all kinds.
- **The Grand style**, reserved for persuasive situations, was eloquent, dramatic, and fiery. However, Cicero cautioned speakers that to use only the Grand style could make them appear demented.

READ THE FOLLOWING SPEAKER COMMENTS AND SELECT THE MORE PERSUASIVE ONE (A OR B):

1. a. Although there are three frequently presented arguments in favor of legalizing drugs, none of them holds up under careful scrutiny. In fact, as you will see, all three arguments are based on faulty reasoning. The first fallacious argument is . . .

   b. Let's look at three arguments in favor of drug legalization. The first argument is . . .

2. a. When legislation on sobriety checkpoints comes up for a vote in your county, think about what I've said in making your decision.

   b. When legislation on sobriety checkpoints comes up for a vote in your county, vote yes. It's time we made our roads safe again.

3. a. There are three points that I'd like to cover today about the Electoral College.

   b. There are three points I'd like to cover today that will demonstrate how hopelessly out of date and ineffective the Electoral College really is.

It wasn't difficult to choose, was it? Persuasive language generally specifies a preferred belief or action and is more forceful than informative language. Now that you have given a number of speeches and are aware of some of the strengths and weaknesses of your delivery, it is time to polish your verbal delivery and perfect your use of language style. As a speaker, your use of language can clarify your ideas, add impact and interest to your message, enhance the audience's perception of you as an ethical speaker, and add forcefulness to your main points or arguments.

Why Language Choices Are So Important

To see how changing a single word can create different emotional reactions, consider the following example:

> A boy called to his mother that he saw a "snake." Hurrying to his aid, the boy's amused mother used a broom handle to dislodge what turned out to be a sleeping garden hose.

Reread the sentences, replacing *amused* with (1) *frightened,* (2) *furious,* and then (3) *long-suffering.* How did these words affect your reaction to the anecdote? Your choice of words influences your listeners' reaction to your speech. The English language gives you plenty of choices. There are approximately 615,000 words in the *Oxford English Dictionary* (Lederer, 1999), and more than 10,000 of them have been added since 1961 (Gozzi, 1990). Your language choices are important for three reasons:

1. *Language can clarify your ideas* by creating vivid mental images for your audience. Even though your listeners may not have personally experienced what you are talking about, they can experience it through the mental image your words create. A good mental image creates both a picture and the accompanying feelings—such as pride, frustration, sadness, or guilt.

2. *Language can influence your audience's attitudes and behaviors.* Advertisers and politicians certainly know the power of language. They know that people

Listeners tend to be attentive to speakers who have perfected their language style.

© Jim Daniels/The Picture Cube

who display bumper stickers, campaign buttons, and T-shirts with their logo are more likely to vote for the candidate or remain loyal to the product because, in using these items, they have already committed themselves (Larson, 2004).

3. *Language can add to audience interest and enjoyment.* Or it can be boring. You don't have to be an expert speaker to make your speeches interesting and enjoyable—just use words that are simple, specific, vivid, and forceful (as discussed in the following section).

Stop reading and take a moment to recall your previous speeches. On the basis of evaluation forms and audience comments, in what ways do you use language that is especially effective? What areas do you feel could use some work?

Effective Language Style

Style is the way you use language to express your ideas. Although language choices must be appropriate to the situation, generally the best language is simple, specific, vivid, and forceful.

Simple Language

Good speakers use simple language. Rarely are listeners impressed by speakers who use long, technical words or who sprinkle each sentence with jargon. In other words, there is no reason to use *precipitation* instead of *rain*. During World War II, President Franklin Delano Roosevelt reacted strongly to the wordiness of this government memo about wartime blackout procedures (O'Hayre, 1966):

> Such preparations shall be made as will completely obscure all Federal buildings and non-Federal buildings occupied by the Federal Government during an air raid for any period of time from visibility by reason of internal or external illumination. Such obscuration may be obtained either by blackout construction or by termination of the illumination.

Roosevelt was so offended by the poor writing that he immediately sent back this rewritten version:

> Tell them that in buildings where they have to keep the work going, to put something over the windows; and, in buildings where they can let the work stop for awhile, to turn out the lights.

Confusing an audience by using $50 words when $1 words will work just as well or using unfamiliar technical words is called **gobbledygook** or bureaucratese (Lutz, 2000). One of the worst offenders in the use of gobbledygook was Alexander Haig, who served as chairman of the Joint Chiefs of Staff and later as secretary of state. Haig, who combined the language of diplomacy with the language of his previous job as a general, confused people with such phrases as "careful caution," "caveat my response," "epistemologically wise," "nuanced departures," "definitizing an answer," and "saddle myself with a statistical fence" (Rackleff, 1987).

 Using InfoTrac College Edition, run a keyword search using *plain language* and note the wide range of professions complaining about the lack of plain language. Especially note the 1998 memo sent by former President Bill Clinton called "Memorandum on plain language in government writing." You might also run a keyword search using *ambiguity* as well as *strategic ambiguity* for additional articles.

Specific Language

Specific words are concrete rather than abstract. **Abstract words** describe intangible concepts that are difficult to picture (such as *devotion* or *health*), whereas **concrete words** describe tangible things that listeners can picture (such as *apple* or *smile*). If your words are specific enough, the audience most likely will have a clear picture of your meaning. Which of the following is easier to picture?

> My dog is mischievous.
>
> *or:*
>
> My West Highland white terrier may look like an angel, but she has a mischievous heart. When she was a puppy, I left her locked in the kitchen for one hour. She peeled off the wallpaper as far up as she could reach, tugged a loose tile off the floor and ripped it to pieces, and chewed holes in the bottom three slats of the miniblinds. One hour—one puppy! How could we name her anything else but Mischief?

Using specific language is especially important when the intent of your message is to persuade. Remember, the purpose of persuasion is to *influence* choices, not to *distort* or *confuse* choices.

Avoid Ambiguous Words Instead of specific words, some speakers use **ambiguous words**—words that have vague, unclear meanings that can be understood in more than one way. When used unintentionally (such as, "My children like our cat more than me"), ambiguous words can be confusing; when used deliberately to sway an audience, they are unethical.

For example, instead of presenting a clear stand on taxation, a senator might use the ambiguous phrase *responsibility in taxation and education,* hoping that it will be interpreted positively by people with differing views. When words have ambiguous meanings, listeners use their own frames of reference to interpret them. In the example just mentioned, voters who believe that teachers are underpaid might think the senator is advocating "spending tax dollars" and vote in favor; those who think that educational spending is too high might think the senator is advocating "cutting educational spending" and also vote in favor (Larson, 2004, p. 128). Although using specific words that make clear the intended fiscal policy could lose votes for the senator, using ambiguous words to deceive listeners into taking an action that they would not normally take is unethical.

Avoid Euphemisms Some speakers try to remove emotional overtones from words by using euphemisms. **Euphemisms** are words with positive overtones (connotations) substituted for words with negative overtones. In some cases, this might be a wise thing for a speaker to do. For example, *special* sounds more accepting than *handicapped,* and *husky* doesn't carry the negative connotation of *fat* or *obese.* Considering how upset Americans were after the explosion of the space shuttle *Challenger,* NASA's decision to refer to the crew's coffins as "crew transfer containers" reflected the agency's (perhaps misguided) attempt to diminish the horror. But when a euphemism is used to mask, mislead, or manipulate audience response, it is unethical. This was the case when the phrase "ethnic cleansing" was used to describe the genocide in Bosnia in 1995 or in the Sudan in 2004.

Vivid Language

In addition to simple yet specific words, effective speakers use vivid language. For the most impact, use the active rather than the passive voice (*active:* "Jorge shoved John"; *passive:* "John was shoved by Jorge"). Vivid speakers avoid vague phrases such as "It is believed," they use a variety of interesting supporting materials, and they speak directly to their listeners as though they were having a private conversation with them. Vivid (concrete) words—especially ones that stimulate mental images in listeners' minds—are also easier to remember (Bryden & Ley, 1983; Hishitani, 1991). For example, words like *friend, snake,* and *corpse* are high-imagery words and are easier to remember than words like *devotion, greed,* and *cost,* which are low-imagery (abstract) words. Adding some vivid adjectives to the concrete words will enhance the imagery even further (for example, a *long, slimy snake*).

Vivid speakers also use words to paint a mental picture in the minds of listeners. In fact, vivid language is a mental visual aid. Returning to our example of the boy and the "snake," which of the following descriptions paints a clearer picture?

> A child claimed that he saw a large snake, but when his mother found it, it was only a garden hose.
>
> *or:*
>
> An 8-year-old boy called to his mother that he saw a huge green snake lurking under the porch. Hurrying to his aid, his amused mother used a broom handle to dislodge what turned out to be a sleeping garden hose.

Picture in your mind what you are describing, and you will find that it is easier to transfer this mental picture to your audience through your language.

Forceful Language

As the examples at the beginning of the chapter illustrate, the words you use in a speech can carry varying degrees of force or strength. **Forceful language** (which

Former Texas Governor Ann Richards is known for her personable and vibrant speaking style.

© Wide World Photos, Inc.

involves effective use of volume, emphasis, and pitch) is especially important in persuasion—it adds to the audience's confidence in the speaker (Bradac & Mulac, 1984; Gibbons, Busch, & Bradac, 1991; Sparks, Areni, & Cox, 1998).

Let's take a closer look at the third set of speaker comments from the beginning of the chapter. *Statement 3a* ("There are three points that I'd like to cover today about the Electoral College") not only implies (incorrectly) that this will be an informative speech, but gives no indication of the speaker's position. However, *statement 3b* ("There are three points I'd like to cover today that will demonstrate how hopelessly out of date and ineffective the Electoral College really is") makes it clear that this will be a persuasive speech, indicates the speaker's position, and through forceful language conveys confidence. The persuasive process has already begun. Even in an informative speech, forceful language can give listeners confidence in you and in your evidence.

Speaking forcefully tends to be harder for women than for men. In a speech called "Taking the Stage: How Women Can Achieve a Leadership Presence," Judith Humphrey (2001), president of the Humphrey Group, gave this advice:

> If you're taking the stage, do so with bold clear language. We find in our work that many women have trouble being direct. Introductory phrases like "in my opinion," "as I see it," or "it's only a thought" downplay our ideas. There's too much apologizing and self-correction in the language women use.
>
> When women do express their ideas directly, they often soften the impact. They use weak verbs: "I think," "I will attempt to," "I'm trying to," "I'm not sure." They use qualifiers: "I'd just like to review." They use past tense. For example: "What I wanted to talk about today was our priorities." (Instead of "I'd like to talk about our priorities.") They also use emotional language and the language of dependency—talking about "being concerned" or "needing that."
>
> In contrast, I listen to the strong words of Margaret Thatcher when she told Britons about the campaign to retake the Falkland Islands: "Now we are present in strength on the Falkland Islands. Our purpose is to repossess them. We shall carry on until that purpose is accomplished."
>
> There's no mistaking her steely resolve. Her sentences are short and to the point. She doesn't qualify, apologize, correct or undercut herself. (p. 437)

Start by concentrating on one or two of these language characteristics. Tape-record a practice speech session and then listen and evaluate it. Replace vague words with specific and vivid ones, and record your speech again. Repeat the process until you are satisfied with your language choices.

Stylistic Devices

In addition to having actual and implied meanings, words can have a texture or "feel"—what persuasion expert Charles Larson (2004) calls the "thematic dimension" of language. This ability of words "to set a mood, develop a feeling, or generate a tone or theme" is "the most important persuasive aspect" of words (p. 134). If your listeners are in the right frame of mind for a particular topic, you will have a better chance of communicating your ideas and concerns to them. Stylistic language devices can help you to establish a mood, both in the introduction and during your presentation.

"Let's change 'Some of the guys' to 'We the people.'"

Stylistic devices gain their entertaining and persuasive power by "departing from everyday language usage" (Cooper & Nothstine, 1992). A **stylistic device** either (1) rearranges sentences in unusual ways or (2) changes "the main or ordinary meaning of a word" (p. 168). This section will cover several of the most popular stylistic devices: alliteration and assonance, antithesis, simile and metaphor, onomatopoeia, repetition and parallelism, hyperbole, and personification. Begin by practicing two or three of these devices. Then add more until you have tried them all. Select the ones that seem to be the most valuable to you and incorporate them into your own style.

Alliteration and Assonance

Alliteration is the repetition of consonants (usually the first or last letter in a word), such as, "Each Wednesday, Willy washes his woolens." **Assonance** is the repetition of vowel sounds, such as, "The low moans of our own soldiers . . ." (Larson, 2004, p. 122). In a speech titled "Conveying the Environmental Message," Peter G. Osgood (1993) used alliteration with the "c" sound in his conclusion:

> It is a matter of culture and it is a matter of conversion. And finally, it is a matter of leadership, commitment and communication. (p. 270)

In his 1961 inaugural address, President John F. Kennedy used several stylistic devices, including alliteration. How many "s" sounds do you hear in this sentence?

> So let us begin anew, remembering on both sides that civility is not a sign of weakness and sincerity is always subject to proof. (Kennedy, 2000, p. 251)

In the same speech, Kennedy also used assonance several times:

> . . . for only when *our arms are* sufficient beyond doubt . . .

> . . . instruments of p*ea*ce, w*e* r*e*new our pledge to pr*e*vent it from b*e*coming . . . (p. 251)

Don't overdo alliteration and assonance, however. Be especially careful with alliteration. You don't want to sound like President Warren G. Harding, who told his audience at the Republican Convention in 1912:

> Progression is not proclamation nor palaver. It is not pretense nor play on prejudice. It is not of personal pronouns, nor perennial pronouncement. It is not the perturbation of a people passion-wrought, nor a promise proposed. (Eigen & Siegel, 1993, p. 467)

Simile and Metaphor

Similes and metaphors compare dissimilar items in order to clarify one of them. **Similes** make direct comparisons using *like* or *as* ("Happiness is like ice cream—both can melt away if you aren't careful"). **Metaphors** are implied comparisons and do not use *like* or *as;* instead, they speak of one item as though it were another ("Happiness is an ice cream cone"). Similes and metaphors create vivid images that improve listeners' understanding and retention of your speech. They can also be very persuasive—they can set a positive or negative tone that influences audience attitudes. ➝ *Similes and metaphors are similar to figurative comparisons discussed in Chapter 6.*

In his conclusion, J. Peter Grace (1993) used the following simile to finalize the tone in a speech titled "Burning Money: The Waste of Your Tax Dollars":

> Now there's a lot of talk coming out of Washington these days about reducing the deficit and, at the same time, increasing government spending. Well, let me tell you, that's like trying to lose weight on a diet of french fries and Big Macs. (p. 566)

In their book *Power Persuasion,* Martha D. Cooper and William L. Nothstine (1992) note that metaphors "gain their power not from altering ordinary sentence structure . . . but from altering usual meanings of words, creating new meaning" (p. 169). In his attempt to unify the Democratic party, the Reverend Jesse Jackson used the metaphor of lions and lambs in his 1988 speech to the Democratic National Convention:

> The Bible teaches that when lions and lambs lie down together none will be afraid and there will be peace in the valley. It sounds impossible. Lions eat lambs. Lambs . . . flee from lions. Yet even lions and lambs find common ground. Why? Because neither lions nor lambs want the forest to catch on fire. Neither lions nor lambs want acid rain to fall. Neither lions nor lambs can survive a nuclear war. If lions and lambs can find common ground, surely we can as well as civilized people. (Cooper & Nothstine, p. 169)

John F. Kennedy's 1961 inaugural address also includes several examples of metaphor (in italics):

> . . . to assist free men and free governments in casting off the *chains* of poverty . . . (Kennedy, 2000, p. 251)

> And if a *beachhead* of cooperation may push back the *jungle* of suspicion, . . . (p. 252)

Onomatopoeia

Although speakers are less likely to use **onomatopoeia**—words that sound like their meanings, such as *buzz, hiss, swish, fizz,* and *ring*—these words can be quite useful in creating a feeling or mood. Martin Luther King, Jr. used onomatopoeia many times

Through onomatopoeia and dynamic delivery in his "I Have a Dream" speech, Martin Luther King, Jr. inspired his listeners.

for effect in his speeches. You are probably most familiar with his use of the word *ring* in his 1963 "I Have a Dream" speech. The way he pronounced the word in "Let freedom ring" created a powerful image of a church bell ringing. And as he repeated it over and over, the ringing seemed to get louder and more intense as he built up to his memorable conclusion:

> So let freedom ring. From the prodigious hilltops of New Hampshire, let freedom ring. From the mighty mountains of New York, let freedom ring, from the heightening Alleghenies of Pennsylvania!
>
> Let freedom ring from the snowcapped Rockies of Colorado!
> Let freedom ring from the curvaceous slopes of California!
> But not only that.
> Let freedom ring from Stone Mountain of Georgia!
> Let freedom ring from Lookout Mountain of Tennessee!
> Let freedom ring from every hill and mole hill of Mississippi.
> From every mountainside, let freedom ring, and when this happens . . .
> when we allow freedom to ring, when we let it ring from every village and every hamlet, from every state and every city, we will be able to speed up that day when all God's children, black men and white men, Jews and Gentiles, Protestants and Catholics, will be able to join hands and sing in the words of the old Negro spiritual, "Free at last! Free at last! Thank God Almighty, we are free at last!" (King, 2000, p. 262)★

Repetition and Parallelism

In King's speech, onomatopoeia wasn't the only stylistic device he used. He also used repetition and parallelism. **Repetition**—repeating a word or series of words in successive clauses or sentences (usually at the beginning)—is an effective way to keep listeners' attention. King's repetition of "Let freedom ring" was very effective.

Parallelism is the grouping of similarly phrased ideas. As you saw in King's speech, parallelism increases the pace and "therefore generates psychological

★Reprinted by arrangement with the Estate of Martin Luther King Jr., c/o Writers House as agent for the proprietor New York, NY. Copyright © 1963 Martin Luther King Jr., copyright renewed 1991 Coretta Scott King.

Technology Tip for Speakers

Adapt Your Presentation to the Media Interview

Businesses and organizations of all sizes are now using media (especially closed-circuit television and teleconferencing) for advertising and for employee education and training. Also, some employees are asked to participate in a news interview or talk show.

Since media presentations can be replayed, it's important that your language usage (as well as your vocal and visual messages) make the right impression. Knowing how to adapt your presentation to the media interview should give you a definite career boost. Carefully consider the following media tips (Blythin & Samovar, 1985; Greaney, 1997; Hamilton, 2005; Howard, 2002; Smudde, 2004; Stephenson, 1997):

- *Always prepare ahead.* As soon as you know the time and purpose of the interview or presentation, plan your agenda. What audience will you be speaking to? What three to five key points do you want to present to the audience? Answer all questions, but transition back to your key ideas with such phrases as "But more important . . ." or "This whole project hinges on . . ." (Stephenson, 1997, p. 147). Also be prepared to offer facts and examples to back up your opinions.

- *Make your comments positive, clear, and brief.* Negative comments might be used in the story, but confusing, jargon-ridden, or long comments won't. Newspapers rarely include comments of more than 25 words; radio and television cut most comments to around 12 seconds.

- *Be conscious of your verbal image.* Make your comments interesting, and give personal examples that fit the frame of reference of the audience.

- *Never lie.* If you don't know, say so. However, avoid saying "No comment," which always makes you sound guilty. And remember that there is no such thing as "off the record."

- *When referring to your organization, use its name, not "we"; when giving an opinion, say "I feel" or "I think," not "we feel."* Own your feelings but present yourself and your company in a positive light. Don't forget to present your own credentials near the beginning of the interview.

---

momentum in listeners" (Hart, 1997, p. 151). In his "American Renewal" speech, President Bill Clinton (1993) used repetition and parallelism:

> Today we do more than celebrate America, we rededicate ourselves to the very idea of America:
> An idea born in revolution and renewed through two centuries of challenge;
> An idea tempered by the knowledge that but for fate we, the fortunate and the unfortunate, might have been each other;
> An idea ennobled by the faith that our nation can summon from its myriad diversity the deepest measure of unity;
> An idea infused with the conviction that America's long, heroic journey must go forever upward. (p. 259)

- *Be conscious of your visual image.* Don't slump or fidget. Maintain direct eye contact with the interviewer. Gesture, lean forward a bit, and show that you have deep feelings on the subject.

- *Choose the color of your clothes carefully.* Avoid white (even as trim) and warm or hot colors such as red, pink, or orange. Avoid stripes, polka dots, or patterns because they tend to bleed together. Solid, neutral, or cool colors are best. A slight contrast in color is desirable, but avoid sharp contrasts or clothes made of shiny material. For example, a light-blue blouse or shirt would look good with a medium-blue suit. Men can add a darker blue tie. Men and women with blond hair should wear a darker blouse or shirt to give a slight contrast. Men and women with dark complexions should select colors that are either darker or lighter than their complexions.

- *Avoid shiny jewelry* (rings, necklaces, tie clasps).

- *Wear slenderizing clothes*—the camera will make you look heavier. Dresses or suits that are fitted or belted at the waist are recommended for women; men also look slimmer in suits that are somewhat fitted at the waist. The lights are hot so you will want to wear cool clothes as well.

- *Men generally do not need makeup.* If they have a heavy beard or a shiny forehead, the producer may suggest applying some powder. Women should wear modest, everyday makeup (eyeliner is suggested).

- *Look directly into the camera* (if there is no audience) as though the camera were a person. If you have an audience, consider the camera as an audience member and include it as you scan the audience. Not looking into the camera will give the appearance that you are not making eye contact with the audience. If the lights are so bright that you are squinting, tell the floor manager so they can be adjusted.

Once you plan possible key ideas, gather supporting facts, dress carefully, speak with sincerity and enthusiasm, and become familiar with the technical speaking environment, your media presentations will be as effective as your regular presentations and maybe even a lot more fun.

President Franklin D. Roosevelt also was fond of using parallelism, which added a rhythm or cadence to his delivery (Zelko, 1970). Consider the following parallel sentences in one of Roosevelt's speeches:

> It cannot be a real peace if it fails to recognize brotherhood. It cannot be a lasting peace if the fruit of it is oppression. . . . It cannot be a sound peace if small nations must live in fear of powerful neighbors. It cannot be a moral peace if freedom from invasion is sold for tribute. . . . It cannot be a righteous peace if worship of God is denied. (p. 194)

In his address to Congress on September 20, 2001, President George W. Bush gave a stirring address, which was interrupted by applause 31 times (Wilson, 2003).

In part, his success was due to the rhythm and momentum created by short, parallel sentences such as: "We will not tire. We will not falter. And we will not fail" (p. 735).

Antithesis

Antithesis occurs when a sentence contains two contrasting ideas in parallel phrases. Antithesis can bring contrasts into sharper focus (Hart, 1997), which is probably why antithesis was one of President Kennedy's favorite stylistic devices. Here are three examples of antithesis from his 1961 inaugural address:

> If a free society cannot help the many who are poor, it cannot save the few who are rich. (Kennedy, 2000, p. 251)

> Let us never negotiate out of fear, but let us never fear to negotiate. (p. 251)

> And so, my fellow Americans, ask not what your country can do for you, ask what you can do for your country. (p. 252)

Another example of antithesis combined with parallelism is found in the conclusion of Peter G. Osgood's (1993) speech about the environment:

> Where many see only additional problems, you need to show them opportunity; where they see unacceptable risk, you have to quantify the benefits; where they think only in terms of added cost, you have to demonstrate the potential savings. (p. 270)

Hyperbole

Hyperbole is extreme exaggeration used for emphasis ("We either vote for this bill, or we die"). In a speech titled "Power, Parity, Personal Responsibility, and Progress," William H. Harris (1993) used both hyperbole and metaphor (both in italics) to impress on his audience the importance of action:

> And the answers will require creativity and discovery. I wish you Godspeed as you create and make your discoveries, but I assure you that *if you neither create nor discover in this essential arena all of us will reap a whirlwind of despair* . . . (p. 536)

Martin Luther King, Jr. (1989) used hyperbole in his "I've Been to the Mountain-Top" speech when he warned his audience:

> And in the human rights revolution, if something isn't done and done in a hurry to bring the colored peoples of the world out of their long years of poverty, their long years of hurt and neglect, *the whole world is doomed.* (p. 311)★

Hyperbole can arouse emotion and stimulate thought, but it must be used carefully so that listeners do not take it at face value or view it as a lie by an unethical speaker.

Personification

Personification is giving human characteristics or feelings to an animal, object, or concept (such as "Mother Nature"). Used in moderation, this device is effective in clarifying ideas. For example, to clarify the importance of keeping computers in top-notch condition, you might personify the computer, as one student did:

★Reprinted by arrangement with the Estate of Martin Luther King Jr., c/o Writers House as agent for the proprietor New York, NY. Copyright © 1968 Martin Luther King Jr., copyright renewed 1996 Coretta Scott King.

Your PC unit will be much more cooperative if you remember to defragment the hard drive regularly, since otherwise your computer exhausts itself rummaging through disorganized bits of files.

Remember

Stylistic devices include . . .

- *Alliteration*—repetition of consonants (usually the first or last letter in a word)
- *Assonance*—repetition of vowel sounds
- *Simile*—direct comparison between two items using the words *like* or *as*
- *Metaphor*—implied comparison between two items without using *like* or *as*
- *Onomatopoeia*—words that sound like their meaning
- *Repetition*—word or series of words repeated in successive clauses or sentences
- *Parallelism*—similarly phrased ideas presented in succession
- *Antithesis*—two parallel but contrasting ideas contained in one sentence
- *Hyperbole*—deliberate exaggeration
- *Personification*—assigning human characteristics or feelings to animals, objects, or concepts

Stop reading and take the following quiz.

Test Your Knowledge Quiz

Testing Your Knowledge of Stylistic Devices

Directions: Here are excerpts from eight speeches. Identify the stylistic device(s) in each excerpt. You can also take this quiz online at the Essentials of Public Speaking website and, if requested, e-mail your responses to your instructor.

_____ 1. "The mother of all wars."—Saddam Hussein

_____ 2. ". . . and that government of the people, by the people, and for the people, shall not perish from the earth."—Abraham Lincoln (1983)

_____ 3. "America is not like a blanket—one piece of unbroken cloth, the same color, the same texture, the same size. America is more like a quilt—many patches, many pieces, many sizes, and woven and held together by a common thread."—Jesse Jackson (2000, p. 274)

_____ 4. "Attitude, not aptitude, determines altitude."—Richard L. Weaver II (1993)

_____ 5. "Fellow citizens, we observe today not a victory of party, but a celebration of freedom. . . ."—John F. Kennedy (2000, p. 250)

_____ 6. "But, in a larger sense, we cannot dedicate, we cannot consecrate, we cannot hallow this ground."—Abraham Lincoln (1863)

_____ 7. "Ours is a nation that has shed the blood of war and cried the tears of depression."—George Bush (1992)

_____ 8. "Tax money flows into Washington, irrigating the bureaucratic gardens."—James P. Pinkerton (2000)

Answers

1. Hyperbole
2. Repetition and parallelism
3. Simile
4. Alliteration
5. Antithesis
6. Repetition and parallelism
7. Personification
8. Metaphor

Biased Language

The only message that counts is the one that gets received. In other words, what you meant to say is less important than what the audience thought you said. Not only can your use of language enhance the effectiveness of your speech, but it can also have negative effects if you aren't careful. Language can indicate speaker bias and create listener bias. Gender and culture are the two most common areas of biased language.

Gender Bias

Avoid using *he* as a generic term to refer to both males and females. Although you may mean both male and female when you use generic terms, *he* conjures up male images in the minds of many audience members (Hamilton, 1988). A study of college students conducted in 1993 found that both male and female students tended to use masculine pronouns when referring to a person who is a judge, an engineer, or a lawyer, and to use feminine pronouns for nurses, librarians, and teachers (Ivy, Bullis-Moore, Norvell, Backlund, & Javidi, 1993). According to Diana K. Ivy and Phil Backlund (2003) in their book *Exploring Gender Speak,* when speakers use generic masculine words such as *he, mankind, sportsman,* and *workmanship,* or feminine terms such as *stewardess, waitress,* and *actress,* they are helping to maintain sex-biased perceptions. ➤ *For more on gender bias, see Figure 10.3 on page 222, which lists some common gender-specific terms and suggested alternatives.*

Culture Bias

Since listeners supply the meaning of words on the basis of their own frames of reference, you must choose your language carefully. The more diverse your audience, the more likely it is that their frames of reference will differ from yours. By the year 2025 in the United States, it is expected that non-Hispanic whites will drop to 60 percent while both the Hispanic and Asian populations will double (Wellner, 2003). The most effective speakers are sensitive to the diverse backgrounds of their listeners and make their language as free of culture bias as possible. ➤ *For more on frames of reference, see Chapter 1; for more on analyzing audience differences, see Chapter 4.*

Sample Student Speech: "No More Sugar!" by Hans Erian

The following persuasive speech, "No More Sugar!" deals with the dangerous sugar consumption of Americans of all ages and was given by Hans Erian as a persuasive contest selection at the 2002 Phi Rho Pi National Tournament. The speech was to be memorized and last no more than 10 minutes. As you read this speech and watch it on the Essentials of Public Speaking website under student resources for Chapter 11, notice Hans's language style. Was his use of language simple, specific, vivid, and forceful? Did he use any stylistic devices? What specific changes would you recommend to make this speech more persuasive?

S A M P L E   S P E E C H

NO MORE SUGAR!

by Hans Erian, 2002 Phi Rho Pi National Tournament

ARNELL SCOTT WAS 15 years old and weighed over 300 pounds. One day his mother noticed that he was losing weight rapidly and was constantly thirsty, so she took him to the hospital. There the doctors diagnosed this 15-year-old with Type 2 Diabetes. According to *Newsday*, July 20, 1999, Type 2 Diabetes—which is usually associated with adults—is now increasing at an alarming rate in children, leaving them open to life-threatening complications like blindness, kidney disease, heart disease, and stroke at ages as young as 30. Dr. Barbara Linder of the National Institute of Diabetes and Digestion and Kidney Diseases attributes this rise in Type 2 Diabetes to a rise in obesity, and obesity is on the rise because of sugar.

According to the *New York Times* of February 16, 2001, of the top 10 most-bought foods at supermarkets, most are sugar-rich junk foods. A Georgetown University study shows that 25 percent of the calories adults consume are from sugar, but for kids it's closer to 50 percent. That means that the average person in this room consumes about 125 to 150 pounds of sugar per year. *Consumer Reports on Health* of August 2001 says that when blood sugar levels rise, so does the risk of disease and even death. Americans are consuming too much sugar, and it's destroying our health but most don't even realize it. Today we'll look at the misconceptions average Americans have regarding their intake of sugar. Next, we'll look at what these misconceptions lead to. And, finally, we'll explore some ways you can overcome your lethal sweet tooth.

So why are Americans consuming all of this sugar? The two main reasons are ignorance and an increased consumption of soda pop. We often consume sugar without even realizing it. This is partly due to the food labeling process. The FDA and the Sugar Association have been fighting a linguistic tug-of-war since about 1970 over the definition of sugar. Let's look at the basics: Fructose is good sugar

(continued)

SAMPLE SPEECH (continued)

that you find in fruits and vegetables. Bad sugar is what you find in most of the items you eat, and these types of sugar go by many different names, including sucrose, dextrose, corn syrup, and high fructose corn syrup. The last one, high fructose corn syrup, may cause some confusion at first because it has the word *fructose* in it, but don't be fooled! This is just another type of refined sugar.

Now, let's take a look at a few common items that you can find at any local Safeway to see the confusion in action. Here we have a cranberry tangerine mix—a juice that we expect to be healthy for us—but notice that the second ingredient is high fructose corn syrup. Now let's take a look at Wheaties, supposedly one of the healthiest breakfast cereals on the market—even their slogan promotes health. Let's look at the ingredients: number one is whole wheat, and number two is sugar. And we also have corn syrup (another bad sugar) and brown sugar syrup (another bad sugar). All of this sugar can't be in the breakfast of champions! These are the kinds of "health foods" that we put into our bodies daily, and we assume that they are healthy for us but they're not.

The other reason Americans consume so much sugar is because of the increased consumption of soda pop. Let's take a look at Coca-Cola. Notice that its second ingredient is high fructose corn syrup and/or sucrose. (Here the manufacturer used the chemical name for sugar, sucrose.) The average can of Coke has about 10 teaspoons of sugar. According to the *San Jose Mercury News* of January 17, 1999, since the mid-80s, soda pop consumption in the United States has increased by 43 percent to more to 85 gallons per American per year. That's 555 cans annually for every American. How much soda do you drink?

Now that we've seen that Americans are consuming too much sugar due to ignorance and an increased consumption of soda pop, let's look at how all this sugar has had a negative impact on our health. The *New York Times* of September 9, 2001, says that there is convincing new evidence about the relationship between weight gain in children and soda pop consumption. The *New York Times* goes on to say that obesity is directly linked to soda pop consumption, regardless of the amount of food you eat or the lack of exercise. Part of the explanation for this may be that the body has trouble adapting to such intense concentrations of sugar taken in liquid form. Obesity has been linked to high blood pressure, high cholesterol, and heart disease. Obesity is also linked to cancer. In fact, obesity is now considered the number-two killer in the United States because of its link to cancer, according to the *New York Times* of October 9, 2001. The *Hindu* of April 26, 2001, says that obese people are 70 percent more likely to get pancreatic cancer, which has a 95 percent mortality rate. The U.S. Department of Health affirms the claim that obesity causes several types of cancer, including post-menopausal breast cancer and colon cancer.

Along with causing cancer, obesity is also a key cause of diabetes. According to the *Hartford Chronic* of September 9, 2001, since 1991 adult obesity has increased by 60 percent and the percentage of overweight kids has doubled in the last decade, helping to put significant numbers of children and adolescents among the ranks of Type 2 diabetics. Type 2 Diabetes usually comes on after the age of 45. Dr. Gerald Bernstein predicts that left unchecked, the onset of more diabetes could have a huge impact, with more than 500 million diabetics worldwide in 25 years. We're looking at a tidal wave of suffering and an avalanche of health-care bills if people don't change their ways.

Now we've seen that Americans are consuming too much sugar, and it's destroying their health, one bite or sip at a time. We obviously need to decrease our sugar intake. So now we'll look at what we could do at a national level. Next, we'll look at what we can do as individuals. On a national level, we need to do two things: increase awareness and decrease soda pop consumption. Kelly Brownwell, director of Yale University's Eating and Weight Disorders, has suggested that we regulate food advertisements directed at children to provide equal time for pro-nutrition and physical activity messages. She also suggests that we change the price of foods to make healthier foods less expensive. Nationwide, schools should mimic what nearly a dozen states are already considering, and that is to turn off school vending machines during class time, stripping them of sweets, or to impose new taxes on soda pop machines. The *New York Times* of February 16, 2001, says that taking these actions will discourage kids from buying sweets. We can even take this proposal one step further and not only impose taxes on school vending machines but also on soft drinks in general. These are a few ways we can create incentives for people to eat healthily and decrease their sugar intake.

Now, we would all like someone else to make us healthy, but what is really needed is a personal commitment to health. You know the answer to the question "How do I get rid of my sugar addiction?" Simple. Start off slow and follow Dr. Ralph Gowen's advice: moderation. The author of *Optimal Wellness* has suggested that dessert a few times a week or a can of pop once or twice a week isn't going to hurt anyone's health. In fact, the World Health Organization has suggested that between 0 to 10 percent of your daily calories can come from sugar, and this will still be considered within a safe range. Try to stick to good foods, though, like fruits, vegetables, and fruit juices that don't have any added sugar. Become a label reader and be aware of what you're eating.

Today we've looked at the misconceptions about sugar, looked at where these misconceptions lead, and have found some solutions to our sugar addiction. Americans have become unhealthy because they're eating too much sugar. Americans need to decrease their sugar intake before more of them end up like 15-year-old Arnell Scott, having to take daily insulin injections just to stay alive.

Summary

Although effective organization, content, and delivery are essential for a successful speech, perfecting your language style adds the polish that makes your speech shine. The most effective language is simple, specific, vivid, and forceful. Language creates mental images in the minds of your listeners, influences audience attitudes and behaviors, and adds interest and enjoyment to your speeches. Professional speakers use a variety of stylistic devices: alliteration and assonance, simile and metaphor, onomatopoeia, repetition and parallelism, antithesis, hyperbole, and personification. These devices are especially important in persuasive speaking because words can set a mood, develop a feeling, or generate a theme. If listeners are in the right frame of mind for a particular topic, you will have a better chance of communicating your ideas and concerns to them. Of course, you must keep your speech free of gender and culture bias.

Essentials of Public Speaking  Online

Use the Essentials of Public Speaking website at **http://communication. wadsworth.com/hamiltoneps3** for quick access to the electronic study resources that accompany this chapter. When you get to the Essentials home page, click on "Student Book Companion Site" in the Resource box. The Essentials website features the Test Your Knowledge quiz on pages 243–244, a video of Hans's speech on pages 245–247, InfoTrac College Edition, the Suggestions for Practice and Critical Thinking activities and the InfoTrac College Edition activities that follow, a digital glossary, and review quizzes.

Key Terms

abstract word 234
alliteration 237
ambiguous word 234
antithesis 242
assonance 237
concrete word 234

euphemism 234
forceful language 235
gobbledygook 233
hyperbole 242
metaphor 238
onomatopoeia 238

parallelism 239
personification 234
repetition 239
simile 238
style 233
stylistic device 237

Suggestions for Practice and Critical Thinking

1. Greek orators were known for using stylistic devices such as hyperbole, metaphor, assonance, alliteration, parallelism, and antithesis. The last three, discussed in Book IV of *Rhetorica Ad Herennium,* were known as the Gorgianic figures. Based on your reading in this chapter, which of these devices is used in this partial sentence from Isocrates' *Letter to Archidamus?* ". . . since I knew, in the first place that it is easier to treat copiously in cursory fashion occur-

rences of the past than intelligently to discuss the future . . ." (Conley, 1990, p. 19; see also Buzzell & Herzberg, 1990, fn. 115, p. 268).

2. In groups of two or three, select a well-known public figure with a distinctive speaking style. Separate the speaker's visual and vocal techniques from his or her verbal language techniques. Try to determine what stylistic devices this person uses. Share your discoveries with another group or the entire class.

3. Use InfoTrac College Edition to conduct keyword searches to find two examples of the following stylistic devices: antithesis, hyperbole, metaphor, personification, and simile.

4. For additional information on media communication discussed in this chapter's Technology Tip for Speakers, use InfoTrac College Edition and run a keyword search using *media interview, media interview★, speak★ and technology,* or *media speeches.*

5. Take a look at Hans's speech on "No More Sugar!" Evaluate his language style and identify any stylistic devices he used. What would you have done differently if you were giving his speech? Share your answers with a classmate.

6. Read the following passage from a speech about health care by James S. Todd (1993), executive vice president of the American Medical Association. How many different stylistic devices can you find? Compare answers with a classmate.

> There is no quick fix. It is essential we do it right, and that will not be easy.
>
> All any of us can do is watch—and wait—and sometimes worry.
>
> If there is one message I have today, it is this: The physicians of America are worried.
>
> Don't get me wrong. We're not worried that change is coming. That we welcome. What worries us is the strong possibility that real change won't occur at all.
>
> We're worried that politics and miscalculation will conspire to keep the Administration from achieving the kind of meaningful reform the President promised during his campaign.
>
> We're worried that the Clinton plan may be too enormous to comprehend, too complex to explain, too expensive to defend. . . .
>
> Senator Phil Gramm says managed competition is like a five-legged animal. It might work, but we sure don't see any running around in nature. . . .
>
> We're worried that the Administration's package of health care benefits could turn into a high-priced Christmas tree, one that's so loaded with ornaments the cost will be prohibitive. (p. 523)

7. Select one argument that you will be using in your persuasive speech. Prepare this argument to present to your class or to a small group of students. Practice using at least two kinds of stylistic devices in this argument.

8. Check out the following websites. *You can access these sites under the Student Resources for Chapter 11* at the Essentials of Public Speaking website.

- Read "United Against Gobbledygook" at PlainEnglishUSA.com. Scroll down and click on "Legalese in the United States."

- For a list of articles from the archives of the journal *Etc: A Review of General Semantics,* see the website for the Institute of General Semantics. When you get to the home page, click on the link "ETC archives" under Online

Library in the right-hand menu. Also, check out the International Society for General Semantics (ISGS) website, GeneralSemantics.org.

- Read the article "How to Prepare Yourself for a Media Interview," *Monitor on Psychology* (March 1998), to learn more about media interview techniques. Use the link provided at the Essentials website or Google "Monitor on Psychology." When you get to the *Monitor*'s home page, search on *March 1998,* click on the "Previous Issues" link, then on "March 1998."

- HistoryChannel.com features many famous speeches in text and audio form, providing many opportunities to read and listen to the language historical speakers have used.

- Read and listen to Martin Luther King, Jr.'s "I Have a Dream" speech at Go to AmericanRhetoric.com.

- For an interesting article on gender and language, read "The Struggle for Gender-Free Language: Is It Over Yet?" by Jane Rea, editor of *The Editorial Eye,* at the EEICommunications.com website. When you get to the home page, click on "EEI Press" in the right-hand menu, then on "The Editorial Eye." At The Editorial Eye home page, click on the "index" link and then scroll down to the "S" titles.

- To get a sense of how diverse the U.S. population is, go to the U.S. Census Bureau's American FactFinder website and search on *overview Hispanic 2000* to find the link to the report "Overview of Race and Hispanic Origin 2000." Consider the diversity of your classroom audience and audiences you may speak to in the future. How does that diversity influence the language choices you make for your speeches?

unit four

Types of Speeches

What do you know about different types of speeches?

The following questionnaire is designed to call attention to common misconceptions you may have about speech preparation.

Directions: If you think the statement is generally accurate, mark it T; if you think the statement is a myth, mark it F. Then compare your answers with the explanations at the end of Chapter 12. You can also take this quiz online at the Essentials of Public Speaking website and, if requested, e-mail your responses to your instructor.

_____ 1. A speech of introduction needs to be fairly long, otherwise the speaker may feel slighted.

_____ 2. Electronic computer visuals (and transparencies) are usually more persuasive if they are in color.

_____ 3. After a question-and-answer session, it is very important to present a final, memorable conclusion in order to reestablish control and leave the audience with a feeling of closure.

_____ 4. Simply mentioning the source of the evidence used makes a speech more persuasive.

_____ 5. It's unethical to use special knowledge of your listeners' needs and wants in order to change their way of thinking.

_____ 6. Good logic will persuade almost anyone.

_____ 7. You can greatly increase low credibility by using professional-looking visual aids.

_____ 8. It is a good idea to avoid using humor in informative speeches unless you are a professional entertainer or are very experienced.

_____ 9. The basic procedure for beginning an informative speech is as follows: You walk to the front, pause for a second, state your topic and purpose, and then present your attention-getter.

_____ 10. When you give the source of your evidence, it is normally more persuasive to mention the source before presenting the evidence.

Informative Speaking

Flashback Quintilian and Cicero believed that regular and careful speechwriting would improve speaker eloquence and carry over into extemporaneous situations. For example, Cicero (*De Oratore,* Book I, Section XXXIII) indicates that the careful language in a written introduction will cause the speech that follows (even when extemporaneous) to "proceed in unchanging style." He compares this process to a boat moving at full steam: even when the crew stops rowing, the boat continues moving in the same direction. How does this advice compare with today's view of speech preparation?

Your speech is an informative speech when you increase awareness by introducing the latest information about a topic or body of related facts; deepen your listeners' knowledge of a complicated term, concept, or process; or aid in your listeners' mastery of a skill. Informative speeches are not meant to influence choices or opinions—that is the purpose of persuasive speeches—but they may be indirectly persuasive. For example, a listener might decide to become a volunteer after hearing an informative speech about various community organizations even though the speaker's intention was not to recruit help. *One of the primary differences between informative and persuasive speeches is the speaker's goal*—the informative speaker's goal is to deepen understanding, to instruct, to teach; the persuasive speaker's goal is to gain agreement, to sell a product, or to encourage an action.

Types of Informative Speeches

There are many ways to categorize informative speeches, but basically, all informative speeches can be divided into two broad categories: demonstration speeches and informational speeches.

Demonstration Speeches

A **demonstration speech** is characterized by showing how to do or make something—right in front of the listeners so that they can see the steps necessary to achieve the same results. Ideally, your audience will learn the skill or procedure well

enough to perform it themselves. For instance, a demonstration speech about flower arranging might include a visual listing the do's and don'ts of making beautiful flower arrangements, but the main focus would be the demonstration of each step, resulting in one or more completed arrangements. You would bring flowers, vases, water, and preservatives—all the supplies that you need to explain and show each step in the creation of a lovely arrangement. Or if you gave a demonstration speech about how to prepare delicious nonalcoholic drinks to serve on special occasions, you would bring in all the ingredients and prepare the drinks in front of the audience, explaining each step as you go. You might also have volunteers try their hand at squeezing lemons or blending the ingredients. Handing out copies of the recipes after the speech might also be a good idea. Figure 12.1 later in this chapter includes sample topics for demonstration speeches.

Be aware that a demonstration speech usually takes more time than an informational speech—especially when audience participation is involved. To make sure that you won't run out of time when you give your demonstration speech, add 1 minute to your practice time. Although the basic steps for planning a speech are discussed later in this chapter, the following items are especially important for demonstration speeches:

- *Visual aids* (such as graphics, charts, pictures, objects, models, and videos) to clarify the development of a skill. ➔ *See Chapters 9 and 10 for specifics on preparing and using visual aids.*

- Effective *supporting materials* (such as explanations, examples, illustrations, comparisons, and expert opinion) to add interest, clarification, and proof. ➔ *See Chapter 6 for specifics on types of supporting materials.*

- The *organizational format* (topical, spatial, chronological, or causal) that will best meet the needs of the audience and your topic. ➔ *See Chapter 7 for more on informative organizational formats.*

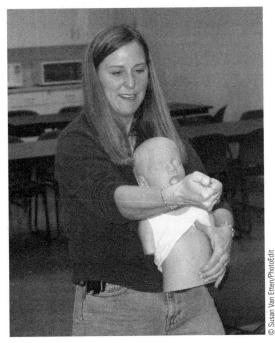

A demonstration speech promotes understanding by showing how to do or make something. This speaker is showing how to use the Heimlich maneuver on a child.

© Susan Van Etten/PhotoEdit

Informational Speeches

An **informational speech** increases awareness by introducing the latest information about a topic or body of related facts, or presents information promoting understanding of a complicated idea, term, or concept. It does not aid in mastery of a skill. The focus of an informational speech is on content and ideas, not on how to do or make something. For example, in an informational speech about flower arranging, you could talk about the aesthetic value of flowers, flower selection, and flower placement while using visual aids (one listing main points, one showing an effective arrangement, and one showing a poor arrangement), and conclude by showing an actual flower arrangement. Most informational speeches (such as the sample student speech on the eye chip later in this chapter) cover topics that are not appropriate for demonstration speeches (for example, youth fads, stress prevention, or vacation suggestions). Figures 12.2 and 12.3 later in this chapter include sample topics appropriate for informational speeches.

Remember

A demonstration speech . . .

- Promotes a skill—making or doing.
- Shows how to accomplish a task step by step.

An informational speech . . .

- Promotes understanding—knowing.
- Focuses on content and ideas; may discuss how something is made but will not actually make it.

Tools to Aid Understanding in Informative Speeches

In addition to varied supporting materials discussed in Chapter 6 and the verbal, visual, and vocal tips summarized in Figure 12.6 later in this chapter, *informative speakers can use four main tools* to aid understanding: *definition, description, explanation,* and *narration.* Which ones you will need to use in your speech will depend on your audience and the speech topic. For example, does your audience already know something about your topic, or will it be new to them? Is your topic fairly simple to understand, or does it involve a complicated term, concept, or process? Will the idea or concept covered in your topic be easy for your "lay" audience to believe intuitively, or are they likely to be skeptical (Rowan, 1995)? Each of these approaches can be used for both demonstration and informational speeches.

Definition

If your audience is unfamiliar with your topic or the topic, one or more definitions will likely be needed. According to the *New World Dictionary,* a **definition** is "a statement of what a thing is; being definite, explicit, and clear; absence of fuzziness." For example, in the sample speech "They Made the Blind to See" (found later in this chapter), Vanessa defines *retinitis pigmentosa* for her listeners in the following way:

> The December 13, 1999, *New York Daily News* explains that retinitis pigmentosa is an inherited disorder affecting 100,000 people yearly. This disease causes

a degeneration of the rods, which control peripheral vision and vision in poor lighting. Consequently, RP sufferers are left with restricted night vision, severe tunnel vision, and eventual blindness.

Usually a definition by itself is not enough to make a concept or term totally clear. Definitions are often followed by one or more of the following: a comparison or contrast, one or two examples, the *etymology* of the word (the origin or root meaning), a *synonym* (word with a similar meaning), or an *antonym* (word with an opposite meaning). Tennyson and Cocchiarella (1986) recommend following a definition with a list of its *essential features* (features that are always present) and comparing/contrasting it to a list of *associated features* (features that are sometimes present and may look like an essential feature, but are not). An example of each feature is also helpful. ➡ *See Chapter 6 for a review of comparisons and other supporting materials.*

Description

Another tool to aid understanding in an informative speech is **description**—painting a vivid, detailed picture of the topic using concrete words and figures of speech such as similes, metaphors, and onomatopoeia (previously discussed in Chapter 11). Vivid, concrete words that paint a clear mental picture for the audience (such as the description of a West Highland white terrier on page 234) not only aid understanding, but they also maintain audience attention and interest. Descriptions are even more compelling when they include similes (that compare items using the word *like* or *as*—"your eyes work like a camera"), metaphors (that are implied comparisons and do not use *like* or *as*—"the pupil of the eye is the camera aperture"), and onomatopoeia (words that sound like their meaning, such as *buzz* or *ring*). ➡ *See Chapter 11 for a review of similes, metaphors, onomatopoeia, and other figures of speech.*

Explanation

When a topic or concept is complex, or is likely to be difficult to believe, or needs a process clarified, one or more explanations (which may include definitions and descriptions) are needed. As discussed in Chapter 6, an explanation is a statement about the relationship between certain items and often answers the questions *how, what,* and *why.* Good explanations are enhanced by quality visual aids, use of clear connecting words (like *because* and *for example*), and comparing old knowledge with new (Mayer, 1989; Rowan, 1995). With complex topics, it's best to start with the "big picture" and then show how the parts or processes work and interrelate (Mayer & Andersen, 1992; Rowan, 1990, 1995). When you present a topic that listeners may find difficult to believe, it is best to first discuss the "lay" theory or belief and why it seems plausible, discuss why it is inaccurate, and then present the more acceptable concept or theory (Brown, 1992; Rowan, 1991). ➡ *See Chapter 6 for more on explanations.*

Narration

Using narratives is an excellent way to improve understanding and grab audience interest (Ballard, 2003; Fisher, 1987; Robinson, 2000). A **narration** is a story about real or imagined things, people, or events told with detail and enthusiasm. Narrations are used in business to enliven "speeches, sales pitches, training sessions, and presentations on otherwise dry or technical topics" (Quinones, 1999). In fact, Quinones reports that executives pay as much as $4,000 for an "executive storytelling" seminar (p. 4).

According to Fisher (1987), an outstanding narration or story has two important qualities: *probability* (the story is easy to follow and makes sense) and *fidelity* (the story

rings true to the audience). Fisher considers former President Ronald Reagan as a master storyteller and suggests that this ability helped earn him the title "Great Communicator" even though his speeches often contained inconsistencies and factual errors (pp. 145–157). If you aren't experienced in using narrations, try telling personal experience stories from your own life. The personal family narrative told by Susan Peterson in Chapter 6, page 119 is a good example. Be sure to pick stories that will relate to your audience with fidelity and probability and don't forget to practice, practice, and practice. → *For more on narratives, see Personalize Your Speeches With Narratives in Chapter 3 and Instances in Chapter 6.*

Sample Student Speech: "They Made the Blind to See" by Vanessa Harikul

The following informative speech, "They Made the Blind to See," was presented by Vanessa Harikul at the State Forensics Championships in Fresno, California. Vanessa was awarded first place in Informative Speaking for her presentation. The following speech has been transcribed from the videotape of the competition. Although Vanessa used visual aids in her speech, they are not mentioned in the text below. What visuals would you suggest? As you read this speech, think about changes you would make if you were speaking about the same topic. Pay special attention to her introduction and conclusion. Did she include all the necessary steps? To watch and analyze a video clip of Vanessa's speech, look under Student Resources for Chapter 12 at the Essentials of Public Speaking website.

SAMPLE SPEECH

THEY MADE THE BLIND TO SEE

by Vanessa Harikul, Moorpark College

Introduction

FROM 1987 TO 1994, Lieutenant Geordi LaForge sat behind his desk following the orders of Captain Picard, helping to bring the Starship Enterprise through mission after dangerous mission, a fact made even more remarkable by the fact that Geordi was completely blind. But as fans of the series will remember, Geordi wore a pair of high-tech sunglasses that enabled him to see, and just look cooler than any other crew member. Of course, such miracles of technology are easy in the world of television; in real life they're a little more difficult. Right? Perhaps not, as this generation's blind may not have to wait for the "Next Generation," for a technological wonder that will restore their eyesight.

According to *Business Week* of January 31, 2000, researchers have developed technology that could enable people with certain types of blindness to be able to see—a feat that the October 28, 1998 issue of the *Times of London* calls "the Holy Grail of eye research." This technology comes to us in the form of the intra-ocular retinal prosthesis, also known as the eye chip—a tiny microchip implanted within the eye—not unlike the cochlear implant which has returned thousands of deaf individuals to the world of the hearing. The *New York Times* of June 24, 1999, argues that for

SAMPLE SPEECH

30 million people worldwide, including 6 million Americans affected with disorders such as retinitis pigmentosa and macular degeneration, this is the realization of a long-awaited dream. And the May/June 1999 issue of the *Technology Review* adds that these two diseases together account for 25 percent of all incidents of blindness.

In order to understand the promises the eye chip holds for the visually impaired, we will first open our eyes to the background of its research. Next, we'll focus on whom exactly this chip can help, and finally we'll process exactly how the chip works.

Body

First Main Point

From eyeglasses to contacts to laser surgery, people have always been trying to find ways to improve their vision, but for those who are completely blind, there has been little hope until now, and for them, the eye chip represents that hope. The *Washington Post* of December 9, 1999, explains that this "Holy Grail" is being pursued by five main research teams. However, the *Times* of October 28, 1998, notes that the team that is leading the race is based in Maryland at Johns Hopkins University. Led by Dr. Mark Humayan and Dr. Eugene deJuan, professors at the University's Wilmer Eye Institute, this team has been working on this project for over a decade. The May/June 1999 issue of the *Technology Review* explains that these two doctors met in the late 1980s at Duke University and began investigating the potential for restoring sight using an electronic chip. A paper written by Dr. Humayan in January of 1999 explains that 15 blind human volunteers have been tested, each of which have been able to see yellow, blue, and green spots of light—as well as simple geometric shapes and letters. Now, while that may not sound like a lot for you or me, 72-year-old Harold Churchey, who had been blind for 15 years, said that "it was just like switching a light on." Churchey told the *Washington Post* on December 9, 1999, "I've never looked at the face of my grandson—but [now] I believe I will before I die." The December 4, 1999 *Houston Chronicle* continues, that the eye chip moved from the laboratory to the national stage when Motown legend Stevie Wonder met with Dr. Humayan to discuss the possibilities the eye chip held for him. He was told, however, that he would not be a good candidate for the eye chip because it is geared to help those with specific types of blindness.

Second Main Point

But if Stevie Wonder can't be helped, who can? Before we can understand the kinds of eye disorders that can be helped by the eye chip, however, a basic understanding of the way the eye works is needed. Dr. Humayan explained the process in January 1999. Light enters the eye through the cornea and crystalline lens, which focus it onto the retina. The retina, a delicate tissue that lines the inside of the eye, is made up of several different cell layers. The first layer is the photoreceptor cell layer—also known as the rods and cones because of the cells' shapes—which captures the light energy and converts it into electrochemical signals. These signals stimulate the cells located in the second layer of neurons, which then transmit the signals to the ganglion cells, which form what is known as the optic nerve. The optic nerve is basically the bridge between the eye and the brain—it transmits the information from the eye to the visual centers of the brain, which process it and form the images that we see.

A disruption in any of these areas can impair sight, but the eye chip can only help those people whose retinas have been damaged. Specifically, Dr. Humayan explained to the *New York Times* on June 24, 1999, "Some patients are blind because of

(continued)

[photoreceptor] cells that have degenerated or died . . . but the rest of the retina is made of neurons that are relatively intact. Our idea was to jump-start the retinal neurons that are waiting in the dark."

The two main disorders that fit this description are retinitis pigmentosa, or RP, and age-related macular degeneration, or AMD. The December 13, 1999 *New York Daily News* explains that retinitis pigmentosa is an inherited disorder affecting 100,000 people yearly. This disease causes a degeneration of the rods, which control peripheral vision and vision in poor lighting. Consequently, RP sufferers are left with restricted night vision, severe tunnel vision, and eventual blindness. AMD, on the other hand, is the leading cause of blindness in people over the age of 50, with half a million new cases reported worldwide each year, according to the *Toronto Star* of February 12, 2000. This disease attacks a small section of the retina, called the macula, which is responsible for sharp central vision. The January 2, 2000, *Detroit News* clarifies that vision becomes blurred or distorted, and a blind spot develops that gradually expands.

Third Main Point   Because the researchers at Johns Hopkins University recognized that in these diseases, only one component of the vision process is damaged, they built the eye chip to bypass that one component and stimulate the rest of the network. The *Toronto Sun* explained on December 4, 1999, that a small camera is mounted on a pair of glasses, not unlike the visor worn by Geordi LaForge. This camera captures images, converting them into a series of electronic signals, and sends them wirelessly to a microchip implanted inside the eye on the retina. From there, according to the November 7, 1998, *The New Scientist,* the chip translates the signals into tiny electric signals that stimulate the ganglia—essentially, the chip is doing the work that the damaged retinal cells would otherwise be doing. The *Times* continues that the image processing then proceeds as it would in a person with normal vision.

It's important to note, though, as Dr. Humayan does in the June 24, 1999, *New York Times,* that this chip cannot be expected to replicate the complexities of natural vision. He explains that the human eye is an incredibly complex image-processing system, with nearly 100 million photoreceptors that allow us to enjoy high-resolution imagery full of colors. The eye chip, in its currently crude stage, is only able to stimulate 100 electrodes. But, he said, "Simply providing mobility-type vision, or the ability to distinguish between light and dark to patients who are completely blind, will have far-reaching consequences." This research marks the start of more research. "The reality is," he predicts, "that we have no idea of the limits of this technology."

Conclusion   Now, while we may look at many of the gadgets of Star Trek's "The Next Generation" as light-years away, as we have seen by looking at the development of the eye chip, who it can help, as well as how it works, at least one of those gadgets may be a part of our immediate future. And I for one would agree with Captain Picard and say, "Make it so."

Steps in Preparing an Informative Speech

The Basic Steps for Preparing a Speech have been discussed in Units Two and Three. Here, we will show how those steps relate specifically to an informative speech. As you read this material, see if your informational or demonstration speech needs any additional work, or perhaps a bit of polishing.

Step 1: Analyze Your Potential Audience

The best informative speeches are designed for a specific audience. Analyzing their situational, demographic, and psychological characteristics will help you figure out what your audience probably knows about the topic and how to make it interesting to them. As you begin preparing an informative speech, ask yourself the following questions:

- What *situational characteristics* of my audience could affect the success of my speech? For example, how much do they know about the topic? What are their general opinions of me? Will anyone be speaking before me? Is the room equipped for the type of speech that I plan to give?

- On the basis of the *demographic characteristics* of audience members (for example, age, marital status, children, major, group memberships, hobbies), how can I make my topic interesting and beneficial to them?

- What *attitudes, beliefs, or values* relevant to my topic do audience members already have? How can I use these psychological factors to communicate my ideas better?

- Is my audience likely to be *friendly, neutral, uninterested, or hostile*? What types of visual aids will impress this audience? What types of attention-getters will interest them (for example, personal instance, startling statement, or quote)?
  → *For more information on audience analysis, see Chapter 4.*

Step 2: Determine Your Topic, Exact Purpose, and Main Points

Since your goal in this course is to learn how to give effective speeches, don't worry about finding the "perfect" topic. As long as it fits the requirements of the assignment, is something that you know about and are interested in, and is of value to your audience, the topic should be fine. Check Figure 12.1 for sample demonstration topics and Figures 12.2 and 12.3 for sample informational topics.

Figure 12.1

Sample Demonstration Speech Topics (How to . . .)

Apply a splint	Dribble a basketball	Make gift bows
Apply clown makeup	Edit your photos on your	Mat and frame pictures
Bid on eBay	computer	Pack a travel bag efficiently
Change a cloth diaper	Fold a flag	Swing a golf club
Clean and store silver items	Give CPR to an adult/child	Take your blood pressure
Decorate holiday cakes	Juggle	Teach your dog a trick
Do origami (Japanese paper-	Keep score in bowling	Use a digital camera
folding)	Make artificial flowers using	Use a metal detector correctly
Do rope tricks	tissue paper	Use the Heimlich maneuver

▼ **Business**

Casual dress and the
  workplace
Changes in the workplace
Credit cards and teen
  market
E-mail abuse
International trade
Job-seeking on the
  Internet
Male/female management
  styles
Sales techniques that
  work

▼ **Family**

Dealing with Alzheimer's
The blended family
Wills and living trusts

▼ **Food/Beverages**

Ethnic foods
Low carb foods
Low-calorie cooking
Mad cow disease
Shopping on a budget

▼ **Health**

Baby Boomers at midlife
Diabetes on the rise
Eating disorders
Fighting Sars
Indoor air pollution
Lowering cholesterol
Medicare reform
Music & relaxation
Nursing shortage
Obesity epidemic
Safe dieting
Sleep disorders

▼ **Holiday/Home**

A vacation spot
Gifts everyone will love
Holiday depression
Holiday safety tips
Home security systems

▼ **Miscellaneous**

A vacation spot
A famous person
Review of a favorite book
Topic related to your job
Topic related to your major
Who benefits from college

▼ **Multicultural**

Diversity training at work
Ethnic traditions in the
  community
Global water shortages
Hatred of Americans
Japanese military
Muslims in America
Rebuilding Araq
US–Mexico relations

▼ **National**

Airline safety problems
Alternative fuels
Homeland security
Media bias
Recent Supreme Court
  decisions
Restructuring Social Security
  benefits
Rethinking NAFTA
Space program future
War on terrorism
Weapons of mass
  destruction

▼ **Personal**

Building lasting marriages
Dealing with stress
Dressing on a budget
Effective resumes
Memory techniques
Overcoming depression
Study techniques

▼ **Pets/Animals**

Animal research
Best pets for children
Discipline & pets

▼ **Social Issues**

AIDS update
Americans with Disabilities Act
Assisted suicide
Charity scams
Fetal tissue research
New immigrants
Sexual abuse & clergy
Stopping genocide
Unwed mothers

▼ **Sports/Hobbies**

Reflective clothing & joggers
Reforming college sports
Soccer fans
Tennis tips
Tips on watching football

▼ **Technology**

Building a web page
Copyright & the Internet
Electric & hybrid cars
Ethics & electronic message
  boards
New computer software
Viruses & hackers

Figure 12.2

**Sample Informational
Speech Topics
(General Categories)**

Once you have selected your topic, narrow it to fit the time limits and decide on your exact purpose. It is better to thoroughly illustrate and support a few points than it is to try to "say it all." Write your exact purpose in one clear and simple sentence beginning with "After hearing my speech, the audience will . . ." As shown in Figure 12.4 later in this chapter, Karen stated her exact purpose as follows: "After listening to my speech, the audience will be aware of the existence of heartworm disease and know how to prevent it."

After stating your exact purpose, select three to five main points. If you are familiar with your topic, you probably already have a good idea of what main points to include. If not, take 5 minutes to brainstorm a list of possible points. Then combine

▼ How	▼ What	▼ Why
How does the eye see colors?	What is the difference between stocks and bonds?	Why is abstract art more difficult than portraiture?
How does radar work?	What is the structure of the federal court system?	Why is perception subjective rather than objective?
How does human vision work?	What is Plato's cave analogy?	Why do natural foods contain dangerous toxins?
How do men get breast cancer?	What are the tenets of Islam?	Why do people yawn?
How do DNA molecules pass on genetic information?	What does "Manifest Destiny" mean?	Why is irradiated food healthy (or dangerous)?

Figure 12.3

Sample Informational Speech Topics—How, What, and Why (adapted from Rowan, 1995)

and eliminate some of them until you arrive at three to five possible ones (you may change your mind after researching the topic).

Step 3: Prepare a Rough-Draft Outline of Main Points and Desired Information

Basically, a rough-draft outline should include a list of possible main points and supporting information. Don't wait until after you do your research to make the rough-draft outline—if you do it first, it will save you research time. If you prefer, you can use storyboards instead. → *See Chapters 6 and 8 for suggestions on making a rough-draft outline, and Chapter 8 for storyboard suggestions.*

Step 4: Research Topic for Material to Support Main Points

Research your topic by looking at printed materials, computer databases, and the Internet; conducting personal interviews; and recalling personal experiences. As you do your research, look for both verbal and visual supporting materials. Effective supporting materials add clarity, proof, and interest to the main ideas in your speech. Using information from respected sources adds to your credibility as a speaker.

Step 5: Select a Variety of Supporting Materials

Effective speakers use a variety of supporting materials—at least two different supports for each main point. For example, to support your first point, you might begin with a definition or explanation, add a detailed factual instance, and conclude with a direct quotation or a visual aid. Your second main point might begin with two or three brief instances followed by a hypothetical instance, and so on. If you can't identify your supports, you are probably using explanation—a type of support that is often overused. Limit your use of statistics and explanation, and increase your use of instances, comparisons, and expert opinions, as well as fables, sayings, poems, and rhymes.

Step 6: Determine How Best to Organize Main Points

Of the four organizational patterns typically used in informative speeches—topical, chronological, geographic, and causal—speakers tend to use the topical pattern most

often, as Vanessa did in her speech on making the blind to see. However, the topical pattern is not necessarily the best for every speech. Since the unusual tends to attract interest, one of the other three organizational patterns may create more listener interest. ➜ *See Chapter 7 for a detailed discussion of the four organizational patterns.*

Test your knowledge of these patterns by taking the following quiz.

Test Your Knowledge Quiz

Testing Your Knowledge of Organizational Patterns

Directions: Here are six mini-outlines, each with a title and main points. Identify how the main points of each outline are organized by selecting (a) topical, (b) chronological, (c) spatial or geographic, or (d) causal. Write the letter in the blank. You can also take this quiz online at the Essentials of Public Speaking website and, if requested, e-mail your responses to your instructor.

_____ 1. "History of the Arabian Horse"
    I. Origin of the breed.
    II. Impact on the desert Bedouins.
    III. Introduction to Europe and North America.
    IV. Modern Arabian horse.

_____ 2. "Traffic Woes"
    I. Traffic accidents have increased.
    II. The chief reason for these accidents is the increaseed speed limit.

_____ 3. "Preparing an Elegant Mincemeat-Pear Tart"
    I. Prepare the pastry.
    II. Prepare the streusel topping.
    III. Bake crust 20 minutes at 350 degrees.
    IV. Arrange mincemeat and pears into partially baked crust.
    V. Add streusel topping and bake 15 to 20 minutes at 425 degrees.

_____ 4. "Eating Breakfast"
    I. Breakfast and academic performance.
    II. Breakfast and weight loss.
    III. Breakfast and attitude.

_____ 5. "Who Was Involved in Building the U.S. Space Station?"
    I. The Goddard Space Flight Center in Greenbelt, Maryland
    II. The Lewis Research Center in Cleveland, Ohio
    III. The Marshall Space Flight Center in Huntsville, Alabama
    IV. The Johnson Space Flight Center in Houston, Texas

_____ 6. "Do You Fit Your Birth-Order Mold?"
    I. "Brilliant" firstborns.
    II. "Forgotten" middle children.
    III. "Get-away-with-murder" lastborns.

Step 7: Plan Introduction and Conclusion

Never begin your speech with a statement of purpose. Always begin with an attention-getter. Also, never end your speech with only a summary of your purpose; instead, after the summary, end with a final memorable attention-getter that will leave your audience thinking about your speech. → *Chapter 7 discusses four basic elements in the introduction of a speech and two basic elements in the conclusion.*

If you decide to use humor, don't use self-disparaging humor (where you make yourself the brunt of a joke)—it has a negative effect on an audience (Hackman, 1988). It is much better to direct humor at your occupation or profession instead—these apparently do not harm your image (Gruner, 1985).

Step 8: Make Preparation Outline (or Storyboards) and Speaking Notes

To make sure your speech flows smoothly, you will need to expand your rough-draft outline into either a preparation outline or several storyboards—either one will help you fine-tune your speech. → *Chapter 8 discusses preparation outlines, storyboards, and speaking notes.*

THE FAR SIDE® BY GARY LARSON

At this point in the speech preparation process, many inexperienced speakers make a *key mistake*: They begin writing out their speech word for word as though it were a paper, but this is more of a handicap than a help. Most speakers discover that brief notes are more helpful. However, some speakers do write out the introduction and conclusion to make sure they begin and end exactly as intended. If you try this approach, make sure you don't sound like you are reading.

Instead of writing out your entire speech, formalize your rough outline into either a phrase or complete-sentence outline or several storyboards. (See a sample preparation outline in Figure 12.4.) Make sure all quotations and statistics are complete. Now, even though the beginning and ending of the speech are missing, read or talk through the body of the speech. If you find that a section is awkward, adjust it and go through the speech again. You may decide to add another example or remove one. You may even decide to do some more research. Whatever you do, don't memorize the speech—an extemporaneous speech should be a little different each time it's given. Finally, add your introduction and conclusion.

Figure 12.4

Karen's Preparation Outline

Karen's Preparation Outline

Title: "Canine Heartworm Disease" by Karen Gemmer
Exact Purpose: After listening to my speech, the audience will be aware of the existence of heartworm disease and know how to prevent it.

	Type of Source
INTRODUCTION	
• **Attention-getter:** What I am holding in my hand—in this jar— is a dog's heart. And this heart is completely infested with worms. This dog died from a very debilitating and deadly disease called Canine Heartworm Disease.	
• **Credibility:** At one time, when I thought I was going to be a veterinarian, I worked as a technician for a veterinarian. According to the journals I've read and the doctors I've talked to . . .	Interviews, Ref. #3
• **Audience motivation:** Approximately fifty percent or one out of every two dogs in our state that are unprotected against this disease will develop it. Now, that's the bad news. The good news is—for you dog owners and future dog owners— that this disease is entirely preventable.	
• **Purpose:** There are three main points that I'd like to cover today about heartworm disease and they are:	
• **Preview:** 1) What exactly is this disease? **[Transparency #1]** 2) How is it spread? 3) How can it be prevented?	
BODY	
I. **What is heartworm disease?**	Ref. #4
A. A parasite in the heart and adjacent blood vessels **[Infected dog heart in jar]**	
B. Facts about adult heartworms *[Explanation]*	
1. 14 inches long	
2. Seven-year life span	
3. Up to 250 in heart at one time	
4. Microscopic offspring called microfilaria	
C. Damage to heart, arteries, and other organs	
D. Results: congestive heart failure and death	
[Transition:] So now that you know what this disease is, how is this disease spread?	

When you decide that your speech is in good shape, you are ready to prepare your speaking notes. Although the format of speaking notes can vary (as discussed in Chapter 8), they are always brief. Speaking notes are key words or phrases to guide you through the speech. Important words are usually underlined in a bright color, and personal cues may be written in the margins. Normally, only quotations are written out word for word. If Lucy had chosen to use note cards for her speech "Our State of Health," the first card might have resembled the one in Figure 12.5. After practicing, she might have decided to use even fewer words on her speaking notes.

Step 9: Prepare Visual Aids

If you organized your speech by using storyboards, you already have a good idea of the visual aids that you want to use. If not, look at your preparation outline and rough out some possible visuals. One could be a text visual listing the main points in your speech—listeners find this to be very helpful. Another might include a graph of some

---

Karen's Preparation Outline
(continued)

II. **How is heartworm disease spread?**
  A. Spread from dog to dog by mosquito *[Explanation and hypothetical instance]*
  B. After bite, six months from microfilaria to adult worms **[Transparency #2]** *[Explanation of disease cycle]*
  C. Spreading rapidly
    1. Disease found in all 50 states and Canada *[Explanation]*
    2. Heavy infestation in eastern and southern states
	Ref. #2

[Transition:] Now that you know how easily heartworm disease is spread, exactly how can we prevent it?	

III. **How is heartworm disease prevented?**
  A. Monthly medication *[Explanation]*
  B. Prescription from veterinarian
	Ref. #1, pp. 1–4

CONCLUSION • **Summary:** Let's just review really fast what we have covered. All right, we know that this is a disease that affects the heart, as well as other body organs, and it's caused by a parasite. It is spread by the mosquito and it's very easily prevented by a monthly medication. **[Transparency #3]**	
• **Refocus:** I have two dogs . . . *[personal instance of healthy dogs]*. Because heartworm disease will strike one of every two dogs here in our state if they are unprotected, right now either Robin or Willie would have heartworm disease. So what I would like you to remember from today is that this disease is out there, and it is deadly. But if the medication is given conscientiously every month, it is entirely preventable.	Personal observation

References: *[APA editorial style]*
1. American Heartworm Society. (1993). *American heartworm society recommended procedures for the diagnosis and management of heartworm infection.* Batavia, IL: American Heartworm Society.
2. Knight, D. H. (1987). Heartworm infection. In R. B. Grieve (ed.), *The veterinary clinics of North America: Vol. 17. Small animal practice* (pp. 1463–1518). New York: W. B. Sanders.
3. Personal interviews with Roger Kendrick, DVM, Eastern Hills Pet Hospital, and Gary Thayer, DVM, MS, Animal Internal Medicine Clinic.
4. Rawlings, C. A., and Calvert, C. A. (1995). Heartworm disease. In S. J. Ettinger and E. C. Feldman (eds.), *Textbook of veterinary internal medicine: Vol. I. Diseases of the dog and cat* (pp. 1046–1068). New York: W. B. Sanders.

Figure 12.4

Karen's Preparation Outline *(continued)*

Technology Tip for Speakers

Put Your Presentation on the Web

PowerPoint 2003 makes it possible for even the most novice speaker to put a presentation on the web. Before we discuss how to do this, let's look at some reasons why you would want to. According to Randall (2000) and Bell (1998), there are many advantages to posting a presentation to the web:

- People can access your information after the presentation is over. This is helpful for those who missed the meeting or want to review certain facts.

- Accessing your presentation from the web eliminates any virus worries—a hazard when file attachments are sent through e-mail—and simplifies updates of material.

- You as speaker have more flexibility and less hassle. You can give your presentation from any computer with Internet access without having to lug a laptop or worry about set-up time. You will always be ready for spur-of-the-moment presentations and could even conduct a long-distance meeting by phone with an individual watching your presentation online.

- Access to hypertext links is fast and smooth. PowerPoint 2000 allows you to incorporate hypertext links into your slides, so that moving between a presentation slide and another web-site requires no long waits.

Now that you see some of the advantages of posting a presentation on the web, let's take a quick look at how Randall recommends we do it.

1. Open your presentation in Power-Point and check to see what the web version will look like (choose **File / Web Page Preview**).

2. When all three screens (slide, outline, and notes) are ready, open the **Save as Web Page** dialog box to save your presentation in HTML. The dialog box allows you to specify the title you want to appear on the browser's title bar.

3. Next open the **Publish as Web Page** dialog box. Here you will decide whether to show speaker notes, select which browsers to use (you'll probably what to select "all" so the viewer's browser can choose the most compatible format), adjust file name, and customize if you wish.

4. When ready, click the **Publish** button. Keep in mind that the presentation will work best on the latest versions of Netscape or Internet Explorer. (If you want to add a voiceover to your presentation, see the PowerPoint Speaker's Guide under Student Resources for Chapter 9 at the Essentials of Public Speaking website.)

statistics or a picture that illustrates a point. Don't forget that computer slides can be very effective. → *Chapter 9 includes information for preparing all types of visual aids.*

Step 10: Rehearse Your Speech

As you know, mentally thinking through your speech will not have the same result as practicing it aloud. A successful speech rehearsal involves standing up and using your

---

#1

"Our State of Health"

Introduction
   Quote: Hippocrates
   Def: "Absence of disease"
   Father—"Health became very..."
   I learned... (C. Everett Koop)
   We pay the price...
   Focus on 3 aspects of health
   (preview main points)   (Visual #1)

Pause
Body
   I. Risk Factors   (Visual #2)
      A. Beyond control
         Levy, Dignan & Shirreffs
      B. In our control
      C. How great a risk?
   Am. Heart   —66 million (1 in 4) —heart disease
   Assoc.   — (1 in 5) die (w) cancer
      [Yet:] 45% — no exercise   NSGA
              Sedentary = 5 times risk   AHA

Figure **12.5**

Part of Lucy's Speaking Notes on a 4-by-6-inch Note Card

speaking notes and visual aids (with equipment if possible) in an environment similar to the one in which you will speak. → *Chapters 10 and 11 include advice on effective delivery.*

> *Lucy rehearsed her speech several times in her living room using the high back of the sofa as a lectern. Her practice included copies of her computer visuals—she even pretended that she was using a computer and practiced using the remote. The first time she practiced, she tape-recorded her speech in order to see how she sounded—she wanted her tone to indicate the seriousness of the topic without sounding glum. Later, her husband and daughter served as her audience and made some valuable comments. For example, her husband said that her hand movements were so expressive that they were distracting; her daughter assured her that her eye contact was excellent. She tried to give her speech in front of a mirror so she could see her facial expressions, but she gave it up when she couldn't keep from laughing. On the day of her speech, she managed to get to class early so that she could run through her speech one time using the overhead projector. Practice made Lucy feel confident that she would do a good job.*

Use InfoTrac College Edition to search for *speechwriting, speech writing, public speaking, oral presentation★,* and *technical presentation★*. Look for articles on preparing and presenting effective speeches written by professionals in your major. Look for speaking suggestions that you can use.

Before You Speak: Last-Minute Checks

Once you have prepared your informative or demonstration speech following the 10 steps, you should conduct three last-minute checks:

▼ Verbal Tips

Use verbal immediacy behaviors (such as personal examples, references to *we* and *our,* reference to individuals by name, and praise).

Use external stimulus to overcome internal listener noise.

Avoid jargon and limit acronyms.

Make language brief, vivid, and specific.

Organize ideas so they flow.

Highlight ideas by using signposting, internal summaries, transitions, repetition, and restatement.

Place the most important points either first or last in your outline.

▼ Visual Tips

Use nonverbal immediacy behaviors (such as relaxed body posture, gestures, and eye contact).

Use powerful visual aids that can be grasped in 3–6 seconds.

Make sure text visuals include:
  fonts that harmonize with content
  type sizes from 18–36 point
  upper- and lowercase type
  no more than six lines
  phrases not sentences
  clip art, color, and large type for emphasis

Make sure graphic visuals:
  limit and group data
  always include headings
  minimize grid lines
  have bars wider than space between them
  avoid too much color or red and green bar graphs

▼ Vocal Tips

Use vocal immediacy behaviors (such as vocal expressiveness and interest).

Use a natural, enthusiastic delivery.

Increase your speaking rate.

Use good vocal variety by varying:
pitch
volume
rate
emphasis

Figure 12.6

Verbal, Visual, and Vocal Delivery Tips

1. *Make sure that all aspects of your presentation are ethical* (Lehman & DuFrene, 1999):
   - Is the information presented in a truthful, honest, and fair manner?
   - Are the ideas expressed clearly?
   - Is the audience treated tactfully?
   - Are embellishment and exaggeration of facts avoided?
   - Are views supported by objective facts?
   - Do graphics present facts accurately and without distortion?

2. *Check for possible equipment problems.* Make sure that the necessary equipment is at your speaking location and that it works. ➔ *Guidelines for conducting a technological rehearsal are covered in the Chapter 10 Technology Tip for Speakers.*

3. *Make sure that your delivery will help your audience understand and remember your speech.* Review the verbal, visual, and vocal delivery tips in Figure 12.6.

If you like, use the Informative Speech Evaluation Form in Figure 12.7 to help you prepare for your own informative speeches, evaluate your speeches after you've given them, and evaluate your classmates' speeches. You can access this form online under Student Resources for Chapter 12 at the Essentials of Public Speaking website.

This chapter has presented a look at what's involved in preparing and presenting an informative speech. The next chapter will apply the Basic Steps for Preparing a Speech to persuasive speeches.

Informative Speech Evaluation Form

Name: _____ Topic: _____ Date: _____

Grades: Outline _____ Presentation: _____

Ratings: 1 (Missing), 2 (Poor), 3 (Fair), 4 (Good), 5 (Excellent)

Comments:

Did **INTRODUCTION**:
1. Begin with attention-getter?   1 2 3 4 5
2. Motivate audience to listen?   1 2 3 4 5
3. Establish credibility?   1 2 3 4 5
4. Make purpose clear?   1 2 3 4 5
5. Preview main points?   1 2 3 4 5

Were **MAIN IDEAS**:
6. Easy to identify and follow?   1 2 3 4 5
7. Arranged in effective pattern?   1 2 3 4 5
8. Characterized by good transitions?   1 2 3 4 5

Was **SUPPORTING MATERIAL**:
9. Well documented during speech?   1 2 3 4 5
10. Adequate in verbal supports? (Use +, ✓, −)   1 2 3 4 5
    _____ Statistics?   _____ Expert opinions?
    _____ Comparisons?   _____ Fables/sayings/poems/rhymes?
    _____ Instances?   _____ Explanations?
11. Adequate in visual supports? (Use +, ✓, −)   1 2 3 4 5
    _____ Interesting?   _____ Professional?
    _____ Easy to see?   _____ Handled well?

Did **CONCLUSION**:
12. Summarize topic and main ideas?   1 2 3 4 5
13. Close in a memorable way and use effective Q&A
    (if appropriate)?   1 2 3 4 5

Was **DELIVERY** characterized by:
14. Minimal (or no) use of notes?   1 2 3 4 5
15. Direct eye contact?   1 2 3 4 5
16. Natural, conversational quality?   1 2 3 4 5
17. Freedom from distracting mannerisms? (Check)   1 2 3 4 5
    _____ "Uh"/"Um"/"And uh"/"You know"/"Well"/"OK"?
    _____ Plays with pencil, clothes, hair, or pointer?
    _____ Nervous laugh or cough?
    _____ Slouches, taps feet, paces, or sways?
    _____ Other?
18. Effective volume, pitch, rate, and emphasis?   1 2 3 4 5

Was **PRESENTATION AS A WHOLE**:
19. Suited to audience?   1 2 3 4 5
20. Suited to time and assignment?   1 2 3 4 5

Total: _____

Figure 12.7

Informative Speech
Evaluation Form

Summary

There are two basic types of informative speeches—demonstration and informational. In a demonstration speech, the visuals become the focus of the speech; in an informational speech, visuals are used only to augment and clarify.

When preparing an informative speech, follow these 10 steps: (1) analyze your audience; (2) determine your topic, exact purpose, and main points; (3) rough out an outline of main points and supporting information; (4) research the topic to find supporting materials; (5) select the best supporting material for each main point; (6) determine how to organize your main points; (7) develop the introduction and conclusion; (8) expand the rough outline into a preparation outline or storyboards and prepare your speaking notes; (9) prepare your visual aids; and (10) rehearse your speech. Until you are an experienced speaker, try to use the steps in the order suggested.

Once your speech is in good shape, give it a final three-point check: make sure that it is ethical, free of equipment problems, and will use good verbal, visual, and vocal delivery skills to help listener understanding and retention.

Essentials of Public Speaking  Online

Use the Essentials of Public Speaking website at **http://communication. wadsworth.com/hamiltoneps3** for quick access to the electronic study resources that accompany this chapter. When you get to the Essentials home page, click on "Student Book Companion Site" in the Resource box. The Essentials website features the Test Your Knowledge quizzes on pages 251 and 262, a video of Vanessa's speech described on page 256, the Informative Speech Evaluation Form on page 269, InfoTrac College Edition, the Suggestions for Practice and Critical Thinking activities and the InfoTrac College Edition activities that follow, a digital glossary, and review quizzes.

Key Terms

definition 254
demonstration speech
   252

description 255
informational speech
   254

narration 255

Suggestions for Practice and Critical Thinking

1. Prepare a 3- to 4-minute demonstration speech. Follow the guidelines in this chapter for preparing your speech. Determine what visuals to use and how to prepare them with maximum effectiveness.

2. Prepare a 4- to 7-minute informational speech to be followed by up to 2 minutes of questions from the audience and a 1-minute (or less) final

summary. Unless your instructor indicates otherwise, prepare a minimum of two transparencies or computer slides—other types of visuals may be used as well. Follow the guidelines in this chapter for preparing your speech.

3. In groups of three to five, prepare the three visual aids Vanessa could have used in her speech "They Made the Blind to See." Use PowerPoint and include color, clip art, transitions, and even sound. Each group should present its visuals (on computer screen or video projector) to the class and then turn in the computer disk or transparencies to the instructor for evaluation.

4. Are you still visualizing the positive statements that you wrote earlier? Twice a day as you read each one aloud, are you picturing yourself successfully accomplishing the skill and feeling confident about it at the same time? Remember, changing negative thoughts and habits into positive ones requires that we "say," "see," and "feel" ourselves succeeding. If you have slacked off on your positive statements, it's not too late to begin working on them again.
→ *See Chapter 2 for suggestions on improving speaker confidence.*

5. Using the Informative Speech Evaluation Form in Figure 12.7, evaluate Vanessa's speech. What grade do you think the speech deserves? Compare your evaluation with that of several other members of your class. If you like, you can watch Vanessa's speech and complete your evaluation online under Student Resources for Chapter 12 at the Essentials of Public Speaking website.

6. Select a subject in your major or minor field of study that is either unknown by most people or misunderstood due to its complexity. Interview class members to determine problems, research the topic, and prepare three of the following: a definition, a description, an explanation, or a narration. Exchange your paragraphs with a class member—include comments and suggestions. If time permits, present your presentation to the class for evaluation.

7. Use InfoTrac College Edition to run a keyword search using *PowerPoint presentations*. How many articles did you find? Read the article "Presentations on the Web" by Neil Randall.

8. Check out the following websites. *You can access these sites under the Student Resources for Chapter 12 at the Essentials of Public Speaking website.*

- For demonstration speeches, check out HowStuffWorks.com, an excellent site with step-by-step procedures and diagrams.

- If you have considered entering an individual events speech tournament, read a description of the 11 events at Lee Mayfield's Events Description web page at the James Madison University site. Lee's site is sponsored by the National Individual Events Tournament.

- For ideas for speech topics, look at the practice topics for this year's informative and persuasive extemporaneous speeches in the University Interscholastic League (UIL). From the UIL home page, click on the "Academics" link, then the "Speech & Debate" link. Scroll down and click on the link "Extemp Practice Topics" under the heading Extemporaneous Speaking.

- For humorous quotations, search Bartleby.com's 86,000 quotations, Quoteland.com, Geocities.com's Humorous Quotations, and Comedy-Zone.net.

- To learn how to post your PowerPoint presentation to a website, read the article "Put PowerPoint on the Web" at the University of Washington's

Catalyst site. From the Catalyst.Washington.edu http site (no www), choose "Build a PowerPoint presentation" from the "I need to . . ." pull-down menu. Scroll down and click on the link "Put PowerPoint Presentations on the Web."

Quiz Answers

Answers to the Unit IV Quiz (page 251): Test Your Knowledge of Different Types of Speeches.

1. *False.* A good speech of introduction focuses attention on the featured speaker, not on the person giving the introduction. Therefore, speeches of introduction are brief—seldom longer than 5 minutes. For hints on preparing an effective speech of introduction, click on "Special Occasion Speaking" at the Essentials of Public Speaking website.

2. *True.* Although much more research needs to be done, it does appear that color (when used correctly) is more persuasive. A study by the University of Minnesota and the 3M Corporation found that color transparencies were more persuasive than black-and-white ones; the Bureau of Advertising found that readers are 80 percent more likely to read a color ad than a black-and-white one and 55 to 78 percent more likely to purchase an item shown in a color ad (Johnson, 1990; Vogel, Dickson, & Lehman, 1986, 1990). ➔ *See Chapter 9 for more information on color visuals.*

3. *True.* Speakers often make the mistake of letting the Q & A period get out of control or run on too long. When this happens, audience members may forget how positive they felt about your speech. To direct the audience back to your speech topic, thank them for their participation, respond to the last question, and then sum up your topic with a final memorable conclusion. ➔ *See Chapter 7 for more suggestions on how to handle Q & A.*

4. *False.* Although you should always cite the source of evidence, research indicates that mentioning only the source but not the qualifications of the source makes the evidence less persuasive than citing no source at all. ➔ *See Chapter 14 for additional information.*

5. *False.* Although manipulation is unethical, analyzing your audience members so that you know their needs and wants is simply good research. How else are you going to make sure that your message fits their frames of reference so that they will give you a fair hearing? ➔ *Audience analysis is discussed in Chapter 4.*

6. *False.* Research has found that few people are persuaded by logic alone. In fact, most people can't even distinguish illogical arguments from logical ones. An argument is logical only if your audience views it as such. And what makes people view an argument as logical is when they can relate to it personally. For example, listeners might be uninterested in giving money to clean up the environment until realizing that the local lake is so polluted that their beloved water sports will be banned unless the county receives enough money to have the lake cleaned before summer.

7. *True.* Professional-looking visual aids impress an audience. Since you obviously worked hard on them, they enhance your credibility. ➔ *Credibility is discussed in Chapter 14.*

8. *False.* There is a big difference between using humor and telling jokes. Few speakers are able to tell jokes effectively. They forget the punch line or leave out a pertinent detail that makes the punch line meaningless. However, most speakers can add humor to their speeches with well-placed examples or un-expected facial or vocal expressions. As long as it is appropriate to your topic, humor has a place in informative speeches. ➤ *See Chapter 7 for more information on humor.*

9. *False.* The correct procedure is to walk to the front, pause, and immediately begin with an attention-getter ("Last week, my favorite uncle was playing basketball with his two teenage sons when . . .") before stating your purpose.

10. *False.* Unless the source is a famous, well-liked person, it is more persuasive to cite the source after presenting the evidence. Apparently it is better to let the audience absorb the evidence before judging it by its source. ➤ *See Chapter 14 for more information about presenting evidence.*

chapter 13

Persuasive Speaking: Individual or Team

Flashback The Greek general Pericles was known for the power of his oratory. Some of the most impressive monuments of ancient Greece owe their existence to his political persuasion. First, he convinced the Delian Defense League to transfer their war treasury to Athens where it would be kept safe. Then he convinced the Athenians that this money should not be used for war, but for peaceful purposes—to rebuild the Acropolis (previously destroyed by the Persians) and to build beautiful marble structures designed to last for generations, such as the Parthenon and the Great Temple of Athena.

THINK OF HOW OFTEN WE USE PERSUASION IN OUR DAILY CONVERSATIONS AT SCHOOL, AT work, and with friends and family. For example, we may

- Convince a professor that our reasons for turning a paper in late are justified.

- Persuade our boss that ordering supplies from a different company would save money.

- Convince our friends that going to a movie would be more fun than going to a hockey game.

- Get our family members so interested in recycling that they pitch in to help.

In other words, we are all familiar with persuasion. That familiarity and your speaking experiences have prepared you for one of the most interesting yet complex types of speaking: persuasive speaking. This chapter will describe the varieties of persuasive speeches and discuss the steps for preparing a successful persuasive speech. The next chapter will focus on specific kinds of persuasive appeals to use whether speaking as an individual or in a team.

Persuasion Defined

Persuasion is communication that is intended to influence choice. This definition includes two important aspects: (1) persuasion is intentional, and (2) persuasion is about influence, not control. Let's look at each of these points in more detail.

First, successful persuasive speakers *intend* to persuade their listeners. They take a definite stand and, through various kinds of persuasive appeals, urge their listeners to take a certain position or action. The ineffective persuasive speaker, in contrast, presents information and options, hoping that the audience will be persuaded, but fails to specify which options are best and avoids taking a definite stand. Which of the following two approaches do you think would be more persuasive?

> **Approach 1**
>
> We've looked at some of the possible solutions to the crisis in our educational system. I hope you will consider them carefully in deciding how best to solve our educational dilemma.
>
> **Approach 2**
>
> We've looked at a variety of plans for solving our educational crisis. However, there's only one that has a record of success in every district where it has been tried. There's only one that appears to please students, parents, teachers, and taxpayers alike. There's only one that deserves our support—and that plan is . . .

The first approach does not indicate which option is best or which solution the speaker advocates. Considering the many different frames of reference in your audience, you cannot assume that listeners will automatically reach the conclusion that you believe is best. On the other hand, the second approach leaves no doubt as to which plan the speaker advocates. This explicit approach decreases the chances of misunderstanding and increases the probability of persuasion. After reviewing the research on the topic, O'Keefe (1990, 1997) concludes: "The overwhelmingly predominant finding is that messages that include explicit conclusions or recommendations are more persuasive than messages without such elements" (1990, p. 160).

The second important aspect of persuasion is that it is meant to *influence,* not control. Taking a stand does not mean that you want to force your listeners to do what you want—there is no coercion in persuasion. Brembeck & Howell (1976) were among the first communication specialists to clarify the differences between *coerce, inform,* and *persuade.* To *coerce* is to eliminate or exclude options. To *inform* is to increase the number of options available (the more listeners know, the more choices they have). To *persuade* is to limit the options that are perceived as acceptable. The only way to know what your audience perceives as acceptable is by researching their attitudes, beliefs, values, and needs. → *See Chapter 4 for specifics in audience analysis.*

Persuasive Versus Informative Speeches

Many speakers seem to think that the main difference between informative and persuasive speaking occurs in the conclusion. But it takes more than a concluding sentence or two to persuade most people. Persuasion begins with your introductory comments and continues through your concluding remarks.

In addition to the goal or intent of the speaker, persuasive speeches differ from informative speeches in four ways: supporting materials, language and style, delivery, and organizational patterns.

Supporting Materials

All speeches need a variety of supporting materials to maintain audience interest and to prove the accuracy of the information. Persuasive speeches must further prove that the recommended position or action is the most desirable. Therefore, it is critical for

persuasive speeches to present supporting materials that prove (such as expert opinion, statistics, brief and detailed factual instances, and literal comparisons).

Language and Style

Although language style (including transitions, word choices, and stylistic devices) is important in all types of speeches, persuasive speakers are more likely to use emotional appeals as well as emotional words in an effort to get their audience to relate personally to their position. Successful persuasive speakers are also more likely to use logical transitions such as *therefore* and *as a result* than informative speakers are. ➡ *See Chapter 14 for specifics on emotional appeals or needs of an audience.*

Delivery

Delivery is more important in persuasive speeches than in other kinds of speeches, because it can affect how an audience judges a speaker's credibility—which, in turn, can affect the speaker's persuasiveness. For example, trustworthiness, a factor in credibility, is affected by eye contact, speaking rate, vocal quality, and vocal variety. In general, persuasive delivery must be more forceful and direct than informative delivery. ➡ *For more on persuasive delivery, see Chapter 14.*

Organizational Patterns

Informative organizational patterns (such as topical, chronological, and geographic) are intended to present information without biasing audience opinions. In contrast, persuasive organizational patterns (such as the claim, problem–solution, criteria satisfaction, and comparative advantages patterns) are intended to influence audience opinions. Effective speakers use organization to help make their speeches more persuasive. ➡ *See Chapter 7 for specifics on organizational patterns.*

Now that we've defined persuasion and discussed the main differences between informative and persuasive speaking, let's take a look at the two basic types of persuasive speeches.

Types of Persuasive Speeches

The two basic types of persuasive speeches are: the speech to convince and the speech to actuate. They differ in the degree of audience reaction sought: the **speech to convince** seeks intellectual agreement from listeners, whereas the **speech to actuate** asks listeners for both intellectual agreement and action of some type.

The Speech to Convince

In a speech to convince, you want your audience to agree with your way of thinking. You aren't asking listeners to "do" anything. For example, in a speech about latchkey children, Maria tried to convince her audience that latchkey children are causing many problems for society and that four relatively simple solutions could alleviate these problems, benefiting both the children and society. Maria didn't ask her audience to write to Congress, vote for a particular bill, or donate money. She just

A woman at a protest rally at UCLA gives a persuasive speech to actuate.

David Young-Wolff/PhotoEdit

wanted to convince her audience that 10 million latchkey children represent a serious—but solvable—problem for society. The speech to convince is also a good choice when listeners disagree with your position and you know that it is unlikely that you can move them to action in a single speech.

The Speech to Actuate

In a speech to actuate, you want your audience to go one step past agreement and take a particular action. First, you must convince listeners of the merits of your ideas; then you want to move them to action. Most speakers try to persuade the audience *to "do" something* that they haven't been doing (such as write a letter to their local representative, volunteer their time, or buy a particular product). In addition, there are three other types of action. You can urge the audience members to

- *Continue* doing something (continue eating balanced meals)

- *Stop* doing something (stop waiting until the last minute to study for exams)

- *Never start* doing something (never start smoking cigarettes)

Depending on your topic and your audience, you may want to include more than one request for action. For example, in a speech about alcohol you might encourage audience members who drink to use a designated driver, urge drinkers who have used designated drivers to continue to do so, and recommend that those who don't drink never start.

Which type of persuasive speech you pick will depend on the assignment, your preferences, and the topic. For example, the "cultural bias of standardized tests," "the breakdown of the family," and "the necessity of teen curfews" are topics that seem

better suited to speeches to convince than to actuate. On the other hand, the "need for volunteers in the community" and "health problems resulting from recycled cabin air in commercial airliners" are topics that seem to lend themselves to audience action. For the first topic, you might urge listeners to spend at least 1 hour a week as a volunteer. For the second topic, you might recommend that listeners write to commercial airlines and the Federal Aviation Administration.

Sample Student Speech: "Drinking and Driving" by Lorna McElaney

The following persuasive speech, "Drinking and Driving," was presented by Lorna McElaney to her public-speaking class, where she was voted best speaker. This sample speech was transcribed from her videotape and then retaped by Peter Boyd because Lorna was not available. The assignment specified a 4- to 7-minute persuasive speech using visual aids. She chose a speech to actuate, in which she tried to persuade the audience to sign a petition and join a "Lights On for Life" campaign. Lorna's speech will be referred to throughout the chapter to illustrate how she went about preparing the speech. As you read her speech, think about the changes you would make if you were speaking about the same subject. To watch and analyze a video clip of Lorna's speech, look under Student Resources for Chapter 13 at the Essentials of Public Speaking website.

SAMPLE SPEECH

DRINKING AND DRIVING

by Lorna McElaney

Introduction to Lorna's Speech by Jeanette

In the holiday season we will be hearing a lot about drinking and driving and alcohol-related accidents. Today I would like to introduce you to a mother of two preteen children who worries about her children's safety each holiday. She has already suffered the loss of a high school friend killed in an alcohol-related accident, and the daughter of a friend who was involved in an alcohol-related accident is confined to a wheelchair for life. Lorna would like tougher penalties for first-time and repeat offenders. So, today I would like to introduce you to Ms. Lorna McElaney.

Lorna's Introduction

Analysis
Since Lorna's speech was given early in December, her reference to the Christmas season and the

THE CHRISTMAS SEASON is the time for sharing and giving and sweet memories of years gone past. There is a lot of celebrating going on, not only now, but all through the year. Everyone seems to be celebrating one thing or another. How many of you when you were out there celebrating have had a drink, or maybe two or more, and then gotten in your

celebrating that occurs during this time was a good attention-getter.

Lorna appeals to safety and social needs in her attempt to motivate her classmates. By asking them if they have ever had one or more drinks and then driven home, she hopes to get her audience personally involved. Immediately after asking the question (most of the class raised their hands), she startles them with the example of Larry Dotson to show them that her topic is relevant. Larry was out celebrating—just like them, and he killed Natalie. Now Natalie's mother grieves—just like their mothers would.

Lorna does not mention her credibility because she was introduced by a classmate, Jeanette.

Since Lorna is using the problem–solution–action pattern of organization, her introduction does not need to include background information on the problem. Also no unusual terms need defining.

Alcohol-Related Facts

- 2 of 5 people in accident
- 17,400 killed in U.S. last year
- 1,800 killed in Texas last year
- Only 20-30% conviction rate

Visual #1

car and driven away? Well, last year in December, Larry Dotson did the same thing and he hit and killed Natalie Gale, a 20-year-old girl, and her companion. Perhaps with greater awareness and tougher laws Natalie would be here today and her mother wouldn't be suffering the pain and anguish that she is this Christmas Season. Last Christmas it was Natalie Gale; this Christmas it could be one of us.

Today I will share with you some startling facts that show how serious a problem drunk driving has become, recommend several workable solutions, and urge you to join me in writing our senators to demand tougher laws to protect ourselves and those we love.

Body

Step I. Problem

According to the National Highway Safety Department **[Visual #1]** two out of five people in their lifetime will be in an auto/alcohol-related accident. That means three or four of you in this classroom will be in an auto accident involving alcohol. Mothers Against Drunk Driving in their Summary of Statistics reports that over 17,000 people in the United States were killed in auto/alcohol-related accidents last year. Now that's a lot, although some of you might not think it's a lot compared to our total population. But if it's your brother or your sister or a friend or an acquaintance, that's one too many.

According to an article in the *Dallas Morning News,* last year we had 1,800 alcohol-related deaths in Texas—1,800 senseless deaths. You know we Texans boast about our number one Cowboys, and our great state, and we are number one in a lot of things. Well, now we are number one in alcohol-related deaths. I don't want to be known for that—do you?

Only 20 to 30 percent of arrests lead to conviction. This sends a clear message to people—you are not going to get caught, or if you do get caught drinking and driving, you are going to get a slap on your hand, maybe a fine, a night in jail and that's it!

Last year at this time Officer Alan Chick was killed by a repeat offender. He was doing his job; he was helping a motorist on the side of the road. And this drunk came along and hit him and killed him. A repeat offender with eight prior convictions! The Chick family won't have new Christmas memories this year. His wife Lisa and two young children will have to rely on past memories. As this example and these statistics show, drunk driving is a serious problem in Texas.

Step II. Solution

What should be done? There's a lot of things that can be done. According to MADD, Mothers Against Drunk Driving, we need to have more sobriety checkpoints. You hear about them at holiday time— at Christmas, July Fourth, Memorial Day—but that's not enough. We

(continued)

Although no optional sub-steps are included in Lorna's introduction, she uses persuasive language effectively in making her exact position known and smoothly previews her three main points: problem, solutions, and recommended action.

In the body of her speech, Lorna not only develops the problems but also establishes her trustworthiness and competency by citing evidence [Visual #1] from a variety of knowledgeable sources such as the National Highway Safety Department, MADD (Mothers Against Drunk Driving), and the Dallas Morning News. *Because these sources were already known to the audience, there was no need to state their qualifications. You will note that Lorna does not mention possible objections to her position—in other words, she presents only one side of the argument. She does this because her poll of classmates showed that most of them were already in agreement with her.*

Even though Lorna concentrates on statistics in her speech,

need them the year round so people will know that they can be stopped any time, not just during the holiday time. Maybe they will think twice before they get behind the wheel.

We also need legislation to lower the legal alcohol level. Right now in Texas before you are considered legally drunk your blood alcohol level must be .10 or higher. MADD is appealing to the legislature to lower that level to .08. The Insurance Institute of Highway Safety says that when a person's alcohol level is at .05, the probability of a crash begins to increase significantly. People are driving around in lethal weapons—their cars. They can't handle .10. It's obvious with all the deaths that we have.

We also need stronger penalties for drunk driving. As reported by the *Dallas Morning News,* Texas has the most lenient DWI penalties in the nation. Our laws must change. For example, Ohio has implemented stricter laws for DWI offenders. First-time offenders can now have their license revoked at the scene or a new license plate is put on their vehicle identifying them as a person who has been pulled over for drinking and driving. Second-time offenders can have their cars impounded. So we see there are things that can be done to lessen the DWI problem.

Step III. Action

Action must be taken now. And we must all take part in that action. December is National Drinking and Driving Awareness Month. On December 16th the National Highway Safety and Traffic Administration is calling for "Lights On for Life" day. Please join in this promotion in remembrance of those killed in alcohol- and drug-related traffic accidents and to show our government representatives that we want change.

You can also make a difference by writing your senators. I have a letter here today that I have written to Senator Kay Bailey Hutchison urging her to take the legal actions I have discussed in this speech. If you agree with me, at the end of my presentation, come up and sign this letter. [Shows letter]

Conclusion

WE MUST DEMAND more sobriety check points, a lower legal alcohol level, and tougher penalties for drunk driving. If we don't, we can look forward to more senseless deaths this Christmas. And next Christmas, like Natalie's mother and Officer Chick's family, it could be us with nothing but memories of someone dear. The time for action is now. Let's stop these senseless deaths. **[Visual #2]** Let's get these drunks off the road before they kill someone we love. I'm going to leave you with a sobering excerpt from a poem called "Prom Night" that was anonymously sent in to a local radio station.

Visual #2

SAMPLE SPEECH

she uses a variety of other supporting materials—detailed and brief instances, comparisons, explanation, a poem, and visual aids. She personalizes the problem by including specific (real) people who died in DWI accidents.

For emotional appeal, Lorna relates to the safety, esteem, and social needs of her audience. For example, she appeals to esteem needs when she asks the audience if Texans want to be known as the state that is number one in alcohol-related deaths.

Lorna does more than describe the problem and recommend a solution—she includes an action step to encourage her audience to get personally involved.

Lorna gives a summary of the three solutions she feels will reduce the accidents caused by drunk drivers. She does not summarize the action she wants from her audience since the action discussion occurred just before the conclusion and because she had already asked her classmates to come up and sign her letter to Senator Kay Bailey Hutchison. Do you think she made the right decision?

Lorna visualizes a future with more senseless deaths and nothing but memories of a loved one. Also, her poem is an indirect but powerful look at this future.

She challenges her listeners to take action before drunks kill a loved one—a good motive appeal.

Finally, Lorna's visual of a tombstone and her concluding poem combine to create a memorable ending.

I went to a party, Mom;
I remembered what you said.
You told me not to drink, Mom,
So I drank soda instead.

I felt really proud inside, Mom,
The way you said I would.
I didn't drink and drive, Mom,
Even though others said I should.

I know I did the right thing, Mom;
I know you are always right.
The party is finally ending, Mom,
And everyone drives out of sight.

As I got into my car, Mom,
I knew I'd get home in one piece
Because of the way you raised me, Mom,
So responsible and sweet.

I started to drive away, Mom;
But as I pulled out onto the road,
The other car didn't see me, Mom,
And hit me like a load.

As I lay on the pavement, Mom,
I hear the policeman say,
"The other guy is drunk," Mom,
And now I'm the one who'll pay.

This is the end, Mom.
I wish I could look you in the eye
To say these final words, Mom,
"I love you and good-bye."

Steps in Preparing a Persuasive Speech

As you already know, the general steps in preparing a speech are similar for informative and persuasive speeches. However, steps 1 and 2 are usually reversed for persuasive speeches because persuasive speakers begin with a topic they feel passionate about and adapt that topic as needed to fit a particular audience. → *For basic information about persuasive speech preparation, refer to Chapters 7 and 8.*

Step 1: Determine Your Topic, Position Statement, and Type of Speech

As mentioned above, although successful persuasive speakers carefully analyze their audiences, they seldom select a topic with a particular audience in mind, as is done in informative speaking. Persuasive speakers usually select a topic because they feel strongly about it. Getting your audience to reevaluate their beliefs is what persuasion is all about. However, because they often speak to more than one audience on the same topic, persuasive speakers' arguments, supporting materials, and persuasive appeals may change depending on the audience's beliefs, attitudes, and values.

To select your topic, position statement, and type of persuasive speech, consider the following guidelines.

Selecting Your Topic If you have been keeping a list of possible speech topics on note cards, you probably know exactly which topic you want to speak about. If you haven't decided on a topic, consider these suggestions:

■ *Select a topic that fits the assignment.* Your assignment may specify a type of persuasive speech, an organizational pattern, or a time limit.

■ *Select a controversial topic.* A controversial topic is one that has at least two conflicting views. The controversy may be over whether a problem exists or what to do about it. For example, everyone may agree that teenage pregnancy is a serious problem but may disagree about how to solve it.

For speeches to convince, the topic must be controversial. For example, the topic "Everyone should exercise for their health" is not controversial. On the other hand, the following topics would be controversial for most audiences: "Parents should encourage their children to participate in peewee football," "Irradiated vegetables are unhealthy," "Sex education should be taught at home, not at school." Even experts disagree about these topics.

For speeches to actuate, controversial topics are preferable but not always necessary. For example, although the need for exercise could not be used as a topic for a speech to convince, you could use it in a speech to actuate. Just because your listeners know that exercise is healthy doesn't mean that they exercise. As Lucy noted in her informative speech about health, 45 percent of Americans don't exercise at all. Therefore, you might wish to persuade your audience to put aside their many excuses and make a commitment to regular exercise.

■ *Select a topic you feel strongly about.* Persuasion includes more than just logic; it also involves feelings. You will be more confident giving a speech about a topic that arouses strong feelings in you. Are there controversial issues in society or politics, the workplace, education or college life, sports or the media, or health or personal topics about which you have definite opinions?

▼ **Business Issues**

Casual dress is affecting work quality

Companies should hire more disabled workers

Homelessness should be a priority business concern

More company training programs are needed

Workplace ethics need an overhaul

▼ **Family Issues**

Children watch too much television (video games)

Condom distribution by schools should be banned

Everyone should have a will or living trust

Parents must exercise more control at home

Sex education should be taught at home, not at school

Sleep deprivation is responsible for lowering grades

▼ **Food Issues**

Alcohol should not be advertised at sports events

Drinking age should be lowered

Healthy people eat low-carb foods

More government controls are needed on imported beef

▼ **Health Issues**

Indoor air pollution can be stopped

Irradiated vegetables are dangerous

Lower your cholesterol now

Nursing shortage is caused by low pay

Popular diets are responsible for obesity in America

Regular exercise is needed for long life

▼ **Multicultural Issues**

America is responsible for rebuilding Iraq

Ethnic traditions should be celebrated in the community

Global water shortages should be a priority of the United Nations

Muslims in America deserve fair treatment

US–Mexico relations need serious improvement

▼ **Personal Issues**

Overcoming depression requires intervention by others

STDs can be avoided by abstinence

Stress is alleviated by regular exercise and proper diet

Taking vitamin supplements is dangerous

Volunteerism is a college student responsibility

▼ **Pet/Animal Issues**

Animal research is a necessary evil

People with pets are healthier than those without pets

Retirement centers should allow pets in private rooms

▼ **Political Issues**

Farm subsidies must be stopped

Homeland security should receive more funding

Mandatory drug testing violates personal rights

NAFTA is producing as expected

National health-care policy is needed in America

One year of military service should be required of all able citizens

Social Security needs restructuring

State polling devices need modernizing

Terrorism is a real threat to citizens

Women should be allowed in combat areas

▼ **Social Issues**

Assisted suicide is an individual right

Clergy charged with sexual abuse should resign

Fetal tissue research is necessary for citizen health

Illegal immigrants should not be granted citizenship

Racial quotas are still necessary to end discrimination

States should determine the legality of gay marriage

Stricter penalties needed for DWI offenses

▼ **Sports/Hobby Issues**

College sports need reforming

Hobbies are good for your health

Salary cap should be implemented in professional sports

Violence at sports events shows moral decline

• **Technology Issues**

College students should have a personal website

Computer hackers deserve stricter punishment

Electric and hybrid cars will lower America's dependence on foreign oil

National regulation of the Internet will decrease pornography

Virus-checker software is worth the cost

Figure 13.1

Sample Persuasive Speech Topics

What changes (if any) in thinking or action would you recommend to your classmates in relation to these issues? Make a list of possible topics. Then check Figure 13.1 for additional ideas. If you feel strongly about any of these topics or if they cause you to think of additional topics, add them to your list. Now select from this list of possible topics the ones that would be the most appropriate for your assigned speech.

Lorna, who gave the sample speech about drinking and driving presented earlier in the chapter, felt so strongly about the problems involved with drunk driving that no other topic seemed appropriate for her persuasive speech. Because of her friends' experiences with drunk drivers and the fact that her two children would be driving soon, Lorna was genuinely concerned about the high number of accidents involving drunk drivers.

■ *Select a topic that you already know a lot about* (if possible). Use this criterion to narrow your list. The topics about which you have the strongest feelings are probably the ones you know the most about either from reading or from personal experience. If you aren't sure which of two issues to select for your speech, you may want to delay your decision until you have written a position statement for each topic. You might also want to poll your audience (see step 2) before making the final decision.

Deciding on Your Position Statement   A **position statement**, like the exact purpose of an informative speech, is a simple sentence that states the speaker's position on the topic. A single word, such as *abortion,* is not enough because it does not specify the speaker's position. A statement such as "Abortion should be illegal in all cases except those in which the woman's life is in danger" makes the speaker's exact position clear.

In his *Rhetoric,* Aristotle divides persuasive issues into four types:

■ *Being* (fact)—Does evidence of harm exist?

■ *Quality* (value)—Does the problem violate basic societal goals or values?

■ *Procedure* (policy)—Is action or change required?

■ *Quantity* (scope)—Is the problem great enough to make it a social issue?

Today, most persuasive writers combine policy and scope—action is only required if the problem is of sufficient magnitude—and categorize position statements as statements of fact, value, or policy:

■ *Statement of fact*—indicates that the speaker will present evidence to persuade the listeners that a debatable point is or is not true. (In contrast, an informative speech is about a topic accepted as true.) Sample statements of fact include "Irradiated vegetables are unhealthy," "Nuclear power plants are a safe energy source," and "Lee Harvey Oswald was part of a conspiracy."

■ *Statement of value*—indicates that the speaker will present arguments and evidence to persuade listeners that an idea, object, or person is or is not good (or ethical, or wise, or beautiful). In other words, the speaker will offer evidence in support of a judgment. Sample statements of value include "The U.S. space program is a wise use of taxpayers' money," "The death penalty is a civilized and moral form of punishment," and "It is immoral to use animals in medical research."

■ *Statement of policy*—indicates that the speaker will use both facts and value judgments to recommend a certain policy or solution. Sample statements of

policy include "Cigarette advertising should be banned from all sports events," "Drugs should be legalized," and "Homeowners should no longer bag their grass clippings."

Unless your assignment specifies the type of position statement to use, brainstorm two or three possible statements of fact, value, and policy for your topic. Looking at the ways in which you could approach your topic will help you narrow it. You may need to do some initial research on your topic before you feel confident making a position statement.

Although Lorna knew that she wanted to speak against drunk drivers, her position statement could have been any of the following:

1. **Statements of fact:** *"Stiff DWI penalties deter drunk driving" or "Drivers with blood alcohol levels higher than .08 are incapable of making safe driving decisions."*
2. **Statements of value:** *"Setting the blood alcohol level at .10 is irresponsible" or "The DWI laws of other states are more responsible than DWI laws in Texas."*
3. **Statements of policy:** *"The state of Texas must implement tougher penalties for drunk driving" or "Texas citizens should demand that local and state representatives take stronger measures against drunk drivers."*

It is important to know whether you are using a position statement of fact, value, or policy because each type of position statement requires different kinds of supporting materials (see step 3) and different types of persuasive appeals. This means that your research will be somewhat different for each. ➜ *Types of persuasive appeals are covered in Chapter 14.*

Deciding on the Type of Speech If you haven't already decided whether you want to convince or to actuate your audience, now is the time to make that decision. Do you want your audience simply to agree with your position, or do you want them to actually do something? The organization of your speech will be somewhat different depending on your goal.

Lorna decided that she wanted her audience to take some responsibility for getting tougher DWI laws—so she chose a speech to actuate. In her research, she looked for specific ways her listeners could lobby state and national representatives to vote for tougher DWI laws.

Once you have decided on your topic, position statement, and type of persuasive speech, you are ready to analyze your specific audience's attitudes toward your position.

B.C. **by johnny hart**

B.C. by johnny hart; B.C. reprinted by permission of Johnny Hart and Creators Syndicate, Inc.

Step 2: Analyze Audience Attitudes Toward Your Position

Since this persuasive speech will be given to the same audience as your earlier informative speech (your classmates), you already know a great deal about them. If you didn't already know your audience, you would need to conduct a detailed analysis like the one you conducted before preparing your informative speech. Review the situational, demographic, and psychological information you gathered and update it if necessary. Then take a look at the following questions that relate to the ethical and emotional appeals you choose to use in your speech:

- Will my classmates' current opinions of me add to my credibility (ethical appeal) or take away from it? What can I do to increase my credibility? ➔ *Establishing credibility is covered in Chapter 14.*

  Lorna felt that her credibility with her classmates was good. She was a few years older than most of them, and they often came to her for advice. They seemed to view her as open-minded and trustworthy. To make sure she appeared competent on her topic, she knew that she would need to cite several respected sources on drinking and driving. She also planned to interview the director of the local MADD (Mothers Against Drunk Drivers) organization. Her one problem was dynamism, an important element of credibility. She was naturally a soft-spoken person and felt embarrassed to show emotion in front of an audience. But she was determined to be more forceful and personal in her delivery and began practicing in front of a mirror; she even videotaped herself several times.

- What are my classmates' beliefs and values about my topic? How can I use these beliefs and values to communicate my arguments better?

  Although Lorna knew that several of the students in her class drank heavily at parties, she had heard them mention the importance of having a designated driver and felt that they believed that driving after drinking is irresponsible. On the basis of speeches that her classmates had given in class, she also knew that they valued family security and self-respect—two values that are threatened by drunk driving.

- What basic needs (physiological, safety, social, self-esteem, or self-actualization) do most of my classmates have that will make the need for my topic obvious?

  Lorna decided that safety, social, and self-esteem needs (emotional appeals) were the audience needs that related best to the topic of drinking and driving. Her classmates wanted their friends and family members to avoid accidents (safety need), yet enjoyed the companionship and sense of belonging that social gatherings bring (social need) and would feel a sense of pride knowing that they had taken steps to ensure their own safety as well as that of their friends and loved ones (self-esteem need).

Once you have reviewed and updated your audience analysis notes, you are ready to assess audience reactions to your position statement. In planning your persuasive arguments, you will want to conduct an audience **attitude poll** to (1) find points on which you and your audience agree (common ground) and (2) learn audience objections to your position (see Figure 13.2). Although an attitude poll is not always appropriate or possible outside the classroom, in the classroom it is an excellent learning tool. The information you collect will help you select the types of arguments and evidence to use in your speech. For example, should you look at both sides of the issue by discussing some objections to your position? (Of course, you will refute these objections by showing why your position is the better choice.) Or should you ignore possible audience objections and present only arguments that support your position? ➔ *Chapter 14 will answer these questions and many others to help you determine the best arguments and evidence to use in your speech.*

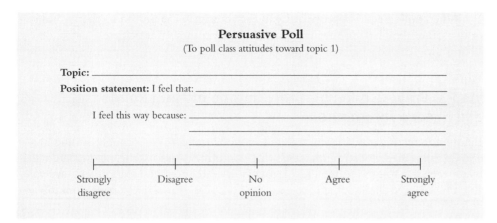

Figure 13.2

Sample Attitude Poll
(enlarge on copier for use in class)

The attitude poll should include your topic, position statement, and the response categories "Strongly disagree," "Disagree," "No opinion," "Agree," and "Strongly agree" (see Figure 13.2). Each potential audience member will read your position statement and check the response category that most closely represents his or her attitude toward it. The more specific your position statement, the more certain you can be of the accuracy of the responses. Therefore, it's a good idea to include a brief explanation in the form of a *because* statement for your position statement. Also, make sure that your solution is completely clear. For example, your audience may agree that stricter laws are needed to deter drug use but may disagree with you on the meaning of *stricter.*

> *Lorna made her position statement very precise by including a "because" statement and describing some of the solutions she had in mind:*

Topic: *Drinking and driving*

Position statement: *I feel that we should demand that our government take stronger measures against drunk drivers (more sobriety checkpoints, loss of driver's license for a specified time, a longer jail sentence, and so on). I feel this way because so many needless deaths occur from drunk driving and because Texas has the most lenient DWI penalties in the nation.*

		✔✔✔✔✔		
✔	✔✔	✔✔✔✔✔✔		✔✔
Strongly disagree	*Disgree*	*No opinion*	*Agree*	*Strongly agree*

Listeners are more likely to be persuaded by your ideas if they consider you credible. Although there are many ways to establish credibility, an important one is to focus on points of *common ground.* Listeners are more likely to be persuaded by speakers whom they view as similar to them in some way (McCroskey & Teven, 1999; McGuire, 1985; O'Keefe, 1990; Perloff, 2003). The more you know about your audience, the easier it is to find points of agreement, such as opinions about related issues, problems you have in common, and values you hold dear.

To learn why people disagree with your position, you may wish to leave a space at the bottom of your attitude poll in which people can briefly describe their objections. By anticipating probable objections, you can plan ways to refute them during the speech.

When polls are not appropriate, you can interview the person in charge and one or two other members of the audience. Or you can merely anticipate possible objections on the basis of the beliefs, attitudes, and values you know the audience holds.

Step 3: Prepare a Rough-Draft Outline of Main Points and Needed Information

Before conducting any serious research on your topic, make a rough outline of the main points and supporting materials that you think you may use. As with informative speeches, a rough outline can narrow your search for information and save valuable time. Also, seeing your speech in visual form can stimulate creative thinking and make it easier to check for problems. Lorna's roughed-out persuasive outline is shown in Figure 13.3.

Figure 13.3

Lorna's Rough-Draft Outline for Her Persuasive Speech, "Drinking and Driving"

Rough Draft Outline

Drinking & Driving

I. Problems
   A. National alcohol-related facts
      • # of people in accidents [source?]
      • # of people killed per yr. [source?]
   B. Texas alcohol-related facts
      • # of people killed per year [source?]
      • Conviction rate   [source?]
      • Instance — Chick, Alan
        [check last week's newpaper]

II. Solutions
   A. More Sobriety Checkpoints [MADD pamphlets?]
   B. Lower legal blood alcohol level
      • Current level in Texas?
      • Desired level? [See health textbook]
   C. Stronger penalties
      • Texas DWI penalties? [source?]
      • Penalties in other states? [source?]

III. Desired Action
   A. "Lights-On-for-Life" Day [MADD pamphlet?]
   B. Write your senators
      [Should I have letter written?]

Step 4: Research Your Topic

Careful research is the key to a successful persuasive speech. Although you will want to include personal experiences to support your arguments, persuasive speeches are supported largely by outside sources such as printed materials, computer databases, and interviews with experts. As you locate these sources, look through them for (1) arguments for and against your position, (2) answers to possible objections from the audience, and (3) benefits of your position.

Research Arguments for and Against Your Position You should research both sides of your position for several reasons. First, it is the ethical thing to do—you can assure your audience that you have done careful research. Second, researching both sides ensures that you are using the "best" arguments in your speech. And finally, researching both sides adds to the list of probable objections you discovered during the audience analysis step. This is especially valuable when you can't poll your audience. ➜ *For additional help on research, see Chapter 5.*

Research Answers to Major Audience Objections Even though you can't answer all objections in your speech, you should be ready for any questions during the Q & A session after the speech. Once you know the basic objections to your position, you can research ways to refute them. Some objections may be based on faulty reasoning—if so, bring it to your audience's attention. Some objections may be based on false or misleading information, so you will need to research for the correct information. And some objections may be valid ones that you can't disprove with reasoning or facts. When this is the case, admit it to your audience. Most audiences are impressed by this type of admission—it shows that you are an ethical speaker who has carefully researched the topic. Of course, you will want to show that the benefits of your position (or plan) far outweigh this single objection. In your research, try to find a quotation from a noted expert explaining why the objection does not weaken your position.

Comparing the benefits of your position to any disadvantages is one way to refute objections. For example, you might say, "Although my proposal has one disadvantage,

Careful research, including personal interviews, is the key to a successful persuasive speech.

© Mary Kate Denny/PhotoEdit

it is an insignificant one compared to its many advantages." Another way to refute objections is to compare the benefits of your proposal with those of a rival proposal. Assuming that both proposals could solve the problem, the more persuasive one would be the one with the greater number of advantages or the more important advantages.

Research Additional Benefits If you can show that your position not only solves the problem under discussion but also provides additional, unexpected benefits, you will be even more persuasive. To increase your chances of persuasion, present these additional benefits during the conclusion. For example, Maria concluded her speech about latchkey children (mentioned earlier in the chapter) by summarizing the problem and reviewing how her solutions would be an effective remedy. She further added to her persuasiveness by presenting a transparency listing six additional benefits of her solutions (such as increased self-esteem and improved social skills of the children).

Step 5: Select the Best Supporting Materials

Persuasive speakers use logic, evidence, emotional appeals, and their own credibility to connect with audience members and persuade them. Although it is good to use a variety of supporting materials to clarify points and maintain audience interest, *persuasive speeches should primarily use materials that prove* (such as expert opinion, statistics, brief and detailed factual instances, and literal comparisons). In addition, materials that are ethically sound are especially important in persuasive speaking because you are asking your listeners to trust you and change their opinions. As mentioned earlier in the chapter, you should never resort to falsifying or misrepresenting information, plagiarizing, or using false reasoning—no matter how "good" your cause might be. Double-check your arguments, evidence, and reasoning to make sure your speech is ethical. Remember to cite your sources during your speech. Lorna's speech on pages 278–281 provides excellent examples of how to cite sources.

Step 6: Determine How Best to Organize Your Main Points

In this step, you will first consider three important aspects about your topic, and second, use these aspects in choosing one of the many available persuasive patterns.

Important Aspects to Consider Which organizational pattern you choose depends on (1) whether you are giving a speech to convince or to actuate; (2) whether your position statement is written as a statement of fact, value, or policy; and (3) your personal preferences and/or assignment requirements. Let's look at each in more detail:

1. *Consider your speech type*—convince or actuate. Recall that a speech to convince seeks to obtain intellectual agreement from listeners, whereas a speech to actuate seeks both agreement and action. If you plan to give a speech to convince, you can choose any of the organizational patterns except problem–solution–action and cause–result–action because they call for action. You would choose one of those two for the speech to actuate (the problem–solution–action pattern is the most popular).

2. *Determine your position statement*—fact, value, or policy. For statements of fact, the claim and the causal patterns (cause–effect–solution and cause–result–

Technology Tip for Speakers

Make PowerPoint Your Ally, Not Your Enemy

Computer-generated visuals can either aid persuasion or they can be so irritating that they work against your persuasive efforts. For example, the Pentagon is waging war on PowerPoint, which has been called a "growing electronic menace" (Jaffe, 2000, p. A1). Apparently, many presentations are too long (100 slides or more), too confusing, too wordy, and cluttered with showy effects (fancy backdrops, distracting slide transitions, spinning pie charts, and "booming tanks"). The real problem may be that "the art of creating a PowerPoint brief frequently has become a substitute for real planning, thoughtful discussion, and cogent analysis" (Wooldridge, 2004, p. 85). The former chairman of the Joint Chiefs of Staff, General Hugh Shelton, attempted to solve the problem by placing restrictions on the use of PowerPoint in military presentations. The business world is experiencing similar problems. One meeting facilitator for a software company became so disgusted that he told attendees "they had to leave their PowerPoint at the door" (Maney, 1999, p. 3B).

Why is this happening? As Simons (2004) indicates in his title, "Bullets May Be Dangerous, but Don't Blame PowerPoint," many presenters make two fundamental—but very serious—mistakes:

1. *They have forgotten the purpose for using visuals*—to aid listener understanding. If your listeners can't grasp the content of a visual in 6 seconds or less, you are forcing them out of a listening mode and into a reading mode. Therefore, limit the amount of words used and don't read from the slides. In addition, nothing on a slide should be random—not the colors, fonts or font sizes, design, images, animation, sounds, or even the number of slides. Using general design principles from Chapter 9 for slide preparation will help you clarify meaning and direct attention.

2. *Their delivery of the visuals is ineffective.* Many speakers make the mistake of giving PowerPoint presentations in a dark room where the audience can barely see the speaker. Effective presenters need to be in some light (even from a simple can-light in the ceiling) so that they can use eye contact, facial expressions, and gestures to add interest and clarity to their presentations.

Make PowerPoint your ally—by using it to enhance rather than diminish communication.

---

action) are especially effective. For statements of value, choose a claim or a criteria satisfaction pattern. For a statement of policy, the problem–solution–benefits, problem–solution–action, and the comparative advantages patterns are recommended.

3. *Follow assignment requirements* and *consider personal preferences.* If the class assignment specifies which pattern to use, make sure your speech type and position statement are compatible. Your preferences should also play a role in which pattern you select.

Remember

For speeches to convince . . .

- When stating your position as a *statement of fact*, use the claim or cause–effect–solution pattern.

- With a *statement of value*, use the claim or criteria satisfaction pattern.

- With a *statement of policy*, use the problem–solution–benefits or comparative advantages pattern.

For speeches to actuate . . .

- With a *statement of fact*, use the claim or cause–result–action pattern.

- With a *statement of value*, use the claim or criteria satisfaction pattern.

- With a *statement of policy*, use the problem–solution–action or comparative advantages pattern.

Check your knowledge of the basic persuasive organization patterns by taking the following quiz. If you have problems with any of the patterns, review that pattern in Chapter 7.

Choosing the Best Persuasive Pattern   You can choose from a variety of patterns to organize the body of a persuasive speech. The patterns discussed previously include the claim, causal, problem–solution, comparative advantages, and criteria satisfaction patterns. → *See the Quick Start Guide and Chapter 7 for a discussion of these organizational patterns.*

Test Your Knowledge Quiz

Testing Your Knowledge of Persuasive Patterns

Directions: Here are six mini-outlines, each with a title and main points. Identify the organizational pattern of the main points as (a) claim, (b) causal, (c) problem–solution, (d) comparative advantages, or (e) criteria satisfaction. Write the letter of your choice in the appropriate blank. You can also take the quiz under Student Resources for Chapter 13 at the Essentials of Public Speaking website and, if requested, e-mail your responses to your instructor.

_____ 1. "Stem Cell Research"

    I. Stem cell research could provide needed pancreatic cells for those with diabetes.

    II. Stem cell research could give further hope for those with Parkinson's disease.

    III. Stem cell research could continue work to help those with spinal cord injuries.

IV. Stem cell research must be supported by the citizens and governments around the world.

_____ 2. "Senseless or Sensible Divorce?" (Hensley, 1994)
I. When divorce is settled in court, it's expensive and lengthy, promotes destructive competition, and clogs the court system.
II. Divorce settled by mediation solves these problems.
III. In addition to solving basic divorce problems, mediation has an important benefit—it allows both parties time to stabilize personally.

_____ 3. "Overweight Americans"
I. Losing weight by dieting has very few advantages.
II. Losing weight by lowering fat intake has several important advantages.

_____ 4. "Becoming a Blood Donor"
I. Blood donors are crucial to alleviating America's blood shortage.
II. Blood donors are essential if new medical treatments (such as heart and bone marrow transplants) are to continue.
III. Blood donors are paramount in disasters such as 9/11.

_____ 5. "Helping the Homeless" (Fitzgerald, 1994)
I. Any workable solution to helping the homeless must meet the following guidelines:
A. Respect the rights and dignity of the homeless.
B. Require that the homeless work for shelter and food.
C. Offer drug and alcohol abuse prevention programs.
D. Offer hope.
II. Our community's attempt to help the homeless by giving them money and housing violates all the above guidelines.

_____ 6. "Good Mothers Care for Their Children at Home"
I. Many single mothers with children must put them in day care during work hours.
II. In several recent cases, the court has taken custody from single mothers who placed their children in day care rather than caring for them at home.
III. Such decisions are irresponsible and must be reversed.

Answers

1. (a) claim pattern
2. (c) problem–solution–benefits pattern
3. (d) comparative advantages pattern
4. (a) claim pattern
5. (e) criteria satisfaction pattern
6. (b) cause–effect–action pattern

In addition to the persuasive patterns already discussed, there is one other popular method of organizing a persuasive speech called the **motivated sequence**. Developed by communications professor Alan Monroe more than 50 years ago, it is similar to the problem–solution–action pattern and is especially effective with speeches to actuate using a statement of policy (Gronbeck, McKerrow, Ehninger, & Monroe, 1994). The motivated sequence includes the introduction and conclusion as

well as your main points. It has five steps: attention, need, satisfaction, visualization, and action. Let's take a brief look at each step.

1. *Attention step.* Grab your listeners' attention (using any of the methods described earlier) and build a desire in them to want to continue listening.

2. *Need step.* Direct the audience's attention to a specific problem. Describe the problem using credible, logical, and emotional appeals, and show how the problem affects your listeners. ➡ *See Chapter 14 for details on persuasive appeals.*

3. *Satisfaction step.* "Satisfy" the need described in the previous step by presenting a solution. The following framework is suggested: "(a) briefly state what you propose to do, (b) explain it clearly, (c) show how it remedies the problem, (d) demonstrate its workability, and (e) answer objections" (Gronbeck et al., p. 209). In demonstrating the feasibility of the solution as well as answering objections by audience members, be sure to use supporting materials that will add proof to your statements. ➡ *See Chapter 6 for examples of supporting materials.*

4. *Visualization step.* Vividly picture the future for your audience, using the positive, the negative, or the contrast method. With the *positive method,* you picture the improved future the audience can expect when your solution is implemented. With the *negative method,* you picture the undesirable conditions that will continue to exist or will develop if your solution is not adopted. The *contrast method* begins with the negative and ends with the positive. The purpose of visualization is to "intensify audience desire or willingness to act—to motivate your listeners to believe, to feel, or to act in a certain way" (Gronbeck et al., p. 211).

5. *Action step.* Conclude your speech by challenging your audience to take a particular action—you want a personal commitment from them. Say exactly what you want them to do and how they can do it. ➡ *See Chapter 7 for suggestions on how to issue a challenge.*

Step 7: Plan the Introduction and Conclusion

An effective persuasive introduction includes (1) an attention-getter, (2) a motivation to listen, (3) evidence of your credibility, and (4) a preview of your purpose and main points. Also, for some of the organizational patterns (such as comparative advantages), you need to mention the background of the problem briefly in the introduction.

An effective conclusion includes (1) a summary of your arguments, position, or recommendations, and (2) a memorable ending (including visualizing the future and a challenge or appeal for action). Don't assume that your audience knows exactly what to do—specify the exact position or action that you want them to take. You will also be more persuasive if your listeners perceive that they are capable of performing the action you are requesting of them (Beck & Lund, 1981). When listeners feel that the problem you have described is serious ("In six months all the landfills in the state will be filled to capacity, and we will have no place to put our garbage") but that they are not capable of solving it ("Even if I do purchase fewer packaged items, one family isn't going to make enough difference"), they are likely to reject your message and even do the opposite of what you recommend (Witte, 1992a). Make it as easy as possible for your listeners to comply with your request. For example, if you ask them to

Kay Bailey Hutchison
703 Hart-Senate Office Building
Washington DC

Dear Ms. Hutchison,

As you are well aware, here in the state of Texas we have a serious problem with drinking and driving. Texas is now number one in the nation with the highest incidence of alcohol-related deaths. People who drink and drive in this state know that their chances of being pulled over for a DWI are slim. If they are stopped and arrested, their punishment is a night in jail or a fine—in other words, a slap on the hand. In order to bring senseless deaths and injury to a halt, we must change our laws. Penalties for first-time and repeat offenders must be stricter to deter people from drinking and driving.

Ohio has implemented stronger penalties for first-time and repeat offenders. For example, first-time offenders can now have their license revoked at the scene or a new license plate put on their vehicle identifying them as persons who have been pulled over for drinking and driving. Second-time offenders can have their cars impounded. Texas and all states in the nation need similar laws.

This is a very serious issue that everyone needs to be aware of— it affects us not only at holidays but all year long. We hope to see more aggressive and immediate action taken before one more death or injury occurs. We are asking you to use your influence to save lives in Texas and the nation.

Sincerely,

write to their senators, provide a handout with each senator's name, address, and phone number. Or, as Lorna did, have a letter already written and ask audience members to sign it. A copy of Lorna's letter (which everyone in her class signed) is shown in Figure 13.4.

Step 8: Make Preparation Outline (or Storyboards) and Speaking Notes

Expanding your rough-draft outline into a preparation outline or several storyboards (see Figure 8.5, page 172) will allow you to check the organization of your speech. See Figure 13.5 for Lorna's preparation outline. Which tool you choose depends on your personal preferences. As you know from your informative speech, the preparation outline is more formally structured, whereas storyboards are less formal and are accompanied by sketches of visual aids. Either tool should include transitions to link your arguments, a list of references (with their page numbers), and brackets to

Figure 13.5

Lorna's Persuasive
Preparation Outline

Lorna's Preparation Outline

Title: *"Drinking and Driving"* by Lorna McElaney
Position Statement: Texas citizens should demand that government representatives take stronger measures against drunk drivers. (Speech to actuate/statement of policy)

	Type of Source
INTRODUCTION • **Attention-getter:** Christmas-celebration. *Question:* How many of you when you are out celebrating have had a drink, or maybe two or more, and gotten into your car and driven away? *Example:* Larry Dotson and Natalie Gale *[Instance]*	Ref. #7
• **Credibility:** *[Presented in student introduction]*	
• **Audience motivation:** Last Christmas it was Natalie Gale and her friend; this Christmas, it could be one of us.	
• **Purpose/Preview:** Today I will share with you some startling facts and hopefully persuade you to join me in writing our senators to demand tougher laws to protect ourselves and those we love.	
BODY I. **[Visual #1] The number of auto/alcohol-related accidents indicates a serious problem. [Problem]**	
A. Nationally, 2 of 5 involved in auto/alcohol accidents. *[Statistics]*	Ref. #3, p. 1
B. Nationally, 17,000 killed in auto/alcohol accidents. *[Statistics]*	Ref. #3, p. 1
C. In Texas, 1,800 killed in auto/alcohol accidents. *[Statistics]*	
1. Texas #1 state in alcohol-related deaths. *[Statistics]*	Ref. #1, p. 11A
2. Only 20–30 percent of arrests lead to conviction. *[Statistics]*	Ref. #1, p. 11A
3. Example of Officer Chick. *[Brief instance]*	Ref. #2, p. 17A
[Transition]: What should be done? There are a lot of things that can be done.	
II. **There are several workable solutions to the DWI problem. [Solution]**	
A. Year-round sobriety checkpoints. *[Expert opinion]*	Ref. #5, p. 7

indicate where you want to use visuals and to identify types of supporting materials.
→ *See Figures 8.3 and 8.4 for more samples of preparation outlines, and Figure 8.6 for a sample storyboard.*

Remember that expanding the body (main arguments) of your speech into a preparation outline or storyboards will improve your flexibility as a speaker far more than writing out your speech word for word. With an outline or storyboards, you will also be able to evaluate your organization and supporting materials at a glance—something you can't do with a manuscript.

Your speaking notes are one of the last things to prepare. For most people, "the fewer words the better" is a good guide. If you have too many words in your speaking notes, you may be tempted to read them—a sure way to decrease your dynamic delivery. Speaking notes can be on a single page, on note cards, or in mind-map form. If you had any problems with the speaking notes you used for your informative speech, try to correct those problems for this speech. → *For more on speaking notes, see Chapter 8.*

B.   Legal blood-alcohol level lowered from .10 to .08. *[Expert opinion and statistics]*   Ref. #3, p. 5
C.   Stronger penalties for drunk driving.
   1. Texas's lenient DWI laws. *[Explanation]*   Ref. #1, p. 11A
   2. Ohio's stricter DWI laws. *[Explanation]*   Ref. #4, p. 11

[Transition]: Action must be taken now. And we must all take part in that action.

III. Action must be taken now. *[Action]*
   A.   "Lights-On-for-Life" promotion on December 16.   Ref. #6
      1. In remembrance of those killed by drunk drivers.
         [Explanation]   Personal
      2. To show government representatives we want change.
         [Explanation]
   B.   Letter to Senator Kay Bailey Hutchison.

CONCLUSION
- **Summary:** We must demand more sobriety checkpoints, a lower blood-alcohol level, and tougher penalties for drunk driving.
- **Visualize:** If we don't—more senseless deaths. **[Visual #2]**
- **Challenge:** The time for action is now. Let's get these drunks off the road before they kill someone we love.
- **Refocus:** I'm going to leave you with a sobering excerpt from a poem called "Prom Night" that was anonymously sent to a local radio station. *[Poem]*   Ref. #8

References:
1. Barlow, Yvonne. "Texas Alcohol Road Deaths Drop but State Has Highest Proportion of Such Fatalities, Study Shows." *Dallas Morning News,* December 3, 1994. Sec. NEWS, p. 11A.
2. Ford, Jacquielynn. "Drunken Driver Gets Life in Death of FW Officer: Widow Gives Emotional Address." *Dallas Morning News,* Sec. NEWS, p. 17A.
3. Mothers Against Drunk Driving. *A 1994 Summary of Statistics: The Impaired Driving Problem.* Irving, Texas: MADD (Mothers Against Drunk Driving), December 1994.
4. Mothers Against Drunk Driving. *Maddvocate: A Magazine for Victims and Their Advocates,* Vol. 6, Fall 1993.
5. Mothers Against Drunk Driving. *20 X 2000: Five-Year Plan to Reduce Impaired Driving.* Dallas, Texas: MADD (Mothers Against Drunk Driving), 1994.
6. National 3D Prevention Month Coalition. *Lights on for Life Handbook.* Washington, D.C.: National Highway Traffic Safety Administration, May 194.
7. North, Kim. "Sobering Message: Woman Whose Daughter Was Victim of Holiday DWI Driver Stresses Perils." *Dallas Morning News,* December 12, 1994, Sec. NEWS, p. 17A.
8. "Prom Night." An anonymous poem read on Sunny 95 FM radio station, Dallas, Texas, October 1994.

Figure 13.5

Lorna's Persuasive Preparation Outline *(continued)*

Step 9: Prepare Visual Aids

If you used storyboards, you probably know exactly what visual aids you want to use. If not, sketch out some possible visuals as you read through your outline. For example, you could make a text visual of an important definition or a list of your main arguments, or you could make a graphic visual of some important statistics.   → *Before finalizing your visuals, review Color Figures C–L in the color insert.*

Step 10: Rehearse Your Speech

Since direct eye contact and a dynamic delivery help determine the audience's evaluation of your credibility, practice is very important. Thinking through your speech is not as effective as practicing it aloud.

> *Lorna kept her speaking outline and a copy of her computer visuals on the kitchen counter, and every time family members wandered into the kitchen, she handed them a stopwatch*

and presented her speech. Each time she tried to be more dynamic and to speak more loudly. Her 13-year-old daughter was also taking a speech course in school, so her comments were especially helpful. For example, she suggested that Lorna relax and slow down a bit. Referring to her mother's tendency to get teary when she read the final poem, her daughter said, "This isn't going to work, Mom—it's too sappy." Lorna's husband told her that she was "doing good." On the day of the speech, Lorna was confident that her delivery would be dynamic (it was) and that she could read the final poem in a personal yet non-teary manner (she did).

Successful speech rehearsal involves standing, speaking aloud, using your notes only occasionally (if at all), and using your visual aids in an environment similar to the one in which you will actually be speaking.

 If you like, use the Persuasive Speech Evaluation Form in Figure 13.6 at the end of this chapter to help you prepare for your own persuasive speeches, evaluate your speeches after you've given them, and evaluate your classmates' speeches. You can access this form online under Student Resources for Chapter 13 at the Essentials of Public Speaking website.

Team Presentations

How do you feel about working in teams or giving team presentations—enthusiastic or full of dread? People who can work effectively in teams are more likely to succeed in today's rapidly changing job market and to be valued by nonprofit organizations as well. Consider these examples of team presentations:

■ You are part of a newcomer orientation team for your department or dorm. Each team member is responsible for briefing new students on a particular aspect of college life.

■ For your final class project, you and three other students decide to give a team presentation on a controversial topic. Each of you will focus on a different aspect of the topic, and then your team will open the floor to audience questions and comments.

■ A complex rezoning issue is up for vote in your community. To help inform the public and answer questions, the city council has asked you and four other community members with special knowledge and differing views to present a panel discussion for broadcast on the local cable channel.

■ College administrators have announced an across-the-board budget cut for next year. Since a portion of the budget cut must come from student activities, the student council has appointed you and six other students to a problem-solving team. Your assignment is to decide which student activities should be cut and to present your decisions to a joint meeting of administrators and student council representatives.

The above examples have probably given you a good idea of what is meant by teams and team presentations. A **team** is normally composed of three to seven members who actively work together toward a particular goal (solving a problem, gathering information, or planning an informative or persuasive presentation). Five is considered the most productive size for a team because it is large enough to supply needed information and to share the work load, yet small enough to give each member a chance for maximum participation.

Successful team presentations require practice, revision, and more practice.

A **team presentation** (whether informative or persuasive) involves the collaborative organization and presentation of material by team members to an audience, often using one of a variety of public discussion formats: forum, symposium, panel, or some combination of the three. Team presentations have the obvious *advantages* of shared responsibility, more expertise during the presentation and Q & A session, and an impressive appearance. However, they also have *disadvantages*—team presentations are difficult to coordinate to fit everyone's schedules, require more time to develop than an individual speech, and call for effective leadership and member cooperation to minimize squabbles and misunderstandings.

Effective Team Presentations

Successful team presentations have three characteristics (Leech, 1992):

- Well-organized, well-supported, smooth-flowing *content*
- Creative, professional, and well-used *visual aids*
- Smooth, polished, and dynamic team *performance*

Content Team presentations should follow the basic steps discussed in Chapter 12 and this chapter. In the initial organization stage, you might benefit by having all members write their ideas on Post-it notes—one idea per note (Epson America, 2003). Use the wall or tabletop to organize the notes, moving them around until a basic outline is formed.

Later, each presenter can prepare storyboards of their part of the presentation—again, tape each person's storyboards to the wall for ease of viewing by other members. While you read them, imagine that you are an audience member. Is each presentation completely clear? Are the main points obvious? Would you doubt any of the main points? What additional information or visual aids would ease those doubts? Does each member's presentation flow smoothly into the next or do transitions need work? Finding and correcting problems early in the planning process is very important. Otherwise, you may be forced to make last-minute changes requiring new visuals. Then, instead of a relaxed dry run of the entire presentation, you'll have a tense, frantic session.

Visual Aids Visual aids of team members should be consistent in appearance throughout the presentation—same logo (if you have one), colors, background or template, fonts and type sizes, as well as use of clip art and graphics. If one member has poorly prepared visuals, the overall team impact is diminished. Unless all team members are aware of and agree on what makes a quality visual aid, it's a good idea to have all final visuals prepared by one group member or by the graphic arts department in your organization. Prepare all visuals early enough so that they will be available for practice and so that any needed corrections can be made. ➡ *Review Chapter 9 for specific suggestions on preparing effective visual aids.*

Team members should practice using their visual aids in front of at least one other team member, who can offer suggestions if needed. Awkward handling of visuals can ruin the effect of a well-organized presentation. ➡ *Chapter 10 gives suggestions for effectively handling a variety of visual aids.*

You can estimate the length of the team presentation by the number of visuals you plan to use. Most people spend at least 1 minute on each visual, so 20 visual aids would make at least a 20-minute presentation. If members take longer for each visual, take that into account. It is important to stay within prearranged time limits.

Performance A polished and dynamic team performance requires practice, revision, and more practice. Each member should practice alone or with a partner, and then the team should have one or more dry runs of the entire presentation. Videotape the practice sessions, if possible.

One team member needs to be the coordinator/leader—preferably a member with past team experience, speaking experience, and leadership abilities. Marjorie Brody (2003) recommends that a team leader should be a "subject matter expert." An effective team leader also needs to be objective in critiquing and directing the presenters. During the actual presentation, the coordinator presents the introduction and conclusion, introduces members, provides transitions if members fail to do so, and directs the question-and-answer session. If you decide to have a Q & A session, plan ahead how you will handle it. Anticipate possible questions and determine who has the most expertise to answer specific topic areas. ➡ *See Chapter 7 for specific suggestions on using Q & A.*

If your team presentation will be videotaped, taped for closed-circuit viewing, or appear on a teleconference, television talk show, or news interview, you will need to adapt your presentation to the media by making strategic verbal, visual, and vocal changes. ➡ *Be sure to follow the suggestions on adapting your presentation to the media in the Technology Tip for Speakers in Chapter 11.*

Team Presentation Formats

Team presentation formats include the symposium, panel, or forum, or any combination of the three. Any of the formats can be used for information sharing, instructional purposes, problem solving, or persuasion.

Symposium In a **symposium** each team member presents a formal, 2- to 10-minute speech on one aspect of the symposium's topic. The purpose may be to inform and instruct or even to persuade. Probably the oldest recorded symposium (described by Plato) took place in Athens around 415 B.C. and consisted of seven participants presenting formal speeches on their views of the nature and definition of love (Jones, 1970).

Panel In a **panel** discussion team members informally discuss a problem or topic of interest in front of an audience. Although no formal speeches are presented, team members contribute freely and equally because they are organized, well prepared, and have a specific purpose. The team coordinator guides members through an organized procedure agreed on ahead of time. It is not unusual to find panelists disagreeing with, correcting, or interrupting each other, which is very enjoyable for the audience.

Forum Open audience participation is referred to as a **forum**. The term is derived from ancient Rome, where a forum referred to a public square where political and legal business was conducted. The traditional New England town meeting is a modern-day forum.

Problem Solving for Team Presentations

Successful team members use the following basic problem-solving procedure, based on John Dewey's (1991) well-known reflective thinking process, as a general tool to help them make decisions—whether in a private planning session (i.e., trying to decide on content for a team presentation) or participating in a panel discussion in front of an audience.

Step 1: Identify the Problem First, the team must agree that a problem exists and define the nature of the problem in a specific, factual, and descriptive manner. Ask questions such as, when did the problem first arise? who is affected? what are the implications? and, when must the problem be solved? Once the problem seems clear, test that understanding by forming the problem into a question and writing it on the board for all to see. Continue discussion until all members are satisfied with the wording.

Since step 1 is so time consuming, team members often choose to complete this step ahead of the public discussion. In this case, the coordinator briefly recaps the previous discussion and reads the team's exact definition of the problem to the audience. Then the team begins their discussion with step 2.

Step 2: Analyze the Problem Begin analyzing the problem by listing the topics and information that the team needs to discuss. Next, narrow down the list to a manageable length and discuss what is known about each item. (Here members share their research and personal knowledge with the team.) Be sure to look at all sides of the problem and include opinions and objections your audience is likely to have. Informative panels use the analysis step to educate audience members; persuasive panels use the analysis step to investigate fallacious reasoning and introduce persuasive evidence. ➨ *See fallacious reasoning in Chapter 14.*

Step 3: Establish Criteria Criteria are guidelines, boundaries, standards, or rules (often in checklist form) that a team agrees to follow in evaluating the solutions to their problem. For example, possible criteria to decide which student activities to cut from the college budget might read as follows:

Any decision we reach about student activities must:

- Be agreeable to a majority of team members.
- Inconvenience the smallest number of students.
- Give preference to low-budget yet high-learning activities.
- Be decided within two weeks.

Begin by making a list of all possible criteria. Then evaluate the importance of each criterion so the team can reduce the list to approximately three to five items. Next, divide remaining criteria into "musts" (required items) and "wants" (desired items) and rank the wants from most to least desired. Keep must criteria to a minimum and check to see that each one is absolutely necessary and not just a high-level want. These must and want criteria will be used later in step 5.

Establishing criteria is a *key step* in the basic problem-solving procedure—it speeds up team decisions and improves the quality of those decisions. In fact, once step 3 is completed, the most difficult part of the process is over.

Step 4: List Possible Solutions List as many alternatives as are feasible within your team's time and budget limitations. As team members brainstorm for ideas, it is tempting to list and evaluate (step 5) at the same time. However, all evaluations should be postponed until step 5 to keep the formation of your list speedy and creative. Don't worry about the quality of your alternatives or whether they meet the criteria now—quantity, not quality, should be the goal in this step.

To speed up this step in panel discussions, each member should have prepared a list of possible solutions ahead of time. Then, one at a time, each member suggests a single solution, which the coordinator writes on the board for all to see. The process continues until all solutions are included. Review the completed list to make sure no important ideas were omitted. Don't forget to include "doing nothing" as an alternative—it serves as a basis of comparison to proposed alternatives.

Step 5: Evaluate Solutions If the team did a good job of establishing criteria, step 5 will be amazingly simple. As you move through this step, be sure to depersonalize the discussion by separating the person from the proposal:

- First, eliminate alternatives that do not meet all the must criteria covered in step 3.

- Next, discuss each remaining alternative's strengths and weaknesses (refer to research presented in step 2 when necessary).

- Determine how well each alternative meets each want criterion by assigning a point value to each—usually from 1 (low) to 5 (high).

- Determine which alternative has the most points and meets the most important criteria. The answer should be obvious, but if not, additional discussion (and even criteria) may be needed in order for a consensus decision to be reached. More than one solution may be desired in some cases.

Step 6: Discuss How to Implement Solutions The final stage is to decide how the agreed-upon solution(s) should be put into practice. In deciding how to implement what the team has endorsed, consider who will be responsible for overseeing implementation, when it will begin, how long it will take, and what resources are needed. This step may be omitted to save time in the panel discussion.

Sometimes, in discussing implementation, a team will find that a solution that seemed excellent on paper is in fact not feasible. For example, if a school board decided to implement uniforms to solve theft of clothing, then discovered that parents refused to comply, the members would need to rethink this decision. In such cases, the team must return to step 5 to select another alternative.

Don't forget that after each presentation, team members should evaluate each other and the presentation as a whole to determine strengths and weaknesses. If at all possible, videotape your presentations to more clearly assess the team's verbal, visual, and vocal communication.

Summary

Persuasion is communication intended to influence choice. Although persuasion is intentional, it should not coerce. Persuasive speeches differ from informative speeches in four aspects: supporting materials, language style, delivery, and organizational patterns. There are two basic types of persuasive speeches: (1) the speech to convince, in which you want audience agreement, and (2) the speech to actuate, in which you want both audience agreement and audience action.

Effective persuasive speeches are carefully organized and supported. The Basic Steps for Preparing a Speech will help you prepare your introduction, body, and conclusion. The introduction includes getting listener attention, motivating the audience to listen, establishing speaker credibility, and stating your position and main arguments.

The body of your persuasive speech may follow any of these organizational patterns: claim, causal (cause–effect–solution or cause–result–action), problem–solution (problem–solution–benefit or problem–solution–action), comparative advantages, or criteria satisfaction. The pattern you choose depends on your goal (to convince or to actuate) and the type of position statement (fact, value, or policy) you are using.

As with informative speeches, the conclusion begins with a summary and ends with refocusing attention in a memorable way. In addition, the persuasive conclusion normally includes two more items: visualizing the future for the audience and issuing a challenge or appeal for action.

Team presentations involve the collaborative presentation of material by several people. Effective team presentations are characterized by well-organized content, professional visual aids, and dynamic team performance, and may take the format of a symposium, panel, or forum. Successful teams use basic problem-solving procedures when planning their presentation and during participation in a panel discussion. Whether you are speaking by yourself or as part of a team, the information covered in this chapter and in this text can help you give interesting, professional presentations.

Essentials of Public Speaking ~~~ Online

Use the Essentials of Public Speaking website at **http://communication. wadsworth.com/hamiltoneps3** for quick access to the electronic study resources that accompany this chapter. When you get to the Essentials home page, click on "Student Book Companion Site" in the Resource box. The Essentials website features a video of Lorna's speech on pages 278–281, the Test Your Knowledge quiz on pages 292–293, the Persuasive Speech Evaluation Form on page 305, InfoTrac College Edition, the Suggestions for Practice and Critical Thinking activities and the InfoTrac College Edition activities that follow, a digital glossary, and review quizzes.

Key Terms

attitude poll 286	persuasion 274	symposium 300
forum 301	position statement 284	team 298
motivated sequence 293	speech to actuate 276	team presentation 299
panel 301	speech to convince 276	

Suggestions for Practice and Critical Thinking

1. Write fact, value, and policy position statements for each of the following persuasive issues. Ask one or two classmates to look over the statements to see if they can identify which type they are. If there are some they can't identify, rewrite them and try again.

   a. Airline safety

   b. Grade inflation

   c. Computer hackers

   d. Care for the homeless

2. Read Hans Erian's persuasive speech on pages 245–247. Identify whether it is a speech to convince or to actuate and what type of position statement Hans appears to be using—fact, value, or policy. Next, evaluate the speech using the Persuasive Speech Evaluation Form in Figure 13.6. Compare your answers and evaluation with several classmates. Verify your evaluation with your instructor.

3. Reread Lorna's persuasive speech on drunk driving. In groups of two, write several additional persuasive transitions Lorna could have used in her speech—especially between her problem and solution steps and between her solution and action steps. Share your transitions with another group; select the best from both groups. If possible, report the best transitions to the entire class. Discuss the importance of transitions to the persuasive process.

4. Prepare a 7- to 10-minute speech to actuate using a position statement of policy following the preparation steps covered in this chapter. Prepare an attitude poll to determine how your audience feels about your topic. Use a copier to enlarge Figure 13.2 (or prepare your own poll). If your instructor doesn't reserve a special day for you and your classmates to poll each other, pass your poll around immediately before class begins. If you find that several students disagree with your position, ask around to see if you can find out why.

5. Select Hans's speech on pages 245–247 or Lorna's speech on pages 278–281, or use InfoTrac College Edition to find a persuasive speech from *Vital Speeches,* or find a speech at the Essentials of Public Speaking website. In groups of two or three, design and produce three professional-looking computer slides or transparencies (graphic and/or text visuals) that the speaker could have used in his or her presentation. On a day scheduled by your instructor, have a copy of all computer slides and transparencies displayed and evaluated by a visiting team of three experts (made up of other instructors and/or design professionals).

6. Using InfoTrac College Edition, locate a recent article on persuasive conclusions (use *persuasive speaking*) or read the article "Standpoint Explicitness and Persuasive Effect: A Meta-Analytic Review of the Effects of Varying Conclusion Articulation in Persuasive Messages" by Daniel J. O'Keefe in *Argumentation and Advocacy,* Summer 1997, page 54. According to research, what type of conclusion is generally considered to be the most persuasive?

7. Each day that persuasive speeches are given in class, each class member should vote for the best speech of the day and the most improved speaker of the day. Give the votes to a designated person to tabulate. At the end of each class

Persuasive Speech Evaluation Form

Name: _____ **Topic:** _____ **Date:** _____
Grades: Outline _____ **Presentation:** _____

Ratings: 1 (Missing), 2 (Poor), 3 (Fair), 4 (Good), 5 (Excellent)

Did **INTRODUCTION:**   **Comments:**
   1. Begin with attention-getter?   1 2 3 4 5
   2. Motivate audience to listen?   1 2 3 4 5
   3. Establish credibility?   1 2 3 4 5
   4. Make thesis/position clear?   1 2 3 4 5

Were **MAIN IDEAS:**
   5. Easy to identify and follow?   1 2 3 4 5
   6. Arranged in effective pattern?   1 2 3 4 5
   7. Characterized by good transitions?   1 2 3 4 5

Was **SUPPORTING MATERIAL:**
   8. Well documented during speech?   1 2 3 4 5
   9. Adequate in verbal supports? (Use +, ✓, –)   1 2 3 4 5

     _____ *Statistics?*   _____ *Expert opinions?*
     _____ *Comparisons?*   _____ *Fables/sayings/poems/rhymes?*
     _____ *Instances?*   _____ *Explanations?*

Did **SPEAKER PERSUASIVELY:**   1 2 3 4 5
   10. Use evidence and logic?   1 2 3 4 5
   11. Establish credibility?   1 2 3 4 5
   12. Relate to psychological needs of listeners? 1 2 3 4 5

Did **CONCLUSION:**
   13. Summarize topic and main ideas?   1 2 3 4 5
   14. Visualize future; ask for audience acceptance? 1 2 3 4 5
   15. Close in a memorable way?   1 2 3 4 5

Was **DELIVERY** characterized by:
   16. Dynamic, yet conversational quality?   1 2 3 4 5
   17. Confidence (in posture, gestures, and eye contact)? 1 2 3 4 5
   18. Freedom from distracting mannerisms? (Check) 1 2 3 4 5

     _____ *"Uh"/"Um"/"And uh"/"You know"/"Well"/"OK"?*
     _____ *Plays with pencil, clothes, hair, or pointer?*
     _____ *Nervous laugh or cough?*
     _____ *Slouches, taps feet, paces, or sways?*
     _____ *Over-reliance on notes?*
     _____ *Other?*

   19. Effective vocal delivery (volume, pitch, rate, and emphasis)? 1 2 3 4 5
   20. Effective language use and at least 1 stylistic device? 1 2 3 4 5
   21. Adequate in visual supports? (Use +, ✓, –) 1 2 3 4 5

     _____ *Interesting?*   _____ *Professional?*
     _____ *Easy to see?*   _____ *Handled well?*

                           Total: _____

Figure 13.6

**Persuasive Speech
Evaluation Form**

period, the winners should be announced and their names posted in the classroom.

8. After each persuasive speech given in class, one member of the class should volunteer or be assigned by the instructor to present a 1- to 2-minute impromptu rebuttal or supporting speech. This is a fun way to practice impromptu speaking.

9. Prepare a 1-minute speech of introduction to give prior to a classmate's persuasive speech. Make sure each speaker in the class has someone to introduce him or her. (Follow the guidelines for speeches of introduction included under Special Occasion Speeches on the Essentials of Public Speaking website.)

10. Check out the following websites. *You can access these sites under the Student Resources for Chapter 13* at the Essentials of Public Speaking website.

- For sample persuasive presentations, check out BusinessTown.com (click on the "Presentations" link) and GiftsOfSpeech.org. The first highlights business speaking, and the second highlights the speeches of women around the world.

- The University of Kansas's Virtual Presentation Assistant offers good speaking advice on a variety of topics.

- See the http site (no www) PowerPointers.com for articles on speaking and using visual supports.

- Acting techniques can be very helpful for speakers. Actor and professional speaker Ed Brodow offers tips in his article "Acting Techniques for Speakers" at Fripp.com (search on *brodow* to find the article).

Persuasive Methods and Theories

Flashback Reasoning by analogy and metaphor have been successful persuasive tools since ancient Greek times. Aristotle believed the use of metaphors indicated a speaker's intelligence, as he said in his *Poetics:* ". . . the greatest thing by far is to be a master of metaphor. It is the one thing that cannot be learnt from others, and it is also a sign of genius, since a good metaphor implies an intuitive perception of the similarity in dissimilars" (Aristotle [translated by Ingram Bywater], 1974, sec. 1459.5).

ONE OF THE MOST ENJOYABLE YET CHALLENGING SPEECHES IS THE PERSUASIVE SPEECH. Persuasive speaking is enjoyable because you get to speak on issues that you feel strongly about, and if you do a good job, you can influence your audience. At the same time, politicians can testify to how difficult people are to persuade—many of them have experienced the "boomerang effect" that can result from misjudging an audience. A **boomerang effect** means that fewer people agree with the speaker at the end of the speech than before it. In his book *Standing Firm,* in a chapter on "How to Lose an Election," Dan Quayle (1994) discusses how he and President Bush failed to communicate effectively with the American public. In the 2004 Presidential election, it appears that Kerry and Edwards may have had the same unexpected experience.

To help you avoid the boomerang effect, this chapter covers three basic factors that will you help convince listeners of the importance and relevance of your ideas: (1) your evidence and logic, (2) your credibility (which includes expertise), and (3) your listeners' psychological needs. Usually all three types of appeals play a role in persuasion, though not necessarily at the same level of importance. This chapter will also summarize valuable persuasive theories and identify unethical types of persuasive appeals that you should avoid when you are the speaker, and recognize and resist when you are the listener.

Using Evidence and Logic Skillfully

Of the three persuasive appeals, the effectiveness of evidence and logic is the most ambiguous. Although we like to think of ourselves as logical, and we expect speakers to use logic and evidence in their speeches, we often are swayed more by other factors, as we will see in this chapter. Nevertheless, when listeners are persuaded, they tend to attribute the persuasion to the superior logic and evidence used by the speaker.

Using InfoTrac College Edition, run a subject guide search on *Aristotle*. Read the following articles: "Ethical Decision Making in Public Relations: What Would Aristotle Say?" by Martinson and "Aristotle's Advice for Business Success" by Laabs.

Successful persuasive speakers use evidence and logic skillfully, establish their credibility in a personal manner, and appeal to listeners' psychological needs.

© Susan Van Etten/PhotoEdit

Evidence and Logic Defined

Evidence consists of factual statements and opinions originating from sources other than the speaker (McCroskey, 1969: Rybacki & Rybacki, 1999). It supports the logical arguments of the speech and includes factual instances, expert opinion, and statistics. **Logic**—from the Greek *logos,* or reason—has been defined as "the study of orderly thinking, the sequence and connection of thoughts and ideas as they relate to one another" (Bell, 1990, p. 262). In other words, logic connects the various pieces of evidence to create a meaningful and persuasive argument. ➞ *See Chapter 6 for additional types of supporting material that can serve as evidence.*

Evidence and Logic as Persuasive Tools

Researchers have begun to realize that evidence and logic may not be nearly as effective at persuasion as was previously thought, and that certain ways of using evidence may even detract from persuasion. Note the following research findings (for a summary, see Reinard, 1988; Reynolds & Reynolds, 2002):

- Listeners have difficulty distinguishing between logical and illogical messages and between high-quality and low-quality evidence (Bettinghaus & Cody, 1997; Dresser, 1963; McCroskey, 1967). Apparently, even though listeners think logic and evidence are important, often they can't identify them in speeches.

- Logical-sounding words and phrases (such as *therefore, as a result, it is only logical that,* and *it is possible to conclude*) have surprising power to convince listeners that a presentation is logical. In general, speeches in which these words are not used are judged to be less logical, no matter what their actual merits may be (Bettinghaus & Cody, 1997). This finding indicates how unethical speakers who use logical-sounding words are sometimes able to fool their listeners.

■ In order for evidence to produce persuasion, listeners must be aware and accept that the evidence exists (Reynolds & Reynolds, 2002). Therefore, speakers and advertisers who make it obvious that evidence is being presented are more persuasive (O'Keefe, 1998; Pfau & Louden, 1994).

■ Low-ability listeners who are not personally involved with the topic will tend to be persuaded when a large amount of evidence is presented—even if the evidence is poor quality (Petty & Cacioppo, 1984, 1996).

■ Listeners who are already in favor of the speaker's proposal or who see the speaker as credible tend to rate the speech as being high in evidence even if no actual evidence is presented (Cathcart, 1955; Dresser, 1963). In most cases, listeners' view of the speaker's credibility and their attitude toward the topic are more important persuasive factors than the evidence presented.

■ Speakers with shaky or unestablished credibility can use evidence effectively to increase their credibility and thereby increase their persuasiveness (McCroskey, 1970; Olson & Cal, 1984). O'Keefe (1998) found consistent confirmation that citing evidence in a speech improves the credibility of most speakers.

■ There is a "significant persuasive advantage for messages providing information-source citations (O'Keefe, 1998, p. 67). When evidence is used, merely mentioning the source of the evidence without explaining who this "expert" is does not make the presentation more persuasive. In fact, unless the source's qualifications are also mentioned by the speaker, citing an unfamiliar source makes the presentation less persuasive (Bostrom & Tucker, 1969; Ostermeier, 1967).

■ Normally, it is more effective to cite the source and his or her qualifications *after* the evidence has been presented. Speakers should cite the source before the evidence only when they know that their listeners consider that source to be highly credible (Cohen, 1964; Reynolds & Burgoon, 1983).

■ Speakers who support their assertions by citing firsthand experiences (self-reference speakers) are considered more trustworthy and more persuasive than speakers who refer only to high-prestige sources (Ginossar & Trope, 1980; Koballa, 1989; Reinard, 1988).

■ Personal examples and experiences tend to be more persuasive than statistical or numerical data (Kazoleas, 1993), especially for listeners who disagree with the speaker (Slater & Rouner, 1996). Personal examples and experiences also seem to have a longer-lasting persuasive effect (Ostermeier, 1967; Papageogis, 1963). Statistical evidence may be more persuasive for audience members who already support the speaker (Slater & Rouner, 1996). In most cases, speakers should include both narrative and statistical evidence (Allen et al., 2000).

■ Research has indicated that audiences are more easily persuaded when the arguments presented are novel or new (Morley, 1987; Morley & Walker, 1987). Listeners who disagree with your topic won't be persuaded by the same arguments and evidence that failed to persuade them in the first place. However, new arguments and evidence, or even old arguments presented in a novel or unusual way, could be successful.

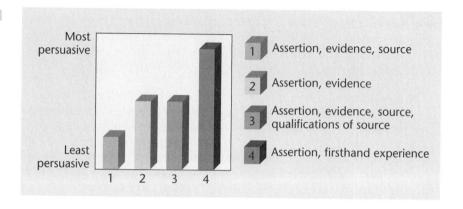

Figure 14.1

Persuasiveness of Evidence Presented in Four Different Methods

Methods of Presenting Evidence

There are four principal ways of presenting evidence, and a summary of the research in the preceding section indicates some important differences among the four methods (see Figure 14.1):

- Method 1—*assertion + evidence + source.* "We need to paint our workroom walls a bright color [assertion] because productivity normally increases by 20 percent [evidence], according to Kenneth Johnson [source]."

- Method 2—*assertion + evidence:* "We need to paint our workroom walls a bright color [assertion] because productivity normally increases by 20 percent [evidence]." Note that the evidence is not linked to a source or documented in any way.

- Method 3—*assertion + evidence + source + qualifications of source:* "We need to paint our workroom walls a bright color [assertion] because productivity normally increases by 20 percent [evidence], according to Kenneth Johnson [source], research director for Business Color, Inc. [qualification of source]."

- Method 4—*assertion + firsthand experience:* "We need to paint our workroom walls a bright color [assertion]. Twice I have been in departments that painted their work areas bright colors and both times productivity increased approximately 20 percent [firsthand experience]."

As Figure 14.1 shows, method 1 is generally the least persuasive of the four methods. As discussed earlier, citing a source without giving the source's qualifications is even less persuasive than presenting evidence with no source at all. Of course, the most persuasive type of evidence is often firsthand experience. So which method should you use?

Best Methods When You Are Unknown to Your Audience   When speaking to an audience who does not know you well (such as your classmates at the beginning of the term), the best methods of presenting evidence are 3 and 4.

There are several reasons for using method 3 (assertion + evidence + source + qualifications of source) for audiences who are unfamiliar with you:

- You can enhance your credibility by citing sources they consider prestigious.

- These listeners will expect you to include documented evidence in your speech. To appear credible (and to improve your persuasiveness), you must meet their expectations.

- Documented evidence can counteract opposing arguments your audience is likely to hear later. Communication researcher James McCroskey (1970) found that audiences are less affected by the opposing view of a second speaker if the first speaker's message contains documented evidence. For example, consider two speeches about year-round schooling—one against that cites authoritative sources and one in favor that fails to cite authoritative sources. If we hear the "con" speech first and are persuaded, when we hear the "pro" speech we are likely to realize that this speaker's sources are inadequate and retain our "con" opinion. But if we hear the "pro" speech first and are persuaded, the chances are that when we hear the "con" speech, we will realize that the "pro" speaker's sources were weak and will side with the "con" speaker.

Method 4 (assertion + firsthand experience) can also be effective when you are unknown to your audience. It is especially effective if the person introducing you presents you as an authority. Would you be more persuaded if you heard about the effects of drugs from a speaker who quoted from a book on the subject or from an ex-addict or relative of a drug addict? However, method 4 should be used only if you have considerable firsthand experience and know more about the topic than most of your listeners. Even so, you should come prepared with more than just personal experience. You should have made an objective and complete search for relevant evidence (both for and against your idea) as part of your speech preparation. If someone asks for additional evidence, you need to be prepared to present it.

Best Methods When You Are Known to Your Audience When speaking to an audience who knows you well (such as a club or work group that you have belonged to for some time), method 2 (assertion + evidence without sources) and method 4 (assertion + firsthand experience) are effective. Method 2 is especially appropriate when your speaking time is limited. Since your audience already knows you (assuming that your credibility and expertise are good), they will view extensive documentation as a waste of time. You also don't need to cite sources when your audience is made up of colleagues who are already somewhat familiar with your topic. Even when the speech is about a new concept or product, your audience will normally have enough general knowledge of the field to determine whether your evidence and conclusions are reasonable.

If you are uncertain about whether you should cite your sources, a compromise might be to name your sources (prestigious sources only) on your visuals. For example, at the bottom of a visual showing the results of a national survey of business trends, you could print simply "Dun and Bradstreet, December, 2005."

Using InfoTrac College Edition, run a keyword search on *persuasion*. Look through the articles and count the number of professions interested in persuasion. Find at least one article on courtroom persuasion.

Whether to Present One or Both Sides of Your Position

Should you present only arguments that support your position or should you introduce and refute opposing arguments (counterarguments) as well? Research indicates these general guidelines (Allen, 1991, 1998; Hovland, Lumsdaine, & Sheffield, 1967; Kamins & Marks, 1987).

Present only your side of the argument when:

- Your listeners agree with your proposal and have a well-developed belief system (in other words, they are not new to the opinion). Presenting negative arguments they have not thought of, even if you refute them well, may create doubt and sabotage your attempt at persuasion. These listeners are more interested in a pep-rally type presentation.

Technology Tip for Speakers

Understand the Power of Persuasion in Electronic Media

Do people react differently to persuasive messages that are sent electronically? It's impossible to answer with certainty, because the research is just beginning in this area. What we do know is that people tend to react differently to different communication channels (Booth-Butterfield & Gutowski, 1993):

■ When persuasive messages are conveyed by *audio or video,* an audience is persuaded more by the communicator's credibility than by any evidence.

■ When persuasive messages are conveyed in *traditional print media* (such as memo, report, and magazine), an audience is more persuaded by the data and quality of evidence than by the communicator's credibility.

Why the difference? Perhaps time is a factor. Print messages can be reread and the evidence can be evaluated more carefully, whereas audio and video messages are usually listened to or viewed only once (Chaiken & Eagly, 1983).

Which type of appeal—evidence or credibility—is more persuasive when *electronic media* carry the message? Preliminary research indicates that we are persuaded more by the communicator's credibility than by the evidence—similar to our reaction to the audio and video channels. Further, when a persuasive message is presented with emotional appeal and fits in with our value system, a type of "instant ethos" occurs (Gurak, 1997). It causes us to trust the message even when we do not know who the author is. Research on victims of fraud (especially Internet fraud) found that most of them gave little attention to the substance of the message once they believed the sender was honest (Priester & Petty, 1995). According to R. B. Cialdini (1993) in his book *Influence: The Psychology of Persuasion,* several irresistible "click-whir" responses lead to instant ethos:

■ *Reciprocation*—If you give me something, I feel obligated to reciprocate.

■ *Commitment and consistency*—Once I have purchased a product or committed myself to an action, I tend to defend that decision consistently (even if the decision was a poor one).

■ *Social proof*—If other people are doing it or believe it, I am more likely to want to do it or believe it.

■ *Likeability*—If I like you (usually because we are alike in one or more ways), I am more likely to be influenced by you.

■ *Authority*—I tend to be influenced by people I perceive to have authority.

■ *Scarcity*—When I perceive an item to be scarce, I value it more.

How many of these techniques do you recognize from messages and ads that you have received in the mail and over the Internet? Obviously, persuasion is a powerful tool. If speakers have an ethical responsibility, persuasive speakers have an even greater responsibility.

- Your listeners know nothing about your topic (too many arguments causes confusion).

- You want them to take an immediate action (such as donating money at the door as they leave).

- There is little chance that they will hear the other side from another speaker or the news media.

Present both sides of the argument when:

- Your listeners are fairly knowledgeable about your topic.

- They agree, but are fairly new to the opinion and have undeveloped belief systems.

- They disagree with your proposal.

- You are not asking for immediate action.

- There is a good chance that they will hear the other side from another speaker or the news media.

Knowledgeable listeners, especially those who disagree with the speaker, are suspicious of speakers who present only one side. Just as presenting documented evidence in your speech can help listeners resist later opposing arguments, presenting both sides also serves to "inoculate" listeners.

The Inoculation Theory According to William McGuire's (1985) **inoculation theory**, "inoculating" a listener against opposing ideas is similar to inoculating a person against a disease. A person who has never heard the other side on a topic will be susceptible to those arguments, just as a person who has lived in a germ-free environment is susceptible to catching a disease. Immunity can be produced by giving a shot containing a weakened form of the disease or, in the case of a speech, by presenting a "brief look" at opposing arguments along with facts and logic disproving them. This "inoculation" helps listeners remain resistant to counterarguments. When they hear opposing arguments, they can say, "Oh, yes, I knew that. However, it's not important (or true) because research shows that . . ."

Presenting both sides also seems to make listeners resistant to arguments that the speaker did not cover (Papageogis & McGuire, 1961; Pfau, 1997; Szabo & Pfau, 2002). Apparently, inoculating listeners even helps them build their own counterarguments. When hearing a new argument, they are likely to say, "Based on what I know, this argument couldn't be true because . . ." Listeners who are highly involved and have critical thinking skills are the best at building these counterarguments (Gass & Seiter, 1999).

The Safest Course: Both Sides Once you poll your classmates, you will have a better idea of whether you should include both sides or only one side of your issue. However, on the basis of the inoculation theory (and since polling is usually not possible), the safest course is to present both sides (Allen, 1991). Whether your listeners agree or disagree with you, they will usually be in a position to hear opposing arguments. Also, presenting both sides shows that you have thoroughly researched the issue—a sure boost to your credibility (Hass & Linder, 1972).

Presenting both sides does not mean giving the opposition equal time. Presenting the "other side" means mentioning one or two objections to your plan and then either (1) showing how each objection is based on inaccurate information or faulty reasoning, or (2) if an objection is accurate, showing how it is minor compared to the

many advantages of your proposal. For example, in a speech about the importance of drinking bottled water, you might admit that cost is a disadvantage but that the small increase in the family budget is minimal compared to the decreased risk to the family's health.

> **Stop reading at this point and decide the following:**
> ■ Should I present one side of my topic or both sides?
> ■ Which of the four methods of presenting evidence will work best for my audience?

Logical Reasoning

Successful persuasive speakers typically use one of four patterns of reasoning—deductive, inductive, analogical, and causal—to organize evidence into logical, persuasive arguments.

Deductive and Inductive Reasoning For your argument to be considered logical, its assumptions (premises) must support its conclusion. Deductive and inductive reasoning patterns are two ways to make sure your premises support your conclusions (Kahane & Cavender, 2002). As discussed in Chapter 7, **deductive reasoning** presents the conclusion first and then proceeds to specific supporting cases; **inductive reasoning** starts with the specific cases before presenting the general conclusion.

For example, suppose you want to argue that your company should provide affordable child care for employees. If you use deductive reasoning, you will state your general conclusion first ("To improve employee satisfaction, Bag It, Inc. should provide child care for the children of its employees"), and then support it with specific cases ("Companies A, B, and C have recently begun providing child care, and each has experienced improved employee satisfaction"). If you use inductive reasoning, you will present the supporting cases first ("Companies A, B, and C have recently begun providing child care, and each has experienced improved employee satisfaction"), and finish with your conclusion ("By providing day care, Bag It, Inc. could increase employee satisfaction also").

The best method depends on your audience. Listeners who are hostile to your conclusion may simply stop listening if you use the deductive pattern. So, even though your evidence might have stimulated them to rethink their positions, you have already lost them. The inductive approach is better when a significant number of audience members is likely to oppose your conclusion, especially if you can catch their interest with powerful stories and vivid personal instances. On the other hand, when most audience members are likely to agree with your conclusion, they will be drawn in by deductive reasoning since they will be interested in hearing your choice of supporting evidence.

Analogical and Causal Reasoning Reasoning by comparison, called analogical reasoning, is used to *explain* and *clarify*. Causal reasoning (especially cause–effect reasoning) is used to *prove*.

Analogical reasoning occurs when you compare a familiar example with an unfamiliar one. For example, suppose you wanted to urge adoption of a state income tax. Using analogical reasoning, you would show several important similarities between your state and state A and then suggest that because state A has benefited from a state income tax, your state would also benefit from one. Reasoning from analogy cannot serve as absolute proof (because the two items being compared are not iden-

tical), but it can be a powerful way to persuade your audience of the merits of your argument. You can use either literal or figurative comparisons in analogical reasoning. Comparing a jogger wearing cheap jogging shoes to a jogger wearing shoeboxes tied onto his feet is an example of a *figurative analogy* (Whately, 1997). Showing similarities between occasional joggers and professional runners and then telling listeners that, like professional runners, they should wear only a special type of shoe is an example of a *literal analogy.*

Causal reasoning occurs when you imply a causal link between two items (for example, fatty foods cause high cholesterol levels in humans). According to persuasion expert Charles Larson (2004), cause–effect reasoning (the most common type of causal reasoning) is used "to identify events, trends, or facts that have caused certain effects" (p. 196). Since causal reasoning is used to prove, you must make sure that what you are claiming as a cause–effect relationship isn't just a chance association. Ask yourself these questions (Herrick, 1995):

- *Do the events occur together consistently?* (For example, Melissa always sneezes violently when a dog comes near her.)

- *Does the cause consistently precede the effect?* (Every time Melissa sneezes violently, a dog is nearby.)

- *Is the cause sufficient to produce the effect by itself?* (Dogs cause excessive sneezing in many people who are allergic to dogs.)

- *Is it possible that a third factor is the "cause" of the events?* (Melissa has taken allergy tests, and she's allergic only to dogs.)

If you can answer yes to the first three questions and no to the final one, you can be fairly confident that your cause–effect relationship is real.

Fallacious Reasoning

Unfortunately, not all reasoning is logical reasoning; some speakers, knowingly or unknowingly, use various types of **fallacious** (false or faulty) **reasoning** (Damer, 2000; Walton, 1998). Seven of the most typical types of fallacious reasoning are discussed in this section, for two reasons: (1) so that you can avoid using them and (2) so that, if in your research you find fallacious objections to your position (or plan), you can recognize them and effectively rebut them in your speech.

Ad Hominem *Ad hominem* is a Latin phrase meaning "to (or against) the person." Speakers using the *ad hominem* fallacy are attempting to divert attention from a weak argument by attacking the person who questions it (for example, "Who are you to question the high cost of my plan—you can't even balance your own checkbook"). The idea is that if the critic can be discredited, chances are that his or her criticism will be discredited too. There is nothing wrong with questioning a person's credibility if it is relevant to the issue at hand. But the *ad hominem* fallacy is much more than a credibility check—it is an unwarranted personal attack (often involving name-calling) designed to distract the audience from a discussion of the issues (Walton, 1998).

Ad Populum The *ad populum* (Latin for "to the people") fallacy is another way to distract attention from an investigation of the issues. However, instead of attacking another person's credibility, the speaker argues, "How could this idea possibly be wrong when public opinion says it's right?" In other words, why waste time with

evidence when "everyone" agrees on the point (for example, "You've asked whether some German shepherds are vicious, but everyone knows that they are the best and most loyal dogs in the world").

Appeal to Ignorance (*Ad Ignoratiam*) Speakers who appeal to ignorance (***ad ignoratiam***) are basically saying that because no one can prove that a claim is false, it must be true. The purpose of this appeal is to put the opposition on the defensive and convince the audience that the burden of proof is now on them ("You can't prove that UFOs don't exist, can you? No one has ever been able to disprove the existence of UFOs. Therefore, it's obvious that they do exist"). When the opposition is unable (or unwilling) to disprove the claim, the claim is obviously true, says the speaker. However, arguing that "because something has not been disproved, it has been proved" (Herrick, 1995, p. 227) is fallacious reasoning.

Begging the Question The fallacy of **begging the question** is a type of circular reasoning; it "asserts that something is because it is" (Bell, 1990, pp. 278–279). A Sony Corporation ad illustrates this type of reasoning. In speaking about the Trinitron XBR television, the ad stated: "The best statement we can make about this television is that it's the best television we've ever made" (Bell, p. 279). This is a "catchy" ad—but it contains no evidence. In begging-the-question arguments, the audience is supposed to assume that the question (considered debatable by most people) has already been answered and no longer requires supporting evidence.

Hasty Generalization The **hasty generalization** fallacy (which is more common with inductive reasoning) occurs when a conclusion is based on too few examples or on isolated examples. This kind of conclusion is based on a sample that is too small to be representative of the population it comes from. The following is an example of a hasty generalization:

> We need to install gun detection equipment in every school in the state.
>
> A survey of students in one inner-city school found that 20 percent carried weapons.
>
> Last month in our own city, there were two incidents involving handguns.

Post Hoc The Latin phrase *post hoc* means "after the fact." The ***post hoc*** fallacy (which is more common with deductive reasoning) occurs when the speaker claims a causal relationship simply because one event followed another event. But just because event B followed event A doesn't prove that A caused B. The following is an example of post hoc reasoning:

> People are drinking more carbonated drinks than they did 30 years ago.
>
> Incidents of cancer have increased in the last 20 years.
>
> Therefore, carbonated drinks cause cancer.

Slippery Slope The **slippery slope** fallacy occurs when a speaker asserts that taking a particular step will lead to a serious and undesirable consequence (for example, listening to rock music will lead to drug use among teenagers), and does not provide adequate evidence to support the assertion. The phrase *slippery slope* implies that if you take one step, you will inevitably slip all the way down the slope and land in an even worse situation.

Remember

Fallacious reasoning includes . . .

- *Ad hominem*—attacking the person rather than the argument.

- *Ad populum*—arguing that since "everyone" knows an idea is right, it can't be wrong.

- *Ad ignoratiam*—arguing that since no one can prove that an idea is false, it must be true.

- *Begging the question*—asserting that something is because it is.

- *Hasty generalization*—basing a general conclusion on too few examples or on isolated examples.

- *Post hoc*—claiming a causal relationship simply because one event followed another event.

- *Slippery slope*—asserting that taking a particular step automatically will lead to a dangerous consequence.

Establishing Credibility

Another important appeal in persuasion is the credibility, or *ethos,* of the speaker. A credible speaker is someone with ethical proof, someone whom listeners perceive as believable—in short, someone in whom they can place their confidence. Aristotle, in his *Rhetoric,* urges speakers to make sure they are perceived to be of good sense, goodwill, and good moral character. Today's research still supports the importance of credibility—in fact, the greater your credibility, the more persuasive you are (O'Keefe, 1990). Consider, for example, candidates running for political office or students competing for your vote for student body president. Or how about an instructor who recommends that you sign up for an additional course that's not part of your degree plan? In all these cases, the credibility of the persuader would likely play a role in your decision.

Credibility as a Persuasive Tool

Researchers are finding that a speaker's credibility depends on such factors as the situation, listeners' involvement with the topic, and their similarity to the speaker. Here are examples of research findings (for a summary, see O'Keefe, 1990):

- Listeners who have *very low involvement* with the topic tend to be more persuaded by the expertise of the speaker than by the quality of arguments or evidence. However, listeners who are *very involved* with the topic are more persuaded by high-quality arguments than by the credibility of the speaker (Petty & Cacioppo, 1986; Ratneshwar & Chaiken, 1991; Tesser & Shaffer, 1990). One explanation for this finding is that involved listeners are more likely to evaluate the arguments presented by the speaker, but uninvolved listeners are more likely to be influenced by their impressions of the speaker (Eagly & Chaiken, 1993; Reardon, 1991). This finding is based on research following the Elaboration Likelihood Model of Petty and Cacioppo (1984,

1996). ➤ *For an explanation of the Elaboration Likelihood Model of Persuasion, see page 325.*

■ When a persuasive message is sent by *audio, video, e-mail,* or the *Internet,* the level of listener persuasion varies depending on the channel used. ➤ *See the Technology Tip for Speakers on page 312 for a detailed explanation.*

■ *Perceived similarity* between audience members and the speaker may enhance persuasion by increasing the perceived trustworthiness or competence of the speaker (O'Keefe, 1990, pp. 148–151). For example, when audience members perceive attitudinal similarities between themselves and a speaker (even when these similarities aren't specifically related to the topic of the speech), they like the speaker better and rate his or her trustworthiness higher (Applbaum & Anatol, 1972; Berscheid, 1985; McCroskey & Teven, 1999). For example, suppose you like pets and discover from the speaker's attention-getter that he or she has two pets. Would this similarity of attitude increase your liking of the speaker—even if the speaker's topic happened to be recycling? Research indicates that this is likely. However, although listeners *like* speakers better when they discover similarities (even when unrelated to the topic), they judge speakers as more *competent* only when perceived similarities are relevant to the topic (O'Keefe, 1990).

Basic Elements of Credibility

A speaker's credibility results from four elements: trustworthiness, competency, dynamism, and objectivity (Smith 1973; Whitehead, 1968). As you read this section, remember that in order for credibility to aid your persuasiveness, being credible isn't enough—you must *also appear* credible in the eyes of your audience.

Trustworthiness Most listeners determine the credibility of speakers by observing all four elements and "averaging" them. But in fact, trustworthiness (honesty, fairness, and integrity) is the most important of the four elements. When speakers appear untrustworthy, their credibility is questioned regardless of their other qualities (Smith, 1973, p. 309).

Several factors seem to affect whether listeners perceive speakers as untrustworthy. For example, speakers who avoid eye contact, shift their eyes rapidly from place to place, or always look over the listeners' heads appear to be ashamed or to have something to hide and may be perceived as untrustworthy. Speakers who don't articulate, who speak in a breathy or nasal voice, or who speak either in a monotone or too rapidly also are perceived as less trustworthy (Addington, 1971). In addition to having an effective verbal delivery style, you can improve your perceived trustworthiness by presenting both sides of an argument and by appearing friendly and likeable (Chaiken, 1986), which includes relaxed delivery, smiling, direct eye contact, and using immediacy behaviors. Hosman (2002) also found that using active instead of passive sentence structure improves the speaker's believability. ➤ *Immediacy behaviors are discussed in Chapter 10.*

Competency Listeners are also more likely to judge a speaker as credible if they perceive him or her as competent (knowledgeable, experienced, expert) on the topic. However, speakers who use **nonfluencies**—inaccurate articulation, vocalized pauses (like *ah* or *uh*), and unnecessary repetition of words—are often judged as low on competence (McCroskey & Mehrley, 1969; McCroskey & Young, 1981). In addition to avoiding nonfluencies, you can appear more competent by citing personal in-

Financial speaker Suze Orman is known for her personable and dynamic style.

© Tim Rue/Corbis

stances that are related to the topic, citing prestigious sources, by speaking in a confident manner, using high-quality visual aids, and wearing more traditional, higher-status clothing (Behling & Williams, 1991).

Dynamism   Another element of credibility is **dynamism**. A dynamic speaker is forceful and enthusiastic and uses good vocal variety. Have you noticed that you can often tell who is in charge simply from the forcefulness of his or her delivery? If you avoid direct eye contact, are soft-spoken, use very little vocal emphasis, and appear hesitant, you will give the impression that you are uncertain about what you are saying (not competent) or that you are trying to deceive your listeners (untrustworthy).

To be fully effective, a dynamic speaker must also sustain a conversational tone. Researchers have found that speakers using low or moderate levels of dynamism are perceived as conversational and judged as credible. However, speakers who overdramatize are perceived as less conversational and more unnatural and phony, and are judged as less trustworthy and less credible (Pearce & Conklin, 1971).

Objectivity   The fourth element of speaker credibility is objectivity. An objective speaker is open-minded and fair and appears to view evidence and arguments in an unbiased manner. You can appear objective by avoiding false reasoning and by discussing both sides of your proposal (of course, you must show why your arguments are best).

If the listeners don't know you, or if they perceive you as having low credibility, review the options listed in the "Improve your credibility by . . ." box on the next page and select several of these to use in your next persuasive speech.

Unethical Use of Credibility

Unfortunately, some speakers give the appearance of credibility in order to hide the fact that their evidence is incomplete or even misleading. The stereotype of the used-car salesperson who gives every outward appearance of being honest in order to get the customer to buy a "lemon" illustrates this point. Unethical speakers who are forceful and dynamic, make direct eye contact, and give every appearance of sincerity may be able to temporarily persuade an audience to agree with their ideas or buy their products. However, when listeners eventually realize that these speakers have based their arguments on inadequate or faulty evidence, they cease to be fooled.

Remember

Improve your credibility by . . .

■ Having a highly credible expert on the topic (or someone of higher rank) introduce you and establish you as a competent and trustworthy speaker.

■ Supporting your assertions with up-to-date, carefully documented evidence and sources considered credible to your listeners.

■ Identifying your views with those of a respected person or institution.

■ Presenting both sides of an issue to show your willingness to be fair and honest.

■ Presenting your ideas in a smooth, forceful, and self-assured manner, while maintaining good eye contact.

■ Establishing a common ground with your listeners by identifying beliefs, organizations, or problems you share.

■ Recognizing (in content and delivery) the formal status and knowledge of your listeners.

Appealing to Listeners' Psychological Needs

Even though you may be a credible speaker and include logic and evidence in your presentations, you will not be successful at persuasion unless you also adapt your arguments to the psychological needs of your listeners (Harris, 1993). In Chapter 4, we defined a *need* as "a state in which some sort of unsatisfied condition exists." Striving to satisfy needs is a great motivator for all people. Because needs are based on values, beliefs, and attitudes, they arouse emotions. A certain amount of emotional appeal, or *pathos,* is needed in a persuasive speech. This doesn't mean that you want audience members to become teary-eyed. It means that you want them to feel that your topic relates to them personally—that they have a stake in the outcome of your speech.

Personalizing Your Persuasive Argument

Why don't more people participate in blood drives or do volunteer work or vote in elections? Many of us fail to participate in these kinds of activities because we don't feel any emotional stake in them. We expect other people to take care of these good works: "I'm too busy working and raising a family" or "My vote won't make any difference." The challenge of the persuasive speaker is to make us realize that his or her issue does relate to us.

Logic and evidence are not enough to convince listeners. For example, you have probably had an argument when you knew that you were right, yet when you presented all the facts, the other person's response was, "I don't care. I don't believe it." As persuasive speakers, we need to remember that it isn't evidence unless audience members think it's evidence. But if we can get our listeners to relate personally to our evidence—to decide that the topic is important to their needs—they are more likely to consider our evidence to be logical and reasonable. ➤ *See Chapter 3 (pages 51–53) for a review of how listeners avoid being persuaded.*

The following example illustrates the importance of relating your message to listeners' personal needs:

> A high-performing vice president decided to retire early, much to the dismay of his co-workers. All kinds of inducements (such as a substantial salary increase, more office help, and a new car) were offered to convince him that it was logical and reasonable to stay with the company. When inducements didn't work, his colleagues pointed out how much he was needed. Nothing was successful. On his last day with the company, he was having lunch in the executive dining room with the president and two other executives. The president began to discuss a completely new and risky project the company was contemplating. Almost in jest, the president suggested that the vice president stay and head the new project. He accepted. None of the other appeals were persuasive because they didn't relate to his personal needs. The challenge presented by the new project was something he could not resist (Hamilton, 2005, p. 344).

Using Maslow's Hierarchy of Needs

Discovering your listeners' basic needs and motives is an essential part of audience analysis. As far back as 1954, psychologist Abraham Maslow presented his hierarchy of needs as one way to identify audience needs: physiological, safety, social, esteem, and self-actualization. As discussed earlier, generally the lower-level needs must be satisfied before the next level becomes important. For example, rarely will you persuade an audience that is concerned mainly with safety needs by appealing to higher-level needs such as esteem or self-actualization (see Figure 14.2). At the same time, needs that have already been satisfied are no longer persuasive. → *See Chapter 4 for more on Maslow's hierarchy of needs.*

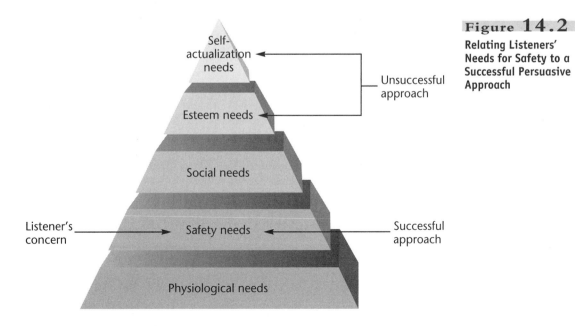

Figure 14.2

Relating Listeners' Needs for Safety to a Successful Persuasive Approach

▼ **Physiological Needs**	Financial and job security	▼ **Esteem Needs**
Bodily comfort (food, shelter, clothing, air, and water)	Freedom from censorship and restraint	Feeling of pride
Physical enjoyment and activity	Freedom from boredom	Recognition from self and others
Sufficient rest and sleep	▼ **Social Needs**	Status, prestige, and reputation
Sexual attraction	Need to give and receive love	Sense of achievement
▼ **Safety Needs**	Companionship and friendship	Sense of value and worth
Freedom from fear and the unknown	Dating, marriage, and family ties	Happiness with appearance
Fear of punishment and conflict	Feeling of belonging	Freedom from guilt
Fear of death	Loyalty	Need for power and control
Need for conformity	Respect for the Deity	▼ **Self-Actualization Needs**
Desire for law and order	Need to give and receive sympathy	Developing one's potential
Protection from injury or poor health	Helping the needy	Responsible for own decisions

(Esteem/Self-Actualization column continued:)

- Recognition from self and others
- Status, prestige, and reputation
- Sense of achievement
- Sense of value and worth
- Happiness with appearance
- Freedom from guilt
- Need for power and control

▼ **Self-Actualization Needs**
- Developing one's potential
- Responsible for own decisions
- Need for creative outlets
- Curiosity
- Reaching worthwhile goals
- Being the best person possible
- Need to be challenged

Figure 14.3

Motivational Appeals for Each of Maslow's Need Categories

To use the hierarchy of needs to figure out how you can be most persuasive, first decide which needs your topic addresses. Next, using the list in Figure 14.3, select the relevant motivational appeals for those needs. Last, develop your persuasive argument around the selected motivational appeals. The following persuasive statements illustrate motivational appeals to various basic needs:

- Exercise regularly for a sexier, slimmer you. [physiological need of sexual attraction]

- It may seem like graduation is a long way off, but anything worth having is worth waiting and working for. [esteem need of sense of achievement]

- Unless we take a leadership role in this international crisis, America will lose its standing among nations. [esteem needs of status, prestige, and reputation]

- Aren't you tired of being afraid to take a car trip with your family during the holidays because of the drunks out on the roads? [safety need of protection from injury]

- Let your children know how you feel about them. Send them to school each day with a nourishing, hot breakfast. [social need to give and receive love]

When using emotional appeal, keep in mind that listeners appear to be "more motivated by the thought of losing something than by the thought of gaining something" (Dillard & Pfau, 2002, p. 520). Therefore, when messages are framed to stress potential losses that may occur if certain action is not taken, persuasion is enhanced. Loss framing is especially effective in situations involving risk and uncertainty (De Dreu & McCusker, 1997; Tversky & Kahneman, 1981).

Fear Appeals

Appeals that are designed to arouse negative emotions are called **fear appeals**. Fear appeals cause listeners to feel threatened or afraid, in contrast to positive emotional appeals, which cause listeners to feel emotions such as pride or sympathy. You'll notice that the motivational appeals listed in Figure 14.3 contain both positive and fear appeals.

Although arousing fear in listeners is not easy (Boster & Mongeau, 1984), research indicates that when it is done successfully, a high level of fear is more likely to result in persuasion than a medium or low level of fear (Sutton & Eiser, 1984). To make your fear appeals successful, research suggests that you do three things in your argument (Maddux & Rogers, 1983; Rogers, 1975):

1. Show that there will be significant consequences if change does not occur.

2. Show how likely the consequences are.

3. Indicate what action(s) the audience can take to halt or minimize the consequences.

For example, if you were giving a speech about the importance of exercising regularly, you would (1) describe personal consequences of not exercising regularly (such as weight gain, heart disease, cancer, and lack of energy); (2) show the audience how likely it is that they will gain weight, lose energy, or get heart disease or cancer if they don't exercise regularly; and (3) explain simple, inexpensive actions they can take to prevent these consequences. Without step 3, listeners are likely to feel that nothing they can do will prevent the problem, and as a result they will avoid being persuaded. In fact, when listeners perceive the likelihood of the threat to be high but the effectiveness of the solution to be low, they may actually do the opposite of what you are recommending—the boomerang effect discussed at the beginning of the chapter (Eagly & Chaiken, 1993; Witte, 1992a, 1992b).

Unethical Use of Emotional Appeals

Emotional appeals are a necessary part of a persuasive speech, but when they are used in place of evidence or are deliberately misused, they are unethical. Here are two unethical psychological appeals that you should avoid using in your persuasive speeches.

Fabrication of Similarities As you have learned, establishing similarities with your audience can increase your credibility and persuasiveness. However, some persuasive speakers fabricate or greatly exaggerate similarities with their audiences. For example, a speaker who has played golf only a few times in his life may try to win over his golfing audience by referring to himself as a "golf fanatic."

Exaggeration Speakers who use exaggeration typically overestimate "the costs, problems, or negative consequences of a new proposal" (Herrick, 1995, p. 230). Rather than giving specifics, they use emotionally loaded terms to draw a response from the audience. For example, the statement "We've received hundreds of phone calls in violent opposition to Senator Johnson's proposal" could get an audience upset enough to forget to look for specific evidence. Exactly how many phone calls? Is this more or less than the usual number of phone calls received? What exactly is "violent" opposition?

Using Persuasive Theory in Speaking

There are many theories about persuasion. Some, such as the inoculation theory, have already been discussed in this chapter and others, such as the Elaboration Likelihood Model, have been briefly mentioned. Table 14.1 summarizes some of the more important persuasive theories. Take a look at each of these theories:

Table 14.1

Important Theories Concerning Persuasion	
Information-Integration Theory	
Basic approach	The way people accumulate and organize information (about a situation, event, person, or object) can result in attitude change (Littlejohn, 2002, pp. 123–126). Attitudes are affected by the valence and weight of information received. *Valence* refers to whether the information supports (+ valence) or refutes (– valence) previous beliefs; *weight* refers to how much credibility is assigned to the information.
Respected theorist	Martin Fishbein (Fishbein & Ajzen, 1975). Your intention to change behavior is determined by: your attitude toward the behavior *times* the strength (weight) of that attitude *plus* your beliefs about what others think you should do *times* the strength of these other opinions.
Consistency Theories	
Basic approach	Because people prefer consistency and balance and feel threatened by inconsistency, attitude change can occur when information creates inconsistency (Littlejohn, pp. 126–130).
Respected theorist	Leon Festinger (1957), *theory of cognitive dissonance.* Dissonance creates stress and tension in people, which cause them to (1) seek to reduce the dissonance, and (2) avoid other dissonance-creating situations.
Respected theorist	Milton Rokeach (1969, 1973), *theory of attitudes, beliefs, values. Attitudes* are feelings of like or dislike, *beliefs* are the reasons we hold the attitudes we do, and *values* are deep-seated principles that direct behaviors. Persuasion may occur when the speaker shows how certain behaviors are consistent with audience values or when a particular value is shown to be less (or more) important now than in the past.
Elaboration Likelihood Theory	
Basic approach	Elaboration likelihood involves the probability that listeners will evaluate arguments critically (Littlejohn, pp. 132–135).
Respected theorists	Richard Petty and John Cacioppo (1986). When evaluating arguments, people either use the *central route* (elaborate carefully and critically) or the *peripheral route* (decide quickly using little critical thinking). For motivated and able people, elaboration leads to attitudes that are resistant to change.
Social Judgment Theory	
Basic approach	People use internal anchors (past experience) as reference points when making judgments about messages (Littlejohn, pp. 130–132). Anchors are more likely to influence the judgments of those who are *ego involved* with the topic.
Respected theorists	Muzafer Sherif (Sherif & Hovland, 1961; Sherif, Sherif, & Nebergall, 1965). A person's ego involvement determines messages that are acceptable (*latitude of acceptance*), totally unacceptable (*latitude of rejection*), or merely tolerable (*latitude of noncommitment*). The larger a person's latitude of rejection, the more difficult he or she is to persuade. Attitude change results when people perceive that an argument fits within their latitude of acceptance. When an argument falls in their latitude of rejection, a *boomerang effect* may occur— the original attitude may be strengthened rather than changed.

Although all these theories contain important information and advice for persuasive speakers, the last two theories offer the most practical, easy-to-use advice for
the beginning speaker. Both theories will be discussed further.

Elaboration Likelihood Model of Persuasion

According to developers Richard Petty and John Cacioppo (1986), the **Elaboration
Likelihood Model** (ELM) of persuasion indicates which of two routes for processing arguments audience members will likely use. If they are motivated (involved and
interested in your topic) and have the ability to process information, they are more
likely to use the *central route,* characterized by careful critical thinking and consideration of arguments and evidence. However, if audience members are not motivated
(have less involvement or interest in the topic) and/or are unable to process information, they are more likely to use the *peripheral route*—taking a shortcut to decision
making that involves less critical thinking and evaluation of arguments and is based
more on senses and cues that aren't directly related to the topic (such as a speaker's
credibility or attractiveness).

So, what does the ELM model of persuasion suggest to speakers? If audience
analysis indicates that your audience is likely to use the central route to processing,
you can expect them to question all that they hear and take an active role in gener-
ating their own arguments (Booth-Butterfield & Welbourne, 2002). Therefore, you
need to present well-supported logic and evidence and even present both sides of the
issue, while still showing how your position is the better one. It's interesting to note
that when highly motivated listeners using the central route are persuaded, their attitudes are "more resistant to counter-persuasion, persistent over time, and predictive
of future behavior" (Booth-Butterfield & Welbourne, p. 157).

On the other hand, if you have audience members who will likely process arguments using the peripheral route, the ELM model suggests that they are less interested in logic and evidence and more influenced by catchy visuals, narratives,
personal experiences, use of immediacy behaviors, and organization using rhymes or
acronyms. Since most audiences include both types of processors, speakers will usually want to relate to both types of audience members ➜ *See Chapter 4 for suggestions
on handling the uninterested audience.*

Social Judgment Theory

First proposed by psychologists Muzafer Sherif and Carl Hovland (1961) and
expanded by Sherif, Sherif, and Nebergall (1965), the **social judgment theory** explains how people evaluate messages based on internal anchors (past experiences)—
the more ego involved we are with a social issue or topic, the more likely our
judgments will be influenced by an internal anchor. Furthermore, according to
Sherif and Hovland, "The individual's stand on a social issue is conceived as a range
or latitude of acceptance" (pp. 128–129). In other words, on an issue, each listener
will view some messages or positions as acceptable (*latitude of acceptance*), some as unacceptable (*latitude of rejection*), and others as merely tolerable (*latitude of noncommitment*). Social judgment theory proposes that the larger a person's latitude of rejection,
the more difficult he or she is to persuade.

Obviously, as with the ELM model of persuasion, audience analysis is crucial
if persuasion is to occur. The audience poll mentioned in Chapter 13 (Figure 13.2)
is one way to determine your audience's views: "Strongly agree" and "Agree"
could represent the latitude of acceptance; "Strongly disagree" and "Disagree" could

represent the latitude of rejection; and "No opinion" could represent the latitude of noncommitment.

So, what does social judgment theory suggest to persuasive speakers? First, attitude change results when people perceive that an argument fits within their latitude of acceptance. It may be up to you to point out that your position does fit in their latitude of acceptance and remind them how important your position is to them and those they love. Second, the larger a person's latitude of rejection, the more difficult he or she is to persuade (especially if the person is personally involved with the topic). In fact, when an argument falls in his or her latitude of rejection, a boomerang effect may occur—the original attitude may be strengthened rather than changed. Therefore, persuasion is more likely if you advocate a change that is only a small step outside the latitude of acceptance or within the latitude of noncommitment—asking for a complete change in opinion will likely fail. Presenting quality evidence, establishing your credibility, and showing how you and the audience have common ground will also aid in persuasion. If time allows, plan a series or campaign of persuasive appeals—attitudes can change over time (Gass & Seiter, 1999).

Both theories—the Elaboration Likelihood Model and social judgment theory—offer additional information for the persuasive speaker that should be used along with the information already covered in this chapter and the previous chapter on persuasion.

Sample Student Speech
"Untreated Depression in America" by Sean Stewart

The following persuasive speech, "Untreated Depression in America," was given by University of Texas communication major Sean Stewart in a speech contest. Sean won first place for this speech. Was this a speech to convince or to actuate? As you read the speech, see if you can determine what organizational pattern was used. Do you think this was the best pattern for this topic? What would you have done differently? To watch and analyze a video clip of Sean's speech, look under Student Resources for Chapter 14 at the Essentials of Public Speaking website.

SAMPLE SPEECH

UNTREATED DEPRESSION
IN AMERICA
by Sean Stewart

For Dr. Leon Rosenberg, the quality of life was something that he never took for granted. With a stellar career as a genetics professor at Princeton University and former dean of the Yale University School of Medicine, Rosenberg's career continued to reach new heights. But, unfortunately, so did his mood disorder. As the *Baltimore Sun* of September 1, 2003, asserts, Rosenberg had suffered

from a mood disorder for more than 30 years but had declined treatment for fear that his career could be adversely affected. Yet Rosenberg isn't the only one suffering silently. According to ABCNews.com of June 17, 2003, some 33 million or more Americans suffer from the debilitating condition of depression. But even more shocking is that over 78 percent receive insufficient care, which means there are some 25 million of us who are victims of the growing epidemic of untreated depression.

So to better understand the damage and devastation of untreated depression, we must first look to the problems surrounding this disease; next, examine the reasons this problem persists so we can finally initiate some solutions to what Dr. Alex Bodkin, Chief of the Clinical Psychopharmacology Department of McLean Hospital of Belmont, Massachusetts, calls on ABC.com the predominant lack of effective treatment that should not be tolerated by our society.

Untreated depression is rampant, and it has astounding effects on us all. The National Mental Health Association website, last updated 2003, mentions that depression tends to affect people in their prime working years, and it can last a lifetime if left untreated. But the impact of untreated depression is far-reaching. In fact, the previously mentioned website notes that untreated depression accounts for more than 200 million days lost from work every year. Additionally, the June 28, 2003, edition of the *Journal of the American Medical Association* notes that some 97 percent of those who reported depression said the disease affected their work, home life, and relationships. Those effects, argues a University of Michigan Health Systems study, released July 17, 2003, cost the United States economy $148 billion annually.

Additionally, depression is also a leading cause of suicide, especially among the elderly. The November 25, 2003, edition of the *Washington Post* explains that the elderly have the highest suicide rate among any group, victims of an act of violence largely due to untreated or mistreated depression. But the elderly are not alone. The previously mentioned National Mental Association Health website notes that untreated depression is the leading cause of suicide and is the third leading cause of death for 15- to 24-year-olds, and the sixth leading cause of death for 5- to 14-year-olds. And untreated depression among children is all too common, as the parents of 12-year-old Timothy O'Clair can attest. The *Post Standard* of Syracuse, New York, on August 14, 2003, mentions that after seeing various doctors for his disorders, Timothy was sent home, seemingly after successful treatment. But 6 weeks later, he went home and hanged himself in his closet, shocking everyone, from his parents to the very doctors that treated him.

Unfortunately, untreated depression persists for two main reasons: the social stigma surrounding depression and the lack of insur-

(continued)

ance coverage. Not surprisingly, many of us never seek treatment out of fear of the stigma associated with the disease. The University of Nebraska's Department of Obstetrics and Gynecology acknowledge on their website, last updated January 6, 2004, that many people still view depression as a weakness, fearing the reaction from friends, family, and coworkers. As a result, millions of those with depression never seek treatment. Even famed *60 Minutes* journalist Mike Wallace never sought treatment for his depressive episodes. According to the book *On the Edge of Darkness,* copyright 1994, Wallace states, "I was ashamed. For years depression meant the crazy house. For years I never sought treatment, and as I look back on it, my depression seems like damned foolishness, which is one of the reasons why I speak of it now."

But, unfortunately, many of us don't speak of it and, in fact, are ashamed. Dr. John Zajecka, Director of Consultation at St. Luke's Medical Center in Chicago notes on Newsday, September 2, 2003, that many people actually view the stigma of receiving treatment as being greater than the stigma of living with the disorder. But even more shocking is that most insurance companies don't cover mental illnesses the same way they do physical illnesses. The *New York Times* of September 1, 2003, asserts that private insurance practices puts stricter limits on mental health care than they do for physical ailments such as cancer and diabetes. This limited health-care coverage, combined with the social stigma surrounding depression, prevents millions of us from seeking the treatment that we so desperately need.

Nonetheless, there are things that we can and must do to relieve the burden surrounding untreated depression: educate those lacking knowledge of depression, combat the medical misdiagnosis, and offer better health-care insurance coverage. Untreated depression has gone rampant in our society, and it's high time that we become educated about it. We can take the time by starting to sit down and read the books *Darkness Visible* by William Styron or *On the Edge of Darkness* by Kathy Cronkite. By actually sitting down and reading these books and making ourselves aware of depression, we can go out and educate others about this devastating disease that has taken far too many lives. The National Mental Health Association website, last updated June 2003, mentions that no two people experience clinical depression in the same manner, and they say that we should look for such behaviors as persistent sad, anxious, or empty moods, or even difficulty concentrating and remembering. Additionally, the *San Diego Union Tribune* of September 28, 2003, mentions that other warning signs of depressive episodes include a lack of sleeping, limited health, and a waning sex drive.

If you suspect that a friend or colleague is suffering from any form of depression, be encouraging and offer to take him to a doctor's appointment, or even sit down with her and speak to her about the nature of depression as a disease and not something indicative of a personality weakness. And if you feel you're suffering from any

SAMPLE SPEECH

form of depression yourself, do yourself a favor and make an appointment with your physician. By actually making yourself as well as others aware about the nature of depression, mainly negative views that some of us have may begin to fade away. Additionally, the *New York Times* of December 18, 2003, brings to light a website about depression for college students. The website, called www.Ulifeline.org, offers contact and help, 24 hours, 7 days a week, for college students, as well as tests for other things such as anorexia, drug dependence, and depression. But websites like that need to be offered and replicated nationwide so that everyone else can actually view the depressive stages.

And finally, mental health care needs to be put on the same level that it is in most other industrialized nations. In the summer of 2003, legislation was tried within the state of New York where legislators devised the bill known as Timothy's Law. You see, it was named after the previously mentioned 12-year-old Timothy O'Clair, and the bill would mandate that mental health-care coverage be put on the same level as all other physical ailments, such as cancer and diabetes, notes the Associated Press of June 5, 2003. And the previously mentioned *Post Standard* remarks that backers of Timothy's Law are asking the public to send New York State Majority Leader Joseph Bruno a letter of support, as well as 1 dollar and 26 cents, just the amount that health-care proponents say insurance rates would increase per person to cover parity for mental illnesses and substance abuse. The state of New York, and all 49 others, must enact such legislation to ensure that depression is finally viewed as the disease that it is.

While Dr. Rosenberg finally received treatment for his mental disorder, there are over 25 million of us who are victims of this disease. But by looking at the problem surrounding untreated depression, glancing at the reasons this problem persists, and enacting some solutions, hopefully one day we can finally end the depressing consequences of our neglect.

Summary

This chapter covered three of the main appeals that lead to persuasion: (1) the evidence and logic of the message, (2) the credibility of the persuader, and (3) the psychological needs of the listeners. Although some people may think that the message's logic and evidence are far more important than other factors, research does not support this notion. In fact, psychological appeals are often needed to convince an audience of the truth and importance of evidence. Successful persuasive speakers consider all three types of appeals when preparing their speeches.

When you present the source of your evidence, give the qualifications of the source. In most cases, presenting the source by itself is less persuasive. Make sure your speeches do not contain the types of fallacious reasoning discussed in this chapter: *ad hominem, ad populum, ad ignoratiam,* begging the question, hasty generalization, *post*

hoc, and slippery slope. In addition, you may be able to refute objections to your position by pointing out fallacious reasoning used in them.

When planning how to improve your credibility as a speaker, keep in mind the four elements of credibility: trustworthiness, competency, dynamism, and objectivity. Remember that persuasion requires more than evidence and credibility—equally important is an emotional appeal to your audience's needs. When planning how to appeal to the psychological needs of your audience, select motivational appeals based on the analysis of your audience's attitudes, beliefs, and values.

Finally, as you plan your persuasive arguments, consider the persuasive theories in Table 14.1. Pay special attention to the Elaboration Likelihood Model of persuasion and the Social Judgment Theory, which give insight on how audience members will likely process and make judgments about your persuasive arguments.

As you now realize, speaking skills, which are important in all fields of life, are not learned overnight—much practice is needed. Once you retake the PRCA and compare your original scores with your current scores, you will likely be amazed at your improvement—the lower the score, the less anxiety you feel. If you are serious about continued improvement of your speaking skills, you must stop avoiding speaking opportunities and begin *volunteering* for them. Becoming a successful speaker will provide you great personal satisfaction, allow you to more easily influence your world, and even advance your career. Best wishes in your future life!

Essentials of Public Speaking  *Online*

Use the Essentials of Public Speaking website at **http://communication. wadsworth.com/hamiltoneps3** for quick access to the electronic study resources that accompany this chapter. When you get to the Essentials home page, click on "Student Book Companion Site" in the Resource box. The Essentials website features a video of Sean's speech on pages 326–329, InfoTrac College Edition, the Suggestions for Practice and Critical Thinking activities and the InfoTrac College Edition activities that follow, a digital glossary, and review quizzes.

Key Terms

ad hominem 315
ad ignoratiam 316
ad populum 315
analogical reasoning 314
begging the question 316
boomerang effect 307
causal reasoning 314

dynamism 319
Elaboration Likelihood
    Model 325
evidence 308
fallacious reasoning 315
fear appeal 323
hasty generalization 316

inoculation theory 313
logic 308
nonfluency 318
post hoc 316
slippery slope 316
social judgment theory
    325

Suggestions for Practice and Critical Thinking

1. With two or three classmates, compose specific illustrations of each of the seven types of fallacious reasoning. When you are done, exchange lists with

another group, read their list, and put a check mark by each instance that you think adequately illustrates the type of reasoning, and an X by each one you don't understand or think needs more work. If time allows, exchange papers with one more group and repeat the process. Then return the papers to the original group. If there are Xs by any of your instances, revise them with your group. If you aren't sure, check with your instructor.

2. Retake the PRCA (Personal Report of Communication Apprehension) without looking at the answers you gave at the beginning of the course. You can find a self-scoring PRCA under Student Resources for Chapter 1 at the Essentials of Public Speaking website. To send your scores to your instructor and yourself, insert the proper e-mail addresses when requested. Compare these scores with your previous scores. Write a brief comparison of the scores and what these scores say about you as a speaker. Show the comparison to your instructor. The lower your totals, the more confident you have become.

3. Select four motivational appeals from Figure 14.3. Find a current radio or television commercial to illustrate each appeal. Share your examples with your instructor, a classmate, or the entire class.

4. Read or watch (on the Essentials website) the Sample Student Speech in this chapter, "Untreated Depression in America" by Sean Stewart. As you can see, Sean did not use visual aids in his presentation. Decide which computer visuals would add to Sean's speech and prepare at least two of them. Show your final PowerPoint slides to your instructor, a classmate, or the entire class.

5. For the persuasive speech you began preparing in Chapter 13 (Practice Suggestion 4), plan specific appeals to logic, credibility, and audience needs that will enhance your persuasiveness. Which of the methods for presenting evidence do you think will work best with your audience? Do you think deductive, inductive, analogical, or causal patterns of reasoning will be most effective? Prepare a brief summary for your instructor.

6. To enhance your persuasiveness by improving your delivery, practice visualizing your positive statements about how effective a speaker you are. Remember that for maximum effect when using positive imagery, you must do more than just read your statements. You need to "say" each positive statement out loud, "see" yourself standing in front of the class performing your speech with ease, and "feel" confident while visualizing your success.

7. Using InfoTrac College Edition, locate a recent article on persuasion from a psychology or speech communication journal. Prepare a 2- to 3-minute review of it to present to the class (clear the article with your instructor).

8. Check out the following websites. You can access these sites under the Student Resources for Chapter 14 at the Essentials of Public Speaking website.

   • See the website for Texas Advertising at the University of Texas at Austin for interesting quotes provided by Professor Jef I. Richards. From the Texas Advertising home page, click on the "People" link. Scroll down and click on Professor Richard's link, then on the "Research" link at the top of the page, then on the link "Advertising Is. . . ."

   • For more on logical fallacies see IntrepidSoftware.com. Click on the "Logical Fallacies" link, then on "Table of Contents."

- For the top campaigns, slogans, jingles, and more of the twentieth century, see AdAge.com/century.

- Listen to President Nixon's resignation address given August 8, 1978, at HistoryChannel.com. Do you think this speech raised Nixon's credibility in the eyes of the American public?

- For an interesting article on using emotional appeals, "Public Speaking: I Get So Emotional," check out the Advanced Public Speaking Institute's site. Search on *emotional appeal,* then click on the link "Article on public speaking and using emotional language."

- Go to Archives.gov to check out several interesting propaganda posters of World War II and the history behind them. Click on the link "Exhibit Hall," then on the link to the exhibit, "Powers of Persuasion: Posters from World War II." Select a poster and determine the persuasive appeals used in it. Do you see any fear appeals?

References

Adams, J. M., Faux, D. D., & Rieber, L. J. (2001). *Printing technology* (5th ed.). Albany, NY: Delmar.

Addington, D. W. (1971). The effects of vocal variations on ratings of source credibility. *Speech Monographs, 38*, 242–247.

Ahles, C. B. (1993, March 15). The dynamics of discovery: Creating your own opportunities. *Vital Speeches, 59*, 352.

Aitken, J. E. (1993, May 15). Light the fire: Communicate with your child. *Vital Speeches, 59*, 473–477.

Alesandrini, K. L. (1982). Image eliciting strategies and meaningful learning. *Journal of Mental Imagery, 6*, 125–140.

Allen, M. (1991, Fall). Meta-analysis comparing the persuasiveness of one-sided and two-sided messages. *Western Journal of Speech Communication, 55*, 390–404.

Allen, M. (1998). Comparing the persuasive effectiveness of one-and two-sided messages. In M. Allen & R. W. Preiss (Eds.), *Persuasion: Advances through meta-analysis* (pp. 87–98). Cresskill, NJ: Hampton.

Allen, M. G. (1994, May 1). Succeeding in Japan. *Vital Speeches*, 60, 432.

Allen, M., & Preiss, R. W. (1997). Comparing the persuasiveness of narrative and statistical evidence using meta-analysis. *Communication Research Reports*, 14, 125–131.

Allen, M., Berkowitz, S., Hunt, S. & Louden, A. (1999). Education on critical thinking. *Communication Education, 48*, 18–30.

Allen, M., Bruflat, R., Fucilla, R., Kramer, M., McKellips, S., Ryan, D. J., & Spiegelhoff, M. (2000). Testing the persuasiveness of evidence: Combining narrative and statistical forms. *Communication Research Reports, 17*, 331–336.

Allen, M., Hunter, J. E., & Donohue, W. A. (1989). Meta-analysis of self-report data on the effectiveness of public speaking anxiety treatment techniques. *Communication Education, 38*, 54–76.

Allen, R. (2000, March). Don't doubt your speaking potential: Public speaking tips for engineering professionals. *Electronic Design, 48*, 165.

Anderson, K. (1999). Stories travel further and faster than facts. *Broadcast Engineering, 41*(9), 88.

Anderson, M. (2002, October 1). Do the right thing: Politics and public policy. *Vital Speeches, 681*, 798–800.

Applbaum, R. L., & Anatol, K. W. (1972). The factor structure of source credibility as a function of the speaking situation. *Speech Monographs, 39*, 216–222.

Arbaugh, J. B. (2001). How instructor immediacy behaviors affect student satisfaction and learning in Web-based courses. *Business Communication Quarterly, 64*(4), 42–54.

Archer, D., & Akert, R. M. (1977). Words and everything else: Verbal and nonverbal cues in social interpretation. *Journal of Personality and Social Psychology, 35*, 443–449.

Argyle, M. (1973). The syntaxes of bodily communication. *International Journal of Psycholinguistics, 2*, 78.

Aristotle. (1971). *Works of Aristotle.* W. R. Roberts (Trans.). Vol. II. London: Oxford University Press.

Aristotle. (1974). *Poetics.* I. Bywater (Trans.). London: Oxford University Press.

Axtell, R. E. (1991). *Gestures: The do's and taboos of body language around the world.* New York: Wiley.

Ayres, J. (1988). Coping with speech anxiety: The power of positive thinking. *Communication Education, 37*, 289–295.

Ayres, J. (1991). Using visual aids to reduce speech anxiety. *Communication Research Reports, 8*, 73–79.

Ayres, J., & Ayres, T. A. (2003). Using images to enhance the impact of visualization. *Communication Reports, 16* (1), 47–55.

Ayres, J., & Hopf, T. S. (1985). Visualization: A means of reducing speech anxiety. *Communication Education, 34*, 318–323.

Ayres, J., & Hopf, T. S. (1989). Visualization: Is it more than extra attention? *Communication Education, 38*, 1–5.

Ayres, J., & Hopf, T. S. (1990, January). The long-term effect of visualization in the classroom: A brief research report. *Communication Education, 39*, 75–78.

Ayres, J., & Hopf, T. S. (1993). *Coping with speech anxiety.* Norwood, NJ: Ablex.

Ayres, J., Heuett, B., & Sonandre, D. A. (1998). Testing a refinement in an intervention for communication apprehension. *Communication Reports, 11*(1), 73–85.

Ayres, J., Hopf, T. S., & Ayres, D. M. (1994). An examination of whether imaging ability enhances the effectiveness of an interview designed to reduce speech anxiety. *Communication Education, 43*, 252–258.

Ayres, J., Hopf, T. S., & Ayres, D. M. (1997). Visualization and performance visualization: Applications, evidence, and speculation. In J. Daly, J. C. McCroskey, J. Ayres, T. S. Hopf, and D. M. Ayres (Eds.), *Avoiding communication: Shyness, reticence, and communication apprehension* (2nd ed.) (pp. 401–422). Cresskill, NJ: Hampton.

Babrick, H. P., Babrick, P. O., & Wittlinger, R. P. (1975). Fifty years of memory for names and faces: A cross-sectional approach. *Journal of Experimental Psychology, 104*, 54–75.

Baird, R. N., Turnbull, A. T., & McDonald, D. (1987). *The graphics of communication* (5th ed.). New York: Holt, Rinehart & Winston.

Baldwin, S. (2000, Winter, Spring). Keep the doors open—2001 commencement address. *Trinity Magazine Online.* Accessed July 9, 2004 at http://www.trinitydc.edu/news_events/mags/summer01/doorsopen.htm

Ballard, B. (2003, June). Six ways to grab your audience right from the start. *Harvard Management Communication Letter, 3*–5.

Baringer, D. K., & McCroskey, J. C. (2000). Immediacy in the classroom: Student immediacy. *Communication Education, 49*(2), 178–186.

Barnlund, D. C. (1989). *Communicative styles of Japanese and Americans: Images and realities.* Belmont, CA: Wadsworth.

Baskette, F. K., Sissors, J. Z., & Brooks, B. S. (1992). *The art of editing* (5th ed.). New York: Macmillan.

Beatty, M. J. (1984). Physiological assessment. In J. A. Daly and J. C. McCroskey (Eds.), *Avoiding communication shyness, reticence and communication apprehension* (pp. 95–106). Beverly Hills, CA: Sage.

Beatty, M. J. (1988). Situational and predispositional correlates of public speaking anxiety. *Communication Education, 37,* 28–39.

Beatty, M. J., Balfantz, G. L., & Kuwabara, A. Y. (1989). Trait-like qualities of selected variables assumed to be transient causes of performance state anxiety. *Communication Education, 38,* 277–289.

Beck, K. H., & Lund, A. L. (1981). The effects of health seriousness and personal efficacy upon intentions and behavior. *Journal of Applied Social Psychology, 11,* 401–415.

Bedard, P. (2004, October 10). Big John goes for some GOP threads. *U.S. News & World Report, 137*(12), 6.

Behling, D. U., & Williams, E. A. (1991). Influence of dress on perceptions of intelligence and expectations of scholastic achievement. *Clothing and Textiles Research Journal, 9*(4), 1–7.

Behnke, R. R., & Sawyer, C. R. (1999). Milestones of anticipatory public speaking anxiety. *Communication Education, 48*(1), 165–172.

Bell, K. (1990). *Developing arguments: Strategies for reaching audiences.* Belmont, CA: Wadsworth.

Bell, S. J. (1998, September/October). Mounting presentations on the Web: Presentation software, HTML, or both? *Online,* 62–70.

Beltran, L. (2004, July 8). Martha Stewart retrial bid again denied. CBS MarketWatch.com. Accessed July 11, 2004 at http://cbs.marketwatch.com/news/story.asp?guid=%7BA4859 B95-BA23-4FFA-BEF6-5BE727FAC045%7D&siteid= google&dist=google

Bergsland, D. (2003). *Introduction to digital publishing.* New York: Thomson Delmar Learning.

Berkman, R. (2000, January 21). Searching for the right search engine. *Chronicle of Higher Education,* B6.

Berscheid, E. (1985). Interpersonal attraction. In G. Lindzey & E. Aronson (Eds.), *Handbook of social psychology* (3rd ed., Vol. 2, pp. 413–484). New York: Random House.

Bettinghaus, E. P., & Cody, M. J. (1997). *Persuasive communication* (5th ed.). New York: Holt, Rinehart & Winston.

Bippus, A. M., & Daly, J. A. (1999). What do people think causes stage fright? Naive attributions about the reasons for public speaking anxiety. *Communication Education, 48,* 63–72.

Blythin, E., & Samovar, L. A. (1985). *Communicating effectively on television.* Belmont, CA: Wadsworth.

Booth-Butterfield, M., & Booth-Butterfield, S. (1992). *Communication apprehension and avoidance in the classroom.* Edina, MN: Burgess.

Booth-Butterfield, S., & Gutowski, C. (1993, Winter). Message modality and source credibility can interact to affect argument processing. *Communication Quarterly, 41,* 77–79.

Booth-Butterfield, S., & Welbourne, J. (2002). The elaboration likelihood model: Its impact on persuasion theory and research. In J. P. Dillard & M. Pfau (Eds.), *The persuasion handbook: Developments in theory and practice* (pp. 155–173). Thousand Oaks, CA: Sage.

Boster, F. J., & Mongeau, P. (1984). Fear-arousing persuasive messages. In R. N. Bostrom (Ed.), *Communication yearbook* (pp. 330–375). Beverly Hills, CA: Sage.

Bostrom, R. N. (1988). *Communicating in public: Speaking and listening.* Santa Rosa, CA: Burges.

Bostrom, R. N., & Tucker, R. K. (1969, March). Evidence, personality, and attitude change. *Speech Monographs, 36,* 22–27.

Bourhis, J., & Allen, M. (1992). Meta-analysis of the relationship between communication apprehension and cognitive performance. *Communication Education, 41,* 68–76.

Bowker, M. (1994, September). Is there gold in your back yard? *Reader's Digest, 145,* 55–56.

Bradac, J. J., & Mulac, A. (1984). A molecular view of powerful and powerless speech styles: Attributional consequences of specific language feature and communication intentions. *Communication Monographs, 51,* 307–319.

Brash, P. W. (1992, November 15). Beyond giving a speech. *Vital Speeches, 59,* 83–84.

Brembeck, W. L., & Howell, W. S. (1976). *Persuasion: A means of social control.* Englewood Cliffs, NJ: Prentice-Hall.

Brewer, G. (2001, March). Snakes top list of Americans' fears. *Gallup News Service.* Accessed June 23, 2004 at http://www.gallup.com/content/default.aspx?ci=1891&pg=1

Brier, N. R. (2004). A $1 million difference. *American Demographics, 26*(6), 10.

Bristow, L. R. (1994, March 15). Protecting youth from the tobacco industry. *Vital Speeches, 60,* 333.

Broadbent, D. E. (1975). The magic number seven after 15 years. In A. Kennedy and A. Wilkes (Eds.), *Studies in long-term memory* (pp. 3–18). London: Wiley.

Brody, M. (2003). Team presentations: A winning combination. *3M Meeting Network.* Accessed December 27, 2004, at http://www.3m.com/meetingsnetwork/articles_advice/marjorie/03-summer.html

Brown, D. E. (1992). Using examples and analogies to remediate misconceptions in physics: Factors influencing conceptual change. *Journal of Research in Science Teaching, 29,* 17–34.

Bryden, M. P., & Ley, R. G. (1983). Right hemispheric involvement in imagery and affect. In E. Perecman (Ed.), *Cognitive processing in the right hemisphere* (pp. 116–117). New York: Academic.

Buchanan, C. (1993). *Quick solutions for great type combinations.* Cincinnati, OH: North Light.

Bufton, N. (2000, January 1). Meeting e-business goals with service providers: The real opportunities of the Internet gold rush. *Vital Speeches, 66,* 177–182.

Burgoon, J. K., & Hoobler, G. D. (2002). Nonverbal signals. In M. L. Knapp and J. A. Daly (Eds.), *Handbook of interpersonal communication* (3rd ed.) (pp. 240–299). Thousand Oaks, CA: Sage.

Burley-Allen, M. (1982). *Listening: The forgotten skill.* New York: Wiley.

Bush, G. H. W. (1992). Transcript of President Bush's radio address on his defeat at the polls. *New York Times,* A26.

Buss, A. H. (1980). *Self-consciousness and social anxiety.* San Francisco: Freeman.

Buzan, T., & Buzan, B. (1996). *The mind map book.* New York: Plume.

Buzan, T. (1991). Use both sides of your brain (3rd ed.). New York: Dutton/Plume.

Buzzel, P., & Herzberg, B. (1990). *The rhetorical tradition.* Boston: Bedford.

Byers, S. (1992). *The electronic type catalog.* New York: Bantam.

Carr-Ruffino, N. (1985). *The promotable woman: Becoming a successful manager* (3rd ed.). Belmont, CA: Wadsworth.

Carrell, L. J., & Willmington, S. C. (1998). The relationship between self-report measures of communication apprehension and trained observers' ratings of communication competence. *Communication Reports,* 11, 87–85.

Carroll, A. B. (2003, June 15). Business ethics in the current environment of fraud and corruption. *Vital Speeches,* 69, 529–533.

Carroll, J. (2003, December). Public rates nursing as most honest as ethical profession. *The Gallup Poll Tuesday Briefing Magazine,* 3.

Castleman, M. (1994, April). Aspirin: Not just for your heart. *Reader's Digest,* 144, 85–89.

Cathcart, S. (1955, August). An experimental study of the relative effectiveness of four methods of presenting evidence. *Speech Monographs,* 22, 227–233.

Chadwick, B. A., & Heaton, T. B. (1992). *Statistical handbook on the American family.* Phoenix: Prux.

Chaiken, S. (1986). Physical appearance and social influence. In C. P. Herman, M. P. Zanna, & E. T. Higgins (Eds.), *Physical appearance, stigma, and social behavior: The Ontario symposium* (Vol. 3, pp. 143–177). Hillsdale, NJ: Erlbaum.

Chaiken, S., & Eagly, A. (1983). Communication modality as a determinant of persuasion: The role of communicator salience. *Journal of Personality and Social Psychology,* 45, 241–256.

Challenger, J. A. (2004, April 1). Boomers at a crossroads: What's the next step? *Vital Speeches* 70, 360–364.

Cialdini, R. B. (1993). *Influence: The psychology of persuasion.* New York: Quill.

Cicero. (1959). *DeOratore.* E. W. Sutton (Trans.). Cambridge, MA: Harvard University Press.

Clanton, J. (1989, April 1). Plutonium 238: NASA's fuel of choice. *Vital Speeches,* 55, 375.

Clinton, B. (1993, February 15). American renewal: We must care for one another. *Vital Speeches,* 59, 259.

Coe, W. C., & Scharcoff, J. A. (1985, April). An empirical evaluation of the neurolinguistic programming model. *International Journal of Clinical and Experimental Hypnosis,* 33, 310–318.

Cohen, A. R. (1964). *Attitude change and social interaction.* New York: Basic.

Colbert, V. (1993, December 15). Successful strategies for achieving your career goals. *Vital Speeches,* 60, 141–143.

Conley, T. M. (1990). *Rhetoric in the European tradition.* New York: Longman.

Conway, A. (1988). The interaction of color code type and information type on the perception and interpretation of visual displays. *Dissertation Abstracts International,* 48, 2123–2124.

Cooper, E., & Jahoda, M. (1966). The evasion of propaganda: How prejudiced people respond to anti-prejudiced propaganda. *Journal of Psychology,* 2, 36–43.

Cooper, M. D., & Nothstine, W. L. (1992). *Power persuasion: Moving an ancient art into the media age.* Greenwood, IN: Educational Video Group.

Cramer, R. B. (1992). *What it takes: The way to the White House.* New York: Random House.

Crook, C. W., & Booth, R. (1977, January). Building rapport in electronic mail using accommodation theory. *Advanced Management Journal,* 62.

Cummins, C. (1995, March 27). Old-timers' at USF now have a place to go. *Tampa Tribune,* 1.

Daly, J. A., & Friedrich, G. W. (1981). The development of communication apprehension: A retrospective analysis of contributory correlates. *Communication Quarterly,* 29, 243–255.

Daly, J. A., Vangelisti, A. L., & Weber, D. J. (1995). Speech anxiety affects how people prepare speeches: A protocol analysis of the preparation process of speakers. *Communication Education,* 62, 383–397.

Daly, J. A., Vangelisti, A. L., Neel, H. L., & Cavanaugh, P. D. (1989). Pre-performance concerns associated with public speaking anxiety. *Communication Quarterly,* 37, 39–53.

Damer, T. E. (2000). *Attacking faulty reasoning: A practical guide to fallacy free arguments* (4th ed.). Belmont, CA: Wadsworth.

Damhorst, M., & Fiore, A. M. (2000). Woman's job interview dress: How the personnel interviewers see it. In M. L. Damhorst, K. A. Miller, & S. O. Michelman (Eds.), *The meaning of dress* (pp. 92–97). New York: Fairchild.

Damhorst, M., & Reed, J. A. P. (1986). Clothing, color value and facial expression: Effect on evaluations of female job applicants. *Social Behavior and Personality,* 14(1), 89–98.

Damhorst, M., & Reed, J. A. P. (1980). *Effects of clothing color on assessment of characteristics of job applicants.* Paper presented at the 71st annual meeting of the American Home Economics Association.

Darling, A. L., & Dannels, D. P. (2003). Practicing engineers talk about the importance of talk: A report on the role of oral communication in the workplace. *Communication Education,* 52, 1–16.

Dauch, R. E. (2004, June 15). Detroit—in the cross hairs: The American auto industry. *Vital Speeches, 70*, 537–541.

Davidson, J. (1993, May 15). Overworked Americans or overwhelmed Americans? You cannot handle everything. *Vital Speeches, 59*, 470–473.

De Dreu, C. K., & McCusker, C. (1997). Gain–loss frames and cooperation in two-person social dilemmas: A transformational analysis. *Journal of Personality and Social Psychology, 72*, 1093–1106.

Decker, B., & Denney, J. (1993), *You've got to be believed to be heard.* New York: St. Martin's.

dePaolo, T. (1985). What are little boys made of? *Mother Goose.* New York: Putnam, 1985.

Detz, J. (2000). *It's not what you say, it's how you say it.* New York: St. Martin's.

Dewey, J. (1991). *How we think* (reprint of 1910 ed.). Buffalo: Prometheus.

Dewsnap, D. (1992). *Desktop publisher's easy type guide: The 150 most important typefaces.* Rockport, MA: Rockport.

Dillard, J. P., & Pfau, M. (2002). *The persuasion handbook: Developments in theory and practice.* Thousand Oaks, CA: Sage.

Drake, A. (2005). Evaluating information found on the World Wide Web. Tarrant County College Library Workshop handout, Fort Worth, Texas.

Dresser, W. R. (1963, August). Effects of "satisfactory" and "unsatisfactory" evidence in a speech of advocacy. *Speech Monographs, 30*, 302–306.

Dulek, R. E., Fielden, J. S., & and Hill, J. S. (1991, January/February). International communication: An executive primer. *Business Horizons, 22.*

Dwyer, K. K. (2000). The multidimensional model: Teaching students to self-manage high communication apprehension by self-selecting treatments. *Communication Education, 49*, 72–81.

Eagly, A. H., & Chaiken, S. (1993). *The psychology of attitudes.* Fort Worth, TX: Harcourt Brace Jovanovich.

Egodigwe, L. (2003). Here come the suits: Raising the style standard in the office. *Black Enterprise, 33*(8), 59.

Eigen, L. D., & Siegel, J. P. (1993). *The Macmillan dictionary of political quotations.* New York: Macmillan.

Ellis, A. (1962). *Reason and emotion in psychotherapy.* New York: Stuart.

Elsea, J. E. (1985). Strategies for effective presentations. *Personnel Journal, 64*, 31–33.

Epson America (2003). Rules for team presentations, basics: Delivery. *Epson Presenters Online.* Accessed February 10, 2003, at http://www.presentersonline.com/basics/delivery/rulesfor team.shtml

Evans, D. L., Beakley, G. C., Crouch, P. E., & Yamaguchi, G. T. (1993). Attributes of engineering graduates and their impact on curriculum design. *Journal of Engineering Education, 82*, 203–211.

Facts on File. (1993, April 8). 52, 250.

Farinelli, J. L. (1994, June 15). Succeeding in business: You can do it with the right strategy. *Vital Speeches, 60*, 533.

Farr, J. V. (2000, November/December). Develop your oral communication skills. *Journal of Management in Engineering, 6.*

February 2004 Web server survey. (2004). Accessed February 3, 2004 at http://news.netcraft.com/archives/web_server_survey. html.

Festinger, L. (1957). *A theory of cognitive dissonance.* Stanford, CA: Stanford University Press.

Fishbein, M., & Ajzen, I. (1975). *Belief, attitude, intention and behavior: An introduction to theory and research.* Reading, MA: Addison-Wesley.

Fisher, W. R. (1987). *Human communication as narration: Towards a philosophy of reason, value, and action.* Columbia: University of South Carolina Press.

Fitzgerald, R. (1994, November). A hand up—not a handout. *Reader's Digest, 145*, 161–165, 168.

Fitzpatrick, K. R. (2004, April 15). U.S. public diplomacy: Telling America's story. *Vital Speeches, 70*(13), 412–416.

Fonte, R. (2003, July 15). *Expanding access to college in America: How the Higher Education Act can put college within reach.* Testimony at the hearing before the Subcommittee on 21st Century Competitiveness, Committee on Education and the Workforce, U.S. House of Representatives. Accessed November 20, 2004, at http://search.epnet.com/login.aspx?direct=true& AuthType=cookie,ip,url,uid&db=f5h&an=32Y2364453545

Forstmann, T. J. (1991, December 1). The spirit of enterprise. *Vital Speeches, 58*, 122.

Francese, P. (2004). Marriage drain's big cost. *American Demographics, 26*(3), 40–41.

Fremouw, W. J., & Scott, M. D. (1979, May). Cognitive restructuring: An alternative method for the treatment of communication apprehension. *Communication Education, 129*–133.

Friedrich, G., Goss, B., Cunconan, T., & Lane, D. (1997). Systematic desensitization. In J. A. Daly, J. C. McCroskey, J. Ayres, T. Hopf, & D. M. Ayres (Eds.). *Avoiding communication: Shyness, reticence, and communication apprehension* (2nd ed.) (pp. 305–330). Cresskill, NJ: Hampton.

Gardano, A. C. (1986, May). Cultural influence on emotional response to color: A research study comparing Hispanics and non-Hispanics. *American Journal of Art Therapy, 24*, 119–124.

Gass, R. H., & Seiter, J. S. (1999). *Persuasion, social influence, and compliance gaining.* Boston: Allyn & Bacon.

Gerhart, P. M. (1994, March 15). The future of the legal profession: The challenge is not public relations, it is human relations. *Vital Speeches, 60*, 347.

Gibbons, P., Busch, J., & Bradac, J. J. (1991). Powerful versus powerless language: Consequences for persuasion, impression formation, and cognitive response. *Journal of Language and Social Psychology 10*, 115–133.

Giles, H., Coupland, J., & Coupland, N. (1991). *Context of accommodation: Developments in applied sociolinguistics.* Cambridge, MA: Cambridge University Press.

Ginossar, Z., & Trope, Y. (1980). The effects of base rates and individuating information on judgements about another person. *Journal of Experimental Social Psychology, 16*, 228–242.

Gioia, D. (1992). Pinto fires and personal ethics: A script analysis of missed opportunities. *Journal of Business Ethics,* 11 (5–6), 379–389.

Goodall, J. (2003, November 15). Dangers to the environment: The challenge lies in all of us. *Vital Speeches,* 70, 71–78.

Gorham, J. (1988, January). The relationship between verbal teacher immediacy behaviors and student learning. *Communication Education,* 37, 40–53.

Gorov, L. (1994, October 16). Simpson prosecutor gets makeover on expert's advice," *Boston Globe* (syndicated).

Goss, B. (1982). Listening as information processing. *Communication Quarterly,* 30, 306.

Gozzi, R. (1990). *New words and a changing American culture.* Columbia, SC: University of South Carolina Press.

Grace, J. P. (1993, July 1). Burning money: The waste of your tax dollars. *Vital Speeches,* 59, 566.

Greaney, T. M. (1997). Five keys to a successful media interview. *Communication World,* 14 (5), 35–38.

Great exaggerations. (2001, December 24). *Sports Illustrated,* 95(25), 32.

Greenleaf, C. T. (1998). *Attention to detail: A gentleman's guide to professional appearance and conduct.* New York: Mass Market Press.

Griffin, E. (1994). *A first look at communication theory.* New York: McGraw-Hill.

Gronbeck, B. E., McKerrow, R. E., Ehninger, D., & Monroe, A. H. (1994). *Principles and types of speech communication* (12th ed.). New York: HarperCollins College.

Gruner, C. R. (1985). Advice to the beginning speaker on using humor: What research tells us. *Communication Education,* 34, 142–147.

Guffey, M. E. (2003). *Business communication: Process and product* (4th ed.). Belmont, CA: Wadsworth.

Gurak, L. J. (1997). *Persuasion and privacy in cyberspace: The online protests over Lotus Marketplace and the Clipper Chip.* New Haven, CT: Yale University Press.

Haber, R. N. (1970, May). How we remember what we see. *Scientific American,* 105.

Hackman, M. Z. (1988, Winter). The reactions to the use of self-disparaging humor by informative public speakers. *Southern Speech Communication Journal,* 53, 175–183.

Hall, E. T. (1992). *The hidden dimension* (reprint ed.). Gloucester, MA: Peter Smith, 1992.

Hall, J. L., Householder, B. J., & Greene, K. L. (2002). The theory of reasoned action. In J. P. Dillard and M. Pfau (Eds.), *The persuasion handbook: Developments in theory and practice* (pp. 259–286). Thousand Oaks, CA: Sage.

Hamilton, C. (1999). The effect of quality and color visual aids on immediate recall, attitude toward speaker, and attitude toward speech. Unpublished dissertation, University of North Texas, Denton, TX.

Hamilton, C. (2005). *Communicating for results* (7th ed.). Belmont, CA: Wadsworth. Used by permission.

Hamilton, L. C. (1988). Using masculine generics: Does generic "he" increase male bias in the user's imagery? *Sex Roles,* 19, 785–799.

Hankin, J. N. (2002, June 1). Make a difference, have no regrets. *Vital Speeches,* 68, 506–508.

Hankin, J. N. (2003, December 1). Two-year colleges: Changes and trends in faculty, students, and missions. *Vital Speeches,* 70(4), 121–128.

Hansen, M.V., & Allen, R. G. (2002). *The one minute millionaire: The enlightened way to wealth.* New York: Harmony Books.

Harari, O. (2002). *The leadership secrets of Colin Powell.* NY: McGraw-Hill.

Harris, T. E. (1993). *Applied organizational communication: Perspectives, principles, and pragmatics.* Hillsdale, NJ: Erlbaum.

Harris, W. H. (1993, June 15). Power, parity, personal responsibility, and progress: The agenda for African Americans in the 1990's. *Vital Speeches,* 59, 536.

Hart, R. P. (1997). *Modern rhetorical criticism* (2nd ed.). Boston: Allyn & Bacon.

Haseley, K. A. (2004, February 1). Dealing with public anger: New approaches to an old problem. *Vital Speeches,* 70, 242–244.

Hass, R. G., & Linder, D. E. (1972). Counterargument availability and the effects of message structure on persuasion. *Journal of Personality and Social Psychology,* 23, 227.

Hauser, M. H., & Hughes, M. A. (1988). Defining the cognitive process of listening: A dream or reality? *Journal of the International Listening Association,* 2, 75–88.

Hegstron, T. (1979). Message impact: What percentage is nonverbal? *Western Journal of Speech Communication,* 43, 134–142.

Heider, F. (1958). *The psychology of interpersonal relations.* New York: Wiley.

Hensley, C. W. (1992, December 1). What you share is what you get: Tips for effective communication. *Vital Speeches,* 59, 117.

Hensley, C. W. (1994, March 1). Divorce—the sensible approach. *Vital Speeches,* 60, 317–319.

Herrick, J. A. (1995). *Argumentation: Understanding and shaping arguments.* Scottsdale, AZ: Gorsuch Scarisbrick.

Hishitani, S. (1991). Vividness of image and retrieval time. *Perception and Motor Skills,* 73, 115–123.

Holcomb, M. W., & Stein, J. K. (1996). *Presentations for decision makers* (3rd ed.). New York: Van Nostrand Reinhold.

Holcombe, M. W., & Stein, J. K. (1983). *Presentations for decision makers: Strategies for structuring and delivering your ideas.* Belmont, CA: Lifetime Learning Publications. (Sample visuals adapted from pp. 86–96).

Holm, J. H. (1981). *Business and professional communication.* Boston: American Press.

Hosman, L. H. (2002). Language and persuasion. In J. P. Dillard & M. Pfau (Eds.), *The persuasion handbook: Developments in theory and practice* (pp. 233–258). Thousand Oaks, CA: Sage.

Houston, J. (1997). *The possible human: A course in enhancing your physical, mental, and creative abilities* (reprint ed.). Los Angeles: Tarcher.

Hovland, C. I., Lumsdaine, A. A., & Sheffield, F. D. (1967). The effects of presenting "one-side" vs. "both sides" in changing opinions on a controversial subject. In R. L. Rosnow & E. J. Robinson (Eds.), *Experiments in persuasion* (pp. 201–225). New York: Academic.

Howard, C. M. (2002). Polishing your spokesperson skills for news media interviews. *Public Relations Quarterly, 47*(4), 18–20.

Humphrey, J. (2001, May 1). Taking the stage: How women can achieve a leadership presence. *Vital Speeches, 67,* 437.

Iacocca, L., & Novak, W. (1984). *Iacocca: An autobiography.* New York: Bantam.

Isaac, A. R., & Marks, D. F. (1994, November). Individual differences in mental imagery experience: Developmental changes and specialization. *British Journal of Psychology, 85,* 479–497.

Isaacson, M. D. (1980, March 15). Public speaking and other coronary threats. *Vital Speeches, 46,* 352.

Itten, J. (1973). *The art of color.* E. van Haagen (Trans.). New York: Van Nostrand Reinhold.

Ivy, D. K., & Backlund, P. (2003). *Exploring gender speak: Personal effectiveness in gender communication* (3rd ed.). New York: McGraw-Hill.

Ivy, D. K., Bullis-Moore, L., Norvell, K., Backlund, P., & Javidi, M. (1993). *The lawyer, the babysitter, and the student: Non-sexist language usage and instruction.* Paper presented at the annual meeting of the Western States Communication Association, Albuquerque, NM.

Jackson, J. L. (2000). The rainbow coalition. In R. L. Johannesen, R. R. Allen, W. A. Linkugel, and F. J. Bryan, *Contemporary American speeches* (9th ed., pp. 271–279). Dubuque, IA: Kendall/Hunt.

Jaffe, G. (2000, April 26). What's your point, Lieutenant? Just cut to the pie charts—the Pentagon declares war on electronic slide shows that make briefings a pain. *Wall Street Journal,* p. A1.

Jaksa, J. A., & Pritchard, M. S. (1994). *Communication ethics: Methods of analysis.* Belmont, CA: Wadsworth.

Johnson, D. D. (1995). Color adaptation for color deficient learners. *Visual Arts Research, 21,* 26–41.

Johnson, V. (1990, February). Picture perfect presentations. *Toastmaster,* 7.

Jones, W. T. (1970). *The classical mind: A history of Western philosophy* (2nd ed.). New York: Harcourt Brace Jovanovich.

Jowett, G. S., & O'Donnell, V. (1999). *Propaganda and persuasion* (3rd ed.). Thousand Oaks, CA: Sage.

Juliussen, E. (2002, December 16). USA tops 160M Internet users. *Computer Industry Almanac.* Accessed January 8, 2004 at http://www.c-i-a.com/pr1202.htm.

Kahane, H., & Cavender, N. (2002). *Logic and contemporary rhetoric: The use of reason in everyday life* (9th ed.). Belmont, CA: Wadsworth.

Kamins, M. A., & Marks, L. J. (1987). Advertising puffery: The impact of using two-sided claims on product attitude and purchase intention. *Journal of Advertising, 16,* 6–15.

Katz, A. N., & Paivio, A. (1975). Imagery variables in concept identification. *Journal of Verbal Learning and Verbal Behavior, 14,* 284–297.

Kaufmann, K. L. (1987). Planning a public presentation. *TechTrends, 32,* 20–23.

Kazoleas, D. C. (1993, Winter). A comparison of the persuasive effectiveness of qualitative versus quantitative evidence: A test of explanatory hypotheses. *Communication Quarterly, 41,* 40–50.

Keaten, J. A., & Kelly, L. (2000). Reticence: An affirmation and revision. *Communication Education, 49,* 165–177.

Kelly, L. (1989). Implementing a skills training program for reticent communicators. *Communication Education, 38,* 85–101.

Kelly, L., & Keaten, J. A. (2000). Treating communication anxiety: Implications of the communibiological paradigm. *Communication Education, 49,* 45–57.

Kelly, L., Phillips, G. M., & Finch, C. (1995). *Teaching people to speak well: Training and remediation of communication reticence.* Cresskill, NJ: Hampton.

Kelsey, D. M., Kearney, P., Plax, T. G., Allen, T. H., & Ritter, K. J. (2004). College students' attributions of teacher misbehaviors. Communication Education, 53(1), 40–55.

Kennedy, J. F. (2000). Inaugural address: John F. Kennedy. In R. L. Johannesen, R. R. Allen, W. A. Linkugel, & F. J. Bryan (Eds.), *Contemporary American speeches* (9th ed., pp. 249–252). Dubuque, IA: Kendall/Hunt.

King, M. L., Jr. (1989). I've been to the mountain-top. In M. C. Leff and F. J. Kauffeld (Eds.), *Texts in context: Critical dialogues on significant episodes in American political rhetoric* (pp. 311–321). Davis, CA: Hermagoras Press.

King, M. L., Jr. (2000). I have a dream. In R. L. Johannesen, R. R. Allen, W. A. Linkugel, & F. J. Bryan (Eds.), *Contemporary American speeches* (9th ed., pp. 258–262). Dubuque, IA: Kendall/Hunt.

Knapp, M. L., & Hall, J. A. (2002). *Nonverbal communication in human interaction* (5th ed.). Belmont, CA: Wadsworth.

Knowlton, S. R. (1997, November 2). How students get lost in cyberspace. *New York Times,* Education Life Supplement. Accessed July 2, 2000 from http://www.nytimes.com

Koballa, T. R., Jr. (1989) Persuading teachers to reexamine the innovative elementary science programs of yesterday: The effect of anecdotal versus data-summary communications. *Journal of Research in Science Teaching, 23,* 437–449.

Koehn, E. (2001, October). Assessment of communications and collaborative learning in civil engineering education. *Journal of Professional Issues in Engineering Education and Practice,* 160–165.

Koester, S., & Pucel, J. (1993). Systematic desensitization. In Communication Apprehension Intervention (a short course offered at the Speech Communication Association convention, Miami Beach in November).

Kosslyn, S. M., Pascula-Leone, A., Felician, O., Camposano, S., Keenan, J. P., Thompson, W. L., Ganis, G., Sukel, K. E., & Alpert, N. M. (1999). The role of area 17 in visual imagery:

Convergent evidence from PET and rTMS. *Science, 284,* 167–170.

Kuriyama, T. (1994, May 1). U.S. and Japan trade relations. *Vital Speeches, 60,* 422.

Lamb, C. W., Hair, J. F., & McDaniel, C. (2004). *Marketing.* Mason, OH: South-Western.

Lamm, R. D. (1993, July 1). New world of medical ethics. *Vital Speeches, 59,* 549–550.

LaRose, R., & Whitten, P. (2000). Re-thinking instructional immediacy for Web courses: A social cognitive exploration. *Communication Education, 49*(4), 320–338.

Larson, C. U. (2004). *Persuasion: Reception and responsibility* (10th ed.). Belmont, CA: Wadsworth.

Lavenson, J. H. (1976). How to earn an MBWA degree. *Vital Speeches, 15,* 411.

Lazarus, D. (2004). Confusing language from SBC. *San Francisco Chronicle.* Accessed August 8, 2004 at http://www.sfgate.com/cgi-bin/article.cgi?file=/chronicle/archive/2004/08/08/BUGAD83PII1.DTL.

Leaper, N. (1999). How communicators lead at the best global companies. *Communication World, 16,* 33–36.

Lederer, R. (1999). *The miracle of language* (rev. ed.). New York: Pocket Books.

Leech, T. (1992). *How to prepare, stage, and deliver winning presentations* (2nd ed.). New York: AMACOM.

Lefton, R. E., Buzzotta, V. R., Sherberg, M., & Karraker, D. L. (1980). *Effective motivation through performance appraisal: Dimensional appraisal strategies.* Cambridge, MA: Ballinger.

Lehman, C. M., & DuFrene, D. D. (2005). *Business communication* (14th ed.). Cincinnati: South-Western.

Lesser, L. M. (1993, August 15). Aid to Russia: Barter transactions. *Vital Speeches, 59,* 651–653.

Lincoln, A. (1983). Gettysburg address. In P. B. Kunhardt, Jr., *A new birth of freedom* (p. 240). Boston: Little, Brown.

Littlejohn, S. W. (2002). *Theories of human communication* (7th ed.). Belmont, CA: Wadsworth.

Loucks, V., Jr. (1993, May 15). Business and school reform: Accountability for educational change. *Vital Speeches, 59,* 466.

Lucas, S. E. (1989). *The art of public speaking,* 3rd ed. New York: McGraw-Hill.

Lucas, S. E. (1992). *The art of public speaking,* 4th ed. New York: McGraw-Hill.

Lundeen, S. W. (1993). Metacognitive listening. In A. D. Wolvin and C. G. Coakley (Eds.). *Perspective on listening.* Norwood, NJ: Ablex.

Lunsford, J. L. (1994, September 4). D/FW signs blamed for more crashes: Three incidents in two weeks attributed to billboards. *Dallas Morning News,* 31A, 36A.

Lutz, W. (2000). Doublespeak. *Journal of Adolescent and Adult Literacy, 44*(3), 230–233.

Maddux, J. E., & Rogers, R. W. (1983). Protection motivation and self-efficacy: A revised theory of fear appeals and attitude change. *Journal of Experimental Social Psychology, 19,* 469–479.

Maltz, M. (1960). *Psycho-cybernetics.* New York: Prentice-Hall.

Mandler, G. (1967). Organization and memory. In K. W. Spence and J. T. Spencer (Eds.), *The psychology of learning and motivation: Advances in research and theory* (Vol. 1., pp. 327–372). New York: Academic.

Manzo, K. K. (2004, June 16). N.C. School Board chairman resigns over plagiarism. *Education Week, 23*(40), 4.

Marcus, A. (1982). Color: A tool for computer graphics communication. In D. Greenberg, A. Schmidt, and V. Garter (Eds.), *The computer image: Application of computer graphics.* Reading, MA: Addison-Wesley.

Marks, D. F. (1999). Consciousness, mental imagery and action. *British Journal of Psychology, 90,* 567–585.

Marshall, J. (2002). Baldwin resigns as USOC president. Associated Press, posted Friday, May 24, 2002 and reported in the *Miami Herald.* Accessed July 12, 2004 at http://www.miami.com/mld/miami/3324754.htm?1c

Maslow, A. H. (1954). *Motivation and personality.* New York: Harper & Brothers.

Maslow, A. H. (1973). A theory of human motivation. In R. J. Lowry (Ed.), *Dominance, self-esteem, self-actualization: Germinal papers of A. H. Maslow* (pp. 153–173). Monterey, CA: Brooks/Cole.

Mayer, R. E. (1989). Systematic thinking fostered by illustrations in scientific text. *Journal of Educational Psychology, 81,* 240–246.

Mayer, R. E., & Anderson, R. B. (1992). The instructive animation: Helping students build connections between words and pictures in multimedia learning. *Journal of Educational Psychology, 76,* 1089–1105.

Maysonave, S. (1999). *Casual power: How to power up your nonverbal communication and dress down for success.* Austin, TX: Bright Books.

McCroskey, J. C. (1967). The effects of evidence in persuasive communication. *Western Speech, 3,* 189–199.

McCroskey, J. C. (1969, April). A summary of experimental research on the effect of evidence in persuasive communication. *Quarterly Journal of Speech, 55,* 169–176.

McCroskey, J. C. (1970, August). The effects of evidence as an inhibitor of counter-persuasion. *Speech Monographs, 37,* 188–194.

McCroskey, J. C. (1972). The implementation of a large-scale program of systematic desensitization for communication apprehension. *Speech Teacher, 21,* 255–264.

McCroskey, J. C. (1982). Oral communication apprehension: A reconceptualization. In M. Burgoon (Ed.), *Communication yearbook 6.* Beverly Hills, CA: Sage.

McCroskey, J. C., & Mehrley, R. S. (1969). Goodwill: A reexamination of the construct and its measurement. *Communication Monographs, 66,* 90–103.

McCroskey, J. C., & Teven, J. (1999). Goodwill: A reexamination of the construct and its measurement. *Communication Monographs, 66,* 90–103.

McCroskey, J. C., & Young, T. J. (1981). Ethos and credibility: The construct and its measurement after three decades. *Central States Speech Journal, 32,* 24–34.

McGarvey, R. (1990, January/February). Rehearsing for success: Tap the power of the mind through visualization. *Executive Female, 35.*

McGuire, W. J. (1985). Attitudes and attitude change. In G. Lindzey and E. Aronson (Eds.), *Handbook of social psychology,* Vol. 2 (3rd ed., pp. 287–288). New York: Random House.

Meichenbaum, D. (1977). *Cognitive behavior modification.* New York: Plenum.

Meichenbaum, D. (1985). *Stress inoculation training.* New York: Pergamon.

Menzel, K. E., & Carrell, L. J. (1999). The impact of gender and immediacy to talk and perceived learning. *Communication Education, 48,* 31–40.

Milem, J. F. (1998, April). Attitude change in college students: Examining the effect of college peer groups and faculty groups. *Journal of Higher Education, 117.*

Miller, G. A. (1956). The magical number seven, plus or minus two: Some limits on our capacity for processing information. *Psychological Review, 63,* 81–97.

Molloy, J. T. (1988). *New dress for success.* New York: Warner.

Molloy, J. T. (1996). *The new woman's dress for success book.* New York: Warner.

Moore, M. (2004, May 11). Bob Love speaks his dream. *ASHA Leader,* 8 & 14.

Morley, D. D. (1987, June). Subjective message constructs: A theory of persuasion. *Communication Monographs, 54,* 183–203.

Morley, D. D., & Walker, K. B. (1987). The role of importance, novelty, and plausibility in producing belief change. *Communication Monographs, 54,* 436–442.

Morrison, P. A. (1993). Congress and the year 2000: Peering into the demographic future. *Business Horizons, 36,* 59.

Motley, M. (1995). *Overcoming your fear of public speaking: A proven method.* New York: McGraw-Hill.

Munter, M. (1993, May/June). Cross-cultural communication for managers. *Business Horizons, 36,* 69.

Napolitano, J. (2003, June 15). Law is a public service. *Vital Speeches, 69,* 533–535.

National Association of Colleges and Employers. (2004). Job Outlook 2004—Student Version. Accessed June 30, 2004 at www.naceweb.org

Nelson, M. C. (2004, March 15). On the path: Business's unfinished journey to diversity. *Vital Speeches, 70,* 336–339.

New York Times. (1980, July 15). As reported in *Current Biography Yearbook,* 1987, p. 259.

Nichols, M. (1996). *The lost art of listening: How learning to listen can improve relationships.* New York: Guilford.

Nickerson, R. S. (1980). Short-term memory for complex meaningful visual configurations: Demonstration of capacity. *Canadian Journal of Psychology, 19,* 155–160.

O'Hayre, J. (1966). *Gobbledygook has gotta go.* U.S. Department of the Interior, Bureau of Land Management. Washington, DC: Government Printing Office.

O'Keefe, D. J. (1990). *Persuasion: Theory and research.* Newbury Park, CA: Sage.

O'Keefe, D. J. (1998). Justification explicitness and persuasive effects: A meta-analysis review of the effects of varying support articulation in persuasive messages. *Argumentation and Advocacy, 35,* 61–75.

O'Keefe, J. (1997, Summer). Standpoint explicitness and persuasive effect: A meta-analytic review of the effects of varying conclusion articulation in persuasive messages. *Argumentation and Advocacy,* 54–60.

Olson, J. M., & Cal, A. V. (1984). Source credibility, attitudes, and the recall of past behaviors. *European Journal of Social Psychology, 14,* 203–210.

Online Writing Lab. (2004). Accessed August 8, 2004 at http:// owl.english/Purdue.edu/handouts/general/gl_nonsex.html.

Oprah Winfrey. (1987). *Current Biography Yearbook,* 610–614.

Osgood, P. G. (1993, February 15). Conveying the environmental message: Getting green is better than seeing red. *Vital Speeches, 59,* 269–271.

Ostermeier, T. H. (1967, June). Effects of type and frequency of reference upon perceived source credibility and attitude change. *Speech Monograph, 34,* 137–144.

Ostling, R. N. (1993). One nation under gods. *Time,* 142(21), 62.

Paivio, A. (1971). *Imagery and verbal processes.* New York: Holt, Rinehart & Winston.

Papageogis, D. (1963). Bartlett effect and the persistence of induced opinion. *Journal of Abnormal and Social Psychology, 67,* 61–67.

Papageogis, D., & McGuire, W. (1961). The generality of immunity to persuasion produced by pre-exposure to weakened counterarguments. *Journal of Abnormal and Social Psychology, 62,* 475–481.

Pastoor, S. (1990). Legibility and subjective preference for color combination in text. *Human Factors, 32,* 157–171.

Pastor resigns after admitting plagiarism. (2004, June 15). *Christian Century,* 121(12)16.

Pearce, W. B., & Conklin, F. (1971). Nonverbal vocalic communication and perceptions of a speaker. *Speech Monographs, 38,* 241.

Peglar, T. (2002, September/October). My reluctant expose. *CJR,* 76.

Pendergrast, M. (1993). *For God, country, and Coca-Cola: The unauthorized history of the great American soft drink and the company that makes it.* New York: Scribner's.

Perecman, E. (Ed.). (1983). *Cognitive processing in the right hemisphere.* New York: Academic.

Perloff, R. M. (2003). *The dynamics of persuasion: Communication and attitudes in the 21st century* (2nd ed.). Mahwah, NJ: Erlbaum.

Peterson, S. (2003, October 1). Top secrets from an expert: How I survived 20 years in the communication business. *Vital Speeches, 69,* 766–768.

Petty, R. E., & Cacioppo, J. T. (1984). The effects of involvement on response to argument quantity and quality: Central and peripheral routes to persuasion. *Journal of Personality and Social Psychology, 46,* 69–81.

Petty, R. E., & Cacioppo, J. T. (1986). *Communication and persuasion: Central and peripheral routes to attitude change.* New York: Springer-Verlag.

Petty, R. E., & Cacioppo, J. T. (1996). *Attitudes and persuasion: Classic and contemporary approaches.* Boulder, CO: Westview.

Pfau, M. (1997). Inoculation model of resistance to influence. In G. A. Barnett & G. J. Boster (Eds.), *Progress in communication sciences: Advances in persuasion* (Vol. 13, pp. 133–171). Norwood, NJ: Ablex.

Pfau, M., & Louden, A. (1994). Effectiveness of adwatch formats in defeating political attack ads. *Communication Research, 21,* 325–341.

Phillips, G. M. (1977). Rhetoritherapy versus the medical model: Dealing with reticence. *Communication Education, 26,* 34–43.

Phillips, G. M. (1991). *Communication incompetencies: A theory of training oral performance behavior.* Carbondale: Southern Illinois University Press.

Philpott, J. S. (1983). The relative contribution to meaning of verbal and nonverbal channels of communication: A meta-analysis. Unpublished Master's thesis, University of Nebraska.

Pinkerton, J. P. (2000). The new paradigm. In R. L. Johannesen, R. R. Allen, W. A. Linkugel, and F. J. Bryan, *Contemporary American speeches* (9th ed., pp. 327). Dubuque, IA: Kendall/Hunt.

Platt, L. (2004, June 15). Accepting risk—daring greatness: An entrepreneurial credo. *Vital Speeches, 70*(17), 541–543.

Pletcher, B. (2000). Plan of reaction: Finding calm from stress lies just a deep breath away. *Fort Worth Star Telegram,* January 10, 11.

Porter, K. (2003). *The mental athlete: Inner training for peak performance in all sports.* Champaign, IL: Human Kinetics.

Porter, K., & Foster, J. (1986). *The mental athlete: Inner training for peak performance.* New York: Ballantine.

Powell, C. L. (1995). *My American journey.* NY: Random House.

Priester, J. R., & Petty, R. E. (1995). Source attributions and persuasion: Perceived honesty as a determinant of message scrutiny. *Personality and Social Psychology Bulletin, 21*(6), 637.

Quayle, D. (1994). *Standing firm: A vice-presidential memoir.* New York: HarperCollins College.

Quinones, E. (1999, August 1). Companies learn the value of storytelling. *New York Times,* p. 4.

Quintilian. (1856). *Quintilian's institutes of oratory; or, Education of an orator.* J. S. Watson (Trans.). London: H. G. Bohn.

Rabb, M. Y. (1993). *The presentation design book: Tips, techniques and advice for creating effective, attractive slides, overheads, multimedia presentations, screen shows and more* (2nd ed.). Chapel Hill, NC: Ventana.

Rackleff, R. B. (1987, March 1). The art of speech writing. *Vital Speeches, 311*–314.

Rae-Dupree, J. (2001, July 2). Finding a needle in the Web. *U. S. News & World Report,* 58.

Randall, N. (2000, May 23). Presentations on the Web. *PC Magazine, 19,* 104–106.

Ratneshwar, S., & Chaiken, S. (1991). Comprehension's role in persuasion: The case of its moderating effect on the persuasive impact of source cues. *Journal of Consumer Research, 18,* 52–62.

Reardon, K. (1991). *Persuasion in practice.* Newbury Park, CA: Sage.

Reinard, J. C. (1988, Fall). The empirical study of evidence: The status after fifty years of research. *Human Communication Research, 15,* 3–59.

Reynolds, C. (2004a). Gen X: The unbeholden. *American Demographics, 26*(4), 8–9.

Reynolds, C. (2004b). Reliable exes. *American Demographics, 26*(3), 10–11.

Reynolds, R. A., & Burgoon, M. (1983). Belief processing, reasoning and evidence. *Communication Yearbook, 7,* 83–104.

Reynolds, R. A., & Reynolds, J. L. (2002). Evidence. In J. P. Dillard and M. Pfau (Eds.), *The persuasion handbook: Developments in theory and practice* (pp. 427–444). Thousand Oaks, CA: Sage.

Richardson, A. (1952). *Mental imagery.* New York: Springer.

Richmond, V. P., & McCroskey, J. C. (1998). *Communication: Apprehension, avoidance, and effectiveness* (5th ed.). Scottsdale, AZ: Gorsuch Scarisbrick.

Richmond, V. P., & Roach, D. (1992). Willingness to communicate and employee success in U.S. organizations. *Journal of Applied Communication Research, 20,* 95–115.

Ring, J. J. (1992, April 1). Global competitiveness: Five steps to failure. *Vital Speeches, 58,* 367.

Robertson, A. K. (1994). *Listen for success: A guide to effective listening.* Burr Ridge, IL: Irwin Professional Publishing.

Robinson, G. J. (2000). *Did I ever tell you the one about the time. . . .* New York: McGraw-Hill.

Robinson, T. E. (1997). Communication apprehension and the basic public speaking course: A national survey of in-class treatment techniques. *Communication Education, 46,* 188–197.

Rogel, S. (2003, April 15). Business ethics and the Boy Scout code. *Vital Speeches, 69,* 403–406.

Rogers, R. W. (1975). A protection motivation theory of fear appeals and attitude change. *Journal of Psychology, 91,* 93–114.

Rokeach, M. (1969). *Beliefs, attitudes, and values: A theory of organization and change.* San Francisco: Jossey-Bass.

Rokeach, M. (1973). *The nature of human values.* New York: Free Press.

Ross, L. D. (1977). The intuitive psychologist and his shortcomings: Distortions in the attribution process. In L. Berkowitz (Ed.), *Advances in experimental social psychology,* Vol. 10 (pp. 173–220). New York: Academic.

Ross, R. K. (2003, November 1). A cry for help: Healthcare: Does anybody care about unequal treatment? *Vital Speeches,* 70, 51–53.

Rowan, K. E. (1990). The speech to explain difficult ideas. *Speech Communication Teacher,* 4, 2–3.

Rowan, K. E. (1991). When simple language fails: Presenting difficult science to the public. *Journal of Technical Writing and Communication,* 21, 369–382.

Rowan, K. E. (1995, July). A new pedagogy for explanatory public speaking: Why arrangement should not substitute for invention. *Communication Education,* 44, 236–250.

Rozema, H. J., & Gray, J. W. (1988). How wide is your communication gender gap? *Personnel Journal,* 66, 98–105.

Rubin, R. B., Rubin, A. M., & Jordan, F. F. (1997). Effects of instruction on communication apprehension and communication competence. *Communication Education,* 46, 104–114.

Russell, A. (1992, May). Fine-tuning your corporate image. *Black Enterprise,* 74–80.

Russell, P. (1979). *The brain book.* New York: Dutton.

Rybacki, D. J., & Rybacki, K. C. (1999). *Advocacy and opposition: An introduction to argumentation* (4th ed.). Boston: Allyn & Bacon.

Sandholtz, K. (1987, Fall). Do you have what it takes? *Managing Your Career,* 10.

Saunders, F. (2000). Web wonders. *Discover,* 21(6), 31–32.

Schab, F. R., & Crowder, R. G. (1989). Accuracy of temporal coding: Auditory-visual comparisons. *Memory and Cognition,* 17, 384–397.

Schnurman, M. (2004, July 11). Ex-Enron chief has lame excuse. *Fort Worth Star-Telegram,* Personal Business Section, 1F & 4F.

Schwartz, S. (1996). Value priorities and behavior: Applying a theory of integrated value systems. In C. Seligman, J. M. Olson, & M. P. Zana (Eds.), *The psychology of values: The Ontario symposium* (Vol. 8, pp. 1–24). Mahwah, NJ: Erlbaum.

Scott, F. (1994, December). Life in these United States. *Reader's Digest,* 145, 83–84.

Scoville, R. (1988, September). Ten graphs (and how to use them). *PC World,* 6, 217.

Sears, W. & Sears, M. (1995, March). Eight reasons spanking doesn't work—and five hands-off techniques that do. *Redbook,* 184, 156, 158–159.

Seiler, W. J. (1971, Winter). The conjunctive influence of source credibility and the use of visual materials on communication effectiveness. *Southern Speech Communication Journal,* 37, 174–185.

Sheikh, A. A. (1983). *Imagery: Current theory, research, and application* (Ed.). New York: Wiley.

Sherif, M., & Hovland, C. I. (1961). *Social judgment.* New Haven, CT: Yale University Press.

Sherif, M., Sherif, C., & Nebergall, R. (1965). *Attitude and attitude change: The social judgment–involvement approach.* Philadelphia: Saunders.

Short tenure: O'Leary out at Notre Dame after one week. (2001, December 14). Associated Press, South Bend, IN. Accessed July 12, 2004 at http://sportsillustrated.cnn.com/football/college/news/2001/12/14/oleary_notredame/

Simons, T. (2004, January 7). Bullets may be dangerous, but don't blame PowerPoint. *Presentations.* Accessed December 27, 2004, at http://www.presentations.com/presentations/search/search_display.jsp?vnu_content_id=2063909

Slater, M. D., & Rouner, D. (1996). Value-affirmative and value-protective processing of alcohol education messages that include statistical evidence or anecdotes. *Communication Research,* 23, 210–235.

Smith, R. G. (1973). Source credibility context effects. *Speech Monographs,* 40, 303–309.

Smith, R. V. (2004). *The elements of great speechmaking: Adding drama and intrigue.* Lanham, MD: University Press of America.

Smith, T. W. (2001). *The emerging 21st century American family.* GSS Social Change Report No. 42. University of Chicago: National Opinion Research Center. Accessed July 3, 2001 from http://www.norc.uchicago.edu/online/emerge.pdf.

Smoak, R. S., Jr. (2001, May 1). Health care coverage for all Americans. *Vital Speeches,* 67, 443.

Smudde, P. M. (2004). The five p's for media interviews: Fundamentals for newbies, veterans and everyone in between. *Public Relations Quarterly,* 49(2), 29–35.

Sparks, J. R., Areni, C. S., & Cox, K. C. (1998). An investigation of the effects of language style and communication modality on persuasion. *Communication Monographs,* 65, 108–125.

St. John, S. (1995, September). Get your act together. *Presentations,* 9, 26–33.

Steil, L. K., Barker, L. L., & and Watson, K. W. (1983). *Effective listening: Key to your success.* Reading, MA: Addison-Wesley.

Steil, L. K., Summerfield, J., & deMare, G. (1984). *Listening: It can change your life.* New York: Wiley.

Stephan, K. M., Fink, G. R., Passingham, R. E., Silbersweig, D., Ceballos-Baumann, A. O., Frith, R. D., & Frackowiak, R. S. J. (1995). Functional anatomy of the mental representation of upper extremity movements in healthy subjects. *Journal of Neurophysiology,* 73, 373–385.

Stephenson, S. (1997). The media and you: 22 ways to get your message across. *HR Magazine,* 42 (6), 146–152.

Stomping turtles. (1987, March). *Tropical Fish Hobbyist,* 35, 77.

Stone, J., & Bachner, J. (1994). *Speaking up: A book for every woman who wants to speak effectively.* New York: Carroll & Graft.

Stoops, N. (2004, June). Educational Attainment in the United States: 2003. U.S. Census Bureau, *Annual Social and Economic Supplement* (ASEC), 20–55.

Streisand, B. (1994). Can he get a fair trial? *U.S. News & World Report,* 117, 62–63.

Students caught lifting material. (2004, May). *Quill Magazine.* 92(4), 31.

Sullivan, D. (2004, April 28). Major search engines and directories. *Search Engine Watch.* Accessed August 25, 2004, at http://searchenginewatch.com/links/article.php/2156221.

Sullivan, M. P. (2004, May 1). How Boomer generational DNA will change healthcare: Creating more satisfied patients. *Vital Speeches, 70*, 443–445.

Sutton, S. R., & Eiser, J. R. (1984). The effect of fear-arousing communications on cigarette smoking: An expectancy-value approach. *Journal of Behavioral Medicine, 7*, 13–33.

Szabo, E. A., & Pfau, M. (2002). Nuances in inoculation: Theory and applications. In J. P. Dillard & M. Pfau (Eds.), *The persuasion handbook: Developments in theory and practice* (pp. 233–258). Thousand Oaks, CA: Sage.

Taylor, J. (2004). A second coming of age. *American Demographics, 26*(5), 36–38.

Tennyson, R. D., & Cocchiarella, M. J. (1986). An empirically based instructional design theory for teaching concepts. *Review of Educational Psychology, 56*, 40–71.

Tesser, A., & Shaffer, D. R. (1990). Attitudes and attitude change. *Annual Review of Psychology, 41*, 479–523.

Thayer, J. (2001, April 15). The purpose of life: Where have all the heroes gone? *Vital Speeches, 67*, 408.

Thompson, B. (2001, December 21). Lyin' O'Leary. *Fort Worth Business Press, 14*(35), 38.

Thompson, L. A., Driscoll, D., & Markson, L. (1998). Memory for visual-spoken language in children and adults. *Journal of Nonverbal Behavior, 22*, 167–187.

Thompson, V. A., & Paivio, A. (1994). Memory for pictures and sounds: Independence of auditory and visual codes. *Canadian Journal of Experimental Psychology, 48*, 380–395.

Tice, L. E. (1980). *Investment in excellence* (cassette series, tape no. 1). Seattle: The Pacific Institute.

Tice, L. E., & Quick, J. (1997). *Personal coaching for results.* Nashville, TN: Thomas Nelson.

Tice, L. E., & Steinberg, A. (1989). *A better world, a better you: The proven Lou Tice "Investment in excellence" program.* Englewood Cliffs, NJ: Prentice-Hall Direct.

Todd, J. S. (1993, June 15). Health care at the brink. *Vital Speeches, 59*, 523.

Tortoriello, T. R., Blatt, S. J., & DeWine, S. (1978). *Communication in the organization: An applied approach.* New York: McGraw-Hill.

Trevino, L. K., & Nelson, K. A. (2004). *Managing business ethics* (3rd ed.). Hoboken, NJ: Wiley.

Tversky, A., & Kahneman, D. (1981). The framing of decisions and the psychology of choice. *Science, 211*, 453–458.

U.S. Bureau of the Census. (2003). *Statistical abstract of the United States.* Washington, D.C.: GPO.

Vest, D., Long, M., & Anderson, T. (1996). Electrical engineers' perceptions of communication training and their recommendation for curricular change: Results of a national survey. *IEEE Transactions of Professional Communication, 12*, 343–370.

Vogel, D. R., Dickson, G. W., & Lehman, J. A. (1986). *Persuasion and the role of visual presentation support: The UM/3M study* (in-house publication, pp. 1–20). St. Paul, MN: 3M Corporation.

Vogel, D. R., Dickson, G. W., & Lehman, J. A. (1990, July 27). Persuasion and the role of visual presentation support: The UM/3M study. In M. Antonoff, Presentations that persuade. *Personal Computing,* 14.

Walters, F. M. (1993, September 1). If it's broke, fix it: The significance of health care reform in America. *Vital Speeches, 59*, 687–691.

Walters, L. (1993). *Secrets of successful speakers.* New York: McGraw-Hill.

Walton, D. (1998). *Ad hominem arguments.* Tuscaloosa: University of Alabama Press.

Warder, M. (1993, August 15). The politics of cultural war. *Vital Speeches, 21*, 653–656.

Warnick, B., & Inch, E. S. (1994). *Critical thinking and communication: The use of reason in argument* (2nd ed.). New York: Macmillan.

Weaver, R. L., II. (1993, May 15). Attitude, not aptitude, determines altitude. *Vital Speeches, 59*, 479.

Weaver, R. L., II. (2003, July 15). What you don't get out of a college education: Personal success skills necessary to exceed in school and in life. *Vital Speeches, 69*, 604–608.

Weisman, L. (2003, August 22). Tice–O'Leary connection goes way back. *USA Today,* Sports, 10c.

Wellner, A. S. (2003). The next 25 years. *American Demographics, 25*(3), 24–27.

Whately, B. P. (1997). Perceptions of rebuttal analogy: Politeness and implications for persuasion. *Argumentation and Advocacy, 33*, 16–19.

Wheeless, L. (1975). An investigation of receiver apprehension and social context dimensions of communication apprehension. *Speech Teacher, 24*, 261–263.

Whitehead, J. R. (1968). Factors of source credibility. *Quarterly Journal of Speech, 54*, 61–63.

Whitworth, J. M. (2003, October 15). We must not forget: Looking back at 9/11. *Vital Speeches, 70*, 25–28.

Wiles, C. (2001). Impromptu speaking: The secret is to prepare for spontaneity. *Harvard Management Communication Letter, 4*(12), 7–9.

Williams, A., & Giles, H. (1998). Communication of ageism. In M. L. Hecht (Ed.), *Communicating prejudice* (pp. 136–162). Thousand Oaks, CA: Sage.

Williams, J. M. (2001). Transformations in technical communication pedagogy: Engineering, writing and the ABET engineering criteria 2000. *Technical Communication Quarterly, 10*(2), 149–167.

Williams, J. M. (2002). Technical communication, engineering, and ABET's engineering criteria 2000: What lies ahead? *Technical Communication, 49*, 89–96.

Williams, R. (2004). *The non-designer's design book: Design and typographic principles for the visual novice* (2nd ed.). Berkeley: Peachpit.

Wilson, A. B. (2003, September 15). In defense of rhetoric: Exercising leadership. *Vital Speeches, 69*, 734–736.

Wise, R., Chollet, F., Hadar, U., Friston, L., Hoffner, E., & Frackowiak, R. (1991). Distribution of cortical neural networks

involved in word comprehension and word retrieval. *Brain,* 114, 1803–1817.

Witte, K. (1992a, December). Putting the fear back into fear appeals: The extended parallel process model. *Communication Monographs,* 59, 329–349.

Witte, K. (1992b). The role of threat and efficacy in AIDS prevention. *International Quarterly of Community Health Education,* 12, 225–249.

Wolff, F. I., Marsnik, N. C., Tracey, W. W., & Nichols, R. G. (1983). *Perceptive listening.* New York: Holt, Rinehart & Winston.

Wolpe, J. (1958). *Psychotherapy by reciprocal inhibition.* Stanford, CA: Stanford University Press.

Wolvin, A. D., & Coakley, C. G. (1985). *Listening* (2nd ed.). Dubuque, IA: Brown.

Wood, J. T. (2005). *Gendered lives: Communication, gender, and culture* (6th ed.). Belmont, CA: Wadsworth.

Wooldridge, E. T., III. (2004, December). Order a PowerPoint stand-down. *Proceedings of the United States Naval Institute,* 130, 85.

Yin, S. (2004). Home and away. *American Demographics,* 26(2), 15.

Zagacki, K. S., Edwards, R., & Honeycutt, J. M. (1992, Winter). The role of mental imagery and emotion in imagined interaction. *Communication Quarterly,* 40, 56–68.

Zayas-Baya, E. P. (1977–1978). Instructional media in the total language picture. *International Journal of Instructional Media,* 5, 145–150.

Zelko, H. P. (1970). Franklin D. Roosevelt's rhythm in rhetorical style. In J. Graham (Ed.), *Great American speeches 1898–1963: Texts and studies* (pp. 191–194). New York: Appleton-Century-Crofts.

Glossary

abstract word Describes intangible concepts that are generally difficult to picture (such as *devotion* or *health*).

acronym A word formed from the first letter of each word of a compound term; for example, TIPS (Tell, Identify, Participate, and Schedule).

ad hominem A type of fallacious reasoning that tries to divert attention from the real issue by attacking the person who presents the argument.

ad ignoratiam A type of fallacious reasoning that appeals to ignorance: because a particular belief cannot be disproved, therefore it must be true.

ad populum A type of fallacious reasoning that appeals to popular opinion as support for an argument.

alliteration The repetition of consonants (usually the first or last letter in a word).

alternate search engine Uses nonstandard means of sorting or ranking the Web pages it finds in a search.

ambiguous word A word with a general, vague, and unclear meaning.

analogical reasoning Reasoning by comparing a familiar example with an unfamiliar one; used to explain and clarify.

antithesis A stylistic device in which two parallel but contrasting ideas are contained in a single sentence.

articulation The clear and distinct production of speech sounds.

assonance The repetition of vowel sounds.

attitude A feeling of approval or disapproval of a person, group, idea, or event.

attitude poll A poll of potential audience members undertaken prior to writing a speech, to gauge their level of agreement or disagreement toward the speech topic and the position statement.

attribution theory Describes how people process information and use it to explain the behavior of others and themselves.

audience type Classification of an audience based on whether they are (1) friendly, (2) neutral or impartial, (3) uninterested or indifferent, or (4) hostile.

begging the question A type of fallacious reasoning that asserts that something is simply because it is.

belief The mental acceptance that something is true even if it can't be proved.

Boolean operator A joining word such as AND, OR, NOT that is used to specify the relationship between search words.

boomerang effect When fewer people agree with the speaker at the end of the speech than before it began.

causal pattern A way of arranging the main topics of a speech so the main points have a cause–effect or effect–cause relationship.

causal reasoning Reasoning that implies a causal link between two items; used to prove.

chronological pattern A way of arranging the main topics of a speech on the basis of time—either in a step-by-step order or by dates.

claim pattern A way of arranging the main topics of a persuasive speech so the main points are the reasons (or claims) for believing a particular fact, holding a particular value, or advocating a particular plan.

cognitive dissonance A feeling of discomfort when evidence is presented that is contrary to what we believe.

cognitive restructuring A method for managing trait anxiety that involves (1) identifying irrational self-talk that produces speaker anxiety, (2) developing alternative coping statements to replace these irrational thoughts, and (3) practicing using the coping statements in stressful situations (such as group discussions or speaking situations).

communication   A process in which people share thoughts, ideas, and feelings in understandable ways.

communication skills   The ability to speak and write well.

comparative advantages pattern   A way of organizing a persuasive speech when the audience already agrees with the problem but may not agree on the solution. This pattern concentrates on the advantages of one course of action over another.

comparison   A type of supporting material that clarifies something unfamiliar by comparing (and/or contrasting) it with something familiar.

complementary hues   Colors that are opposite one another on the color wheel.

concrete word   Describes tangible things that listeners can picture easily (such as *red apple* or *cheerful smile*).

credibility   The quality of a speaker that inspires the feeling that he or she is believable, ethical, and a person in whom listeners can place their confidence.

criteria satisfaction pattern   A way of arranging the main topics of a persuasive speech in which criteria are presented for evaluating possible plans or solutions, followed by a plan to meet or exceed the established criteria.

customize   To take a basic idea or PowerPoint template and adapt it so it becomes one's own.

decoding   The process listeners go through in interpreting a sender's meaning.

deductive reasoning   Presenting the position or general conclusion first and then providing the supporting evidence.

definition   A statement of what a thing is.

deliberative speaking   One of Aristotle's three categories of speaking; political or legislative speaking.

demographic information   Information about audience characteristics, such as age, gender, marital status, education, economic status, occupation, college major, political beliefs, religion, cultural background, and group identification.

demonstration   Using objects or people to explain or clarify an idea.

demonstration speech   A type of informative speech that shows how to do or make something.

description   A vivid, detailed picture of a topic that uses concrete words and figures of speech such as similes, metaphors, and onomatopoeia.

distortion   Misrepresenting or twisting facts, or stating that something is true when it is only partially true or not true at all.

dynamism   A speaking style characterized by forcefulness, enthusiasm, and good vocal variety.

Elaboration Likelihood Model   A theory of persuasion that indicates which of two routes for processing arguments (central or peripheral) audience members will likely use.

emoticon   A sequence of keyboard symbols, such as :) for "happy," used to add meaning and emotion to e-mail messages.

emphasis   Stressing a word with the voice in order to give the word significance.

encoding   The process of deciding how best to organize and convey a message to a specific audience or person.

environment   The time, place, and physical and social surroundings in which the speech occurs.

epideictic speaking   One of Aristotle's three categories of speaking; ceremonial speaking.

ethical speaker   One who researches information carefully and completely, presents only truthful information, and gives credit for all ideas and words that are not original.

euphemism   An abstract word or phrase with positive overtones substituted for a specific word with negative overtones (such as *ethnic cleansing* in place of *murder*).

evaluating stage   The third stage of listening, in which listeners think about, evaluate, and judge the speaker and the message.

evidence   Factual statements and opinions originating from a source other than the speaker, which support the logical arguments of a speech.

exact purpose   A clear, simple sentence that specifies exactly what the audience should gain from an informative or demonstration speech. For example, "After hearing my speech, the audience will . . ."

exaggeration   Overstating or presenting something as greater or more important than it is.

expert opinion   Supporting material that refers to the ideas of another person who is an expert on the topic of the speech.

explanation   Supporting material that defines or gives more information about a term or topic, gives instructions on how to do something, or describes how something works or the relationship between certain items.

extemporaneous speech   A speech that is not memorized or written out word for word, but is developed and presented from brief notes or visual aids.

external noise   Distractions in the environment, such as people talking or dim lighting, that interfere with communication.

external stimulus   A person or object external to the listener that triggers an idea in the listener.

fallacious reasoning   False or faulty reasoning.

fear appeal   A persuasive appeal that causes listeners to feel threatened or afraid.

feedback   The audience's verbal, visual, and vocal responses to the speaker's message.

figurative comparison   Supporting material that shows similarities or differences between two or more items from different classes or categories (such as comparing an individual to a snowflake).

forceful language   Involves the effective use of volume, emphasis, and pitch.

forensic speaking   One of Aristotle's three categories of speaking; speaking in court.

forum   A type of team presentation that includes open audience participation.

frame of reference   A person's experience and background.

framing   Fitting your message to audience needs.

friendly audience   An audience that has heard you speak before, has heard positive things about you, or is simply sold on your topic.

general design principles   Guidelines used to construct the elements of all well-designed visuals. Principles include contrast, repetition, alignment, and proximity.

geographic pattern   See spatial pattern.

gobbledygook   Using complex words or jargon in place of simple words. Also called bureaucratese.

graph   A visual representation of numeric data. Examples include line graphs, bar graphs, stacked bar graphs, pie charts, and pictographs.

graphic visual   A visual aid that consists mainly of graphic elements with just enough words to clarify the visual. Examples include organizational charts and flowcharts, diagrams and schematic drawings, maps, pictures, and graphs.

harmonizing hues   Colors that are relaxing and calming when used together.

hasty generalization   A type of fallacious reasoning that occurs when a conclusion is based on too few examples or on isolated examples.

hierarchical index   A system, used by some search engines, in which Web sites are organized into categories.

highlight main points   To make the important ideas in a speech stand out so it is easier for listeners to follow and remember them.

hostile audience   An audience that is predisposed to dislike you, your topic, or both.

hue   Any color on the color wheel.

hyperbole   An exaggerated or distorted statement that is deliberately used to draw attention to a situation or problem.

immediacy behavior   Any verbal, visual, or vocal behavior that a speaker uses to promote a sense of closeness and personal interaction with the audience.

impartial audience   See neutral audience.

impromptu speech   Speaking without prior preparation and without notes or manuscript.

indifferent audience See uninterested audience.

inductive reasoning Presenting specific evidence first before building up to a general conclusion.

informational speech A type of informative speech that promotes understanding-knowing; focuses on content and ideas; may discuss how something is made, but will not actually make it.

informative speech A speech that increases awareness by introducing the latest information about a topic or body of related facts; deepens listeners' knowledge of a complicated term, concept, or process; or aids in listeners' mastery of a skill. Includes two types—demonstration and informational.

inoculation theory States that inoculating a listener against opposing ideas is similar to inoculating a person against a disease.

instance Supporting material involving an example or illustration that is used to clarify, add interest, and (in some cases) prove a point.

instrumental value A guide for conduct in fulfilling a terminal value.

internal noise Conditions within listeners, such as headaches or lack of knowledge about a topic, that interfere with communication.

internal stimulus A thought generated by the listener that triggers additional thought or action.

interpreting stage The second stage of listening, in which listeners supply meaning to the messages that they have seen, heard, or felt.

keyword search Locates Web sites that match a specific word or phrase entered by the user.

literal comparison Supporting material that shows similarities or differences between two or more items in the same class or category (such as comparing two species of saltwater fish).

logic The sequence of thoughts and ideas that connects the various pieces of evidence to create a meaningful and persuasive argument.

metaphor An implied comparison that speaks of one item as though it were something else, without using *like* or *as*.

metasearch engine A search engine that searches other search engines.

mind map A visual aid for the mind that starts in the center of a paper with the major idea, and works outward in all directions, producing a growing and organized structure composed of key words and key images.

motivated sequence A method of organizing a persuasive speech that involves five steps: attention, need, satisfaction, visualization, and action.

narration A story about real or imagined things, people, or events told with detail and enthusiasm.

need A state in which some sort of unsatisfied condition exists.

neutral audience An audience that considers itself objective, rational, and open to new information. Also called impartial audience.

nonfluency A speech mannerism, such as inaccurate articulation, vocalized pauses (like *ah* or *uh*), or unnecessary repetition of words, that interrupts the flow of a speech and makes the speaker appear less competent on the topic.

onomatopoeia A word that sounds like its meaning, such as *buzz*, *hiss*, or *fizz*.

overlay A piece of clear or colored acetate containing text material that is taped to the frame of an overhead transparency and folded back out of view until needed (such as during a Q & A session).

panel A type of team presentation in which team members informally discuss a problem or topic of interest in front of an audience.

parable A fable that illustrates a moral or religious principle.

parallel points Points that include similar phrasing and sentence structure as well as the same voice (active or passive).

parallelism The grouping of similarly phrased ideas.

paraphrase Putting another person's statements into different words.

pause A short, medium, or long silence between words; sometimes referred to as *live silence*.

personification   Giving human characteristics or feelings to an animal, object, or concept.

persuasion   Communication that is intended to influence choice.

persuasive speech   A speech that seeks to influence beliefs, choices, or opinions.

phrase   A group of words preceded and followed by a pause.

pitch   The highness and lowness of vocal tones.

plagiarism   Using the ideas of others, whether paraphrased or word for word, without giving them credit.

position statement   In a persuasive speech, a simple sentence that states exactly how the speaker feels about the issue covered in the speech.

positive imagery   A technique in which the mind is used to create a positive, vivid, and detailed mental image of accomplishment.

post hoc   A type of fallacious reasoning that occurs when the speaker claims a causal relationship simply because one event followed another event.

preparation outline   A detailed outline of a speech that is prepared after research is completed. In addition to main points and supporting information, it should include an introduction and a conclusion, transitions, and references.

problem–solution pattern   A way of arranging the main topics of a persuasive speech by first stating a problem and then proposing solutions.

pronunciation   Speaking words with all the sounds and accents that are in general usage in a population.

rate   The speed at which one speaks.

remembering stage   The fifth and final stage of listening, in which listeners decide what parts of the speech to retain and then attempt to store them in memory.

repetition   A stylistic device in which words or series of words are repeated in successive clauses or sentences (usually at the beginning).

responding stage   The fourth stage of listening, in which listeners give feedback verbally and nonverbally.

restatement   Rewording of a key concept to make sure listeners grasp it.

rhetoric   The art of persuasive public speaking.

rhetorical question   A question that is designed to make the audience think—no real answer is expected.

rhetoritherapy   A method of managing trait anxiety that focuses on speaking skills: the speaker identifies speaking goals and then determines specific behaviors or practices needed to complete the goals.

rough-draft outline   A brief outline (or list) of the main points of a speech and possible supporting information, which is prepared before research is begun.

sans serif typeface   A geometric-looking, easy-to-read typeface. Examples include Helvetica, Arial, and Optima.

saturation   The amount of color in a hue.

search engine   A tool (such as Yahoo, AltaVista, HotBot, or Excite) that searches the Internet and downloads requested information.

sensing stage   The first stage of listening, in which listeners select or ignore one or more stimuli from the multitude of stimuli that bombard us continually.

serif typeface   A typeface with small lines or finishing strokes that extend from letter stems. Examples include Times Roman, Palatino, Bodoni, and Century Schoolbook.

signpost   A specific type of transition (like a road sign) that clearly indicates where the speaker is going next.

simile   A comparison that uses the word *like* or *as*.

situational anxiety   A type of anxiety caused by factors present in a specific situation (for example, speaking before a new audience or being graded or critiqued while speaking).

situational information   Information about the audience size, members' general expectations about

the topic, and the inclusion of other speakers at the event.

slippery slope   A type of fallacious reasoning that occurs when a speaker asserts that taking a particular step will lead to a serious and undesirable consequence.

social judgment theory   A theory of persuasion that explains how people evaluate messages based on internal anchors (past experiences)—the more ego involved people are with a social issue or topic, the more likely their judgments will be influenced by an internal anchor.

spatial pattern   A way of arranging the main topics of an informative or demonstration speech according to location in space, such as front to back, left to right, first floor to third floor, or north to east to south to west. Also called geographic pattern.

speakers' bureau   An organization within a company that is composed of employees who have expertise in some aspect of the company and are willing to share it with interested groups looking for a guest speaker.

speaking notes   Brief key words or phrases, written on note cards or paper, that guide the speaker through the speech.

special occasion speech   A speech that gives a sense of distinction to important events, such as funerals and award ceremonies.

spectral hues   Colors that are next to each other on the color wheel.

speech to actuate   A type of persuasive speech that asks listeners for both intellectual agreement and action of some type.

speech to convince   A type of persuasive speech that seeks intellectual agreement from listeners.

standard search engine   Uses computer "robots" to search the Web, index the pages found, and determine the relevance of the pages by mathematical calculation.

statistics   Supporting material involving numbers that show relationships between items.

storyboard   An alternate way to organize a speech (other than an outline), consisting of informal visual

as well as verbal representations of the main points and supporting information.

style   The way a speaker uses language to express ideas.

stylistic device   Any departure from everyday language usage, such as rearranging sentences in unusual ways or altering the ordinary meaning of a word, in order to establish a mood or feeling. Examples include alliteration and assonance, antithesis, simile and metaphor, onomatopoeia, repetition and parallelism, hyperbole, and personification.

subject search   A search that locates Web sites that fit a subject in a directory of general topics.

supporting materials   Any type of verbal or visual information used to clarify, prove, or add interest to the ideas presented in a speech.

symposium   A type of team presentation in which each team member presents a formal 2- to 10-minute speech on one aspect of the symposium's topic.

systematic desensitization   A method for managing trait anxiety that utilizes deep muscle relaxation and breathing, and visualization of speaking situations that gradually progress from low anxiety to high anxiety.

T-bar   The horizontal bar to which most flipchart pads attach.

team   Three to seven members who actively work together toward a particular goal (solving a problem, gathering information, or planning an informative or persuasive presentation).

team presentation   Involves the collaborative organization and presentation of material by team members to an audience.

terminal value   An ideal state of being.

text visual   A visual aid that includes mainly text or printed words with one or two pieces of clip art, drawings, or pictures.

theory of reasoned action   Describes how people rationally calculate the costs and benefits of engaging in a particular action and think carefully about how others will view the behavior under consideration.

thesis statement   In the introduction of a speech, a statement that clarifies the specific purpose of the speech and previews the main points.

topical pattern   A way of arranging the main topics of an informative speech in which each main point is one of several aspects of the topic.

trait anxiety   The internal anxiety an individual brings to the speaking situation (for example, feelings of inadequacy when in a group or fear of looking like a fool in front of others).

transition   Word, phrase, or brief sentence used to link ideas, main points, or major parts of a speech.

uninterested audience   Listeners with a short attention span, who wish they were someplace else. Also called indifferent audience.

upspeak   An upward pitch inflection that is often used at the end of declarative sentences and phrases, which gives the impression that the speaker is asking for verification or approval.

value   A deep-seated principle that serves as a personal guideline for behavior.

verbal code   The form in which messages are carried by spoken and written words.

visual code   The form in which messages are carried by nonverbal means, such as personal appearance and visual aids.

vocal code   The form in which messages are carried by vocal means, such as tone of voice and emphasis.

vocal variety   Achieved by varying volume, pitch, emphasis, rate, and pauses in a natural manner, as well as articulating and pronouncing words clearly.

volume   The loudness and softness of the voice. It can be increased by adding to the amount and force of the air expelled while speaking.

white space   Space that contains no text or graphics.

Index